GLOBAL WINE TOURISM:
RESEARCH, MANAGEMENT AND MARKETING

GLOBAL WINE TOURISM:
RESEARCH, MANAGEMENT AND MARKETING

Edited by

Jack Carlsen

and

Stephen Charters

www.cabi.org

CABI is a trading name of CAB International

CABI Head Office
Nosworthy Way
Wallingford
Oxon OX10 8DE
UK

Tel: +44 (0)1491 832111
Fax: +44 (0)1491 833508
E-mail: cabi@cabi.org
Website: www.cabi.org

CABI North American Office
875 Massachusetts Avenue
7th Floor
Cambridge, MA 02139
USA

Tel: +1 617 395 4056
Fax: +1 617 354 6875
E-mail: cabi-nao@cabi.org

A catalogue record for this book is available from the British Library, London, UK.

A catalogue record for this book is available from the Library of Congress,
Washington DC, USA.

ISBN 1 84593 170 X
ISBN 978 1 84593 170 4

Produced and Typeset in 10/12pt Optima by Columns Design Ltd, Reading
Printed and bound in the UK by Biddles Ltd, Kings Lynn

Contents

Contributors

Michael Q. Adams is a partner at Sheldrake Point Vineyard and is also a Managing Director of a wine exporting and marketing firm in Australia, which focuses on opening up emerging markets in Asia for wineries. Currently, he is completing a post-graduate programme in Wine Marketing at the University of Adelaide, where he focuses on viticulture, wine tourism, consumer behaviour research, and winery brand building. From 1999–2002, Michael and his wife, Marjorie, lived in Beijing, China, where he established the first chapter of the American Wine Society outside North America, with a focus on introducing wine education to the emerging Chinese wine trade and new wine consumers. Michael holds post-graduate degrees from The American Graduate School of International Management, Syracuse University and the University of Wales, and is active in several international wine professional associations.

Abel Alonso is a visiting lecturer at the Wellington Institute of Technology in New Zealand. Abel received his PhD from Lincoln University. Prior to taking up an academic career, Abel worked in the hospitality industry, mainly in Switzerland, and managed his own language school in Japan. His research interests include rural small and medium enterprises, particularly those involving the wine and hospitality industries.

Graham Brown is the Professor of Tourism Management at the University of South Australia. He gained his PhD from Texas A&M University and has been involved in tourism education for over twenty years, teaching at universities in England, Canada and Australia. Research projects in Wine Tourism have included examinations of the relationship between wine involvement and visitation to wine regions, factors that affect the attractiveness of wine destinations and the potential for wine lodge development. The findings have appeared in reports, leading tourism journals and as presentations at wine marketing conferences.

Liping A. Cai is a Professor and Director of Purdue Tourism and Hospitality Research Center in the Department of Hospitality and Tourism Management, Purdue University, USA. His research interests include destination branding and management, visitor socio-economic and behavioural profile, and international tourism development. His current research focuses on destination branding and rural tourism.

Jack Carlsen is Chair in Tourism and Hospitality Studies, Curtin University of Technology, Western Australia. He facilitates the tourism research programme at Curtin, which includes tourism development, planning and management. Jack has an excellent research track record, and has produced more than 50 scholarly publications on tourism economics, management, planning, development and evaluation. Jack has conducted extensive research and publications in niche tourism markets of wine tourism and events tourism. Jack has co-authored one other book with Professor Donald Getz and Professor Alison Morrison titled *The Family Business in Tourism and Hospitality* (CABI, 2004).

Stephen Charters lectures in Wine Studies at Edith Cowan University, Western Australia – courses which cover the understanding and appreciation of wine, its varying worldwide styles, the cultural and social context of its consumption and the processes of marketing wine. He is an active researcher, with interests in drinker perceptions of quality in wine, the mythology surrounding wine consumption, the motivation to drink, and the motivations and experience of the wine tourist. He is a member of the editorial board of the *Journal of Wine Research* and is one of only 240 members of the Institute of Masters of Wine in the world.

Luís Correia holds a Master in Management and Development in Tourism from the University of Aveiro, and a BA (+ 2-years) in Hospitality Management from the University of Algarve, Portugal. Luís has been working for Leiria Institute Polytechnic since 2005 in the School of Maritime Technology. He is responsible for teaching Hotel Management and Restaurant Management. Besides lecturing, he also is the practical training coordinator. Luís also lecturers at Felgueiras Higher Institute of Educational Sciences studies in tourism, hospitality and thermal spas. Prior to commencing his academic career he acquired extensive experience as a consultant and trainer in Hotel, Restaurant and Tourism industries.

Richard A. Fraser is a Senior Lecturer in the Commerce Division at Lincoln University, New Zealand where he teaches strategic management. He received his PhD from Massey University and has been involved with tourism education for 30 years. His research interests have included career selection and development in the tourism industry but he is now investigating the wider issues relating to SME ownership and development. In his spare time Rick runs a nut orchard where he and his wife operate a bed and breakfast business and tourist attraction.

Joanne Fountain has been employed as a Lecturer at Lincoln University, New Zealand since 2005. Before this appointment, she taught at Edith Cowan

University in Western Australia and at a number of other Australasian universities. While wine tourism dominates her research interests, Joanna has recently commenced a research project exploring the potential of Chinese goldmining heritage in New Zealand as a tourism product. The location of much of this heritage – Central Otago – just happens to be one of her favourite wine regions.

Dick Friend has worked in research, management and marketing in universities, private businesses, government enterprises, and industry organizations, as well as running small businesses. He has specialized in start-ups and business development in horticulture, mariculture and aquaculture, food wholesaling, wine retailing and distribution, publishing and tourism. Dick currently works as a consultant in innovation, marketing and business development. He is continuing to develop events and produce publications in the food, wine and tourism sectors in order to fund development of content for location-based services, to be deployed on computer, hand-held and mobile platforms for wine tourism.

John G. Gammack is Professor of Information Systems at Griffith Business School, Australia, previously directing a research centre at Murdoch University. His research has examined tourism operator clusters, virtual tourism and destination website effectiveness. Having served on the Australian management committee of the International Federation for IT and Tourism he currently supervises doctoral work in destination marketing. Ongoing research (with Professor Stephanie Donald, at UTS) concerns the branding of Asia-Pacific cities. In 2002 the APEC International Centre for Sustainable Tourism commissioned him to lead an international study on development needs for tourism SMEs, which produced a major report covering the APEC region.

Donald Getz is a Professor in the Haskayne School of Business at the University of Calgary, Canada. He teaches, conducts research, writes and consults in the field of events, tourism and hospitality management. He has developed an international reputation as a leading scholar and proponent of event management and event tourism. Other areas of expertise include destination management and marketing, family business and entrepreneurship, rural tourism, impact assessment, and special-interest travel. Don is author of the book *Explore Wine Tourism* (Cognizant, 2000) and has worked with a number of collaborators on wine tourism research projects.

Karen Graham has a background in the wine industry, both as a manager at a leading winery in British Columbia's Okanagan Valley, and operating her own wine marketing consulting business. She recently completed the Master of Public Policy Program at Simon Fraser University, Vancouver, Canada. Her interest in public policy and wine tourism resulted in collaboration with SFU's Centre for Tourism Policy and Research, and its ongoing work on sustainable wine tourism. She is presently an analyst with the Business Council of British Columbia, and travels in Pacific Northwest wine country as often as possible.

Tony Griffin is a Senior Lecturer in Tourism Management in the School of Leisure, Sport and Tourism at the University of Technology, Sydney. His professional background is in environmental planning, and he has published extensively on subjects ranging from hotel development to alternative tourism. Much of his recent research has focused on understanding the nature and quality of visitor experiences in a variety of contexts, including urban tourism precincts, national parks and wine tourism.

John Hall is an Associate Professor of Marketing at Deakin University, Melbourne where he is a director of the Centre for Business Research. His research interests include market segmentation, consumer behaviour, social marketing and the development and application of marketing research techniques and technology. He has a particular interest in the area of hospitality and tourism research.

Norbert Haydam is a senior lecturer in Marketing Research at the Cape Peninsula University of Technology, South Africa. Between 1996 and 2004, he was the Head of the Tourism Research Unit at the Cape Technikon, South Africa, where he managed and executed a number of research projects for both national and international clients. He is the author of two textbooks on Economics and has written a number of academic papers. Furthermore, in 1994 he was awarded the best paper in *research methods* at the American Marketing Association (AMA) Summer Marketing Educators Conference in San Francisco (California, USA). Since 1994, he also run a successful marketing and tourism research consultancy and is currently studying towards his PhD in business tourism.

David Hurburgh is Managing Partner of Myriad Research Associates (MRA), a Hobart (Tasmania) based communications consultancy. From an earth sciences and resource economics background, in the early 1990s David pioneered the use of Global Positioning System (GPS) technology in the management of mining exploration in remote and harsh northern Canadian environments. David now intends to fuel the spectacular recent growth of the wine tourism industry by the application of modern technologies to navigating the wine trail. His fieldwork for The VineFinders™ Project has taken him to over 2600 cellar doors and wineries throughout Australia in the past three years.

Leo Jago is Deputy CEO and Director of Research for Australia's Cooperative Research Centre for Sustainable Tourism and a Professor in Tourism at Victoria University. He has eclectic research interests that include wine tourism, event evaluation, tourist behaviour and small enterprise management. For three years, Leo was been the Chair of Australia's Council of Australian University Hospitality and Tourism Educators and is a director of a number of public and private organizations in the tourism industry. He is on the editorial board of six international journals.

SooCheong (Shawn) Jang is an Assistant Professor in the Department of Hospitality and Tourism Management, Purdue University, USA. His research interests are three-fold: hospitality finance, hospitality and tourism marketing, and strategic management. His recent research subjects focus on capital structure in the hospitality industry, service quality and loyalty, and business diversification.

Sally J. Linton is the Marketing and PR Specialist for the Indiana Wine Grape Council, an association created to enhance the economic development of wine and grape industry in the state of Indiana. She is the creator and coordinator of the Vintage Indiana Wine and Food Festival, an annual event attracting more than 5000 people.

Larry Lockshin is Professor of Wine Marketing at the University of South Australia. Dr Lockshin has spent more than 20 years working with the wine industry, first as a viticulturist and now as a marketing academic. He received his Masters in Viticulture from Cornell University and a PhD in Marketing from Ohio State University. His research interests are consumer choice behaviour for wine and wine industry strategy.

Alice Loersch is currently employed as Events Coordinator for onesixsigma.com, an independent information portal and networking organization, providing a gateway for Six Sigma professionals in Europe. Prior to this she worked for two years at Axis Sales and Marketing as an Account Executive covering the UK and Ireland conference and incentive markets. Before relocating to London she graduated with distinction with a BA in Tourism Management at the University of Technology, Sydney, where she researched the quality of visitor experiences within the Canberra wine region.

Jane Malady works as a research assistant with Griffith University's Department of Tourism, Leisure, Hotel and Sport Management and is an administrative officer with the Sustainable Tourism CRC Education Program. She holds a Bachelor of Business in Tourism and Hospitality Management and has worked on a number of research projects in the area of food and wine tourism, itinerary planning and study tourism.

Louella Mathias has a Masters in Public Policy from Simon Fraser University, Vancouver, Canada. She has extensive experience in policy development, policy implementation and programme evaluation in the public and non-profit sectors. Louella is deeply interested in municipal government's role in promoting sustainability. Her tourism research has involved assessing tour operator initiatives to implement sustainability policies, as well as examining land use policies related to wine tourism at the University's Centre of Tourism Policy and Research. She is currently the Manager of Policy, Planning and Evaluation at the Canadian Cancer Society, British Columbia and Yukon Division.

Richard Mitchell, a Senior Lecturer at the University of Otago Department of Tourism, has been researching wine tourism since 1998. His research includes winery visitor consumer behaviour, tracking of post-visit behaviour, profiling of winery visitors, wine tourism and regional development, and his research has focused on New Zealand, Australia, Europe and the Mediterranean. He is a member of the management committee of the New Zealand Food and Wine Tourism Network and has been invited as the inaugural holder of the 'Champagne Chair' (a visiting chair at Reims Management School and funded by the CIVC and five major Champagne houses).

Alastair M. Morrison is a distinguished Professor of Hospitality and Tourism Management, Purdue University, USA. He holds the position of Associate Dean for Learning and Director of International Programs in the School of Consumer and Family Sciences. His research interests include destination marketing, Internet marketing and e-commerce, international tourism market development, and consumer behaviour in tourism. His current research focuses on special interest tourism markets, destination image measurement, website satisfaction and evaluation, and wireless applications in tourism.

Jamie Murphy earned an MBA, Masters in Communication, and PhD. After earning his PhD, he has worked, researched, taught and published – *New York Times, Wall Street Journal, Journal of Interactive Marketing, Tourism Management, European Journal of Marketing, Cornell Quarterly, Information Technology and Tourism,* and *Australasian Marketing Journal* – about the Internet. His university experience includes full-time positions in the USA and Australia, visiting positions in Austria, Canada, France and Switzerland, and speaking engagements in Asia, South America, the Middle East, Europe and the USA.

Barry O'Mahony is Associate Professor and Director of the Centre for Hospitality and Tourism Research at Victoria University, Melbourne, Australia. Dr O'Mahony has had extensive international experience in the hospitality industry having held a broad range of positions in hotels, restaurants and commercial catering organizations His research interests include event management, food and beverage management and consumer behaviour and he has published in a number of leading international journals including the *Cornell HRA Quarterly,* the *International Journal of Hospitality Management* and the *International Journal of Contemporary Hospitality Management.*

Martin A. O'Neill is an Associate Professor of Hotel and Restaurant Management with Auburn University, Alabama, and has published widely on hospitality, services marketing and wine tourism. He previously worked with both Edith Cowan University, Western Australia and the University of Ulster in Northern Ireland. It was during his time in Western Australia that he undertook the research for the chapter in this book in collaboration with the Margaret River Wine Industry Association. He is presently collaborating with colleagues and the wine industry in the United States to replicate the research in Californian wine regions.

Mário Passos Ascenção is a Principal Lecturer at the School of Hotel, Restaurant and Tourism Management in International Tourism Marketing at HAAGA University of Applied Sciences, Finland, where he lectures on marketing studies to undergraduate and postgraduate students. He began his studies in his native Portugal where he graduated with a BA in Hospitality

Management and subsequently, a DESE (Diploma of Specialized Higher Studies) in Marketing (majoring in tourism). In 1999 he achieved an MA in Marketing at the University of Ulster in Northern Ireland and in 2005, he was awarded a Doctorate of Philosophy (DPhil) in Marketing. In addition to his lecturer activities, Mário undertakes research work at HAAGA Research on international tourism marketing and marketing for tourism protected areas, such as World Heritage Sites.

Linda Roberts is an Associate Professor in the School of Hospitality, Tourism and Marketing. She holds a BSc (First Class Honours), Postgraduate Certificate of Education (First Class), MSc and a PhD. She is Head of the Hospitality Discipline Area and Course Director for the Master of Business in Hospitality Management and the Master of Business in Hospitality Management (Professional Practice) at Victoria University, Melbourne. She has thirty-six years of experience as an educator and academic with twenty-seven years in higher education in the hospitality field. Her research interests encompass the areas of: new product development and innovation; new product adoption and the factors affecting decision making in the adoption and purchasing of new products; food and wine tourism; identification of innovative strategies to meet visitors needs in the motel industry; and innovation change management in small and medium tourism enterprises. Her research in recent years has been largely focused on Sustainable Tourism Cooperative Research Centre projects in Australia in the capacity of both team member and project leader.

Beverley Sparks is a Professor with the Department of Tourism, Leisure, Hotel and Sport Management at Griffith University. She holds a Bachelor of Arts, Graduate Diploma of Business and a PhD. Beverley is an active researcher in the area of tourism and hospitality marketing and management, and has several publications in top quality journals. She is on the editorial board of several journals including *Cornell HRA Quarterly* and the *Journal* of *Hospitality and Tourism Research*. She has received a range of grants for her research work. Her current research projects include food and wine tourism, study tourism, customer derived value and service quality.

Dimitri Tassiopoulos is currently finalising his doctoral thesis, holds a Masters degree in Business Administration, and a BA (Hons.) in Political Science from the University of Stellenbosch, South Africa. Since 1993, he has been involved in various national and international tourism research projects, of a multidisciplinary and multi-institutional nature, concerning agri-, event, cultural and wine tourism, amongst other. He is the author and editor of a first and second edition text on Event Management, and, has written a number of academic articles and chapters on various tourism related topics. He specialises in tourism entrepreneurship and strategic management and is currently an Associate Director at the Centre of Excellence in Leisure and Tourism, Walter Sisulu University, South Africa.

Ruth Taylor is the Academic Programme Area Head of Services, Small Business and Tourism Management at the School of Management, Curtin University of Technology, Western Australia. She holds Master of Educational

Management and Bachelor of Science degrees from the University of Western Australia, and is currently undertaking PhD studies at Monash University in service operations management. Ruth's research and teaching areas include tourism and events management, and service operations management.

Peter W. Williams is a Professor in the School of Resource and Environmental Management at Simon Fraser University, Vancouver, Canada. At the School's Centre for Tourism Policy and Research, he directs a team of graduate researches in policy and planning research which nurtures the development of more sustainable forms of tourism. Past wine tourism research that he and the Centre's researchers have conducted include: examinations of policies shaping the development of wine tourism regions; analyses of the efficacy of wine tourism value chains; and assessments of travel market preferences and behaviours in wine regions.

Jingxue (Jessica) Yuan is an Assistant Professor in the Department of Nutrition, Hospitality and Retailing, Texas Tech University. Her research interests include wine tourism, special interest tourism, consumer behaviour for hospitality and tourism, and e-marketing and Website evaluation. Her current research focuses on typology and modelling of wine tourists.

Acknowledgements

The editors would like to acknowledge the assistance of Michael Hughes, Shirley Bickford and Elspeth Callender of Curtin University in preparation of this volume.

They would also like to thank all of the chapter reviewers for their excellent feedback on the manuscripts.

Chapters 4 and 6, by Roberts and Sparks and Sparks and Malady, respectively, are based on *'Good Living' tourism: An analysis of the opportunities to develop wine and food tourism in Australia*, which is a Sustainable Tourism CRC research project conducted by Beverley Sparks, Marg Deery, Linda Roberts, Jenny Davies and Lorraine Brown. Jane Malady worked as a research assistant on this project and her contribution is acknowledged. The authors would also like to acknowledge the people in both regions who kindly gave their time to be interviewed for this project. Their commitment, drive and passion for food and wine is outstanding.

Chapter 5, by Gammack, was supported by the APEC International Centre for Sustainable Tourism, to whom thanks are given. The author thanks Shin Nee Teoh, Christopher Hodkinson and Paula Goulding for help in data collection from wine tourism operators, and two anonymous reviewers for helpful suggestions.

Chapter 9 was presented as an invited manuscript at the 2004 American Marketing Association's Summer Educators' Conference. Pearlin Ho, Calvin Chan and Edward Walters contributed to earlier versions of this manuscript.

Chapter 10 by O'Mahony, Hall, Lockshin, Jago and Brown is based on a Sustainable Tourism CRC research project titled 'Understanding The Impact of Wine Tourism On Future Wine Purchasing Behaviour'. The authors would like to thank the Sustainable Tourism CRC for their support.

The research for Chapter 11 was supported in part by Border Technikon and by the Western Cape Tourism Board. The researchers also wish to acknowledge the useful contribution made by the following: Nancy

Phaswana-Mafuya (Human Sciences Research Council, South Africa); Brian Knowles of Tourism Tasmania, Australia; and Nimish Shukla and Dinesh Vallabh of Border Technikon. Earlier versions of this research were presented in 2004 before the International Wine Tourism Conference and published in 2004 in the *Journal of Wine Research*.

The authors of Chapter 12 would like to thank The Vines resort in the Swan Valley for their invaluable hospitality in carrying out this research, and Freya Powell for her assistance in preparing the study.

Chapter 13 the authors would like to acknowledge the assistance of Susan Knox for her help in carrying out the research on which this chapter is based.

The acknowledgements for Chapter 14 go to the Swan Valley Tourism Council for enabling successive teams of research students to have the opportunity to be involved with a window of 'real world learning' in the area of events management.

Chapter 16 authors acknowledge the input of the Margaret River Wine Region Festival Association and the Festival Director Perpetua (Petti) McInnes in preparation of the strategic plan and case study.

Preface

This is the first research-based book on wine tourism and, as such, makes a significant contribution to wine tourism research, management and marketing. Considering the emergence of wine tourism globally, and the consequent growth of academic and practitioner interest in this topic area, it is a timely publication.

All of the contributed chapters in this book (apart from Chapters 1 and 20) have been double-blind reviewed prior to publication. Earlier versions of some of these chapters also appeared in the proceedings from the First International Wine Tourism Conference held in May 2004 at Margaret River, Western Australia (Carlsen and Charters, 2004).

All of the contributors were required to discuss the implications of their research findings for wine tourism generally, so that practical and applied outcomes of the research could be presented. In this way, the book bridges the gap between theoretical and practical research outcomes and provides insights for academics and practitioners alike.

Hence it is envisaged that a number of groups will use this book, including:

- Wine and tourism students in undergraduate and postgraduate programmes.
- Wine tourism destination management organizations.
- Wine tourism planners and policy makers.
- Wine tourism research agencies and consultants.
- Wineries, cellar door and restaurant managers.
- Wine and tourism marketing agencies.
- Wine festival and event organizers.

It is anticipated that this book will provide the basis for further research into the many facets of wine tourism in the future, and suggestions as to the direction of that research are proposed in the conclusion. Wine tourism research poses many challenges but also provides rich rewards for those that are attracted to this field.

Cheers
Jack Carlsen and Stephen Charters (editors)

1 Introduction

JACK CARLSEN[1]* AND STEVE CHARTERS[2]

[1]Curtin University, Perth, Western Australia, Australia;
[2]Edith Cowan University, 100 Joondalup Drive, Joondalup,
Western Australia 6027, Australia; E-mail: s.charters@ecu.edu.au
*E-mail: jack.carlsen@cbs.curtin.edu.au

Introduction

This volume is the first significant contribution to the wine tourism literature since the initial work of Getz (2000) and Hall *et al.* (2000), despite a proliferation of interest in the topic. Over the last 5 years, wine tourism research has become more specialized and eclectic, evolving from conceptual and case study approaches to more comprehensive and expansive investigation of the wine tourism phenomenon. The chapters in this volume extend beyond descriptive case studies of wine tourism, to investigate the links between wine tourism and sustainable regional development, land-use policy, planning, marketing and wine tourist demographics, behaviour and experiences. The proceedings from the First International Wine Tourism Conference held in May 2004 in Margaret River (Carlsen and Charters, 2004) were the genesis for some of these chapters.

Definitions

Wine tourism has been defined as 'visitation to vineyards, wineries, wine festivals and wine shows for which grape wine tasting and/or experiencing the attributes of a grape wine region are the prime motivating factors for visitors' (Hall *et al.*, 2000). This market-based definition has informed a proliferation of consumer studies of wine tourists and wine festival visitors (Hall and Macionis, 1998; Foo, 1999; Nixon, 1999; Cambourne *et al.*, 2000; Dodd, 2000; Getz, 2000; Hall *et al.*, 2000; Mitchell *et al.*, 2000; Carlsen, 2002a; Charters and Ali-Knight, 2002; Heaney, 2003; Alant and Bruwer, 2004; Fountain and Charters, 2004; Mitchell and Hall, 2004; Tassiopoulos *et al.*, 2004; Taylor, 2004; Weiler *et al.*, 2004).

Many wine regions and tourism destinations have realized that the benefits of wine tourism extend well beyond the cellar door to virtually all areas of the regional economy and into the urban areas that generate the majority of wine tourists. Wine, food, tourism and the arts collectively comprise the core elements of the wine tourism product and provide the lifestyle package that wine tourists aspire to and seek to experience.

This product-based approach is exemplified by the definition given in the Winemakers' Federation of Australia (1998) National Wine Tourism Strategy: 'visitation to wineries and wine regions to experience the unique qualities of contemporary Australian lifestyle associated with enjoyment of wine at its source – including wine and food, landscape and cultural activities.' This definition and approach has given rise to a range of studies of the many products and places that comprise wine tourism (Carlsen and Dowling, 1999; Getz, 2000, 2002; Hall *et al.*, 2000; Dodd and Beverland, 2001; Telfer, 2001; Williams, 2001; Lane and Brown, 2004; Loubser, 2004; Roberts and Deery, 2004; Sanders, 2004; Sparks and Malady, 2004).

Wine Tourism Research

Research into wine tourism has accelerated over the last decade to a point where there is now an extensive body of knowledge on wine tourism markets and products. Most of this research has been descriptive in nature, drawing on different data sources, case studies and events to investigate or demonstrate the wine tourism phenomenon. Jennings (2001) found that most tourism research uses the descriptive approach, addressing the basic 'who' and 'what' questions of the topic, but stopping short of addressing the 'how' and 'why' questions – best addressed using more complex explanatory, causal, comparative, evaluative or predictive research approaches.

Two attempts to frame wine tourism research have emerged in the literature, which could be classified as being: (i) macroeconomic; or (ii) microeconomic in their approach (Carlsen, 2004). Carlsen and Dowling (1999) suggested a macroeconomic, hierarchical framework for strategic wine tourism research at the national and regional levels. Strategic research issues were identified as follows:

- Wine tourism research at the national level – marketing and branding; export revenue; tourism trends; taxation and regulation; funding; and industry integration, accreditation and awards.
- Wine tourism research at the regional level – regional identity, image and branding; marketing and facilities audits; infrastructure; tourist expenditure and the role of local government.

This hierarchical approach was useful in communicating broad wine tourism issues to government and industry groups, but did not extend to the level where wine tourism takes place – the winery and consumer – the microeconomic level.

Getz (2000) proposed that the research priorities for wine tourism should be based on wine consumers, wine tourists, marketing effectiveness, success factors for wineries and destinations (see Getz *et al.*, 1999). Dodd and Beverland (2001) also took a microeconomic, organizational life cycle view of winery tourism to identify strategies for successful wine tourism development. In case studies of three wineries (in Australia, New Zealand and Texas) they developed a five-stage model 'from the ground up' of winery tourism life cycle stages and the internal and external characteristics of each stage. The five stages identified were:

- Winery establishment.
- Winery recognition.
- Regional prominence.
- Maturity.
- Tourism decline.

The factors that characterize each stage were based on visitor types, facilities provided, community networking, sales and pricing, brand awareness, size and structure and cellar door media coverage. This model was found to have some limitations in that some wineries may have unique development paths depending on their size and ownership, so further testing of the model was recommended.

A suggested approach (Carlsen, 2004) is to recognize that wine production and tourism are essentially at opposite ends of the industrial spectrum, and the characteristics of each activity are essentially different in a microeconomic sense. At one end wine production is mainly a primary and partially a secondary industry-based activity, characterized by being supply led, price-taking, and producing a standardized, homogenous product, cost-minimizing and reliant on capital growth to create wealth.

At the other end of the industrial spectrum, tourism as a service industry is characterized as being a demand-driven, price-making, heterogeneous product/service, profit-maximizing and relying on profits to create wealth.

There is much work to do in understanding further how these two industries – wine and tourism – diverge, and indeed converge, across a range of economic, technical, cultural, geographic and vocational factors. One area of convergence is that of ease of entry and low barriers to entry and exit. This is exerting considerable pressures on existing wine and tourism enterprises at a regional as well as at an international level. This framework can thus be used to examine wine tourism research issues at a regional, national or international level, thereby overcoming the limitations of the existing frameworks. This framework is analysed in more detail in Fig. 1.1.

These are fundamental issues that confront all wineries and wine regions. Within this framework the range of production-based and consumer-based research conducted to date can be located. The next challenge for wine tourism researchers is the integration of wine tourism product and consumer knowledge to develop a more comprehensive view of the strategic and pragmatic issues in wine tourism. It is anticipated that this volume will make a contribution to the emergent knowledge base of wine tourism.

Primary industry → ← Secondary industry → ← Tertiary industry →	
← Wine industry	Tourism industry →
Supply led – subject to seasonal, temporal, global, technical and agricultural factors that set the supply of grapes and wine	Demand driven – subject to economic, consumption-led, competitive, demonstrative and demographic forces that determine demand for wine tourism
Price takers – single price is determined by wine producers, global wine prices, price of other alcoholic beverages (substitutes)	Price makers – price range is determined by nature of product/service offered, seasonal demand, value-added to experiences
Homogenous product – highest quality standard varietals or blends, long lead times for changes in production, consistent over time	Heterogeneous product/service – a range of options and offerings and short lead times to develop new products, changing over time
Cost Minimizers – seek more efficient production methods, technology intensive, innovate to maximize yield	Profit maximizers – seek maximum returns through extensive marketing; labour intensive; imitate, renovate or renew rather than innovate
Wealth creation through capital growth in value of land and buildings in the long term	Wealth creation through profits and return on investment in the short term

Fig. 1.1. A framework for wine tourism research (from Carlsen, 2004).

Themes in Global Wine Tourism Research

In order to provide a scholarly overview of literature in the field of wine tourism, an analysis of the most extensive tourism literature database in the world was conducted. The database is housed at the Centre International de Recherches et d'Études Touristiques (CIRET) in Aix-en-Provence, France. This database, developed over the last five decades by retired academic René Baretje-Keller, categorizes all tourism publications according to theme, and there are over 1300 themes in the tourism database. CIRET has created a website (http://www.ciret-tourism.com) and provides a worldwide directory of academic institutions (some 629 in 95 countries) and individual researchers (some 3218 in 106 countries), specializing in tourism, leisure, outdoor recreation and hospitality education and research.

Over the years, Monsieur Baretje-Keller has analysed some 131,452 documents including books, conference proceedings, journals and reports. These documents are searchable by theme words (in French) through a thesaurus (with French to English and English to French translations) as well as by a geographical index. The thesaurus, the geographical index and a model of the analysis of a book and of an article of a journal are found on CIRET's website. Academic institutions and individual researchers have access free of charge to the database (but not directly) and a search by theme(s) and (or) country can be organized via e-mail. Researchers can contact CIRET by e-mail (http://www.ciret@free.fr) to submit their tourism research topics and receive in return by e-mail the selected references of the documents, the originals of which are all located in CIRET's library.

In total, 282 references on wine tourism were analysed for the purposes of providing this overview of extant literature. A qualitative analysis software package (NUD*IST) was used to analyse the theme word frequencies occurring in the reference list. Note that the themes are recorded in French, but a thesaurus is available on the CIRET website for translation into English.

Interestingly, the most frequent grouping of themes to emerge in the wine tourism literature could best be described as *wine tourism culture and heritage*, where these publications included themes related to heritage enhancement, conservation, culture and authenticity. This reflects the fact that the CIRET database is international, hence 'Old World' and 'New World' wine tourism publications are represented and many old (and some new) world wine regions are also cultural and heritage tourism destinations. The next most frequent grouping is *wine tourism business* and includes themes such as commercialization, development, management, economic impact, international tourism, festivals, forecasting and cost–benefit analysis.

There has been a proliferation of wine tourism research by academics within university business faculties in countries such as Australia, New Zealand, South Africa, the USA and Canada over the last decade, and this is reflected in the CIRET database. There have also been a number of wine tourism conferences in Australia and New Zealand which have generated publications in the form of conference proceedings.

A third grouping is *wine tourism marketing*, which includes themes such as special-interest markets, destination, marketing, market study, promotion, image, brand, attractiveness, identity, perception and distribution. Wine marketing and tourism marketing are closely aligned in that they both rely on creating awareness of a destination and brand loyalty and operate in a highly competitive business environment, so it is not surprising that wine tourism marketing research is a common theme in the literature.

A fourth grouping is *wine tourists' behaviour* and includes consumption, frequency of visits, behaviour, decision choice, motivation, expenditure, experience and preference as themes. As for any new tourism phenomenon, it is necessary to understand the consumer behaviour and characteristics of that particular market and considerable effort has been exerted in identifying, profiling and segmenting wine tourists in the literature.

Lastly, a grouping of publications on wine tourism regions, models, policy, politics, life cycle, partnerships and cooperation could be described as wine tourism systems for the purposes of providing an overview of the extant publications in the CIRET database. These overarching and integrative themes are important in understanding the theoretical and practical issues associated with wine tourism, and the literature in this area is growing.

Hence, these five thematic groupings: (i) wine tourism culture and heritage; (ii) wine tourism business; (iii) wine tourism marketing; (iv) wine tourists; and (v) wine tourism systems capture most of the research publications on the topic of wine tourism. Perhaps reflecting a bias toward 'New World' wineries, the chapters in this volume make virtually no reference to the first grouping, nor any specific reference to culture and heritage. This highlights both a limitation of current research and an opportunity for a greater research effort in wine tourism research beyond the 'New World' perspective, to include more of the traditional wine regions of Europe.

A logical starting point (in addition to literature in the CIRET database) would be a review of wine regions that host culinary and cultural study tours and the groups that organize, promote and participate in these tours. A search using the Internet reveals over 20 directories, portals and sites dedicated to culinary culture study tours, yet little is known about the groups that are involved in these tours, or the planning, programming and perceptions of those that take these tours. It is evident that hospitality institutions and universities are the target market for these tours and that Italy, France, Spain, Portugal and Germany are the countries where this form of wine tourism takes place.

Thankfully, the other thematic groupings identified in the CIRET database analysis are covered to a greater or lesser extent by the chapters in this volume, and will add another 18 references to the valuable CIRET database on wine tourism once Monsieur Baretje-Keller has conducted his analysis of their content. For the purposes of organizing the chapters in this volume, the six sections and the chapters in each section are introduced below.

Book Structure

The book is divided into six parts – with three chapters in each part. Each part of the book is introduced as follows:

    Part I – The wine tourism setting.
    Part II – Wine tourism and regional development.
    Part III – Wine marketing and wine tourism.
    Part IV – The cellar door.
    Part V – Wine festivals and events.
    Part VI – Wine tours and trails.

The wine tourism setting

The three chapters in Part I set the context for wine tourism from a business, a land use and a customer perspective. Whilst wine tourism can be researched from multiple perspectives, these three chapters address key issues in the context of the wine tourism landscape. First, in Chapter 2, Fraser and Alonso address the most fundamental research question for wineries: that is, what motivates them to get into wine tourism? This question of winery owners' reasons for non-involvement has been addressed before (Leiper and Carlsen, 1998) as well as the motivations of small, family businesses (including wineries) for involvement in tourism (Getz *et al.*, 2004).

However, this chapter provides a quantitative investigation of this important question and provides insights into the suggested approach of Carlsen (2004) in addressing how wineries make the transition from primary producers to service providers. Without pre-empting the findings of this chapter, it is apparent the New Zealand wineries are focused on the production and sale of wine and maintenance of their lifestyle rather than on wine tourism, so wine production and tourism are not always complementary.

Land-use planning and policy is also an immensely important contextual issue for wine tourism, as it is often the rural landscapes as much as quality of the wine that sustains wine tourism. In Chapter 3 Williams *et al.* address the question of appropriate land use policy for wine tourism in three beautiful regions of North America – British Columbia's Okanagan Valley, Washington's Yakima Valley and Oregon's Willamette Valley. In researching and reviewing land use policies in these regions, they find evidence of an integrated and strategic approach to avoid compromising the rural essence and ambience of these regions. Using the analogy of a winemaker balancing flavours to make a good blended wine, the authors provide a lesson in balancing economic and environmental dimensions of wine tourism development.

Wine tourism would not occur without wine tourists, so the customer's perspective is critical in wine tourism research. In Chapter 4, Roberts and Sparks provide us with insights into the factors that enhance the wine tourist's experience, as part of a larger study by the Australian Sustainable Tourism Cooperative Research Centre's (see http://www.crctourism.com.au) study of 'Good Living Tourism'. Through focus groups, they identify eight enhancement factors which provide context to the wine tourism experience, namely:

- Authenticity of experience.
- Value for money.
- Service interactions.
- Setting and surroundings.
- Product offerings.
- Information dissemination.
- Personal growth – learning experiences.
- Indulgence – lifestyle.

Thus, the setting for wine tourism presents challenges for wineries, land use planners and policy makers and others involved in designing, developing and delivering the wine tourism experience. The chapters in Part I address these challenges through their timely and important research in four countries – Australia, New Zealand, Canada and the USA – and set the scene for further international wine tourism research.

Wine tourism and regional development

Wine regions do not automatically transform into wine tourism destinations; a significant investment of time, money and effort is needed to develop a successful wine tourism region. This part examines the issues in developing wine tourism in the context of regional development, using reviews and case studies of emergent Australian wine regions. In some states of Australia there has been a concerted effort to support the development of wine tourism at the regional level, with state government and tourism and wine agencies playing a coordinating role. Their strategy is generally to facilitate increased investment, income and employment in both the wine and tourism sectors in the region and to encourage tourists to visit wine regions and experience all that they have to offer.

At the regional level, there is an array of infrastructure (both hard and soft) required to support the development of wine tourism, as well as a range of support systems for the many small wineries that tend to populate the wine tourism landscape. Getz (2000) provided some excellent insights into the hard infrastructure required for developing successful wine tourism destinations, so this part focuses on the 'soft' infrastructure for wine tourism, including knowledge, communication, networking, innovation, information and strategies. In Chapter 5, Gammack provides some insights into the issues associated with developing wine regions and identifies a 'knowledge infrastructure' for regional wine tourism development. The importance of networking between wineries and tourism operators at the regional level is highlighted in this chapter, as well as the technology that provides the platform for developing and sustaining wine tourism.

Case studies provide excellent insights into the development of wine regions and the wine tourism experience and help to put the real issues confronting wine tourism into context. In Chapter 6, Sparks and Malady glean valuable lessons from emergent wine regions in Queensland, perhaps the most salient being that wine tourism regions need local 'champions'. The recurring themes of planning, networking and collaborating to deliver a successful wine tourism product are integral to this chapter, but there will be many barriers to overcome before this can occur. This is where the presence of champions with the leadership and vision to build a successful brand from a sometimes disparate cluster of wine, food and tourism businesses is critical.

Even when the networks and products are in place, regional wine tourism must deliver more if it is to meet and exceed the expectations of visitors. This will involve developing quality experiences, delivered by knowledgeable and trained staff. In Chapter 7, Griffin and Loersch find that people are the key in delivering quality wine tourism experiences in emergent wine tourism regions in Canberra, Australia. As with all wine tourism regions, quality wine is the core product, but the setting for and ambience of the wine also appears to be critical in attracting, satisfying and retaining wine tourists.

The issues around, and challenges and barriers to, developing wine tourism in wine regions are formidable, but with a sound knowledge base, coordination, leadership, communication and the right people success can be attained – as the chapters in this part attest.

Wine marketing and wine tourism

Wine tourism is often perceived as the means to increase sales of wines at good margins through the cellar door, and most wine tourism marketing includes that sales objective. However, wine tourism can also provide new opportunities for wine distribution as well as for building positive brand image and identity for the many small wineries competing in an increasingly crowded market. One of the key research questions in wine tourism marketing is whether a visit to a winery generates brand loyalty, subsequent sales and positive word of mouth for a wine region and its wineries. Two of the chapters in this section address the key question of post-visit wine purchase behaviour of wine tourists, in New Zealand and Australia.

In Chapter 8 Mitchell provides some analysis of reasons for purchase (and non-purchase) by wine tourists after visiting wineries. He interprets winery visitation as 'consumer experience tourism' and finds that it is indeed the experience elements of the visit – such as service and social aspects – that are most influential in post-visit purchase behaviour. He also points out the importance of 'hygiene factors' that, if absent, can compromise the experience but in themselves do little to enhance the experience. In contrast to previous studies, Mitchell finds a high likelihood of brand loyalty amongst New Zealand winery visitors, especially if they visit more frequently, which results in increased post-visit purchases. Mitchell also provides the first insights into reasons for post-visit non-purchase by winery visitors.

The role of electronic marketing of wine is described by Murphy in Chapter 9. Wine websites present a virtual space for the initial interaction between a winery and a consumer, so it is imperative that this interaction is as informative and interactive as possible. Murphy identifies website design features and the importance of prompt and polite responses to e-mail queries and requests as key to developing a competitive advantage in the electronic marketing of wineries.

The role of wine tourism marketing is essentially to transform wine from being a low-involvement product to a high-involvement experience. In Chapter 10, O'Mahony *et al.* find that high involvement correlates with higher post-visit purchases of wine, but the relationship is a complex one. Without over-reliance on market segmentation (which can be misleading when based on a single factor such as demographics), it is evident from this research that there is a continuum of wine involvement from low to high that may or may not change after a winery visit. Perhaps more than any other topic area in wine tourism marketing, it is the questions of wine involvement, winery visitation and subsequent wine purchase behaviour that deserve further research.

The cellar door

When one thinks of wine tourism, images of cellar door tastings spring to mind. However, whilst cellar doors are ideal places to study the initial interactions of tourists with wineries and to capture samples of wine tourists, it is a mistake to confine wine tourism research exclusively to the cellar door. It is the wider experiences in wine regions that are now being sought by wine tourists, so the cellar door becomes a portal through which to view the wine tourism phenomena and the wine tourists.

From the wineries' perspective the cellar door has become a major point of sale of their wines, particularly for the smaller 'boutique' wineries that find the wine retail and export market too difficult to supply and service profitability. There has been a proliferation of small vineyards and wineries in countries such as Australia, leading some commentators to claim there is an impending wine glut, which will force small wineries to sell their wines mainly through the cellar door. In such a competitive environment, understanding wine tourists and delivery of quality service and experiences through the cellar door has become an absolute imperative.

In Chapter 11, Tassiopoulos and Haydam provide some insights into South African wine tourists. They find that most wine tourists are younger female professionals, on day trips from within the Western Cape region. They travel (in their own vehicles) in small groups with family and/or friends or with their spouse and visit wineries to purchase wine and socialize. This profile of wine tourists bears some similarity to other studies in Tasmania and South Australia, although the extent to which the findings can be generalized is limited by the sample size and timing of the study.

Looking at the next generation of wine tourists, who have to follow in the wake of the baby boomer generation that has fed the growth in demand for wine and wine tourism, is crucial to the long-term wine tourism outlook. In Chapter 12, Charters and Fountain profile younger wine tourists and the generational differences in cellar door experiences. Using 'mystery shopper' research methods, they do indeed find important differences in expectations and experiences not only between older and younger wine tourists but between Generation X and Generation Y. Again, without being definitive, it appears that preferential treatment is given to older cellar door visitors in terms of the attention they receive, so there may be some need to consider the needs of younger wine tourists in future cellar door research.

As with most social research, there is always a lot of 'noise' in data sets that can mask the clarity of findings. Amorphous concepts such as service quality expectations, experience and perceptions are often influenced by a range of intrinsic and extrinsic variables that may be beyond the scope of researchers and cellar door managers.

In Chapter 13, O'Neill and Charters find that one variable in particular, that of the timing of visitor surveys, does indeed influence perceptions of cellar door quality. They find support for their hypothesis that perceptions of cellar door quality decline over time, having conducted one of the few longitudinal studies of cellar door visitors in Margaret River, Western Australia. This instability of both customer expectations and perceptions over time should alert researchers to the limitations of cross-sectional studies and the need for a more longitudinal approach to understanding cellar door visitors. There are also some salient implications for cellar door operators that need to ensure the highest quality service, as customer satisfaction and loyalty over time are important.

For some, particularly the young and inexperienced wine consumer, the cellar door can be a daunting and intimidating environment. The challenge for researchers and operators is to understand the needs of their customers and how best to meet them, make the experience educational, enjoyable and memorable for all the right reasons. In this way, favourable word of mouth, brand image and loyalty and wine sales will result. Indeed, the future of many small wineries may depend on getting the cellar door experience right, based on sound visitor research and monitoring over time.

Wine festivals and events

Wine festivals and events present an opportunity to research the wine tourism market segments. Wine festivals are also an appropriate environment in which to study wine tourism because visitors are mainly motivated by the opportunity to experience wine and wine-related activities, in line with popular definitions of wine tourism (Carlsen, 2002). The celebration of wine, food and the arts of a region is the essence of wine tourism, and wine festivals and events encapsulate all that a region has to offer wine tourists.

In this section, visitors to wine festivals in the USA and Australia are profiled, in terms of their motivations (USA) and satisfaction (Australia). The last chapter investigates some strategic issues in developing wine festivals in the case of Margaret River, Western Australia.

In Chapter 14, Taylor uses multiple methods to investigate the motivations and satisfaction of visitors to the 'Spring in the Valley' wine festival in the Swan Valley, Western Australia. Using a longitudinal data set, visitor profiles give insights into wine festival visitor demographics and characteristics. Content analysis of open-ended survey responses from 4 years of visitor research also provides an indication of likes and dislikes, invaluable information for festival organizers. Using a third method, that of observation for investigating service quality, services mapping is employed to identify those critical service settings and encounters that form the tangible and intangible elements of service quality at events. There are many implications for wine festival and event managers from this research, as well as some innovation in using multiple methods of research.

In Chapter 15, Yuan *et al.* also conduct a very comprehensive investigation of a wine festival visitor's segments and motivations, but extend their research into the promotional effects on their decision processes. Segmentation according to visitor motivations reveals four motivational factor groupings related to 'escape', 'wine', 'socializing' and 'family', and three groups of 'wine focused', 'festival seekers' and 'hangers-on' visitors. Wine festival quality and satisfaction were found to have positive promotional effects for the wineries associated with the regional festival, in this case in Indianapolis, Indiana. The significant promotional opportunities for attracting and retaining visitors to wineries through wine festivals are highlighted in this chapter.

The substantial social and economic benefits of wine festivals and events are not realised incidentally, but need to be carefully planned, managed and monitored to ensure that the visitors' and the stakeholders' involvement is optimized. In Chapter 16, Carlsen and Getz provide an overview of the strategic planning process for a long-running wine festival in Margaret River, Western Australia. The process of researching current visitor profiles, identifying stakeholders' aspirations and visions and then developing strategies for re-positioning the festival in the following 5 years is described. It was evident that the festival association has evolved into a more professional organization and that strategic planning can place it on a firmer footing to pursue their vision and mission and take action in the areas of positioning, programming, marketing, communications and membership.

Wine festivals and events harbour innovation, creativity and synergy in wine regions and provide a stage upon which the collective talent of the winemakers, chefs, artists, performers and producers of the region can be showcased. Clearly there are opportunities for innovative research using the captive audiences at these gatherings and the conduct of new techniques for investigating the important characteristics, motivations and satisfaction with the range of carefully planned and managed offerings in these settings.

Wine tours and trails

In this final section, we revisit perhaps the oldest form of wine tourism, the concept of wine trails and tours, but in a very modern and contemporary context. Wine tours and trails (and directional signage) are now ubiquitous in wine regions, yet there has been a limited amount of research into their effectiveness and function as part of the wine tourism experience. Nor have there been any insights into new and alternative ways of participating in self-organized wine tours, so this field of wine tourism is literally wide open to new research insights.

In Chapter 17, Adams describes the process of developing private boating facilities at wineries wanting to host 'nautical' wine tourists. The Finger Lakes in the New York State Canal System is the setting for developing this 'new' form of wine tourism (although it could be argued that the canal systems of Europe have been used to transport visitors to wine regions for many years). With a huge and affluent market of 50 million people within one hour's drive of the Lakes, increasing rates of boat ownership and a range of waterfront tourist attractions and wineries available, the potential for nautical wine tourism is immense, as Adams' study confirms. However, visitor flows, needs and physical facilities will need to be monitored very carefully if this form of wine tourism is to be successful.

In Chapter 18, the development of wine routes in Portugal is investigated by Correia and Passos Ascenção. Specifically, the development of the Bairrada Wine Route (BWR) is case studied and some evaluation of the success of the wine route is conducted. In-depth interviews with the 14 wineries along the BWR indicate that success to date has been limited due to lack of funding, focus and dynamism. Despite their dissatisfaction with the BWR, participating wineries remain optimistic about the future of wine tourism for the region, particularly if a new management structure to manage and promote more effectively the BWR is implemented.

In the penultimate chapter, Hurburgh and Friend demonstrate the innovative use of new Global Positioning System (GPS) software for locating and profiling wineries. Their Australian company, Vinefinders®, has employed new mobile technologies and digital imaging technology to enable wine tourists to plan and coordinate their wine tours before departure by loading the ground-truthed maps and directions to over 2600 wineries and points of interest across Australia. Information on individual winery locations, opening hours, wines and useful links can also be downloaded onto appropriate in-car and hand-held devices to ensure that navigating the wine trail becomes a smooth and seamless exercise. Hence, Chapter 19 demonstrates the role of new technologies in addressing the challenges of developing wine trails.

Summary

The six sections in this volume group together 18 chapters on topics that should be of great interest to wine tourism researchers and stakeholders in the wine and tourism sectors. Most chapters address the key questions in wine tourism confronting both 'Old World' and 'New World' wine regions, yet most of the answers are developed from a 'New World' perspective. It is self-evident that there is much that we can learn from the traditions, culture and heritage of 'Old World' wine regions, and from the millions of tourists who are motivated to visit these famous regions on organized and self-directed culinary study tours and wine tours. The 'New World', perspective is a reflection of the physical location of the wine tourism research community and the impetus that has been developed in the last decade in wine tourism at the national and state level in Australia, New Zealand, South Africa, the USA and Canada.

The research insights, methods and findings in this volume present both a knowledge base for existing wine tourism researchers and a platform upon which the next wave of wine tourism research can be developed. The research opportunities are many and wine regions, cellar doors, festivals and trails are proliferating world-wide – so use this book to refine your research and thinking about wine tourism in a global context.

References

Alant, K. and Bruwer, J. (2004) Wine tourism behaviour in the context of a motivational framework for wine regions and cellar doors. In: Carlsen, J. and Charters, S. (eds) *International Wine Tourism Research. Proceedings of the International Wine Tourism Conference*, Margaret River, Western Australia, May 2004. Vineyard Publishers, Perth, Australia.

Ali-Knight, J. and Carlsen, J. (2003) An exploration of the use of extraordinary experiences in wine tourism. In: Lockshin, L. and Rungie, C. (eds) *Proceedings of the International Colloquium in Wine Marketing*, Adelaide, Australia; Wine Marketing Group, University of South Australia, Adelaide, Australia.

Beverland, M. (2001) Generation X and wine consumption. *Australian and New Zealand Wine Industry Journal*, 16(1), 91–96.

Bruwer, J. (2002) Marketing wine to Generation X consumers through the cellar door. *The Australian and New Zealand Grapegrower and Winemaker*, December, 67–71.

Bruwer, J. (2003) South African wine routes: some perspectives on the wine tourism industry's structural dimensions and wine tourism product. *Tourism Management* 24, 423–425.

Cambourne, E.B., Macionis, N., Hall, C.M. and Sharples, L. (2000) The future of wine tourism. In: Hall, C.M., Sharples, L., Cambourne, B. and Macionis, N. (eds) *Wine Tourism Around the World: Development, Management and Markets*. Elsevier Science, Oxford, UK, pp. 297–320.

Carlsen, J. (1999) The first Australian Wine Tourism Conference. *Tourism Management* 20(4), 367–368.

Carlsen, J. (2002) Segmentation and profiling of the wine festival visitor market. In: Cullen, C., Pickering, G. and Phillips, R. (eds) *Bacchus to the Future: The Inaugural Brock University Wine Conference*, St Catharines, Ontario, Canada. Brock University Press, St Catharines, Ontario, Canada, pp. 257–278.

Carlsen, J. (2004) A review of global wine tourism research. *Journal of Wine Research (Special Issue: Wine Tourism)* 15(1).

Carlsen, J. and Ali-Knight, J. (2004) Managing wine tourism through demarketing: the case of Napa Valley, California. In: Carlsen, J. and Charters, S. (eds) *International Wine Tourism Research. Proceedings of the International Wine Tourism Conference*, Margaret River, Western Australia, May 2004, Vineyard Publishers, Perth, Australia.

Carlsen, J. and Charters, S. (2004) International wine tourism research. In: *Conference Proceedings of the International Wine Tourism Conference*, Margaret River, 2–5 May. Vineyard Publications, Perth, Australia.

Carlsen, J. and Dowling, R. (1999) Acquiring a taste for tourism research. In: Molloy, J. and Davies, J. (eds) *Tourism and Hospitality: Delighting the Senses*. Bureau of Tourism Research, Canberra, Australia, pp. 100–109.

Carlsen, J. and Dowling, R. (2001) Regional wine tourism: a plan of development for Western Australia. *Tourism Recreation Research* 26(2), 45–52.

Charters, S. and Ali-Knight, J. (2002) Who is the wine tourist? *Tourism Management* 23, 311–319.

Charters, S. and O'Neill, M. (2000) Delighting the customer: how good is the cellar door experience? *Australian and New Zealand Wine Industry Journal* 15(4), 11–16.

Charters, S. and O'Neill, M. (2001) Service quality at the cellar door: A comparison between regions. *International Journal of Wine Marketing* 13(3), 7–17.

Correia, L., Ascenção, M.J.P. and Charters, S. (2004) Wine routes in Portugal: a case study of the Bairrada Wine Route. In: Carlsen, J. and Charters, S. (eds) *International Wine Tourism Research. Proceedings of the International Wine Tourism Conference*, Margaret River, Western Australia, May 2004, Vineyard Publishers, Perth, Australia.

Dodd, T. (2000) Influences on cellar door sales and determinants of wine tourism success: results from Texas wineries. In: Hall, C.M., Sharples, L., Cambourne, B. and Macionis, N. (eds) *Wine Tourism Around the World: Development, Management and Markets*. Elsevier Science, Oxford, UK, pp. 136–149.

Dodd, T. and Beverland, M. (2001) Winery tourism life-cycle development: a proposed model. *Tourism Recreation Research* 26(2), 11–21.

Dowling, R. and Carlsen, J. (1998) Introduction. In: Dowling, R. and Carlsen, J. (eds) *Wine Tourism: Perfect Partners. Proceedings of the First Australian Wine Tourism Conference*, Margaret River, Western Australia, May 1998. Bureau of Tourism Research, Canberra, Australia.

Foo, L.M. (1999) A profile of international visitors to Australian wineries. *BTR Tourism Research Report* (vol. 1, no. 1, autumn). Bureau of Tourism Research, Canberra, Australia, pp. 41–44.

Fountain, J. and Charters, S. (2004) Younger wine tourists: a study of generational differences in the cellar door experience. In: Carlsen, J. and Charters, S. (eds) *International Wine Tourism Research. Proceedings of the International Wine Tourism Conference*, Margaret River, Western Australia, May 2004. Vineyard Publishers, Perth, Australia.

Getz, D. (2000) *Explore Wine Tourism: Management, Development and Destinations*. Cognizant Communication Corporation, New York.

Getz, D. (2002) Wine tourism in Canada: development, issues and prospects. In: Cullen, C., Pickering, G. and Phillips, R. (eds) *Bacchus to the Future: The Inaugural Brock University Wine Conference*, St Catharines, Ontario, Canada. Brock University Press, St Catharines, Ontario, Canada, pp. 331–356.

Getz, D., Carlsen, J. and Morrison, A. (2004) *The Family Business in Tourism and Hospitality*. CAB International, Wallingford, UK.

Getz, D., Dowling, R., Carlsen, J. and Anderson, D. (1999) Critical success factors for wine tourism. *International Journal of Wine Marketing* 11(3), 20–43.

Griffin, T. and Loersch, A. (2004) The determinants of quality experiences in an emerging wine region. In: Carlsen, J. and Charters, S. (eds) *International Wine Tourism Research. Proceedings of the International Wine Tourism Conference*, Margaret River, Western Australia, May 2004. Vineyard Publishers, Perth.

Hall, C.M. (2004) Small firms and wine and food tourism in New Zealand: issues of collaboration, clusters and lifestyles. In: Thomas, R. (ed.) *Small Firms in Tourism: International Perspectives*. Elsevier Science, Oxford, UK.

Hall, C.M. and Johnson, G. (1999) Wine and tourism: an imbalanced partnership? In: Dowling, R. and Carlsen, J. (eds) *Wine Tourism: Perfect Partners. Proceedings of the First Australian Wine Tourism Conference*, Margaret River, Western Australia, May 1998. Bureau of Tourism Research, Canberra, Australia, pp. 51–71.

Hall, CM., Longo, A.M., Mitchell, R. and Johnson, G. (2000) Wine tourism in New Zealand. In: Hall, C.M., Sharples, L., Cambourne, B. and Macionis, N. (eds) *Wine Tourism around the World: Development, Management and Markets*. Elsevier Science, Oxford, UK, pp. 150–176.

Hall, C.M. and Macionis, N. (1998) Wine tourism in Australia and New Zealand. In: Butler, R.W., Hall, C.M. and Jenkins, J.M. (eds) *Tourism and Recreation in Rural Areas*. John Wiley and Sons, Sydney, Australia, pp. 267–298.

Hall, C.M., Sharples, L., Cambourne, B. and Macionis, N. (eds) (2000) *Wine Tourism Around the World: Development Management and Markets*. Elsener Science, Oxford, UK.

Heaney, L. (2003) Tapping the barrel: profiling domestic wine tourists, 1998–2001. *BTR Tourism Research Report* (vol. 5, no. 1, autumn). Canberra: Bureau of Tourism Research, Canberra, Australia, pp. 39–43.

Jennings, G.R. (2001) *Tourism Research*. John Wiley, Brisbane, Australia.

Lane, D. and Brown, G. (2004) The strategic development of wine tourism in South Australia. In: Carlsen, J. and Charters, S. (eds) *International Wine Tourism Research. Proceedings of the International Wine Tourism Conference*, Margaret River, Western Australia, May 2004. Vineyard Publishers, Perth, Australia.

Leiper, N. and Carlsen, J. (1998) Strategies for winery managers contemplating tourist markets; a case history: what happened to a winery positioned to remain on the fringe? In: Dowling, R. and Carlsen, J. (eds) *Wine Tourism: Perfect Partners. Proceedings of the First Australian Wine Tourism Conference*, Margaret River, Western Australia, May 1998. Bureau of Tourism Research, Canberra, Australia, pp. 197–208.

Loubser, S. (2004) The role of wine tourism in establishing a successful South African wine industry. In: Carlsen, J. and Charters, S. (eds) *International Wine Tourism Research. Proceedings of the International Wine Tourism Conference*, Margaret River, Western Australia, May 2004. Vineyard Publishers, Perth, Australia.

Macionis, N. (1999) Wineries and tourism: perfect partners or dangerous liaisons? In: Dowling, R. and Carlsen, J. (eds) *Wine Tourism: Perfect Partners. Proceedings of the First Australian Wine Tourism Conference*, Margaret River, Western Australia, May 1998. Bureau of Tourism Research, Canberra, Australia, pp. 35–49.

Mitchell, R. and Hall, M. (2001) Lifestyle behaviours of New Zealand winery visitors: wine club activities, wine cellars and place of purchase. *International Journal of Wine Marketing* 13(3), 82–93.

Mitchell, R. and Hall, C.M. (2004) The post-visit consumer behaviour of New Zealand winery visitors. In: Carlsen, J. and Charters, S. (eds) *International Wine Tourism Research. Proceedings of the International Wine Tourism Conference*, Margaret River, Western Australia, May 2004. Vineyard Publishers, Perth, Australia.

Mitchell, R., Hall, M. and McIntosh, A. (2000) Wine tourism and consumer behaviour. In: Hall, C.M., Sharples, L., Cambourne, B. and Macionis, N. (eds) *Wine Tourism Around the World: Development, Management and Markets*. Elsevier Science, Oxford, UK, pp. 115–135.

Nixon, B. (1999) The changing face of the winery tourist. In: Dowling, R. and Carlsen, J. (eds) *Wine Tourism: Perfect Partners. Proceedings of the First Australian Wine Tourism Conference*, Margaret River, Western Australia, May 1998. Vineyard Publications, Perth, Australia.

Roberts, R. and Deery, M. (2004) Good living tourism: case studies of two food and wine regions in Victoria Yarra Valley and the Macedon Ranges. In: Carlsen, J. and Charters, S. (eds) *International Wine Tourism Research: Proceedings of the International Wine Tourism Conference*, Margaret River, Western Australia, May 2004. Vineyard Publications, Perth, Australia.

Sanders, D. (2004) Wine tourism and regional development: a case study of the Margaret River wine region, Western Australia. In: Carlsen, J. and Charters, S. (eds) *International Wine Tourism Research, Proceedings of the International Wine Tourism Conference*, Margaret River, Western Australia, May 2004. Vineyard Publications, Perth, Australia.

Sparks, B. and Malady, J. (2004) Developing wine and food regions: product, people and perseverance. In: Carlsen, J. and Charters, S.

(eds) *International Wine Tourism Research, Proceedings of the International Wine Tourism Conference*, Margaret River, Western Australia, May 2004. Vineyard Publications, Perth, Australia.

Tassiopoulos, D., Nunstsu, N. and Haydam, N. (2004) Wine tourists in South Africa: a demographic and psychographic study. In: Carlsen, J. and Charters, S. (eds) *International Wine Tourism Research. Proceedings of the International Wine Tourism Conference*, Margaret River, Western Australia, May 2004. Vineyard Publishers, Perth, Australia.

Taylor, R. (2004) Wine tourism and festivals and events: a longitudinal analysis of visitor characteristics and satisfaction measures. In: Carlsen, J. and Charters, S. (eds) *International Wine Tourism Research. Proceedings of the International Wine Tourism Conference*, Margaret River, Western Australia, May 2004. Vineyard Publishers, Perth, Australia.

Telfer, D. (2001) From a tiny tourism village to a regional wine route: an investigation of the competitive advantage of embedded clusters in Niagara, Canada. *Tourism Recreation Research* 26(2), 23–33.

Weiler, B., Truong, M. and Griffiths, M. (2004) Visitor profiles and motivations for visiting an Australian wine festival. In: Carlsen, J. and Charters, S. (eds) *International Wine Tourism Research. Proceedings of the International Wine Tourism Conference*, Margaret River, Western Australia, May 2004. Vineyard Publishers, Perth, Australia.

Williams, P. (2001) Positioning wine tourism destinations: an image analysis. *International Journal of Wine Marketing* 13 (3), 42–58.

Winemakers Federation of Australia (WFA) (1998) *National Wine Tourism Strategy* WFA, Adelaide, Australia.

Part I
The Wine Tourism Setting

2 Do Tourism and Wine Always Fit Together? A Consideration of Business Motivations

RICK A. FRASER* AND ABEL ALONSO

*Commerce Division, PO Box 84, Lincoln University, Canterbury,
New Zealand
E-mail: fraserr1@lincoln.ac.nz

Introduction

Although several authors comment in passing about resources for the activities of marketing and wine production, legal restrictions on land use, sign posting and other infra-structural matters, there is seldom any clear discussion about the winery owner's or winemaker's ability or interest to become involved in wine tourism. Dodd (1995) and Beverland (1998) appear to be the only authors to clearly identify that wine tourism may present significant downside aspects to the business of making and marketing wine. Though there may be a marketing advantage from cellar door sales, not every grower will necessarily want to be involved, and indeed may not be able to afford to become involved. To this end, the researchers began exploring some of the parameters that might influence wine tourism involvement.

Literature Review

The tourism and wine industries are increasingly identified as natural symbiotic partners. This relationship is now embraced in the term 'wine tourism', which has received elevated awareness, if not importance, through the relatively recent advent of specialist wine tourism conferences in Australia and New Zealand. Many authors point to the potential benefits from this relationship (Dodd, 1995; Dodd and Bigotte, 1997; Hall et al., 1997; Hall and Johnson, 1998; Getz et al., 1999). Beverland (1998) argues that some authors seem to be saying that wineries should be involved in wine tourism. It has also been argued that in some cases the sale of wines locally to visitors will be more profitable by avoiding high transport costs and retailer mark-ups (Kingston, 2000). But Kingston's claim of 'tourism – essential for success' may be going too far, as such a strategy may be neither sufficient, nor necessary, to achieve profitability or growth of wine sales and brand recognition.

Much has been written about facets of wine marketing opportunities for producers diversifying into wine tourism. Examples include the wine education expectations of wine tourists (Charters and Ali-Knight, 2000); what needs to happen at the cellar door (Pitcher, 2002); relationship marketing dimensions with young wine tourists (Treloar, 2002); their generational characteristics (Mitchell, 2002); and lifestyle behaviours (Mitchell and Hall, 2001). Hall *et al.* (2002), have suggested that local resources in the food and wine areas constitute intangible capital that could bring benefit to the wider community. A lengthy list is provided by Getz *et al.* (1999) as to what is needed to attract wine tourists, and to cater for and satisfy their needs. These contributions all add refinement to the arguments presented by Hall *et al.* (1997), that there is a need to develop information and networks to inform potential tourists and create the economic synergies within a particular region.

It is at least implicit in all these writings that wine tourists will generally experience an opportunity for wine tasting, perhaps a tour of the vineyard and winery or a chance to meet the winemaker. A fairly consistent theme is the opportunity to buy the wine, or at least to be introduced to it in order to enhance the probability of later purchase. However, the argument that winery visits will create enhanced brand loyalty among visitors, and thus future purchases by them, is cast into doubt by King and Morris (Beverland, 1998). Seldom mentioned, furthermore, are aspects such as Occupational Health and Safety or Food Safety Programme requirements, both of which present significant operational challenges. There also seems to be no suggestion of adopting wider-ranging ideas to attract the potential tourist, such as grape-stomping competitions, demonstration vineyards, blending your own wines, or participation in actual winery processes – as offered in the Sonoma Valley (Himelstein, 2002). Such ideas may add to the experience or even attract other tourists not necessarily interested in the wine per se, but who might be tempted to pay for such activities.

Offering any tourist activities moves the vineyard manager from a singularly primary industry focus, dealing with crop management activities such as preventing predation by birds or damage by freak weather events, to having to include a tertiary sector focus where customer service skills are more critical. That some wineries do not want to be involved in wine tourism was acknowledged by Hall *et al.* (1997) when they wrote: 'the negative attitudes of some of the wineries may not be entirely misplaced, some … may receive little direct benefit from tourism' (p. 24). They argue that there may well be considerable effort needed to inform and persuade wineries to become involved in wine tourism.

Research Method

As this was largely an exploratory investigation and there happens to be a convenient cluster of vineyards and wineries immediately nearby, we arranged to interview the owners of the nearest nine wineries. These interviews allowed us to develop a fuller understanding of both the motivations and business challenges faced than was obtainable from the literature.

We then developed a survey instrument with a mix of closed and open items that could be left with other local owners prepared to take part but unable to spare the time for a personal interview. Telephone contact, and in some cases personal visits, resulted in a total of 48 vineyards in the Canterbury region agreeing to participate. In 17 cases the initial contact also became the data collection stage, with the researcher recording responses directly on the survey instrument. While these were virtually structured interviews, they were not as in-depth as the initial nine interviews had been. None the less, the additional comments made by owners and managers proved very insightful, as much for how they spoke, as what they spoke about. The other 22 questionnaires completed by Canterbury respondents were distributed through the mail.

The focus of this stage was to determine the nature of the various business ventures, owner expectations and perceptions of both the wine and the tourism industries, along with motivations for being involved in either or both. It became clear from the responses that there were two distinct sub-groups: those who saw winery visitors as a useful adjunct to their operations and those who saw them as creating a negative impact on their business.

Based on the initial data and feedback, we decided to expand the study to include all New Zealand wineries and, therefore, slightly modified the questionnaire to take the form of a mailed, self-completion instrument. This was then mailed, along with an explanatory letter, to a further 242 vineyards and wineries throughout New Zealand for which mail addresses could be identified using an industry-sourced mailing list and cross-checking through telephone directories, Visitor Information Centres, wine tour operator brochures and web listings. This gave a total sample of 290. We considered this to be a more than acceptable proportion of the industry based on the 334 wineries reported as being in existence in 1999 (Beverland and Lockshin, 2001). By relying on mailed surveys and not making direct personal contacts, however, we accept that many vineyards were not identified and thus excluded.

A total of 144 usable responses were collected by these various means. Of these, 137 were included in the study after eliminating three publicly owned companies and four very long-established businesses. While, arguably, each of these eliminated respondents are, or potentially could be, involved in wine tourism, they were considered to be driven by commercial market branding reasons or they had always traditionally sold their wine at the cellar door, and in one case had done so since the 19th Century. This represents a used response rate of 47.2%. As part of another subsequent study the researchers also had varying degrees of personal contact with owners in the Otago, Nelson, Marlborough and Waikato regions. These provided additional opportunities to discuss with owners and managers their personal views about wine marketing and wine tourism in particular.

Responses were analysed using the SPSS statistical package and descriptive statistics were produced.

Findings

Given that 93 (67.9%) respondents work full-time in their winery, it was clear that these are serious business ventures. For many respondents though, the business is either not sufficiently robust to support them fully, or they are currently unable or not needing to commit all their energies to it. While 81 respondents (59.1%) reported a passion for wines and 63 (46.0%) cited a desire to change their lifestyle as their main reasons for their business choice, having a business was the dominant rationale. Making money, or that it was a business venture, were the reasons given by 99 (72.3%) respondents. These respondents and their businesses seem generally similar to the descriptions of Australian winery owners as developed by Charters and Loughton (2000) and Charters (2001), especially in terms of such ventures being a lifestyle choice and personal development direction.

The view in the literature that wine tourism adds a strong business element was well supported, with 79 (57.7%) respondents being part of a wine trail, and 37 of these also operating a restaurant or café. A further five respondents who are not involved with wine trails also have either a restaurant or café. The relative importance of the wine itself as compared to the tourism element can be seen in Table 2.1 of mean importance scores for a number of business foci items rated on a five-point, Likert-type scale. The number of responses varies as a number of items were not relevant to some operators. Clearly, the dominant foci are the growing of grapes and making of their own wine, followed by various forms of wine sales. While still somewhat important, it is notable that selling food and catering to passers-by are among the least important reasons for being in the industry; the wine itself standing out as the dominant focus.

From these results we argue that the respondents are in this industry primarily because of an interest in wine and that it is a business and motivated by monetary reasons. This fits the general view contained in the literature.

Table 2.1. The importance ratings for possible business foci.

	Mean	SD	n
Growing grapes/making own wine	4.90	0.41	132
Selling wine nationally (e.g. to retailers/wholesalers)	4.37	1.07	108
Exporting wine	4.27	1.39	103
Wine sales at cellar door	4.08	1.35	106
Wine sales at own restaurant	4.08	1.43	59
Wine sales through mail order	3.84	1.29	100
Wine sales through tastings	3.62	1.27	91
Catering to passers-by and wine tours	3.55	1.28	77
Food sales	3.46	1.45	52
Buying grapes elsewhere and making wine in own winery	3.39	1.48	75

1, totally unimportant; 5, vitally important; SD, standard deviation.

Given this commercial focus and the implicit view in the literature that wine tourism is a good fit with such objectives, we had expected considerable involvement with wine trails, or similar. But while on a regional basis this is generally true, with 57–89% of respondents in each region being involved, there was an exception. In Canterbury, only 20% of respondents reported being involved with wine trails. In part, this is probably due to the more recent development of wine production here, but we believe two other factors moderated the result.

First, through local knowledge, the researchers had been able to identify a large number of local vineyards not involved in tourist activities. Secondly, a positive bias in favour of wine tourism was inevitably introduced outside Canterbury, as the sampling process relied in part on brochures, websites and various other tourist publications. Based on the more detailed local knowledge we developed from the personal interviews and other qualitative information, we believe that there are many other wineries that are not included in the national sample and whose owners also have no wish to be involved in wine tourism.

When asked why they belonged to a wine trail, respondents clearly favoured commercial reasons. Of the 79 who are already part of a wine trail, the majority (64, 81.0%) cited 'economic benefits', with another 26 (32.9%) giving 'imperative business need' as their reason. However, the fundamental driver appears to be 'a means of selling more wine', given that this was reported by 92.0%. Providing a means of diversifying their business was also reported by 14 (17.7%) of these respondents. These reasons all point to compelling financial drivers behind the decision.

Despite these reasons for some businesses becoming involved with wine trails being compelling, they were not sufficient for all to do so. Therefore, the reasons for not doing so, as given by the 58 respondents from across New Zealand who are not part of wine trails, were of particular interest to the researchers. Their responses are summarized in Table 2.2.

Respondents indicated that their decision was an informed one in that they did not cite a lack of knowledge as a reason for not belonging to a wine trail. They also indicated that they were aware of the potential. Eighteen respondents cited either insufficient economic benefit or lack of demand as the reason for not belonging to a wine trail. Of these 18, seven also cited a

Table 2.2. Reasons why vineyard owners have not joined a wine trail.

Reason	f	%
Lack of infrastructure to host wine tours	19	33.9
It would disrupt existing business operations	18	32.9
Insufficient economic benefit	10	17.9
Not enough wine supply to cope with possible demand	8	14.3
I don't see the demand for it	7	12.5
I am unaware of wine trail business potential	1	1.8
Lack of knowledge or lack of research about wine trails	1	1.8

f, frequency; *n*, 56; not all respondents answered this item and some gave more than one lack of infrastructure and another six wished to avoid disruption to their existing business as additional reasons for not belonging to wine trails. It had been expected that some smaller and newer operators would be concerned that they had insufficient product to meet demand if they were to open to visitors, but only eight respondents gave this reason.

Clearly, some respondents might alter their position if sufficient economic benefit could be demonstrated, or they could be confident that their winemaking would not be disrupted. However, there would still be a need to address the infrastructure issues. Where the issues lie outside the businesses themselves, such as road accessibility, signage, accommodation or other local attractions, regional authorities and planning agencies may then need to become involved. However, if the issues relate to on-site infrastructure such as insufficient development of access, buildings and facilities on the vineyard, it would be the task of owners to address these. The causes may include a lack of capital, inadequate initial planning and layout of the property, limited available land or planning requirements restricting land usage. Some of these issues may be effectively insurmountable, at least in the short term, while other matters may also be an issue of cost *versus* potential benefit.

The qualitative data provided some further insight into this. For one owner, the cost for the necessary road access was prohibitive, while another five cited the lack of tasting, food or accommodation facilities. Only three owners specifically indicated a lack of infrastructure external to the property as an impediment. While one business owner indicated that they viewed the local regional wine tourism fees as too costly for the benefits gained, eight saw wine tourism as distracting them from their main business of wine production. This latter group also commented that they did not have the time, nor perceived sufficient returns from tourists, to justify becoming involved.

There was also a distinct theme that being involved in wine tourism would interfere with the respondents' lifestyles. The lifestyle associated with grape growing was a common and important reason for entering the wine industry. Having to spend time attending to visitors was seen as taking valued time away from producing a good product and would further reduce already scarce free time, especially for those also having to work away from the property to support its development. Clearly, many winery owners simply do not want to know about visitors.

Implications for Wine Tourism

While research has increasingly been undertaken on consumer profiles, expectations, levels of satisfaction and expenditures, which all point to business opportunities, this study has found that many potential wine tourism suppliers do not want to become involved. Some of the reasons identified reaffirm those argued by Dodd (1995), but it is also argued here that the alleged benefits of wine tourism are seen by many as insufficient to encourage engagement. It has also been identified that many operators see wine tourism as negatively impacting on their lifestyle and main business focus. Therefore, while adding a tourist dimension to a winery or vineyard may increase regional tourism appeal and economic benefit, it may not provide much in the way of net benefit for the individual winery business. There is even the possibility that if producers are distracted from making a quality product, they may then also find it difficult to sell what they do produce.

There may well be a need to provide more education about the wider social benefits that are argued to accrue from wine tourism, and possibly even business support, if some current winery owners are to become involved. However, given that several wineries in this study reported that they are successful without tourism involvement, it must be recognized that there are other successful business models. Future research could be directed towards this aspect to ensure that a balanced perspective is offered to owners, especially to those individuals whose passion lies in producing the wine and enjoying the associated lifestyle without distractions.

It may be of particular benefit to investigate the relationships between owner interests and personal and business life-cycle stages compared with business achievements to date, and even to investigate what constitutes success in the wine or wine tourism businesses. A possible research direction could be to combine and extend the studies by Charters and Loughton (2000) and Corkindale and Welsh (2003), who looked at various concepts of small business and success in the wine industry, dimensions seldom referred to in the wine tourism literature. Such further work could provide a clearer evaluation of any benefits arising from engaging in wine tourism.

References

Beverland, M. (1998) Wine tourism in New Zealand – maybe the industry has got it right. *International Journal of Wine Marketing* 10(2), 24–34.

Beverland, M. and Lockshin, L. (2001) Organizational life cycles in small New Zealand wineries. *Journal of Small Business Management* 39(4), 354–362.

Charters, S. (2001) The structure of business in the wine industry. *Australian and New Zealand Wine Industry Journal* 16(1), 97–100.

Charters, S. and Ali-Knight, J. (2000) Wine tourism – a thirst for knowledge? *International Journal of Wine Marketing* 12(3), 70–80.

Charters, S. and Loughton, K. (2000) Attitudes to small business in the wine industry. Presentation to the 45th International Conference on Small Business, World Conference, Brisbane, Australia.

Corkindale, D. and Welsh, A. (2003) Measuring success and marketing in small wineries in Australia. *International Journal of Wine Marketing* 15(2), 4–24.

Dodd, T. (1995) Opportunities and pitfalls of tourism in a developing wine industry. *International Journal of Wine Marketing* 7(1), 5–17.

Dodd, T. and Bigotte, V. (1997) Perceptual differences among visitor groups to wineries. *Journal of Travel Research* 35(1), 46–51.

Getz, D., Dowling, R., Carlsen, J. and Anderson, D. (1999) Critical success factors for wine tourism. *International Journal of Wine Marketing* 11(3), 20–43.

Hall, J., Sharples, L. and Smith, A. (2002) Local initiatives for regional development: The role of intangible capital in food and wine tourism. *New Zealand Tourism and Hospitality Research Conference Proceedings*, Rotorua, New Zealand, p. 335.

Hall, M., Cambourne, B., Macionis, N. and Johnson, G. (1997) Wine tourism and network development in Australia and New Zealand: review, establishment and prospects. *International Journal of Wine Marketing* 9(2/3), 5–31.

Hall, M. and Johnson, G. (1998) Wine and tourism: an imbalanced partnership? *Proceedings of 1998 First Australian Wine Tourism Conference*, Margaret River, Western Australia, pp. 51–71.

Himelstein, L. (2002) Wine lovers: want to get your feet wet? New tours offer vineyard visitors more action. *Business Week* 3797, 100.

Kingston, C. (2000) Central Otago going for new gold – wine grapes: HortResearch study measures impact. *New Zealand Winegrower* 3(4), 23–25.

Mitchell, R. (2002) The generation game: Generation X and baby boomer wine tourism. *New Zealand Tourism and Hospitality Research Conference Proceedings*, Rotorua, New Zealand, pp. 115–127.

Mitchell, R. and Hall, M. (2001) Lifestyle behaviours on New Zealand winery visitors: wine club activities, wine cellars and places of purchase. *International Journal of Wine Marketing* 13(3), 83–93.

Pitcher, L. (2002) Interpretation of wine: a cellar door perspective. *New Zealand Tourism and Hospitality Research Conference Proceedings*, Rotorua, New Zealand, p. 336.

Treloar, P. (2002). An investigation into the significance of relationship marketing on the young winery tourist. *New Zealand Tourism and Hospitality Research Conference Proceedings*, Rotorua, New Zealand, pp. 128–139.

3 Land Use Policy and Wine Tourism Development in North America's Pacific Northwest

PETER W. WILLIAMS,* KAREN GRAHAM AND
LOUELLA MATHIAS

*Centre for Tourism Policy and Research, Simon Fraser University, Burnaby,
British Columbia, Canada, V5A 1S6*
*E-mail: peter_williams@sfu.ca

Introduction

The long-term viability of wine regions as tourism destinations depends on implementing regional policies that sustain landscapes conducive to producing top-quality wines and attracting appropriate numbers of visitors. Most wine tourism regions promote and sell the image of experiencing wine in its geographical and cultural context (Senese, 1999; Williams, 2001; Bruwer, 2003). Establishing policies which encourage the maintenance of regional sense of place in such areas is critical to the wine industry and other tourism stakeholders (Hall and Jenkins, 1998; Skinner, 2000). More specifically, policies that conserve the integrity of rural landscapes and their associated cultural attributes are essential ingredients in the mix of elements needed to create a viable wine tourism system (Getz, 2000). Developing such guidelines requires the collaboration and sound planning of many wine industry partners (Williams and Dossa, 2003). Frequently, rural regions forget this practice and rush to capitalize on growing market interest and enthusiasm for wine tourism opportunities.

Much research and discussion has focused on examining the characteristics and evolution of product development, marketing and management dimensions of wine tourism operations in various geographic regions (Macionis and Cambourne, 1998; Aloysius and Lee, 2001; Dodd and Beverland, 2001; Telfer, 2001; Demhardt, 2003). However, comparatively little work has addressed the policy regimes that guide such developments (Hall *et al.*, 2000). This chapter examines the mix of land use policies and related permitted activities that shape wine tourism development. The findings contribute to a recognized need for more policy-oriented and benchmarking research related to wine tourism destination policy and development practices (Getz and Brown, 2006 (in press)).

Literature Review

Wine tourism is often viewed as an economic engine capable of generating benefits for a variety of regional and local stakeholders. Its potential contributions include increased markets and sales for winery operators; jobs and income for residents engaged in complementary service activities (e.g. wine product sales and services, restaurants, accommodation); and tax revenues for government agencies supporting broader rural development initiatives (Busby and Rendle, 2000; Getz, 2000; Hall *et al.*, 2000). While such contributions have been explored within individual wine tourism enterprises (e.g. Dodd and Bigotte, 1995; Hall and Macionis, 1998; Macionis and Cambourne, 1998; Hall *et al.*, 2000), they are seldom examined in a regional destination context. The extent to which these benefits occur is shaped significantly by the type of policy regime guiding and managing the development of wine tourism at state, provincial and local levels (Hackett, 1998; Martin and Williams, 2003).

In contrast to promoting policies that support development, limited attention is afforded to anticipating or mitigating the potential adverse implications of wine tourism growth (Carlsen and Ali-Knight, 2004). Potential drawbacks to wine tourism development include: (i) urbanization pressures associated with various forms of residential development in agricultural zones (Cambourne *et al.*, 2000); (ii) excessive tourist use of such regions (Getz, 1999); (iii) displacement of traditional agricultural practices (Sharp, 1992, Poitras and Getz, 2006 (in press)); (iv) conflicts between winery operators and residents concerning appropriate farm management practices (Martin and Williams, 2003); and (v) encroachments of non-agricultural activities onto prime farming lands (Penner, 2006).

Skinner's paper (2000) on the evolutionary stages of wine tourism development in California's Napa Valley clearly flags up the importance of developing policies for managing the industry's growth and effects. Without carefully targeted policies, the cumulative pressures of wine tourism may limit the capacity of wineries to provide positive tourism experiences for patrons, and adversely alter the attractiveness of regional winescapes at the core of the tourism product (Boxall, 1999). In a growing number of cases, unrealistic expectations of the benefits of wine tourism have overshadowed the emerging adverse effects of such development and resulted in less than ideal long-term impacts (Skinner, 2000; Carlsen and Ali-Knight, 2004).

A better balance and integration of policies is needed between those facilitating wine tourism developments and others conserving lands strictly for more traditional agricultural uses (Hall *et al.*, 2000). As Getz (2000) suggests, the long-term sustainability of wine tourism systems rests on a foundation of not only sound business management capabilities and coordinated supplier–visitor interactions, but also on natural resource management practices that nurture and sustain the production of quality wines and the landscapes that host them. Sustainable wine tourism systems in this context require policies and institutional arrangements that integrate resource conservation goals that maintain critical ecological habitats and landscapes, with those supporting forms of facility and service development that reflect and respect rural culture and character (Lane, 1994; Hall *et al.*, 2000). Indeed, a supportive and responsive policy regime that provides clear guidance for wine tourism land use, related infrastructure development and programming decisions is an important cornerstone in sustaining the competitiveness of wine regions. In too many cases, such policy is limited and the full impact of its absence only emerges when destinations reach crisis point.

Clearly, there is a need for systematic and comparative analyses of policy regimes used to guide wine tourism development in rural regions (Getz and Brown, 2006 (in press)). The following comparison of land use policies in North America's Pacific Northwest Wine Country illustrates institutional strategies that currently guide the evolution of this emerging industry. Several wine-related publications regularly cover British Columbia, Washington and Oregon: wine and food magazines such as *Wine Press Northwest, Northwest Palate* and the web-based publication *Wines Northwest* (www.winesnw.com) all consider these three regions to be part of greater Pacific Northwest wine country. They have published useful discussions on issues common to all three zones. Officials from each zone increasingly communicate with each other to share experiences and initiatives (Oregan Wine Board, 2004, personal communication).

Research Method

Encompassing viticultural zones in the American states of Oregon and Washington and in the Canadian province of British Columbia, the Pacific Northwest Wine Country region is gaining a favourable reputation for the quality of its wines and attractive winescapes (O'Hara, 2006). Cumulatively, viticultural zones within this region now occupy about 19,600 ha of land, which generate in excess of 142,000 tonnes of grapes and 79.2 million l of wine annually (Table 3.1). From a tourism development perspective, each area has strategies to facilitate greater visitation and travel expenditures. Linked to those strategies are specific initiatives promoting wine tourism. Similarly, each area has a sizeable portion of its wineries participating in wine tourism pursuits (Table 3.1).

Land use policies affecting the development of wine tourism vary in their emphasis and application across the region. A comparison of these policies in British Columbia's Okanagan, Valley Washington's Yakima Valley and Oregon's Willamette Valley illustrates this diversity of approaches. These areas fall, respectively, within the more localized political jurisdictions of the Regional District of the Central Okanagan (RDCO) for the Okanagan Valley, Yakima County for the Yakima Valley and Yamhill County for the Willamette Valley (Fig. 3.1). While each area has its own economic and socio-cultural characteristics, they all have growing wine industries, commitments to increasing wine tourism opportunities and well-established agricultural land use traditions.

Table 3.1. Wine and wine tourism industry characteristics of case study regions (1999–2004).

Indicator	British Columbia		Washington		Oregon	
	1999	2004	1999	2004	1999	2004
Grape production (tonnes)[1]	10,957	16,672	70,000	107,000	16,523	18,620
Vineyard acreage (prov./state)[1]	4,184	5,462	24,800	30,000	9,800	13,700
Vineyard acreage (regional district/county)[2]	505	537[3]	8,540	9,650[4]	3,040	4,380
Vol. of wine sales (prov./state, million l)[3]	2.4	4.7	38	62.9	7.0	11.6
No. of wineries (prov./state)[4]	n/a	97	n/a	323	n/a	201
Driving time from regional district/county to most proximate major urban travel market (h)		4.5 (Vancouver)		3.25 (Seattle)		1.0 (Portland)
Regional district/county share of provincial/state tourism revenues (%)[5]	3.7	4.0	2.3	2.3	0.9	1.0
Increase in regional district/county tourism revenues, 1999–2004 (%)[5]		9		21		36
No. of wineries (regional district/county)[6]	24	50	22	49	35	81
No. of wineries offering tourism (regional district/county)[7]	n/a	46	20	43	18	33

[1] BC, Oregon, Washington estimates derived from: British Columbia: BCWI, 2004/5; Oregon: Oregon Agricultural Statistics Service, 2004 (www.nass.usda.gov/or); Oregon Wine Board, 2005, personal communication; Washington: Washington Agricultural Statistics Service, 2005 (www.nass.usda.gov/wa); Washington Wine Commission, 2005.
[2] RDCO, Yamhill, and Yakima estimates derived from: RDCO: MAFF, 2005; Yamhill County: Oregon Wine Board, 2005, personal communication; Yakima: Washington Wine Commission, 2005.
[3] BC, Oregon, Washington estimates derived from: British Columbia: BCWI, 2005; Oregon: Oregon Wine Board, 2005, personal communication; Washington: Washington Wine Commission, 2005.
[4] BC, Oregon, Washington estimates derived from: British Columbia: BCWI, 2005; Oregon: Oregon Wine Board, 2005, personal communication; Washington: Washington Wine Commission, 2005.
[5] BC estimates based on data from BC Ministry of Finance and Corporate Relations 1997–2001; Washington and Oregon estimates based on data from Dean Runyan Associates, Portland, Oregon, 2004.
[6] Estimates of RDCO, Yamhill and Yakima wineries derived from: RDCO: Okanagan Wine Festivals Society, 2005; Yamhill: Willamette Valley Wineries Association, 2005; Yakima: Wines Yakima.
[7] Estimates of RDCO, Yamhill and Yakima wineries derived from: RDCO: Okanagan Wine Festivals Society, 2005; Yamhill: Willamette Valley Wineries Association, 2005; Yakima: Wines Yakima.

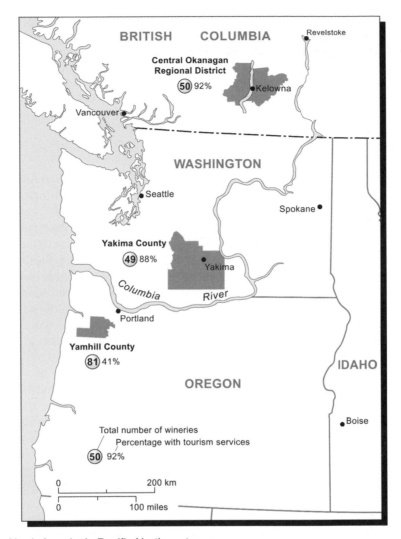

Fig. 3.1. North America's Pacific Northwest area.

A combination of quantitative and qualitative data informs this investigation. In particular, quantitative information collected from government and industry documents describes the relative shifts in wine production, tourism and wine tourism development occurring in each case study area between 1999 and 2004. Subsequent to this, key informant interviews and document reviews concerning provincial/state and regional/county level acts and by-laws provide the qualitative basis for assessing the wine tourism policy approaches in each region.

Land use policies affecting wine tourism development in the Pacific Northwest relate primarily to two distinct but complementary themes: the production and sale of wines on agricultural lands, and tourism uses of winery/agricultural lands. This paper focuses on policies affecting tourism uses of winery/agricultural lands, as well as liquor regulations governing on-site activities at wineries. An adapted version of Clarke's rural tourism land use framework (1996) identifies the key wine tourism activity, accommodation and amenity elements that are typically affected by policy decisions. The extent to which such elements exist in current land use policy forms the basis for the comparative analysis that follows (Fig. 3.2).

Findings

A variety of indicators help assess the extent of tourism in rural regions (Busby and Rendle, 2000). Indicators of wine tourism development include not only measures of wine industry investment (e.g. vineyard acreage, wine production, marketing resources, wineries) but also developments related to wine tourism facilities and services (e.g. wine tasting facilities, restaurant services, accommodation, entertainment areas) (Getz and Brown, 2006 (in press)). While data concerning wine production is available for each case study area, limited information exists concerning wine tourism's traits. Reflecting the emerging character of wine tourism in these areas, the industry's contributions to overall provincial and state level revenues is limited to a few anecdotal indicators of its size and performance.

Overall, wine tourism development in these areas is primarily comprised of many small businesses providing products and services to visitors on a seasonal basis (Table 3.1). While many of them are interested in expanding their wine tourism operations, most are only in the formative stages of such development. However, as domestic and international interest in wine tourism continues to grow, provincial/state and local tourism associations are

Attractions – permanent	Attractions – events
On-site wine shops/ tasting rooms	Guided tours (vineyard and winery)
Special event facilities	Festivals
Off-site wine museums	Educational demonstrations
Self-guided vineyard walks	
Access – rural	Activities
Wine routes (brochures and signage for vehicles)	Guided multiple winery tours
Wine routes (bicycle)	Cycling tours to wineries
Accommodation	Amenities
On-site bed and breakfast	Restaurants
Agri-tourism accommodation	On-site picnic areas

Fig. 3.2. Wine tourism land use elements (from Clarke, 1996).

increasingly incorporating the presence of such products into their destination and promotional strategies.

Wine and tourism industry performance

British Columbia

British Columbia's wine industry has grown substantially in recent years. It is second only to Ontario's Niagara Region in the production of Canadian wines. Between 1999 and 2004, vineyard acreage in this region increased by 31% to 2180 ha, and grape production grew by 52% from about 10,900 to 16,700 tonnes. This translated into a 96% increase in the number of litres of wine sold. By 2004, there were about 97 operating wineries. Significant investments in wine marketing and wine tourism development complemented this expansion (BCWI, 2004).

Between 1999 and 2004, Okanagan Valley wineries more than doubled – from 24 to 50 operations (Table 3.1). In response to growing domestic and international tourist demand (Williams and Kelly, 2001; Williams and Dossa, 2003), and an increasingly competitive tourism marketplace, almost of all of them (92%) promoted various forms of wine tourism (OWFS, 2005). This translated into increased winery visitation levels and other related tourist events. For instance, the region's Okanagan Wine Festival Society spring and autumn wine festivals drew about 138,500 attendees and generated an estimated Cdn$3 million in 2004. This was the ninth straight year of growth in both measures (OWFS, 2005). Building on this performance, the wine industry's official marketing agency (i.e. British Columbia Wine Institute) stated its intent to 'create a wine tourism industry second only to California' (BCWI, 2003).

Washington

Washington is second only to California in overall US wine production. The state's wine industry grew significantly between 1999 and 2004; vineyard acreage increased by 21% to 12,000 ha and grape production grew by 53% from 70,000 to 107,000 tonnes during this time. This translated into a 66% increase in the number of litres of wine sold (Table 3.1). By 2004, there were 323 wineries producing wine in the state. The vast majority of these were small, family-owned wineries. Yakima Valley's growth of wineries matched general growth rates for the wine industry in Washington State. Between 1999 and 2004, the number of wineries stretched from 22 to 49 – a 223% increase. Building on a desire to generate greater cellar door sales, about 88% of them operated some form of wine tourism business (Table 3.1). As in British Columbia, the state's leading wine industry organization intends to compete directly with California and position the area as North America's premier wine tourism destination (Gaudette, 2000; WWC, 2004, personal communication).

Oregon

Oregon's wine production trailed only that of California, Washington and New York in the USA in 2004; only California had more wineries than Oregon at that time (Yamhill Valley Visitors Association, 2006). As with the two preceding regions, much of its wine industry growth occurred recently. Between 1999 and 2004, vineyard land increased by 40% to 5480 ha. In that same period, grape production grew by 13% from 16,500 to 18,600 tonnes. This translated into a 66% increase in the number of litres of wine sold (Table 3.1). By 2004, there were about 200 wineries in operation in the state.

Yamhill County produces many of Oregon's top-quality wines. Its growth in wineries reflects expansion trends elsewhere in Oregon. Between 1999 and 2004, wineries in the county increased from 35 to 81 – a 231% increase (Table 3.1). The wine industry's stakeholders specifically focused on creating smaller-scale, farm-focused operations as opposed to more industrialized wineries (Darlington, 1999; Shara Hall, 2001). In addition, a much smaller proportion of them established wine tourism enterprises. Less than half (41%) of the wineries in Yamhill County offered regular visiting hours and on-site amenities for wine tourists in 2004. This reduced focus on farm-based wine tourism development was partially offset by the creation of community-based retail outlets, gift shops, restaurants and accommodations typically associated with wine tourism (Yamhill County Winery Association, 2004).

In all three regions, planners and policy makers face growing pressures to transform agricultural lands into venues for producing wine- and tourism-related revenues. Tourist demands to visit wineries and pursue related tourism opportunities at the cellar door continue to escalate. Such pressures have met with varying policy responses. The following sections compare the policies and approaches to wine tourism land use management that have emerged. Tables 3.2 and 3.3 summarize these policies for each of the case study areas.

British Columbia land use policies

In British Columbia, the Ministry of Agriculture, Food and Fisheries (MAFF is now the Ministry of Agriculture and Lands) governs land use issues related to the wine industry. It established the Agricultural Land Reserve (ALR) and the Agricultural Land Commission (ALC) in 1973 to oversee agricultural land uses in British Columbia. MAFF and the ALC are central actors in the development of British Columbia's land use policies associated with wine tourism.

The ALC's mandate is to protect agricultural land and encourage farming on it. The ALC General Order (Policy No. 3) relating to wineries and cideries makes clear that its jurisdiction with respect to permitted uses takes precedence over other provincial or local government regulations. Other agencies may not prohibit winery or cidery activities approved by the ALC (ALC, 2003a). Furthermore, the ALC's General Order (Policy No. 4) expressly designates agri-tourism activities as a permitted farm activity in the ALR. This situation exists 'provided the activity promotes or markets farm products

Table 3.2. Pacific Northwest wine industry: state/provincial land use policy comparisons.

Land use policy	Policy presence and strength[1]		
	BC	Washington	Oregon
Agriculture/farming			
Agricultural lands protected for farming use	Yes/Medium	Yes/Strong	Yes/Medium
Winery is a permitted farm use	Yes/Strong	Yes (conditional)/Strong	Yes/Strong
Non-farm use: permitted uses			
Ancillary buildings for commercial purposes:	Yes/Strong	Yes/Medium	Yes/Strong
Retail	✓	(devolved to county)	✓
Restaurant	✓ (conditional)	(devolved to county)	✓
Agri-tourism activities	✓	✓ (conditional)	✓
Accommodation			
Agri-tourist	Yes (10 rooms)	No	No
Bed and breakfast	Yes (4 rooms)	No	Yes (variable)
On-site activities			
Retail items must be produce of farm or related merchandise	Yes/Medium	Yes/Strong	Yes/Strong
Wine tastings (in wineshop)	Yes ✓	Yes ✓	Yes ✓
Special events	Yes ✓	No	Yes (3 per year)
Food and beverage service	Yes ✓	Yes (conditional)	Yes (conditional)

[1] Yes, a policy exists; No, there is no policy in place; ✓, permitted activity; Strong, significant intent of policy to protect agricultural uses and prevent over-development of the resource; Medium, moderate intent of policy to protect agricultural uses; Weak, low intent of policy to protect agricultural uses.

Table 3.3. Pacific Northwest wine industry: regional/county land use policy comparisons.

Land use policy	Policy presence and strength[1]		
	Central Okanagan	Yakima County	Yamhill County
Agriculture/farming use			
Protects agricultural lands for farming use	Yes/Strong (minimum parcel requirements)	Yes/Strong (minimum parcel requirements)	Yes/Strong
Non-farm use – permitted uses			
Ancillary buildings for agri-tourism	Yes/Medium	Yes/Strong	Yes/Medium
Accommodation			
Agri-tourist	Yes (large parcel: 10 rooms, small parcel: 4 rooms)	No	No
Bed and Breakfast	Yes (4 rooms)	Yes (5 rooms)	Yes (9 rooms)
On-site activities			
Retail	No	Yes	No
Wine tastings	No	Yes	No
Special events	No	No	Yes (3 per year)
Food and beverage service	No	No	Yes (conditional)

[1] Yes, a policy exists; No, there is no policy in place; Strong, significant intent of policy to protect agricultural uses and prevent over-development of the resource; Medium, moderate intent of policy to protect agricultural uses; Weak, low intent of policy to protect agricultural uses.

produced on that farm. These activities are accessory and, at the same time, related to the principle use of the farm or ranch and must promote or market farm products from the farm or ranch' (ALC, 2003b).

While the ALC regards wineries and vineyards as permitted agricultural uses, it has the power to limit the quantity, scale and use of buildings for such purposes. The ALC's policy on non-farm use permits ancillary, wine-related buildings on the site, as long as the principal winery building is established. Tasting rooms and wine shops are permitted. The ALC also permits up to ten bedrooms for agri-tourist accommodation if all or part of the parcel is zoned for farm use. Bed and breakfasts (B&B) are considered a separate category of accommodation, and up to four bedrooms are allowed in such on-site facilities. The ALC generally permits tours, events and other ancillary activity on lands designated for winery use, but has the power to limit them if necessary. Few ALC guidelines dictate how to manage such activities.

The Liquor Control and Licensing Branch (LCLB), under the jurisdiction of the Ministry of Public Safety and Solicitor General, governs all retail liquor sales in BC. As such, it controls the conditions under which wineries can serve and sell wine. These regulations affect land use with respect to the amount of property that can be used for winery lounges, wine shops and special event sites such as outdoor theatres or picnic grounds. The LCLB is the key provincial agency governing all public on-site activities, including wine festival events and dinners. Most events hosted on-site at winery lounges are not subject to Special Occasion License approval, as long as they do not exceed capacity or duration permitted in the general license. Wineries that do not have a winery lounge can host the same types of events upon receiving a Special Occasion License (LCLB, 2004). The LCLB also governs the meal service permitted on winery property. The current winery licence includes the right to prepare and serve food (Surich, 1999; LCLB, 2004).

Cumulatively, the preceding policies create a management environment that is relatively permissive and proactive in encouraging the development of winery and wine tourism opportunities on BC's agricultural lands. These policies are now shaping the way in which wine industry land use decisions are taking place in BC's prime viticultural region – the Okanagan Valley. They are influential both within and outside the Agricultural Land Reserve (ALR).

Regional District of Central Okanagan (RDCO) land use policies

The RDCO encompasses most of the land in the central Okanagan Valley and the regions surrounding local urban centres that are subject to local government regulations. Among other things, it is responsible for land use decisions on rural agricultural lands outside and adjacent to the ALR as well as some lands in the ALR. These lands are under tremendous urbanization pressures. Between 1996 and 2001, the total farm land in the RDCO declined by 24% – from 78,500 to 59,476 acres (EDC, 2005). Pressures for wine tourism development intensified the demand to convert the area's agricultural lands to other uses.

The RDCO relies primarily on Zoning By-law No. 871 to address land use issues. This by-law identifies permitted and prohibited uses, parcel size, setbacks from ALR lands and appropriate wine tourism uses. For the most part, this complements those of the ALC with respect to permitted agricultural and non-farm uses and to the general environment around farm-related tourism. One aspect on which it differs is that outside the ALR, the RDCO sets two minimum parcel sizes, depending on the zone. Wineries that are zoned 'Rural 1' (RU1) must have a minimum parcel size of 30 ha, while wineries zoned RU2 require a minimum land parcel size of 4 ha. This policy encourages those rural lands outside the ALR to remain rural, and resistant to residential subdivision development or other uses.

There are differences with respect to non-farm uses. The RDCO permits one residential building per parcel, regardless of zoning, and allows for various on-site wine tourism activities. The RDCO also differs slightly from the ALC with respect to agri-tourist accommodation allowances. The ALC permits ten bedrooms per agri-tourism accommodation per parcel in the ALR, as long as the accommodation is related to tourism activities on the farm. In contrast, the RDCO specifies a limit of four bedrooms on parcels of 3.8 ha or less. This limitation is designed to maintain the agricultural character of the land, by preventing large or numerous accommodation buildings dominating the landscape. In addition, the RDCO land use policy recognizes permanent attractions, including on-site wine shops, as an accessory use of the land. The term wine shop encompasses the tasting room activities. Wine museums and wine centres in the Okanagan are off-site, and are managed by the BC Wine Institute. They are located in town centres such as Kelowna and Penticton, and are subject to local zoning and commercial by-laws.

Overall, RDCO land use policies bolster those of the ALC. They encourage wine tourism while restraining other forms of urban development that might diminish the scenic quality of the rural landscape important to tourism. While the zoning by-law provides a good framework for identifying appropriate agriculturally related activities, there is growing recognition that a broader strategic plan is needed to manage agricultural diversification options related to activities such as wine tourism. In response to this concern, the RDCO launched a multi-stakeholder planning process in 2005 to develop a regional Agriculture Plan which enhanced 'the viability of the agricultural sector in the Regional District by addressing farm viability issues arising from resource potential, diversification opportunities, urbanization conflicts and competition for agricultural land' (RDCO, 2005, p. 1). This initiative reflects a growing awareness of the need to manage growth of the industry in ways that respect the inherent and long-term values of the rural and agricultural landscape.

Washington State land use policies

Washington State's most pervasive rural land use policies are associated with its Growth Management Act (GMA), which was created in 1990. The Act and its regulations are tools for assisting and guiding local governments, state agencies and others in land use planning and related initiatives designed to manage growth and development. Conserving, maintaining and enhancing agricultural resource lands are key goals of the GMA. Land designated for agriculture cannot be converted to intensive, non-agricultural uses such as residential subdivisions or commercial development. Rather, it can be used specifically for agriculture operations and some other accessory uses.

For instance, zoning ordinances allow home occupations in agriculture zones. Strict laws ensure that this category of land use remains true to personal accommodation functions. Historically, the GMA has not directly addressed other 'accessory' uses such as ancillary buildings for agri-tourism or accommodation. Only recently have efforts to open such lands for broader agricultural opportunities emerged. In 2004, Senate Bill 6237 was approved, providing opportunities for accessory uses that support, promote or sustain agricultural operations and production. This includes compatible commercial and retail uses that involve agriculture or agricultural products related to grape and wine production.

As in the case of British Columbia, Washington's Liquor Control Board (LCB) controls the distribution, consumption and sale of wines within the state. It influences wine tourism land uses via jurisdiction over decisions concerning the distribution of permits for wineries, on-site tasting rooms and the sales of wines at on-site stores. It also determines the extent to which wineries may provide picnic areas and/or restaurants where wines of the property are sold and consumed.

Overall, Washington State's policies governing wine tourism development are restrictive – especially with respect to the use of agricultural lands. No policies promote the development of commercial accommodation within agricultural zones. Similarly, there is limited specificity concerning wine tourism uses such as wine shops and restaurants on agricultural lands. The state's LCB holds most of the control over such pursuits. It plays a significant role in determining the location and character of winery-related, permanent attractions such as wine shops, restaurants and picnic areas. Decisions concerning wine tourism land use rest far more with local and regional government comprehensive planning policy regimes.

Yakima County land use policies

Yakima County is primarily an agricultural area significantly involved in grape and wine production. Under the GMA, county lands devoted to long-term viticultural uses – including wineries – are designated as 'Agricultural Resource Lands'. This designation is intended to preserve and protect the agricultural land base of the area. The Yakima County Comprehensive Plan promotes protection of agricultural land for the area's long-term sustainability, and discourages land uses incompatible with agricultural resource areas. County ordinances permit B&B buildings on some sites, subject to a lengthy review and a number of conditions. The County may elect to restrict the number of rooms to less than the five currently prescribed, but there is presently no zoning ordinance to address the specifics of this variance. The number of rooms permitted is dependent on the outcome of individual reviews, which are based on the proposed project's impacts on local traffic patterns and road capacities connecting the winery with the marketplace. In Yakima County, few standards exist to determine threshold acceptance levels for on-site building permits and approvals for permitted non-farm uses.

This policy environment is challenging for wine tourism proponents seeking opportunities to develop ancillary attractions and facilities for their cellar door operations. Wine tourism stakeholders claim that state stipulations and county regulations cause untimely delays and, in the long run, inhibit the growth of their businesses. However, as awareness of the economic opportunities associated with wine tourism increases so do pressures to develop friendly amendments to the county's Comprehensive Plan. There is a need for policies that recognize and clearly guide the development of wine tourism facilities and activities, on-site restaurants, retailing and events on agricultural land. Both state and county policies currently lack any systematic ability to respond proactively to growing pressures to accommodate wine tourism. Largely, existing policies reflect a limited awareness of either the development constraints or potential impacts of wine tourism. As a result, policy lags behind the market with respect to nurturing sustainable forms of wine tourism development.

Oregon land use policies

As with British Columbia and Washington, Oregon's wine tourism land use is primarily controlled by policies not only regulating winery use of agricultural land, but also rules guiding the operation of wineries and the wines they produce. Oregon's progressive 1973 Land Use Act established the Land Conservation and Development Commission (OLCDC) and the Department of Land Conservation and Development (ODLCD) to manage land use issues in the state. These agencies are responsible for developing state-wide planning goals, reviewing and certifying local comprehensive plans and facilitating planning efforts by local governments. A key role of the ODLCD is to 'preserve and maintain agricultural land for farm use, consistent with existing and future needs for agricultural products' (ODLCD, 2004).

Wineries and vineyards in Oregon are exclusive farm uses. Policies permit ancillary buildings for residential, retail or commercial purposes on these lands. These policies also provide conditional approval for B&B accommodation provided it is located within a residence on the agricultural property. These buildings must be situated on lands deemed marginally productive. The ODLCD allows counties to implement Comprehensive Plans and make decisions that meet local needs and circumstances within the state's broader land use framework.

Like its counterparts in the two other case study regions, the Oregon Liquor Control Commission (OLCC) licenses wineries and governs production and sales of wines produced and sold within the state. It also governs, in conjunction with other jurisdictions, the type and scale of wine-related activities that may occur at the winery locations. Examples include tasting rooms, special events and wine tours. Currently, the OLCC permits the development of on-site tasting rooms, retail sales of winery produce and some ancillary gift operations. Three special events per year are permitted at each winery, as well as a limited-service restaurant (Tables 3.2, 3.3).

Historically, traditional agricultural land uses in Oregon were encouraged by strict pro-farming land use policies and a tax regime that provided incentives for keeping such lands in agricultural functions. However, in 2004 Oregon passed Measure 37, which permits property owners who have had the value of their property artificially reduced because of adverse land use regulations to seek monetary compensation or reversion to previous uses (Oregon Secretary of State, 2004). This has opened the door to potentially sweeping changes in the development options available to local agricultural and winery operators. Decisions concerning those changes that may affect the development of wine tourism will be reflected in future Comprehensive Plans created at the county level.

Yamhill County land use policies

Yamhill County positions itself as a leader in Oregon land use strategies addressing agriculture in general, and wineries in particular. Its regulatory environment is characterized by a general culture of deregulation, as long as the spirit of the Comprehensive Land Use Plan is respected, and uses are compliant with ODLCD regulations. Zoning ordinances are skeletal and not overly restrictive. Oregon's approach to land use planning considers wineries as an exclusive farm use at both state and county levels, including some ancillary activities.

Yamhill County permits some small-scale amenities on winery property. Included are attractions such as B&Bs, light snack facilities, tasting rooms and wine tourism retail space. Local stakeholders drive decisions concerning the focus and interpretation of such policies. For instance, in recent years several zoning ordinances – including restrictions on the frequency of on-site events and number of bedrooms per agricultural lodging unit – were modified. The perspectives of many winery operators and local stakeholders who have lived in the area for decades drove these incremental changes. All of these changes were guided by a locally nurtured and commonly held vision of the intent of the County's Comprehensive Plan with respect to wine tourism and other forms of land use.

Implications for Wine Tourism

The insights gained from this research prompt several interrelated observations concerning wine tourism development and land use policy. First, land use policies in these regions reflect different predispositions towards wine tourism. British Columbia's provincial framework is quite responsive and decidedly committed to the development of wine tourism. Recent changes by the LCLB make it easier for wineries to serve wine by the glass, host events and establish on-site restaurants. ALC General Orders recognize the rising importance of agri-tourism as a means of diversifying and promoting the sale of locally grown agricultural products. Indeed, they have established an agri-tourist accommodation land use policy, separate from B&Bs, that is not apparent in other regions.

Similarly, LCLB regulations concerning the appropriate land uses at BC wineries make the delivery of special events far less cumbersome than in the other two jurisdictions. While Washington, Oregon and BC have wine tourism policies similarly rooted in broader land use planning and liquor control management regimes, BC's policies are far more wine tourism development-friendly. This reflects a growth-oriented strategy in which agricultural lands are placed under ever-increasing pressures for non-traditional forms of use.

At the other extreme, Washington is significantly less engaged in creating policies that promote the use of agricultural land for wine tourism. At a relatively early stage in the development of this industry, its land use policies are not particularly aligned and more ad hoc with respect to nurturing wine tourism development. Faced with growing economic pressures to capitalize on increasing demand for wine tourism, its state and county land use agencies need to work with local and regional stakeholders (tourism operators, vinters, grape growers, local residents, etc.) to create a more integrated policy approach to land use decisions influencing the development of this industry.

In contrast, Oregon's approach is between the BC and Washington extremes. With balanced and more integrated land use policies, Oregon encourages small winery development with off-site ancillary services that are key to the development and promotion of wine tourism. Oregon's policies support small-scale wine tourism whilst protecting the viticultural core of the wine tourism product.

Secondly, there are distinct variations in the extent to which policies are harmonized in each region. BC's wine tourism policies are relatively harmonized but distinctly top-down in character compared to the other two regions. For the most part, regulations developed at the provincial level are reinforced in more localized RDCO policies. In Washington, state policies are limited with respect to wine tourism land use and most polices are interpreted in a patchwork fashion at the county level.

In Oregon, state policies provide the general framework for more localized decision-making. However, localized policies reflect broader community values and perspectives. Comprehensive Plans at the county level provide the specific guidance used by local decision makers. Locally driven perspectives concerning growth and the vision of wineries inform the regulations that are developed. While economic pressures may encourage proposals calling for greater levels of wine tourism development, a strong local ethic rooted in agricultural land conservation and an anti-Napa Valley growth philosophy continue to shape the industry's development.

In each of the preceding cases, the extent and focus of wine tourism land use policy reflects varying perspectives and awareness of wine tourism's potential contributions to broader regional development objectives.

Thirdly, pressures for wine tourism development in all regions continue to put traditional agricultural land use policies under strain. Despite ongoing losses of agricultural land to various non-farming activities, the push for opening the cellar gates to increasing levels of tourism development continues to grow. Each of the case study areas responds in a different fashion to these pressures. In BC, the strategy involves embracing such initiatives and creating policy that facilitates such expansion at all levels. In Oregon, there is localized policy support for moderate expansion of wine tourism opportunities as long as it occurs within a commonly accepted growth framework. In Washington, policy supporting wine tourism growth is limited and decidedly uneven in its application. The emphasis of policy is still entrenched in agricultural land use protection, despite industry calls to create a wine tourism industry competitive with that of California.

Fourthly, an industry and region with a common vision helps create a more systematic and balanced approach to wine tourism development. While all the case study areas are relatively small and emerging in character, Oregon's wine industry has been in operation for a longer period of time and is arguably more mature in its approach to wine tourism development. Experience provides a useful lens for developing wine tourism policy. For instance, in Yamhill County the demand for wine tourism amenities such as lodging, restaurants and gift shops continues unabated, despite the lack of such facilities on many winery sites.

While current policies constrain on-site developments, they also help to redistribute such demand to other non-agricultural locations. Longstanding proponents of wine tourism in the region note that many amenities and services are emerging off-site in local communities. As a result, wineries themselves simply do not need to offer such attractions in order to draw wine tourists, which helps preserve the land for more traditional vineyard purposes. This type of knowledge is built into a common ethic and vision found in policies concerning the role of wine tourism on agricultural lands.

Such perspective and community engagement in decisions concerning the development of wine tourism are less pronounced in the other case study regions. In BC, the need to engage multiple stakeholders in establishing priorities for agricultural land use has emerged as the pressures for wine tourism and other forms of non-traditional agricultural land use have surged in the RDCO. In Washington, the need for such a vision with respect to agricultural land use has not surfaced to the same extent.

Conclusions

The overriding land use challenge for proponents of wine tourism is to avoid the headlong development of amenities to the detriment of idyllic winescapes and the agricultural capacity of the land, whilst creating policies that encourage local operators to develop their wine tourism opportunities (Hall *et al.*, 2000; Skinner, 2000). A balanced and sensitively applied policy regime helps meet this challenge. In all of the case study areas, efforts are underway to create more integrated wine tourism development approaches. In some cases, these initiatives have strong land use management elements. In other instances, the focus is on market and product development opportunities.

In Oregon, winery stakeholders and local governments have recently agreed on policies that allow more flexibility with respect to accommodation and special events on agricultural land. In Washington, more strategic approaches to wine tourism development based on lessons learned from Californian destinations are developing to guide policies in emerging wine regions. In BC, the RDCO is developing a multi-stakeholder-based agricultural plan that will provide a common vision and clear guidelines for the use of agricultural lands (including those associated with wine tourism).

In all of these cases, it is important to balance policies that support agricultural land conservation with those that meet the needs of winery, tourism and local community stakeholders. Weak polices that encourage a 'creeping incrementalism' in wine tourism land use development must be avoided if the core viticulture and aesthetic assets of regions are to be sustained. Similar to the challenge for the vintner of balancing flavours to produce a fine wine, there is a need to create equilibrium between the benefits of economic development and environmental protection in order to produce sustainable wine tourism.

References

ALC (Agricultural Land Commission) (2003a) *Activities Designated as Farm Use: Wineries and Cideries in the ALR.* Policy No. 3. March. http://www.alc.gov.bc.ca/legislation/legislation_main.htm#orders

ALC (Agricultural Land Commission) (2003b). *Activities Designated as Farm Use: Agritourism in the ALR.* Policy No. 4. March. http://www.alc.gov.bc.ca/legislation/legislation_main.htm#orders

Aloysius, L. and Lee, D. (2001) Strategic management of the Geographe wine region. *Tourism Management* 26 (2), 81–97.

BC Ministry of Finance and Corporate Relations (1997–2001) *Tourism Properties, Rooms and Revenues, Hotel Room Tax Database.* Consumer Tax Branch, BC Ministry of Finance and Corporate Relations, Victoria, British Columbia, Canada.

BCWI (British Columbia Wine Institute) (1999–2005) *Annual Reports.* British Columbia Wine Instiute, Vancouver, Canada.

Boxall, B. (1999) Vineyard neighbours see only wrath from grapes. *The Los Angeles Times,* 18 February, A1, A21.

Bruwer, J. (2003) South African wine routes: some perspectives on the wine industry's structural dimensions and wine tourism product. *Tourism Management* 24 (4), 423–435.

Busby, G. and Rendle, S. (2000) The transition from tourism on farms to farm tourism. *Tourism Management* 21 (6), 635–642.

Cambourne, B., Macionis, N., Hall, C.M. and Sharples, L. (2000) The future of wine tourism. In: Hall, C.M., Sharples, L., Cambourne, B. and Maciones, N. (eds) *Wine Tourism Around the World: Development, Management and Markets.* Butterworth Heinemann, Oxford, UK.

Carlsen, J. and Ali-Knight, J. (2004) Managing wine tourism through demarketing: the case of Napa Valley, California. In: *International Wine Tourism Research, 2004. Proceedings of the Margaret River, Australia, International Wine Tourism Conference.* Vineyard Publishing, Guildford, Western Australia, Australia..

Clarke, J. (1996) Farm accommodation and the

communication mix. *Tourism Management* 17 (8), 611–620.

Darlington, D. (1999) Burgundy West: between Oregon's Cascade Mountains and its Coast Range sits an unlikely rival to one of France's pre-eminent wine districts. *VIA*, September 1999, http://www.viamagazine. com/top_stories/articles/orwin99.asp

Dean Runyan and Associates (2004) *Washington and Oregon State Travel Impacts by County (Travel Spending), 1999–2004*. Dean Runyan and Associates, Portland, Oregon.

Demhardt, I. (2003) Wine and tourism at the Fairest Cape: post-apartheid trends in the Western Cape Province and Stellenbosch (South Africa). *Journal of Travel and Tourism Marketing* 14 (3/4), 113–130.

Dodd, T. and Beverland, M. (2001) Winery tourism life cycle development: a proposed model. *Tourism Recreation Research* 26 (2), 11–21.

Dodd, T.H. and Bigotte, V. (1995) *Visitors to Texas Wineries: their Demographic Characteristics and Purchasing Behavior*. Texas Wine Marketing Research Institute, Texas Tech University, Lubbock, Texas.

Economic Development Commission (EDC) (2005) *Economic Profile: Agriculture and Wine Sector*. http://www.edccord.com/pdf/ economic_profile/agriculture_wine.pdf

Gaudette, K. (2000) Washington makes plans to challenge Napa Valley. *Wall Street Journal*, 12 July, p. NW1.

Getz, D. (1999) Wine tourism: global overview and perspective on its development. In: Dowling, R.K. and Carlsen, J. (eds) *Wine Tourism: Perfect Partners*. Proceedings of the First Australian Wine Tourism Conference, Margaret River, Western Australia, 1998. Bureau of Tourism Research, Canberra, Australia, pp. 13–33.

Getz, D. (2000) *Explore Wine Tourism: Management, Development and Destinations*. Cognizant Communications, Elmsford, New York.

Getz, D. and Brown, G. (2006) Comparison and benchmarking between wine tourism destinations: lessons from a case study of the Okanagan Valley, British Columbia. *International Journal of Wine Marketing* **(in press)**.

Hall, C.M. and Jenkins, J. (1998) The policy dimensions of rural tourism and recreation. In: Butler, R.W., Hall, C.M. and Jenkins, J.M. (eds) *Tourism and Recreation In Rural Areas*. John Wiley and Sons, New York, pp. 19–42.

Hall, C.M. and Macionis, N. (1998) Wine tourism in Australia and New Zealand. In: Butler, R.W., Hall, C.M. and Jenkins, J.M. (eds) *Tourism and Recreation in Rural Areas*. John Wiley and Sons, New York, pp. 267–298.

Lane, B. (1994) Sustainable rural tourism strategies: a tool for development and conservation. In: Bramwell, B. and Lane, B. (eds) *Rural Tourism and Sustainable Development*. Channel View Publications, Clevedon, UK, pp. 102–111.

Hall, C.M., Johnson, G. and Mitchell, R. (2000) Wine tourism and regional development. In: Hall, C.M., Sharples, L., Cambourne, B. and Macionis, N. (eds) *Wine Tourism Around the World: Development, Management and Markets*. Butterworth Heinemann, Oxford, UK, pp. 196–225.

Liquor Control and Licensing Branch (LCLB) (2004) *Winery Licence Regulation*. http://www.pssg.gov.bc.ca/lclb/publications/ guides-licensee/Winery.pdf

Macionis, N. and Cambourne, B. (1998) Wine tourism: just what is it all about? *The Australian and New Zealand Wine Journal* 13 (1), 41–47.

Martin, E. and Williams, P.W. (2003) Directions in British Columbia wine tourism policy. *International Journal of Contemporary Hospitality Management* 15 (6), 317–323.

ODLCD, Oregon Department of Land Conservation and Development (2004) http://www.lcd.state.or.us/

O'Hara, S. (2006) *Wines Northwest*, http://www.winesnw.com/bchome.html

Oregon Agricultural Statistics Service (2004) http://www.nass.usda.gov/or

Oregon Secretary of State (2004) Text of Measure 37.

OWFS, Okanagan Wine Festivals Society (2005) *Annual Report*, http://www.owfs. com/ aboutus/ hostanevent.htm

Penner, D. (2006) Condo-resort project draws allure of a vineyard setting. *Vancouver Sun*, 5 January, p. B-10.

Poitras, L. and Getz, D. (2006) Sustainable wine tourism: the host community perspective. *Journal of Sustainable Tourism* **(in press).**

RDCO, Regional District of the Central Okanagan (2005) *Agricultural Plan*. June.

Senese, D. (1999) Wine tourism and the evolution of cultural landscapes of the Okanagan. Paper presented at the *Western Division Canada Association of Geographers Annual Meeting*, 3 March, Kelowna, British Columbia, Canada.

Shara Hall, L. (2001) *Wines of the Pacific Northwest*. Mitchell Beazley, London.

Sharp, K. (1992) Sour grapes over tourist boom. *Los Angeles Times*, 3 December, A3.

Skinner, A. (2000) Napa Valley, California: a model of wine region development. In: Hall, C.M., Sharples, L., Cambourne, B. and Macionis, N. (eds) *Wine Tourism Around the World: Development, Management and Markets*. Butterworth Heinemann, Oxford, UK.

Surich (1999) *Liquor Policy Review Final Report and Recommendations*, 20 May. Office of the Attorney General, Government of British Columbia, Victoria, British Columbia, Canada.

Telfer, D. (2001) From a wine tourism village to a regional wine route: an investigation of the competitive advantage of embedded clusters in Niagara, Canada. *Tourism Recreation Research* 26 (2), 23–33.

Washington Agricultural Statistics Service (2005) http://www.nass.usda.gov/wa

Washington Wine Commission (2005) http://www.washingtonwine.org/facts.cfm

Williamette Valley Wineries Association (2005) http://www.williamettewines.com/

Williams, P.W. (2001) Positioning wine tourism destinations: an image analysis. *International Journal of Wine Marketing* 13 (3), 42–58.

Williams, P.W. and Dossa, K. (2003) Non-resident wine tourist markets: management implications for British Columbia's emerging wine tourism industry. *Journal of Travel and Tourism Marketing* 14 (3/4), 1–34.

Williams, P.W. and Kelly, J. (2001) Cultural wine tourists: product development considerations for British Columbia's resident wine tourism market. *International Journal of Wine Marketing* 13 (1), 59–76.

Wines Yakima Valley (2005) http://www.wineyakimavalley.org/

Yamhill County Winery Association (2004) http://www.yamhillwine.com/index.shtml

Yamhill Valley Visitors Association (2006) http://www.yamhillvalley.org/

4 Enhancing the Wine Tourism Experience: the Customers' Viewpoint

Linda Roberts[1]* and Beverley Sparks[2]

[1] School of Hospitality, Tourism and Marketing, Victoria University, Victoria, Australia; [2] Services Industry Research Centre, Griffith University, PMB 50 Gold Coast Mail Centre, Queensland, Australia
*E-mail: linda.roberts@vu.edu.au

Introduction

The research reported in this chapter is part of a wider Sustainable Tourism CRC study entitled *Good Living Tourism*. *Good Living Tourism* incorporates the essential features of wine tourism as a total experience, not only emphasizing wine but also food and other lifestyle components. The research question under investigation for the part of the study reported here was to develop a greater understanding of the factors that are important or enhance the experiences of tourists visiting wine regions.

Literature Review

Tourism offers wine growers, and the associated region where the vineyards are located, an opportunity for financial development. As wine tourism evolves there is a need to better understand the consumers who travel to these regions, as well as the factors that enhance their overall experiences. Hall and his colleagues (2000) have argued that visitation to a wine region is frequently motivated by 'grape wine' specifically or 'the attributes of a grape wine region' referred to as the winescape. These winescapes are characterized by three main elements: the presence of vineyards, the wine-making activity and the wineries where the wine is produced and stored (Telfer, 2000).

Getz (1998) also argues that attributes of a wine region, such as the scenery and open spaces, also provide an incentive to visit the region. It has been argued (Beames, 2003) that an important challenge facing regions is to be able to create a total experience for tourists rather than merely the opening of cellar doors. Thus, a deeper understanding of the consumer is required.

Recent attempts to define wine tourism in broader terms have been made, and Charters and Ali-Knight (2002) have noted the characteristics that have been incorporated, including 'lifestyle experience, supply and demand, an educational component, linkages to art, wine and food, incorporation with the destination image and as a marketing opportunity which enhances the economic, social and cultural values of the region'. Indeed, a number of these characteristics also emerge in Beverland's (2005) definition of authenticity in the context of luxury wines as:

> ... a story that balances industrial (production, distribution and marketing) and rhetorical attributes to project sincerity through the avowal of commitments to traditions (including production methods, product styling, firm values, and/or location), passion for craft and production excellence, and the public disavowal of the role of modern industrial attributes and commercial motivations.

Furthermore, O'Neill and Charters (2000) considered quality service at the cellar door as another crucial aspect of wine tourism and noted that it may be 'a vital antecedent to any purchase being made'. However, despite the growing interest in the area of wine (and food) tourism, relatively little research into consumer perceptions and motivations has been undertaken. This research focuses upon what types of experiences enhance a consumer's overall evaluation of a visit to a wine region.

Research Method

Since there has been little research conducted into consumer perceptions and motivations when visiting a wine region regarding the total experience, a qualitative approach was used to develop a greater understanding of what aspects of wine tourism enhanced the experiences that people have undertaken. Focus groups were conducted with people who visited wine regions and who considered themselves to be lovers of wine and food in order to discuss what they were looking for in terms of the total experience of the visit.

Selection of participants

A purposive approach was taken to recruit participants who considered themselves to be 'lovers of wine and food'. A total of nine focus groups were conducted: four in Victoria, three in Queensland and two in South Australia. For four of the focus groups, participants were recruited through local wine or food clubs in the three states, while for the other five focus groups participants were recruited from both general and academic staff via the university email systems at the three participating universities, Victoria University in Victoria, Griffith University in Queensland and the University of South Australia.

In total there were 78 participants: 37 in the four focus groups held in Victoria, 25 in the three focus groups held in Queensland and 16 in the two focus groups held in South Australia. A mix of both males and females from within the broad age range of 18–65 years was involved.

Procedure

The focus groups were conducted in a relaxed environment with refreshments provided before the focus groups started, to enable participants to meet each other informally. Each focus group lasted for one hour and proceedings were tape-recorded. Recordings were transcribed and notes were also taken by a person other than the moderator to ensure that a complete record would be available for analysis.

A semi-structured approach was adopted, with questions relating to the participants' interest in wine and food tourism, the kinds of people they perceived to be interested in it and to what attracts people to a wine and food region. There was then discussion on the types of experiences that were sought by the participants when visiting a wine and food region and what they associated with 'good living' tourism. Subsequent discussion centred on products for sale in a wine and food region, the attractions visited and what was learned during the visit.

Results and Discussion: Enhancement Factors

The contents of the focus groups' transcriptions were classified using NVivo qualitative data analysis software. The classifications, referred to as nodes, identified key themes associated with wine tourism experiences that came out of the participants' detailed observations. Passages from the transcripts relevant to the nodes were coded under the relevant node/sub-node. The passages that were relevant to more than one node/sub-node were coded under each of these nodes. In order to ensure validity of the coding scheme the data were analysed by three researchers. When coding, assigned by the three researchers, were found to differ they were discussed and the best and most appropriate coding selected, as agreed.

From the focus group results a wide-ranging model of themes emerged. Enhancement factors that help to make the experience of visiting a wine and food region more enjoyable was one of these themes. From an integrative process of analysis eight key enhancement factors were identified comprising authenticity of the experience, value for money, service interactions, the setting or surroundings, product offerings, information dissemination, personal growth and indulgence or lifestyle. A concept map of the enhancement factors is shown in Fig. 4.1.

Authenticity of experience

The first theme to emerge was typified by visitors looking for an authentic experience and was labelled authenticity. The theme of authenticity incorporated a number of aspects, from the broader perspective of the location itself, where the winery was 'in the middle of nowhere', or through activities and events like music festivals and agricultural fairs held in a 'huge

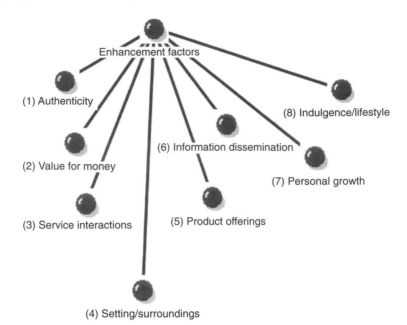

Fig. 4.1. Model of focus group themes (enhancement factors) (from Sparks *et al.*, 2005).

paddock' behind the winery. Authenticity may also include the finer details of what can be seen and what is happening at the winery or the pleasing experience of talking to the winemaker. In summary, participants indicated that they wanted their experience to feel 'real' and yet also, to a certain extent, to be unique to them.

From the food perspective, attention may be attracted by displays of unusual produce, particularly when the produce is related to the dishes served in the restaurant. Furthermore, to be able to purchase wines from boutique wineries that cannot be purchased elsewhere was another aspect contributing to a wine region's authenticity. As one participant noted: 'It's that sense of ... developing a kind of affinity with the place that is established by those personal contacts and that lack of packaging, and that sense that you're getting somebody's particular speciality rather than just the stuff with a label on it.' This also applies to local produce, as another participant observed: 'I actually prefer local ingredients.'

Value for money

Another theme that was evident was labelled value for money and involved getting a 'good deal' or feeling the experience was worth the cost contributed to enhancement of the overall experience. However, value for money did not mean that people wanted cheap products; rather it involved the feeling that they were getting value for the money they spent. For many visitors there was still the expectation that there would be complimentary wine tasting, as this had become accepted as 'part of the ethos' of visiting a winery.

However, a charge was considered to be more acceptable if there was something extra offered, such as a complimentary wine glass. Participants also assessed the price of wine at the cellar door against what the cost of the same wine would be in the local supermarket, but also taking into account the added experience of the winery visit, as illustrated by the comment: 'And you think, is the five dollars (extra) worth the experience of having been to the winery? Sometimes it is, and sometimes it isn't.'

None the less, if something extra is offered, such as a 'cooler pack', that could soften the impact of the higher price. Furthermore, reasonable shipping costs were also encouraging for interstate visitors to purchase more wine. In the same way similar factors affected participants' attitudes to food prices as, for some, a higher price paid for local produce at markets was acceptable if the experience was an enjoyable one: 'Money is not the problem. You don't look at price ... I'm having fun ... It's the value that you put on it.'

Service interactions

Another theme that became evident based on the respondents' dialogue was to do with service interactions. Service interactions were indicative of the level of customer service extended to tourists. Personal interactions with the winemaker and winery staff and others on a social level had an important function in creating the total experience. Personal attention was wanted and was expressed in terms of a preference for visiting smaller winery operations where interactions were more personal, rather than being in a large crowd waiting for attention.

Furthermore, first impressions of a winery reflecting responses to the initial contact person were important and, subsequently, if the service was good, this could be the determining factor for repeat visits. As one respondent noted: 'To me it's definitely a service thing. If I go somewhere and it's great wine and great food but the service is no good, there's no way I'll go back.' Similarly: 'I like the experience of meeting people; that's something that I have always enjoyed rather than being just herded in and out.'

Setting and surroundings

Another area that was widely discussed was the location and natural surroundings of the winery. Participants reported that the setting attracted them to a region and enhanced their experiences, while the weather and the atmosphere could also help to create or enhance the setting. Regional maps of the locality that identified the wineries were liked, as they could be used to plan the day and allow scenery to be incorporated – as well as the wineries – into the itinerary. Picnic facilities at the winery, where visitors could take their own food and purchase wine to drink, were looked for by some.

Thus, it was evident that participants were looking for interesting or attractive settings as part of the overall experience. In describing an ideal setting, one respondent described an ideal setting in the following terms:

> It is usually relatively small areas … so you are talking about a fairly compact area with usually some sort of mapped out approach to it so you can get some logic to what you are driving around, you can decide to visit two wineries before you have lunch and you can drive literally through the hills and look at the scenery as part of the process.

Product offerings

Wine tasting may have been the focus of the visit for some, but many people looked for a choice from a range of product offerings beyond the wine to local food produce, like cheeses, that could be purchased to take home. For others a variety of eating places like restaurants and cafés were sought where they could dine alfresco on local produce. The expectation was that the wine would be from the local region and, especially for accompanying wine tastings, seasonal food platters and information about matching wine and food were appreciated. In addition to wine and food, other products were sought and may be related to craft activities in the region like woodworking, painting and pottery.

As one respondent noted:

> Most people are looking for a total package considering Australia is so big, and if you are going to drive from here [one state] to South Australia you are not going to go there just to drink the wine, are you? You are going to want to see and enjoy everything else that part of the country has to offer.

Though 'gift items' were sought, not all were necessarily approved of, especially if the main focus of the 'gifts' was to advertise the winery. As one respondent commented in relation to other merchandise: 'And I haven't been back since; I thought no, I don't like this and also they had a whole big display of their own merchandise … caps, awful!'

Information dissemination

It was evident that the availability of adequate information about a region was an important enhancement factor for visitors. Respondents identified three major sources of information: (i) print media, including newspapers like *The Age* with the Epicure supplement and 'glossy' brochures; (ii) visitor information centres; and (iii) 'word of mouth', through talking with winery staff and other visitors to wineries. As one person observed: 'It's got a lot to do with the brochure. I'll go "Oh, that looks interesting, that doesn't". It's got a lot to do with glossy pictures … and whether someone else has said, "Oh this place is good".'

The importance of adequate information dissemination became clear when respondents recounted some of the difficulties they had experienced finding wineries, observing that some regions needed better maps and more signage. Information about whether visitors were accepted at the winery and opening times of cellar doors was also necessary and was not always readily available. While an aspect of authenticity was for the wine to be available only for purchase at the cellar door, respondents did see the negative perspective, as some wines that they did wish to purchase later after they had returned home were also hard to find for purchase outside the winery. For this reason lists of where the wines were sold, besides at the cellar door, were considered to be useful.

Personal growth: learning experiences

For many of the participants, a visit to a wine and food region was not just about wine, but was also a learning experience. As one respondent noted, it was: 'The experience of the new area, the beauty of the area, the history of the area, of the whole thing. It's just a whole learning experience.' Learning about the region, eating and drinking in restaurants and getting to know the people were all part of the experience, just as interactions with the winemaker and staff, learning about the history of the winery, how the wine was made and matching wine and food all helped to build memories that could be revived later.

The following comment reflects this: 'I would be disappointed if there wasn't a large element of that [the educational aspect] there, that you are going away knowing quite a bit more than you did, that's part of why you go there, otherwise you would just go down to the bottle shop.'

Thus, for many, learning experiences contributed to personal growth and were valued in the wine and food experience.

Indulgence: lifestyle

Finally, lifestyle and indulgence in the experience constituted a theme. In the context of wine and food regions, respondents described lifestyle and indulgence aspects of their visit in terms of a totally pleasing experience that takes them away from the hard work of the week and the stress of the city. Words used by the respondents to describe the experience included 'country', 'freedom', 'change of pace', 'no pressure', 'indulgence', 'pampering', 'relaxing', 'self-indulgence', 'decadence', 'comfort', 'cosy', 'service/being waited on', 'nurturing', 'social' and 'shopping'. One respondent summed up: 'You know, we've done the hard stuff and now we're pleasuring ourselves a bit.'

This indulgence aspect may range from simply making a day of it to staying in the region and enjoying the accommodation, wine and food or the overall experience with 'almost that element of decadence'. As this respondent observed:

There is something really indulgent, taking off on a Sunday and going up to the Yarra Valley, and sitting somewhere like Domaine Chandon, beautiful gardens, glass of wine, a bit of cheese or something, talking, chatting. I don't know whether it's because I grew up in the country or it's just getting out, away from the hustle and bustle.

Implications for Wine Tourism

The findings from the focus groups in this project indicate that there are many aspects to the experience that can be collectively described as enhancement factors. The wine tourist is rarely interested simply in wine tasting, rather – as also observed by Beames (2003) – the total experience is of utmost importance.

The scenery surrounding the winery, as also noted by Getz (1998), the location and entrance to the winery itself as well as the people at the winery – their manner of greeting and welcoming the visitor – all made a difference to the overall experience. Value for money was important and some visitors may make trade-off decisions regarding how much they will spend on one aspect, for example accommodation, in order to spend more on another, for example dining out at good restaurants in the region.

However, for others money is not necessarily a problem, especially if tourists are 'having fun' and enjoying a quality experience indicating the need for a region to offer products across a range of prices to allow trade-offs to be made by visitors in achieving their own desirable total experience. In addition, without adequate information like maps and brochures or information from visitor information centres for visitors to plan their trip this is more difficult. Once in the region, 'local knowledge' – including information from winery or visitor information centre staff – makes an important contribution and can further assist visitors in planning their itinerary.

Visitors, if made to feel welcome, are recognized and can enter into discussion with the winemaker to learn more about the winery and winemaking in an enjoyable way without feeling intimidated, then they feel special. This is particularly the case if visitors feel they are personally invited to taste a certain wine or are given information 'just for them'. There is a trend for self-development through learning more about wine production and styles, as noted by Charters and Ali-Knight (2000). Thus, it may not be just about a pleasant visit to a cellar door but rather a self-enhancing experience that provides an opportunity to enhance one's own knowledge. Thus, by being innovative in developing new products the winemaker may be able to build upon this sort of experience and attract more visitors to the cellar door.

Good service, as also noted by O'Neill and Charters (2000), was a determining factor for subsequent visits, once again highlighting the importance of personal interactions. It is the memories that the visitors take away with them of the unique aspects of their visit, as well as the familiarity that they have developed with the people of the region, that help to bring them back for return visits. Even the purchase of local produce for later consumption can rekindle these memories, thereby ensuring that memories of the region are refreshed, making it more likely that the region will be visited again and/or recommended to friends.

Thus, the range of factors enhancing the experience of visitors to wine (and food) regions was identified in this study consistent with findings of earlier research. There is now a need for more quantitative research to be carried out on consumer perceptions and motivations to further investigate these factors and their relative importance or weightings in enhancing the total visitor experience to a wine region.

References

Beames, G. (2003) The rock, the reef and the grape: the challenges of developing wine tourism in regional Australia. *Journal of Vacation Marketing* 9 (3), 205–212.

Beverland, M. (2005) Crafting brand authenticity: the case of luxury wines. *Journal of Management Studies* 42 (5), 1003–1029.

Charters, S. and Ali-Knight, J. (2000) Wine tourism – a thirst for knowledge? *International Journal of Wine Marketing* 12 (3), 70–80.

Charters, S. and Ali-Knight, J. (2002) Who is the wine tourist? *Tourism Management* 23, 311–319.

Getz, D. (1998) Wine tourism: global overview and perspectives on its development. In: *Wine Tourism – Perfect Partners: the First Australian Wine Tourism Conference*, May 1998, Margaret River, Australia, pp. 13–33.

Hall, C.M., Sharples, L., Cambourne, B. and Macionis, N. (2000) *Wine Tourism Around the World: Development, Management and Markets.* Butterworth-Heinemann, Oxford, UK.

O'Neill, M. and Charters, S. (2000) Service quality at the cellar door: implications for Western Australia's developing wine tourism industry. *Managing Service Quality* 10 (2), 112–122.

Sparks, B., Roberts, L., Deery, M., Davies, J. and Brown, L. (2005) *Good Living Tourism Lifestyle: Aspects of Food and Wine Tourism.* CRC for Sustainable Tourism Pty Ltd, Gold Coast, Queensland, Australia.

Telfer, D.J. (2000) Tastes of Niagara: building alliances between tourism and agriculture. *International Journal of Hospitality and Tourism Administration* 1 (1), 71–88.

Part II
Wine Tourism and Regional Development

5 Wine Tourism and Sustainable Development in Regional Australia

JOHN G. GAMMACK

Department of Management, Griffith Business School, Griffith University, Nathan 4111, Queensland, Australia
E-mail: j.gammack@griffith.edu.au

Introduction

Tourism associated with wineries has been a major area of recent growth in regional Australia (Charters and Ali-Knight, 2002). The Winemakers Federation of Australia (WFA) recognized this in developing a national wine tourism strategy in 1998 (www.wfa.org.au/planning/tourstrat.html, accessed 14 March 2004). WFA predicted a value of nearly Aus$1 billion (WFA, 2002), comprising money spent at wineries and elsewhere by domestic and international winery visitors: figures since borne out. The benefits to associated businesses in regional economies are clear.

While the growth rate in wine tourism is potentially greater than that in other tourism areas, Beames (2003, p. 207) adds the important proviso 'providing that both infrastructure and attractions are available'. He outlines challenges facing the sector, including: (i) the cottage-industry mentality of current wine-tourism operators; (ii) creating an overall tourist experience rather than just cellar-door sales; (iii) local planning and development consents; (iv) investment funds; and (v) lack of available data, information and research.

Other issues (Macionis, 1998) include the lack of appropriate market research, lack of tourism understanding among winemakers, and general lack of integration among relevant industry sectors. This latter is recognized by industry groups and by state governments, and is attributed to: (i) the industry's relative infancy, with associated lack of information and research; (ii) a dominant product focus, making tourism a subsidiary area of the wine industry; and (iii) lack of experience and entrepreneurial skills in tourism and marketing among winemakers. Hall and Johnson (1998) also note that tourism operators lack understanding of viticulture and the conflicting demands for resource use, presenting further barriers.

Like other tourism businesses, the sector primarily comprises small and medium enterprises (SMEs), who face recognized development barriers (SMIDEC, 1998). Other challenges, related to enterprise scale, linkage formation and requisite knowledge, also apply. SMEs are considered vulnerable in an economic climate of industrial agglomeration (Marceau *et al.*, 1997), and industry-specific policies are required. Wine tourism, however, may allow 'small producers to overcome the barriers associated with market consolidation on a global scale' (WFA, 2002). This chapter investigates some current barriers to developing a sustainable Australian wine tourism industry from the understanding both of operators and industry professionals.

Literature Review

Research suggests that investment in 'knowledge infrastructure' will be critical for regional areas' success in the new economy (Kennedy and Forman, 2003). A knowledge economy involves infrastructure factors including industry clusters and other inter-organizational linkages, effective use of information and communication technologies (ICTs), and linkages between education, business, community and government. Increasing the external focus of regions through leveraging greater connectedness, sharing best practice for organizational and community learning, relevant, rapid innovation and research dissemination and knowledge sharing are all indicated.

The industry also recognizes the importance of its marketing strategy (WFA, 2002), with the suggestion that new wineries' ability to tap wine tourism will 'determine their viability'. Branding linkages concern regional tourism networks, and engage the national brand. Discussing 'Brand Australia', Fraser (2001) encouraged the wine industry to continue developing the wine tourism experience, benefiting from wider branding and integration with other regional attractions.

In a New Zealand study (Hall and Johnson, 1998), however, participation in alliances was low, further hampered by the wine producers' perspective that wine had more to offer tourism than vice versa. Perhaps relatedly, regional branding was not yet standard practice. Hall *et al.* (2000a) provide examples of inter-organizational linkages at various stages of (wine tourism) network development. For example, a regional wine route may be designated, developing into a joint promotional activity, and evolving to a fully developed network, embracing other attractions. These authors note that such networks not only represent flows of business information, but also possible tourist flows on the ground. Inter-organizational relationships range from dyads, through organization sets and action sets (a purposive coalition of interacting organizations) to a bounded network (e.g. a federation). Hall's group (Hall *et al.*, 2000a) reviewed network development in this sector in Australasia, and noted that prospects will only be improved by substantial persuasion, education and information provision activity, and internally rather than by government-driven initiatives.

Studies within Australia (Sellitto *et al.*, 2003a, b) have shown that smaller wineries are more likely to be innovative and to use a wider range of Internet technology. Powerful stakeholders in the supply chain, such as large supermarkets and federal government, heavily influence e-business usage. Major retailers 'dictate' adoption of synchronized global data as an Internet mechanism for transferring standardized product information and images, obliging wineries to follow suit. Wineries report that this affects their business to consumer (B2C) strategies, effectively locking out direct online sales, explaining apparent lack of innovation and absence of online sales for many larger wineries (Roberts and Fitzgerald, 2003). Consolidation among smaller wineries and cluster technology-sharing initiatives may face similar issues in future, and in general it is possible that the technology choices mandated by major distribution organizations may be expected to drive e-business adoption more than perceived intrinsic benefits, but concomitantly stifling innovation.

Knowledge, marketing activity and technology sharing are all facilitated through the Internet and ICTs generally, and by clusters of operators and other stakeholders working together. The knowledge infrastructure within regional inter-organizational settings is thus of particular interest in the present research.

Research Methods

A key strategy of the WFA is to improve wine tourism research (WFA, 2002). There is general agreement that wine tourism is under-researched (e.g. WFA, 2002; Beames, 2003), impacting on the knowledge required for business development. Major academic research includes that of Dowling and Carlsen (1998), Getz (2000) and Hall *et al.* (2000b). Industry and government bodies also conduct or commission research, and a knowledge base is gradually becoming established. Forward-looking research to drive the industry's decision making is seen as strategically required, and its relevance, accessibility and utility to business operators are crucial.

This study employed face-to-face, semi-structured interviews with wine tourism operators throughout Australia and with other tourism business operators involved in related industry networks. This was done in parallel with interviews of key representatives of state tourism bodies responsible for industry development. South Australia, New South Wales, Western Australia and Queensland were chosen as including a range of mature and emerging wine regions.

Interviews, normally lasting about one hour, addressed previously identified priority areas for SME development (SMIDEC, 1998), including human resource development, access to finance, access to markets and market development, access to information and technology and technology sharing. Participants were generally owners/operators of wineries. A mini-focus group was used in one case to supplement individual interviews, providing extra depth and richness of understanding:

Opening questions regarding the interviewee, their background and current business built rapport, leading naturally to the specific areas. These were covered as they occurred conversationally, with a checklist protocol ensuring completeness. Notes taken were handwritten or tape-recorded by permission. Themes and issues were extracted directly: detailed content analysis and modelling was not considered necessary.

Operators and industry professionals were purposely sampled in each region – aiming for a qualitative overview expressed in participants' own words, using a convergent interviewing technique (Dick, 1998). Here, the number of interviews is determined when participants consistently give similar responses: normally between four and 16 data sources suffice and, when prior literature is also available, sample size can be smaller (Nair and Riege, 1995). This approach meant that, once redundancy was achieved, further interviewing was considered unproductive. Eleven wine tourism operators were interviewed, and convergence among interview data was often achieved after only a few interviews. Once an issue was validated, the researcher could be confident that it applied beyond a single operator. This allows inductive and deductive research to be combined and refinement of the inquiry as it evolves (Perry and Jensen, 2001).

Findings

For space reasons, only issues relating to knowledge infrastructure are reported. Specific issues relating to branding, finance (e.g. double taxation), lack of relevant research and human resource development were also identified. Some operators considered that more networking and local planning initiatives were required, since some areas were oversupplied with accommodation, and there was a need to co-market attractions with other facilities in the area. One region had 11 wineries near the accommodation supply but no link, nor tourist route designation, was provided.

Australia generally has high technological awareness, and even regionally – where infrastructure is less advanced – most wineries sampled had Internet presence and e-mail. Within this, however, a range of activity was apparent. Some wineries had their own website with e-commerce functionality, such as online ordering: others outsourced this as part of a cooperative marketing strategy. One winery had a website at their vineyard location (elsewhere), but had no plans to introduce one at the cellar door operation.

Responses on e-commerce, e-readiness and industry linkage and clustering issues were of particular relevance. Some state governments would facilitate, but not operate, educational sessions on e-commerce, delivered by private providers. Such events were difficult to run effectively outside the metropolitan areas in some states due to large distances, and the time and costs involved for potential attendees affirming the 'digital divide' as a general issue for a knowledge-based economy's success.

One state government official believed that 'mentoring' talks by leading operators in successful regions worked better than conventional public sector educators. Another thought that tourism extension officers, subject to resources, would be useful. One operator said that whilst his group of wineries shared the employment of a winemaker, family members who were 'paying attention' were becoming usefully prepared in the absence of a formal qualification. Business and education links specific to wine tourism were being established, with tertiary qualification programmes available in some states.

Wine tourism sustainability is closely aligned to that of the winemaking industry. Bruwer (2002) noted that in Australia '51% of all wineries have a production capacity of less than 4000 cases per year while 66% … produce less than 7500 cases per year'. New Australian wineries have emerged rapidly, recently as frequently as one every three days (Australian Wine and Brandy Corporation, figures cited in Bruwer, 2002). Unless contracted to a big purchaser, this would position a majority of wineries in niche segments, thus favouring direct sales through cellar doors or online. This industry structure differentiates those operators primarily concerned with product from those for whom tourism-associated revenue is a significant part of the business mix.

Industry groups had already formed in each state surveyed. One group was just forming at the time of the study, and one new winery in another state was not affiliated to any group. In one state with a relatively recent tradition of wine tourism, a group of wineries had formed to share all aspects of their expertise, and saw a critical mass of new ideas benefiting all in the region rather than conferring competitive advantage at local level. One emerging area saw itself as essentially primary production, but recognized the need for value-added (service) industries, with the need for attractions beyond wine seen as critical for developing a sustainable regional tourism economy.

Established regions had websites embracing several wineries in their region, some also having their own sites. These portal sites charged memberships but all members benefited from a brand identity. One website (http://www.winediva.com.au) provides a database of Australian wineries and contact details, helping build industry presence and enabling route designations or package designs. The Australian Tourism Data Warehouse also provides extensive listings, though state tourism officials noted some uptake issues.

Other linkages were evident in more established regions, addressing wine-associated products, particularly gourmet foods. Such groups recognized complementarity among their products in marketing an experience to the wine tourist. One emerging wine region was in the process of forming an industry group, primarily as an awareness-raising marketing initiative since 'nobody knew that region had wineries'.

Technologies other than ICTs apply in the sector. Wine production entails relevant environmental technologies that also affect sustainable tourism. Unrestrained growth in wineries naturally impacts on the land and water, and extra traffic and associated use of amenities impacts on infrastructure capacity. Salinity and wastewater in wine regions are major issues, and education sessions at expositions, plus the trade press, are mechanisms for sharing technological know-how. Currently sustainable and indigenous practices – including permaculture approaches – are considered by some operators to be an important part of sustaining Australia's environment.

Genetically modified (GM) products and other practices aimed at global markets were viewed with suspicion, although not ignorance: the wine industry is officially opposed to GM use. Local governments also impose environmental requirements through planning approvals and inspections, although, in more than one state, inconsistencies in application were reported. State tourism authorities recognized the need for a coordinating role in, for example, route development, and in ensuring environmental and capacity issues were properly considered at regional levels.

Implications for Wine Tourism

The new economy is characterized by inter-organizational networking and cooperation across sectors, by diffusion of knowledge and learning, and by innovation (not price) as the basis of competitive advantage. The present study revealed various issues pertaining to the sustainable development of wine tourism in Australia, particularly highlighting new economy practices.

Many wine regions are not in the mass tourism business, but regional branding and related destination management become applicable. Operators in emerging regions recognized the comparative value that Margaret River, Barossa and Hunter had established. Following more mature regions, some entrepreneurs had begun to form action sets to promote their emerging regions. Such industry associations will need to move from sector-specific to cross-industry alliances.

A promotional or marketing relationship through industry group portals was prevalent among wine tourism operators interviewed. For smaller wineries not involved in exporting, this entry-level approach may be appropriate since they will benefit from regional-level branding and promotion.

In emerging wine-tourism areas, industry groups' aims were modest. Some other tourism business operators were more proactive in forming industry linkages and arguing for joint promotions. Accommodation providers have much to gain from a short break or other targeted market for winery attractions, and could take a lead in developing destinations. Overall, barriers appeared associated more with a basic need to realize the importance of collaboration in facing global competition, and using and sharing technologies with a view to effective destination promotion and branding.

Increased external focus is aided by Internet presence and computer-supported collaboration. Internet and e-commerce use varied: most wineries have some Internet presence, and some exporters were adopting a staged approach to e-commerce activity (e.g. with online ordering but manual order fulfilment).

States found it more effective to facilitate private e-business education providers than to supply it themselves. Effective partnerships in these areas could be further examined. An understanding of the capacity of a region to support tourism may also be better left to a knowledgeable authority than to market forces, with public private partnership models also applicable.

The research reported here validates views expressed in trade media by industry figures and suggests that the increased presence and external focus gained through new economy practices of branding, clustering and e-business adoption is likely to affect the ongoing viability of wineries and associated tourism. The significant potential of wine-tourism in Australia, and indeed emerging wine regions elsewhere, will be conditioned by the effectiveness of the partnerships formed by operators for branding, knowledge sharing and sustainable practice.

References

Beames, G. (2003) The Rock, the reef and the grape: the challenges of developing wine tourism in regional Australia. *Journal of Vacation Marketing* 9, 205–212.

Bruwer, J. (2002) Marketing wine to Generation-X consumers through the cellar door. *The Australian and New Zealand Grapegrower and Winemaker*, December (http://www.grapeandwine.com.au/dec02/07.htm, accessed June 2005).

Charters, S. and Ali-Knight, J. (2002) Who is the wine tourist? *Tourism Management* 23, 311–319.

Dick, B. (1998) *Convergent interviewing: a technique for qualitative data collection* (http://www.scu.edu.au/schools/gcm/ar/arp/iview.html, accessed June 2005).

Dowling, R. and Carlsen, J. (eds) (1998) *Wine Tourism, Perfect Partners: Proceedings of the First Australian Wine Tourism Conference*, Margaret River, Western Australia, May 1998, Bureau of Tourism Research, Canberra.

Fraser, C. (2001) Brand Australia. Australian Tourist Commission presentation given at *Australian Wine Marketing Conference*, Adelaide, July 2001.

Getz, D. (2000) *Explore Wine Tourism: Management, Development and Destinations.* Cognizant Communication Corporation, New York.

Hall, C.M. and Johnson, G. (1998) Wine tourism: an imbalanced partnership. In: Dowling, R. and Carlsen, J. (eds) *Wine Tourism, Perfect Partners: Proceedings of the first Australian Wine Tourism Conference*, Margaret River, Western Australia, May 1998, Bureau of Tourism Research, Canberra, pp. 51–72.

Hall, C.M., Johnson, G. and Mitchell, R.D. (2000a) Wine tourism and regional development. In: Hall, C.M., Sharples, E., Cambourne, B. and Macionis, N. (eds) *Wine Tourism Around the World: Development, Management and Markets.* Butterworth-Heinemann, Oxford, UK, pp. 196–225.

Hall, C.M., Sharples, E., Cambourne, B. and Macionis, N. (eds) (2000b) *Wine Tourism Around the World: Development Management and Markets.* Butterworth Heinemann, Oxford, UK.

Kennedy, N. and Forman, D. (2003) *A New Angle on Regional Infrastructure*, Australian Business Foundation Limited, Sydney, Australia (http://www.abfoundation.com.au/ext/ABFound.nsf/all/917526EDA4C5392F4A256D4400208FF8/$FILE/Infrastructure+Commentary+Report,+August+2003.pdf, accessed June 2005).

King, C. and Morris, R. (1998) Wine tourism: an Australian/New Zealand case study of cellar door decision making at small and medium-sized wineries. *International Council for Small Business Conference Proceedings*, Singapore (http://www.sbaer.uca.edu/Research/1998/ICSB/o002.htm, accessed March 2004).

Macionis, N. (1998) Wineries and tourism: perfect partners or dangerous liaisons? In: Dowling, R. and Carlsen, J. (eds) *Wine Tourism, Perfect Partners: Proceedings of the First Australian Wine Tourism Conference*, Margaret River, Western

Australia, Bureau of Tourism Research, Canberra, pp. 35–49.

Marceau, J., Manley, K. and Sicklen, D. (1997) *The High Road or the Low Road? Alternatives for Australia's Future*, Australian Business Foundation Limited, Sydney, Australia.

Nair, G. and Riege, A. (1995) Using convergent interviewing to develop the research problem of a postgraduate thesis. Cited in: Master, H. and Perry, C. (eds) *Product and Promotional Strategy Development in Database Marketing Types, Proceedings of ANZMAC,* 1998 (http://smib.vuw.ac.nz: 8081/www.ANZMAC1998/Cd_rom/Master 91.pdf, accessed 13 May 2006).

Perry, C. and Jensen, O. (2001) Approaches to combining induction and deduction in one research study. *Proceedings of the Australian and New Zealand Marketing Academy Conference,* 1–5 December 2001. Massey, NZ (http://130.195.95.71:8081/WWW/ANZMAC2001/anzmac/AUTHORS/pdfs/Perry1.pdf, accessed June 2005).

Roberts, B. and Fitzgerald, E. (2003) An investigation of e-business use by Australian wineries. In: Burn, J. (ed.) *Proceedings of the 14th Australasian Conference on Information Systems,* Perth, Western Australia, 26–28 November 2003.

Sellitto, C., Burgess, S. and Wenn, A. (2003a) The developing websites of Australian wineries. Paper presented at the *4th International Working with e-Business Conference,* Perth, Western Australia, November 2003 (CD ROM).

Sellitto, C., Wenn, A. and Burgess, S. (2003b) A review of the websites of small Australian wineries: motivations, goals and success. *Information Technology and Management* 4, 215–232.

SMIDEC (1998) Integrated Plan of Action for SME Development (SPAN). *Fifth Meeting of APEC Ministers Responsible for SMEs,* Malaysia, 7–8 September1998, Small and Medium Industries Development Corporation (Malaysia) (http://www.apec-sec.org.sg/ecotech/span.html, accessed March 2004).

Winemakers Federation of Australia (WFA) (2002) *Wine Tourism Strategic Business Plan 2002–2005* (http://www.wfa.org.au/PDF/NWTS%20Strategic%20Plan.pdf, accessed March 2004).

6

Emerging Wine Tourism Regions: Lessons for Development

BEVERLEY SPARKS* AND JANE MALADY

Services Industry Research Centre, Griffith University, PMB 50 Gold Coast Mail Centre, Queensland 9726, Australia
*E-mail: B.Sparks@griffith.edu.au

Introduction

This chapter describes and analyses two developing wine regions located in Queensland, Australia. A number of key themes emerged from this research. First, the importance of developing tourism clusters to attract tourists to a region is required. Such strategies rely on collaboration between operators within a compact geographic area that provide products that enhance the overall wine and food experience (Telfer, 2001). Second, there is a need to develop marketing and business skills of operators wanting to enter the tourism business. Third, the development of tourism product relies on those entering the industry to be committed, and thus available at all opening hours on a consistent basis. Fourth, regional champions, leaders and individuals with an entrepreneurial spirit are vital to the development and growth of a regional wine tourism product.

Australia has many wine growing areas and many of these have developed (or are developing) strong tourism product. More recently, many traditional farming or rural areas have sought out tourism for increasing economic development opportunities. Wine and food tourism has played a key role in such developments. The wine industry and wine tourism are emerging industries in Queensland. The Queensland Government Tourism, Fair Trade and Wine Industry Development identifies eight wine tourism regions in Queensland outlining wine grape plantings at the end of 2004 to be as follows:

- The Granite Belt, 790 ha.
- The South Burnett, 420 ha.
- Darling Downs, 120 ha.
- Inglewood and Maranoa, 50 ha.
- Gold Coast Hinterland, Brisbane, Brisbane Valleys and the Scenic Rim, 50 ha.

- Central Queensland and North Burnett, 40 ha.
- Sunshine Coast and Hinterland, 20 ha.
- D'Aguilar Ranges and Somerset Valleys, 20 ha.

(Queensland Government Tourism, 2005a). The locations of Queensland's wine tourism regions are depicted in Fig. 6.1.

This research uses a case study approach to explore the developing wine and food tourism industry in two Queensland regions: the Sunshine Coast and the South Burnett. Both regions are new to the development of a wine industry and, therefore, provide a good setting for an analysis of the emerging wine tourism product. In addition, these two regions provide a contrasting view of different positioning and stages of tourism development within Queensland. The Sunshine Coast region is a well-established tourist destination, with Noosa being widely recognized as a lifestyle destination. It is now seeking to add wine tourism to its more established tourism product.

The South Burnett region, in contrast, is Queensland's second largest wine producing region (Queensland Department of State Development, 2004), with a well-established agricultural base but with an emerging tourism industry based on its historical perspective and natural attractions. This

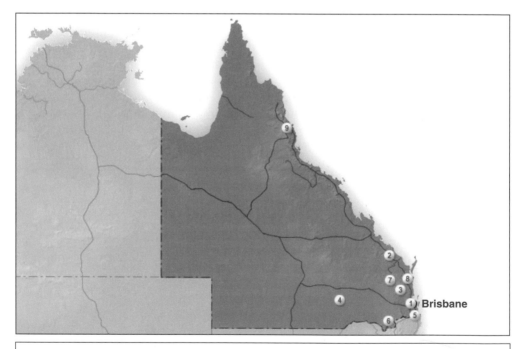

1.	Brisbane City (not a wine region)	6.	Granite Belt
2.	Central Queensland and North Burnett	7.	South Burnett
3.	D'Aguilar Ranges and Somerset Valleys	8.	Sunshine Coast Hinterland
4.	Darling Downs, Inglewood and Maranoa	9.	Tropical North Queensland
5.	Gold Coast Hinterland		

Fig. 6.1. Queensland wine regions. Source: Wine-region-tours.com (2005).

research seeks to gain a better understanding of the development of the wine and food tourism product, including unique features of the two Queensland regions and challenges faced. In addition, this research focuses on the role played by people (key stakeholders) from the region in the development of wine tourism.

Literature Review

Dowling and Getz (2000, p. 57) suggest that the wine tourism experience is made up not only of the provision of good wine, but also requires 'quality dining opportunities and other attributes to create a unique experience and ambience' and note that Australians value the 'preservation of architecture and heritage as part of the wine country product'. Significantly, Hall *et al.* (2000) suggest that the development of networks is critical to the development of wine tourism in a region as there is a need for businesses that previously have not identified themselves as being part of the same industry to work collaboratively with stakeholders in the tourism industry.

Dodd and Beverland (2001) note that in the life-cycle development of wine tourism regions, as the region grows the establishment of networks between wineries and other tourism-related business becomes more prevalent to assist in the marketing and promotion of the region. In addition, Hall (2003) argues that the roles of 'champions' and local government are important in the development of wine and food networks. Dowling and Getz (2000, p. 58) state that 'leadership is an important issue and may come from wineries, industry associations or government agencies'. An important dimension of wine and food tourism for regional communities often extends beyond the pure financial aspect into a community pride and sense of local identity and culture (Hall, 2003).

Research Method

This study adopted an instrumental case study approach (Stake, 2000) to examine regional development of wine- and food-based tourism. An instrumental case study approach assumes an interest in providing insight to a general issue, such as, in this instance, the development of regional tourism. This case analysis is based on three sources of data: archival statistical data, field visits and in-depth interviews conducted with key stakeholders and leaders within each region. Sites visited and stakeholders selected were based on perceived prominence within the regions' tourism industry as identified from regional tourism association websites, promotional material analysed and initial discussion with stakeholders from regional tourism associations and the tourism industry.

The case studies included information on the regions' wine and food tourism attractions; the infrastructure, in particular accommodation and restaurants; marketing of the region; regional wine and food development groups; and various characteristics of the regions in terms of their development and leadership. The interviewees were selected based on an audit of local tourism organizations. In total, eight in-depth interviews were conducted with key informants, together with more informal shorter interviews with operators. In analysing the collected interview information, a content analysis was undertaken using NVivo software to assist in the codification of information from the interviews.

Findings and Discussion

The two regions studied in this project both have an emerging wine tourism industry, but differ considerably, however, in geographic location and maturity of their tourism industry. The Sunshine Coast region is a mature tourist destination with Noosa, the largest tourist destination in this region, experiencing visitor numbers of 1.7 million in 2002 and a resident population on 44,000 (EMDA, 2003). Noosa has long been recognized as a lifestyle destination, with more restaurants per head of population than anywhere else in Australia and 194 accommodation operators and 711 food outlets.

Furthermore, the beaches and local hinterland provide a rich tourism draw card for natural tourism. In contrast, the South Burnett region is an emerging tourist destination with a resident population of 35,836 and approximately 47,917 visitors in 2002 (South Burnett Local Government Association, 2003). The tourism infrastructure within South Burnett region is somewhat less developed, with 76 accommodation operators and 49 food outlets.

Sunshine Coast region

The Sunshine Coast, although well developed as a tourism destination, has a newly emerging wine tourism industry. At its most southerly point this region is approximately 90 km from Brisbane, the capital city of Queensland. The wine industry on the Sunshine Coast accounts for approximately 20 ha of wine grape plantings in Queensland, with 12 vineyards, most of which have cellar door facilities or are in the process of building a cellar door facility. The wineries of the Sunshine Coast operate first and foremost as tourism enterprises. All the wineries on the Sunshine Coast are small boutique operators, the largest being only 11 ha in area and the majority being less than 5 ha, relying primarily on cellar door sales to distribute their wine.

However, with small production yields, continuous year-round supply can be problematic for some wineries due to low production. Many of the wineries on the Sunshine Coast are newcomers to the wine industry, often owned by people that have moved to the Sunshine Coast for a lifestyle change. Table 6.1 provides an overview of the existing wineries located in this region.

Table 6.1. Sunshine Coast wineries (from Queensland Department of State Development 2004).

Winery	Established	Location
Delaney's Creek Winery and Vineyard	1997	Caboolture Shire
Maleny Mountain Wines	2000	Maleny
Settlers Rise Winery	1999	Montville
Flaxton Gardens Wine Cellar and Vineyard	2000	Flaxton
7 Acres	1985	Forest Glen
Eumundi Winery and Vineyard	1996	Eumundi
Maroochy Springs Winery	2003	Eerwah Vale
Kenilworth Bluff Wines	1993	Kenilworth
Dingo Creek Vineyard	1997	Traveston
Glastonbury Estate	2000	Gympie
Glengariff Historic Estate Vineyards	1996	Dayboro
Noosa Valley Winery	2000	Noosa Shire

The Sunshine Coast Wineries Association was identified as being an influential group in the development of this region's wine tourism industry. The Sunshine Coast also has an increasing number of local food producers, which complement the wineries. Some have incorporated tourism into their business, in some cases to increase the sustainability of their business. The combination of food outlets together with the wineries is a productive step in creating a wine and food trail experience for tourists in the Sunshine Coast region. This is supported by a brochure *Noosa Food Trail*, produced by Tourism Noosa.

The Sunshine Coast Wine region, while in close proximity to Brisbane, is spread over a relatively large distance with the most southerly winery being 83 km from the most northerly winery, and distances between wineries ranging from 12 to 70 km. Wine trail maps for this region, such as that shown in Fig. 6.2, can often be misleading when estimating distance between wineries.

South Burnett region

The South Burnett region is the second largest wine growing region in Queensland, accounting for 400 ha of wine grape plantings with 26 vineyards in the area, ranging in size from experimental plots of 0.4 ha to large commercial vineyards. Clovely Estate, situated in the South Burnett region, is the largest vineyard in Queensland, with more than 222 ha under vine producing 1298 t of wine grapes (Queensland Department of State Development, 2004; Stuart Range Estate Wines, 2005).

The South Burnett Region is situated 2.5 hours' drive north-west of Brisbane and was established as Australia's newest winemaking region in 1994. Again, the wineries in this region are spread across a wide region, with 60 km between the most southerly and most northerly wineries; however,

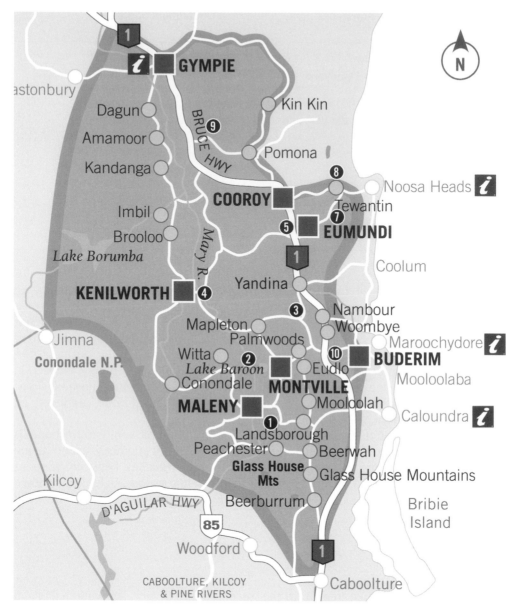

Fig. 6.2. Sunshine Coast wine trail map. Courtesy of Tourism Queensland.

unlike the Sunshine Coast regions there is some clustering of wineries, as depicted in Fig. 6.3. Once again, however, this wine trail map does not provide a true indication of the distances between key wineries in this region; for example the distance between Stuart Range Estate and Clovely Estate is approximately 58 km.

Vineyards were established in the South Burnett region in response to the recognition that there was a need for diversification within the agriculture

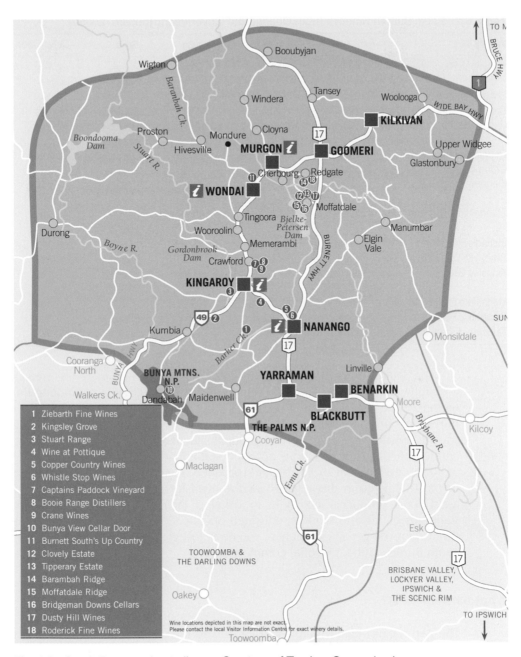

Fig. 6.3. South Burnett wine trail map. Courtesy of Tourism Queensland.

industry. As a result, the South Burnett region potentially has 'a lot of dairy farmers that are trying to be cellar doors' (D. Postle, South Burnett, 2004, personal communication). Table 6.2 provides an overview of the South Burnett wineries.

Table 6.2. South Burnett wineries (from Queensland Government Tourism, 2005d).

Winery	Established	Location	Size	Style	Cellar Door
Barambah Ridge Winery	1995	Redgate	500 t	Large commercial	Yes
Bridgeman Downs Cellars	1996	Moffatdale			Yes
Captains Paddock Vineyard	1995	Kingaroy	4 ha	Boutique	Yes
Clovely Estate	1997	Murgon	1298 t 220 ha	Large commercial	Yes
Copper Country	1997	Nanango	1 ha	Boutique	Yes
Crane Winery	1993	Booie	4 ha	Boutique	Yes
Kingaroy Ridge Winery	2003	Booie	Limited quantities	Boutique	
Stuart Range Estates	1997	Kingaroy	400 t	Large complex	Yes
Ziebarth Fine Wines	1998	Goodger			Yes
Dusty Hill Vineyard	1996	Moffatdale	7 ha	Boutique	Yes
Kingsley Grove	1998: first release 2003	Kingaroy	8.7 ha	Boutique	Yes
Moffatdale Ridge	1995	Moffatdale	105 ha		Yes
Roderick's Fine Wine	2004	Redgate	18 ha	Boutique	Yes
Tipperary Estate Vineyard	2004	Moffatdale		Boutique	Yes

The South Burnett Wine Industry Association aims to promote the area as a quality gourmet wine and food region and is very active in promoting the region's wine growing status to locals and tourists. As part of the South Burnett's tourism development strategy new customer markets are being sought utilizing existing tourism product, such as golf courses, wineries, antiques, heritage and boutique accommodation.

The development of the region's produce is paramount, and a common theme to emerge in this regard was the need for education programmes to assist local producers not only to develop their product to high-quality standards but also to work as educated operators 'so that when you go to a cellar door you get an experience, you don't just get a wine tasting' (D. Postle, South Burnett, 2004, personal communication).

What barriers exist?

The two regions face a number of barriers to the development of successful wine and food tourism industries. First, the geographical dispersion of the wineries is noteworthy, with distances between outlets being quite large in some cases. There is a need to promote the wine and food attractions within a small geographical area clustered with related attractions such as galleries, historic buildings, markets and natural attractions.

Lesson 1: find ways to link tourism wineries (and other offerings) together within small geographical areas. Take the opportunity to present these to consumers in a clearly mapped-out way.

Secondly, many of the operators, though exhibiting enthusiasm, lack formal training, as identified by one Sunshine Coast interviewee: 'I guess that's an impediment … the lack of formal training of our members.' A similar problem identified in the South Burnett region is the need for education for winery operators: 'This is an education process that we are trying to get over, for them to realize that they are in the tourism industry and therefore they should be open.' In order to develop the region there is a level of professionalism required that moves beyond the 'hobby' feel to serious business.

Lesson 2: the provision of training to those entering the industry in fundamental business, including marketing principles, is vital.

A third problem identified through this study was associated with emerging tourism regions such as the South Burnett, where the process of collaboration has not yet been achieved among industry stakeholders. One stakeholder commented: 'The lack of cooperation, competitiveness within the region is very fierce …' Another stated that they felt there was a 'lack of product, lack of awareness, lack of people heading in the right direction'. For any region attempting to establish and develop a tourism product like wine and food, there is a need for the business owners to work collaboratively.

Further to this problem, both regions are spread across several shires, making collaboration and coordination a challenge and a necessity to successful planning and development. As one interviewee on the Sunshine Coast stated when discussing what makes for strong regional development: '[it's] the sense of community and without that you can go nowhere.' On the other hand, the South Burnett is in its infancy as a tourism area and overcoming competitive tendencies and allowing the development of collaborative partnerships between sectors of the tourism industry is a key challenge. Recognition that the tourist is looking for a destination with enough products to make it a worthwhile experience is still required.

Lesson 3: there is probably more to be gained through the collaboration of tourism entities within the region and between other regions close by.

A fourth issue has to do with the size of the wineries. For the Sunshine Coast region this was seen as an impediment to development; as one stakeholder stated: 'We don't grow enough grapes. One of our members has been out of all wine for about a month.' A further problem related to size is the effect that the Wine Equalization Tax (WET) (a value-based tax applied to wine consumed in Australia) has on these small operators as economies of scale are not there to help them absorb this tax – instead, they have a high price on their wine: 'Our wine is expensive. If you go to the Hunter Valley you can buy a $7–8 bottle of wine; well, you would have to double that up here.'

Lesson 4: emerging regions may face a challenge with small operators and there may be a need in the early days to give consideration to how to manage the supply of product throughout the year.

A fifth issue that is a barrier to development is that of commitment to the tourism industry. For example, as tourism is in its infancy in the South Burnett region, not all operators consider they are part of the tourism industry. Many have an agricultural background or operate at a retail level while others recognize that tourism needs to be developed in the region; however, the bottom line (making a profit) is the more important issue. The differing commitment among wine industry operators is a further barrier to collaborative planning between the wine industry and tourism stakeholders:

> I guess I look at this site – that we've got not only the opportunity to grow that tourism side of things, but if we can make the wine commercially very successful and develop some export and wholesale business and get some of our food ingredient business working really strongly, it will actually provide some cash income to continue that tourism development to get the region well known. So it's an interesting balance of finding what's commercially workable but still helping tourism. Tourism can make you a lot of money but because we're an emerging region you can't rely on it 100 per cent, so you have to augment that with other aspects of the business.

The Sunshine Coast, on the other hand, has a solid tourism base and new and existing winery operators have set up their business to cater for tourism. The wineries on the Sunshine Coast operate as tourism entities, relying on cellar door sales for revenue, and as such are actively promoting themselves to tourists.

Lesson 5: wine growers need to decide whether they are in or out of the tourism industry. Half-hearted approaches can damage more that just one enterprise.

Related to the last barrier is the flow to tourism promotion. As Hall and his colleagues have noted (2000), winemakers often know a lot about the production of wine but less about tourism. Similarly, some of the operators in the South Burnett do not appear to be fully committed to operating as tourism operators and, as a result, much of the promotional material doesn't have all the necessary information, for example whether there is food available, opening times, what product is on offer, etc. This is an important issue given the wide geographic dispersion of these wineries – people need this sort of information to plan their itinerary.

Both regions are largely self-drive markets yet the road signage is still lacking. Both regions have developed maps of wine and food trails, yet these could be further developed with additional content and better information on distances between venues. Decisions based on poor information can be costly if the tourist has to travel 35 or 40 km between venues. The region needs to give further thought to what the tourism product comprises and how to best communicate that accurately to potential tourists.

The people operating the wineries in the South Burnett region are from an agricultural background and are very authentic, although lacking tourism experience. One stakeholder in the South Burnett commented on the cellar door operator's attitude 'to know that you just can't go out into the cow yard and come in and sell wines in no shoes and a really ratty t-shirt, that's just not a good image'. Similarly, several interviewees commented on the need to have consistent opening hours and actually to be open when advertised. Planning seems to present a challenge for many newly organized network groups, as one Sunshine Coast interviewee noted: 'The way that most collectives of people operate is "oh, did you hear about this ... next week lets see if we can do something about it". Always too late, always chasing your tail, people are panicking and they spend a lot of the time running around in circles and that's not professional.'

Lesson 6: make sure information that is used to promote a region is accurate and kept current, especially where the product is geographically dispersed.

A key to success usually lies with the people of the region. We identified individuals with a passion for a particular vision for the region who are the driving force in the development of a regional identity and are encouraging collaboration and commitment from industry members. However, this can be a barrier when operators are motivated by self-interest, as one stakeholder identified: 'Again it comes back to the fact that everyone gets busy and it all starts to fall down if someone isn't keeping it alive and going.' Nevertheless, in many of the interviews we conducted we found evidence of an entrepreneurial and pioneering attitude. For example, one of the stakeholders interviewed, although often employed on a voluntary basis, outlined her vision for the region's organic food producers and plans to bring together the organic producers with restaurateurs to help grow the organic produce of the region, expressing great passion for this project.

Lesson 7: harnessing the energy of all concerned is important to overcome the factional barrier.

For both regions the continuing challenge is to develop the authenticity of the region and deliver this to potential tourists in a consistent and reliable manner. If tourists are going to visit a destination for a wine and food experience there needs to be enough products available to satisfy the desire for a range of unique and interesting experiences. For example, the South Burnett region is rich in history and a number of farm stays feature the original farm house and outhouses, serving breakfast in the original kitchen, telling stories of the history of the farm and the original owners of the property, thereby providing an authentic and unique experience to the tourist. The cultural heritage of this region could be further integrated into the tourist experience and, ideally, restaurants and food outlets needed in the region could also draw on the cultural heritage of the region and utilize the region's product rather than provide an experience that has no link to the region itself.

Lesson 8: every region needs its own authentic identity with product to complement that identity.

Implications for Wine Tourism

This chapter presents the work of two case studies that sought to investigate the level of development in the emerging wine tourism industry within Queensland. Several notable implications for the development of regional wine tourism to emerge from this study include first, that attention to product development is required and the positioning of the various regions as wine tourism destinations is still challenging. Our interviews revealed a high degree of commitment by many community or business personnel, but it was not without a sense of competition.

Second, this investigation highlighted the important role of clusters and networks in building the tourism product. This seems particularly vital at the early lifecycle stage of these regions. Third, further consideration of linking wine and food tourism to other tourism product may be required in order to target different market segments and provide diversity. As an example, heritage tourism or wildlife tourism could be incorporated into promotional materials. Finally, improved promotional information – especially information about opening times and what is available at the wine venue – is vital to existing visitors to the region as well as to attracting new markets. Attention to signage and concise tourist maps are also required.

This study has identified the importance of regional champions and leaders to the development and branding of the food and wine product of that region and the presence of such seems essential to the successful development of food and wine tourism. As south-east Queensland continues to grow at a rapid rate the opportunity to attract more day-trippers and tourists to regional locations exists. However, most of this growing population has extensive tourist experience and, consequently, high expectations about the tourism experience and the level of service. In summary, the case studies identified a number of barriers that lead to some possible lessons in developing emerging regions.

References

Dodd, T. and Beverland, M. (2001) Winery tourism life-cycle development: a proposed model. *Tourism Recreation Research* 26 (2), 11–21.

Dowling, R. and Getz, D. (2000) Wine tourism futures. In: Faulkner, B., Moscardo, G. and Laws, E. (eds) *Tourism in the Twenty-first Century: Reflections on Experience.* Continuum, London, pp. 49–66.

EMDA (Economic and Market Development Advisers) (2003) Tourism Noosa 2002/03 *Tourism Monitor – Q3*, June 2003, Canterbury, Victoria, Australia.

Hall, C.M. (2003) Consuming places: the role of food, wine and tourism in regional development. In: Hall, M., Sharples, L., Mitchell, R. and Macionis, N. (eds) *Food Tourism.* Butterworth and Heinemann, Melbourne, Australia.

Hall, C.M., Johnson, G. and Mitchell, R. (2000) Wine tourism and regional development. In: Hall, C.M., Sharples, L., Cambourne, B. and Macionis, N. (eds) *Wine Tourism Around the*

World: Development, Management and Markets. Butterworth-Heinemann, Oxford, UK, pp. 196–225.

Queensland Department of State Development (2004) (http://www.sd.qld. gov.au/dsdweb/htdocs/global/content.cfm? id=73, accessed 24 February 2004).

Queensland Government Tourism (2005a) *Fair Trade and Wine Industry Development* 2005(a) (http://www.dtftwid.qld.gov.au/ Wine/ Industry+Overview, accessed 25 November 2005).

Queensland Government Tourism (2005b) *Fair Trade and Wine Industry Development* 2005(b) (http://www.dtftwid.qld.gov.au/_ Documents/Wine-Wineries/Sunshine Coast_Map_TQ.pdf, accessed 25 November 2005).

Queensland Government Tourism (2005c) *Fair Trade and Wine Industry Development* 2005(c) (http://www.dtftwid.qld.gov.au/_ Documents/Wine-Wineries/SouthBurnett_ Map_TQ.pdf, accessed 25 November 2005).

Queensland Government Tourism (2005d) *Fair Trade and Wine Industry Development* 2005(d) (http://www.dtftwid.qld.gov.au/Wine/Wineries+and+Regions/South+Burnett, accessed 25 November 2005).

South Burnett Local Government Association (2003) (http://sblga.asn.au/news).

Stake, R. (2000) Case Studies. In: Denzin, N.K. and Lincoln, Y.S. (eds) *Handbook of Qualitative Research*, 2nd edn. Sage, Thousand Oaks, California.

Stuart Range Estate Wines (2005) (http://www.srewines.com.au, accessed 25 November 2005).

Telfer, D.J. (2001) From a wine tourism village to a regional wine route: an investigation of the competitive advantage of embedded clusters in Niagara, Canada. *Tourism Recreation Research* 26 (2), 23–33.

Wine-region-tours.com (2005) (http://www.wine-region-tours.com/queensland.php, accessed 25 November 2005).

The Determinants of Quality Experiences in an Emerging Wine Region

TONY GRIFFIN* AND ALICE LOERSCH

School of Leisure, Sport and Tourism, University of Technology, Sydney, Australia
E-mail: tony.griffin@uts.edu.au

Introduction

In recent years, wine production has increased substantially in Australia, and with this expansion has come the emergence of new wine regions. As each new region develops a critical mass of wineries, an awareness of it generally leads to a flow of visitors who are curious to sample the product. The subsequent pace of growth of tourism to the region is dependent to some extent on the experiences of the pioneer tourists, who will then develop some loyalty, or not, to the new region and pass their impressions, positive or negative, on to friends and acquaintances. The quality of experience that the emerging region offers in its early years is thus crucial to its future as a wine tourism destination. This paper is based on one such region, the Canberra District, which embraces the Australian Capital Territory (ACT) and surrounding districts of New South Wales (NSW). In particular, the research sought to determine the key attributes that contributed to quality experiences in this emerging region.

The research was undertaken in conjunction with Australian Capital Tourism Canberra (ACTC), as part of a process of developing a quality auditing procedure that could be applied to a variety of tourism industry sectors. The purpose of this overall exercise was to identify indicators of quality that could be efficiently and effectively observed in order to audit the service quality performance of various tourism operators. Wineries were selected as the basis for a pilot project to develop a methodology that could then be modified and applied to other sectors. The initial task was to identify a set of possible indicators and then to refine this list to comprise those that were considered most important in influencing the quality of tourists' experiences. By identifying any deficiencies in quality, ACTC would then be able to implement product and service training programmes, partnerships and/or enhancement programmes that could be tailored to address these deficiencies and, ultimately, to increase the overall quality of the local tourism industry.

The Case Study Region

The Canberra District comprises the ACT and surrounding areas of NSW. At the time of the research there were 28 wineries operating within a 50 km radius of Canberra. Of these, 21 offered cellar door tastings and sales, while another two received visitors but by appointment only.

In 2001, Tourism NSW (2002) estimated that wineries in the Canberra, Southern Highlands and Snowy region received just over 50,000 visitors, making it the eighth most visited wine region in NSW (see Table 7.1). Virtually all of the wineries in that region are within the Canberra District. All other wine regions in the state lagged well behind the leading region, the lower Hunter Valley, which received nearly 3 million visitors in 2001. In terms of visitor numbers the Canberra District significantly exceeded those received by some other emerging regions, such as Orange, which has a similar number of wineries but lags well behind others, such as Shoalhaven/South Coast.

Literature Review

The increasing importance of service quality in gaining competitive advantage has led to the development and application of attribution base measurement techniques (Parasuraman *et al.*, 1985, 1991; Cronin and Taylor, 1992). The majority of these methods have adopted the expectancy–disconfirmation paradigm, which seeks to explore the relationship between a customer's expectations and perceptions of service performance. The difference between what customers expect and their perceptions of what they actually receive

Table 7.1. Estimated visitation to wineries with cellar door tastings and sales in NSW wine regions, 2001 (from Tourism New South Wales, 2002).

NSW wine region	Estimated visitor numbers
Lower Hunter Valley	2,901,512
Mudgee	368,096
Sydney/Nepean/Hawkesbury	292,118
Shoalhaven/South Coast	174,393
New England/North West/Northern Hastings	84,846
Riverina/Griffith	84,596
Upper Hunter	53,253
Canberra/Southern Highlands/Snowy	50,932
Murray/Darling/Perricoota	35,600
Orange	19,767
Hilltops/Young	17,115
Cowra	11,925

leads to either satisfaction when the performance exceeds expectations or dissatisfaction when performance falls short.

A number of methods have been developed which apply this paradigm to the measurement of service quality and which also attempt to serve as a diagnostic tool for management by pinpointing aspects of a service that requires attention. The SERVQUAL instrument developed by Parasuraman *et al.* (1985) measures performance in a range of service attributes across five dimensions: responsiveness, assurance, tangibles, empathy and reliability. Cronin and Taylor (1992) subsequently developed a more direct approach using an absolute rating of customers' attitudes towards service quality, called the SERVPERF technique. SERVPERF scores could also be weighted by measuring the importance of the quality attributes being tested. A related development is importance–performance analysis, which simultaneously seeks to measure the importance of various attributes and the customers' perceptions of performance in relation to those attributes (Lovelock *et al.*, 2001). Attributes that receive low importance scores are likely to play a lesser role in affecting overall perceptions of quality, while high scores are likely to play a more critical role (O'Neill *et al.*, 2002).

Several recent attempts have been made to identify indicators of service quality specifically in wine tourism operations. O'Neill and Charters (2000) focused on service quality at the cellar door in the Margaret River region and consequent implications for developing Western Australia's wine tourism. They argued that wineries needed to differentiate themselves to tourists and the best way to do this was through providing superior quality experiences. In order to assess service quality at wine tourism establishments, O'Neill and Charters (2000) first needed to establish the key service attributes. This was achieved using a two-stage methodology of operator and customer interviews based on the SERVQUAL scale. Once the service attributes had been identified, a questionnaire was administered to winery visitors, asking them to rate each attribute according to their perceptions of the quality experienced. Visitors were also asked to indicate the level of importance they ascribed to each attribute. The questionnaire responses were analysed using the five dimensions of SERVQUAL, and weighted SERVPERF scores were used to rank the attributes. Some critical success factors for wineries discovered in this study included accessibility, promotion, reputation and quality of service. Furthermore the criteria that directly related to the quality of experience at the cellar door were identified as layout, appearance and friendliness of staff.

Charters and O'Neill (2001) subsequently replicated this approach in the Barossa Valley and drew comparisons with the earlier study in Margaret River (O'Neill and Charters, 2000). While there were differences between the two regions, the service quality dimension of responsiveness emerged as the most important and most significant in terms of influencing future behaviour, such as intention to revisit.

A more recent study looked at the effects of service quality on wine sales. O'Neill *et al.* (2002) developed a 22-item quality attribute questionnaire, similar to the standard SERVQUAL instrument, focusing on the dimensions of contact, tangibles and responsiveness. Respondents rated the attributes on both their importance and performance. This enabled the use of weighted SERVPERF scores to measure the service quality of each attribute.

A number of other studies have focused on the importance of the cellar door experience for wine tourists and for subsequent wine sales (Bruwer, 2002; Ho and Gallagher, 2005), and on identifying the key motivations for winery visits (Alant and Bruwer, 2004). Bruwer (2002) stressed the importance of the quality of the first-time visitor's cellar door experience, as this would largely determine repeat visitation and positive word-of-mouth promotion. He viewed this as particularly important in the Australian context as small wineries, predominant in emerging regions, were increasingly reliant on cellar door sales as their major means of retail distribution. Alant and Bruwer (2004) measured the relative importance of a wide range of motivational factors to wine tourists in two regions of South Australia. Factors that related to the quality of the cellar door experience, such as 'to have a nice tasting experience' and 'to experience the atmosphere at the winery', rated very highly. The curiosity of visitors that might motivate a visit to an emerging wine region was reflected in the high rating assigned to 'to enjoy different wines'.

Research Method

In this study, the 22-item SERVQUAL scale was used to ascertain the general indicators that might be useful for measuring quality at the cellar door, along with the adapted version developed by O'Neill *et al.* (2002). Specific performance indicators for cellar door experiences were gathered by reviewing various wine and tourism industry fact sheets and checklists (Tourism NSW, 2003a, b, c; Winemakers' Federation of Australia, 2003a, b, c; Winter, 2003). Further attributes were elicited via interviews conducted with six winery operators in the Canberra District. These operators represented a cross-section of wineries within the district, according to type and size. A checklist of questions for the interviews was developed based on the literature and industry advisory information referred to above, and the interviews were recorded for subsequent analysis.

The service quality attributes that were subsequently tested were identified by conducting a meta-analysis of the SERVQUAL instrument, the industry advisory information and the results of the winery operator interviews. Ultimately, the most commonly recurring quality attributes were selected as offering the best potential for measuring the quality of Canberra District wineries. The results of this analysis are presented in Table 7.2. In total, 23 quality attributes were identified as being worthy of testing, across six dimensions: exterior, interior, service, staff, wine and convenience attributes. Exterior and interior attributes related to the physical qualities of the winery, with the former being associated with the winery's setting and surroundings, and the latter concerned with the layout and character of the tasting room.

Table 7.2 shows the relationship between the selected attributes, the SERVQUAL dimensions, the wine and tourism industry advisory information and the operator interview results. The choice of attributes was also partially

Table 7.2. Winery quality indicators (from Lovelock *et al.*, 2001; Tourism NSW, 2003a, b, c; Winemakers' Federation of Australia, 2003a, b c; Winter, 2003; authors' survey of wine operators).

Winery attributes	SERVQUAL dimensions	TNSW WFA WBM	Winery 1	Winery 2	Winery 3	Winery 4	Winery 5	Winery 6
Exterior attributes								
Views of surroundings	Tangible		✓				✓	✓
Attractive setting and environment	Tangible	✓	✓	✓		✓	✓	✓
Interior attributes								
Clean and well presented	Tangible	✓	✓			✓	✓	✓
Uncluttered and comfortable	Tangible	✓			✓	✓	✓	✓
Visually appealing	Tangible	✓	✓			✓		✓
Enjoyable atmosphere	Tangible	✓	✓			✓	✓	✓
Service attributes								
Prompt service	Responsiveness				✓		✓	✓
Ability to talk to winemaker	Assurance		✓	✓	✓		✓	
Informative and educational	Assurance	✓	✓		✓	✓	✓	✓
Restaurant or café	Tangible	✓	✓			✓	✓	✓
Staff attributes								
Friendly and welcoming	Responsiveness		✓	✓	✓		✓	
Professional and knowledgeable	Assurance	✓				✓	✓	
Understand visitor needs	Empathy	✓	✓			✓	✓	✓
Provide individual attention	Empathy	✓				✓		✓
Wine attributes								
Wine quality	Tangible	✓	✓		✓	✓	✓	
Wine variety	Tangible	✓	✓			✓		
Reasonably priced	Tangible				✓			✓
Convenience attributes								
Adequate signage and easy to find	Tangible	✓		✓	✓	✓	✓	
Adequate car parking	Tangible	✓		✓			✓	
Convenient opening times	Tangible					✓		✓
Tasting notes	Assurance	✓	✓		✓			
Price list	Assurance	✓			✓	✓		
Ability to join a mailing list	Tangible	✓	✓			✓	✓	

TNSW, Tourism New South Wales; WFA, Winemakers' Federation of Australia; WBM, Wine Business Monthly.

constrained by the ultimate purpose of the exercise, that is, to develop a simple method for conducting a quality audit by ACTC. Thus the focus was on attributes which could be observed rather than on those which would rely on customer evaluations of quality.

The quality indicators presented in Table 7.2 were then incorporated into a questionnaire survey administered to visitors of Canberra District wineries. The questionnaire asked visitors to indicate the following: (i) their expectations with respect to each of the 23 attributes on a five-point scale ('low' to 'high'); (ii) the importance they ascribed to each attribute on a five-point scale ('not' to 'very' important); and (iii) the performance of each attribute, again on a five-point scale, based on the extent to which their experience fell below or exceeded their expectations.

The survey was conducted at six wineries over a six-week period in July and August 2003. At some wineries the survey was administered by cellar door staff and at others by a member of the research team, with visitors being asked to complete the questionnaire upon their arrival and return it at the end of their visit. Winery staff were asked to assist with the survey administration because of the logistical difficulties of covering all six wineries within a relatively short time frame and of generating a reasonable number of responses. The intention was to approach all visitors present during the sampling period, however this was rather inconsistently done at a number of the wineries. If visitors went to a number of the surveyed wineries during their trip, they were asked to complete the questionnaire at only one winery.

Ultimately, a total of 173 visitors completed the questionnaire, relatively evenly divided between males (51.7%) and females (48.3%). Ages ranged from 18 to 65+, with the greatest number of respondents being in the 25–34 and 55–64 year age groups (31% and 25%, respectively).

To test how representative the survey sample was of wine tourists to the Canberra District in general, respondents were asked to categorize themselves by indicating which of a series of statements best described them in terms of their interest in visiting wineries. The resulting profile of respondents, as predominantly 'wine interested' or 'dedicated visitors/wine lovers', accorded closely with the general wine tourist profile developed by the Canberra Tourism and Events Corporation (2001). The sample can thus be said to be reasonably representative of winery visitors to the Canberra District.

Findings

The key results from the visitor survey are presented in Tables 7.3, 7.4 and 7.5. Each table presents the mean score for each attribute, based on the five-point scale that was used to measure expectations, importance and performance. In all cases the higher the score, the higher the rating ascribed to each attribute. The attributes are grouped according to the dimension with which they were associated.

Expectations

Visitors were asked to indicate the level of expectations they held in relation to their visit to the particular winery where they completed the questionnaire. Generally, visitors held the highest expectations in relation to the staff and the interior attributes of the cellar door/tasting room (see Table 7.3). 'Friendly and welcoming' staff and a 'clean and well-presented' tasting room were the

Table 7.3. Visitor expectations of winery attributes.

Attributes (n)	Mean score
Exterior attributes	
Views of surroundings (165)	3.52
Attractive setting and environment (160)	3.73
Interior attributes	
Cellar door/tasting room	
Clean and well presented (167)	4.08
Uncluttered and comfortable (166)	3.96
Visually appealing (166)	3.90
Enjoyable atmosphere (166)	4.06
Service attributes	
Prompt service (167)	4.02
Ability to talk to winemaker (161)	3.60
Informative and educational (163)	3.67
Restaurant/café (137)	3.62
Staff attributes	
Friendly and welcoming (165)	4.08
Professional and knowledgeable (160)	4.02
Understand visitor needs (161)	4.00
Provide individual attention (160)	3.88
Wine attributes	
Quality (163)	3.77
Variety (163)	3.57
Reasonably priced (159)	3.61
Convenience attributes	
Adequate signage and easy to find (163)	3.92
Adequate car parking (162)	4.00
Convenient opening times (162)	3.89
Tasting notes (139)	3.40
Price list (143)	3.62
Ability to join a mailing list (135)	3.16

single attributes with the highest average expectations. Visitors also had high expectations that staff would be 'professional and knowledgeable' and 'understand visitor needs', and that the tasting room would provide an 'enjoyable atmosphere'.

All these attributes achieved a mean score of 4 or greater on the five-point scale, with only two attributes from other than the staff and interior attribute dimensions – 'prompt service' and 'adequate car parking' – receiving scores of a similar magnitude. Most of the attributes with scores approaching 4 were similarly found within the staff and interior attribute dimensions, although moderately high expectations were also held with respect to the winery having 'adequate signage and [being] easy to find' and 'convenient opening times'.

The lowest expectations were generally associated with the exterior attributes and the wine itself. The latter finding may be a reflection of the Canberra District being a relatively new wine region that has yet to establish a reputation for quality product, and of the current visitors having very little experience or knowledge of that product. Visitation would appear to be currently motivated more by curiosity than an expectation of encountering fine wine. Visitors also did not have high expectations that they would encounter attractive views or settings as part of their experiences. The lowest expectations, however, were reserved for a number of the convenience attributes, notably 'tasting notes' and the 'ability to join a mailing list', with very few visitors having high expectations in regard to these.

Importance

Visitors were asked to indicate the level of importance they attached to each attribute when visiting wineries in general. There were strong parallels with the findings on expectations, with staff and interior attributes generally being highly important (see Table 7.4). The highest ratings were assigned to 'friendly

Table 7.4. Importance ratings of winery attributes.

Attributes (n)	Mean score
Exterior attributes	
Views of surroundings (168)	3.64
Attractive setting and environment (164)	3.88
Interior attributes	
Cellar door/tasting room	
Clean and well presented (166)	4.34
Uncluttered and comfortable (165)	4.15
Visually appealing (165)	4.12
Enjoyable atmosphere (165)	4.40
Service attributes	
Prompt service (166)	4.22
Ability to talk to winemaker (163)	3.83
Informative and educational (164)	3.95
Restaurant/café (141)	3.87
Staff attributes	
Friendly and welcoming (166)	4.52
Professional and knowledgeable (164)	4.42
Understand visitor needs (163)	4.29
Provide individual attention (160)	4.24
Wine attributes	
Quality (163)	4.34
Variety (163)	4.00
Reasonably priced (160)	4.08
Convenience attributes	
Adequate signage and easy to find (164)	4.14
Adequate car parking (162)	4.12
Convenient opening times (162)	4.14
Tasting notes (141)	3.67
Price list (144)	3.91
Ability to join a mailing list (135)	3.09

and welcoming' and 'professional and knowledgeable' staff and an 'enjoyable atmosphere' in the tasting room. However, unlike the findings on expectations, visitors also placed a high degree of importance on the wine attributes, particularly its quality, which was rated as the fourth most important attribute overall. A majority of visitors (51%) rated the quality of wine as very important, compared to the one-in-four (27%) who held high expectations of quality when visiting the particular winery. A number of convenience attributes relating to signage, car parking and opening times were also rated as being relatively important, along with 'prompt service'.

The attributes that were perceived to be of least importance were those which related to the exterior setting of the winery or were convenience factors, such as tasting notes, price lists and the opportunity to join a mailing list, which may be supplementary to the experience but not regarded as of more than moderate importance by the vast majority of visitors. The service attributes of 'ability to talk to winemaker', 'informative and educational' and 'restaurant/café' were also rated as being of moderate importance only.

Performance

Overall, Canberra District wineries appeared to be performing very well from a customer perspective. When asked to rate the overall quality of the winery, 49% of visitors rated it as 'good' and 44% as 'excellent'. The remaining 7% of visitors assigned an 'average' rating, with no-one considering it 'poor' or 'very poor'. In terms of overall satisfaction, 32% of visitors were 'satisfied' and 64% 'very satisfied' with their visit.

The highly satisfactory overall results are mirrored in the levels of satisfaction that visitors reported in relation to the specific winery attributes (see Table 7.5). Generally, the wineries performed best on those attributes that were considered to be the most important and for which visitors had the highest expectations. The visitors' experiences exceeded their expectations most in relation to staff attributes, particularly 'friendly and welcoming' staff and the interior attributes of the tasting room. Visitor expectations were also substantially exceeded for service attributes, especially for the highly important attribute of 'prompt service'. For all attributes, apart from the relatively unimportant 'ability to join a mailing list', a majority of visitors indicated that their expectations had been exceeded. Upwards of 80% of visitors indicated this in relation to a number of the most important attributes. Generally, the lowest levels of satisfaction were recorded for those attributes that were considered least important.

A very positive result for the wineries was the high proportion of visitors who considered that the quality of the wine had exceeded their expectations. As alluded to previously, visitors regarded this generally as a highly important attribute, but they did not hold particularly high expectations of the Canberra District product. The majority would appear to have been pleasantly surprised, which augurs well for repeat visitation and positive word-of-mouth.

Table 7.5. Extent to which visitors' experience of attributes matched expectations.

Attributes (n)	Percentage whose expectations were exceeded	Mean score
Exterior attributes		
Views of surroundings (172)	62	3.84
Attractive setting and environment (169)	68	3.95
Interior Attributes		
Cellar door/tasting room		
Clean and well presented (167)	74	4.13
Uncluttered and comfortable (167)	76	4.13
Visually appealing (167)	73	4.05
Enjoyable atmosphere (167)	77	4.19
Service attributes		
Prompt service (169)	80	4.27
Ability to talk to winemaker (158)	68	4.03
Informative and educational (160)	69	4.03
Restaurant/café (129)	71	4.09
Staff attributes		
Friendly and welcoming (168)	90	4.50
Professional and knowledgeable (167)	84	4.38
Understand visitor needs (165)	79	4.21
Provide individual attention (167)	83	4.31
Wine attributes		
Quality (168)	71	4.01
Variety (167)	62	3.78
Reasonably priced (164)	54	3.66
Convenience attributes		
Adequate signage and easy to find (169)	73	4.04
Adequate car parking (169)	69	3.99
Convenient opening times (163)	59	4.00
Tasting notes (123)	53	3.63
Price list (126)	55	3.67
Ability to join a mailing list (99)	47	3.51

Implications for Wine Tourism

Generally, the attributes that appeared to be most significant in determining the quality of experience in this emerging wine region were those relating to the staff and the interior of the tasting room. Visitors had both high expectations of, and placed considerable importance on, the staff being friendly, knowledgeable, understanding of visitor needs and capable of providing individual attention, suggesting that appropriate staff recruitment and training are paramount if quality experiences are to be provided. In this sense the key requirements for an emerging wine region would appear to differ little from those of more established regions, as Charters and O'Neill (2001) similarly concluded that training staff to deal efficiently and effectively with customers was fundamental to the success of a wine tourism operation.

Tasting rooms need to be clean and well presented and provide an enjoyable atmosphere. Prompt service is also highly valued, as are factors such as adequate signage and car parking, which enable visitors to maximize the time they devote to wine-tasting as opposed to moving between wineries.

The quality of the wine is also an extremely important attribute, even though the visitors in this instance did not have terribly high expectations of Canberra District wines. They appeared to be at least willing to take a risk on this factor in order to satisfy their curiosity about the region's wines. Presumably, as the region moves from being an emerging to an established region, its future as a wine tourism destination will be heavily dependent on the quality and value-for-money of its wines, as well as on the maintenance of current high standards of service being provided by winery staff.

References

Alant, K. and Bruwer, J. (2004) Wine tourism behaviour in the context of a motivational framework for wine regions and cellar doors. *Journal of Wine Research* 15 (1), 27–37.

Bruwer, J. (2002) The importance and role of the winery cellar door in the Australian wine industry. *The Australian and New Zealand Grapegrower and Winemaker*, August, 96–99.

Canberra Tourism and Events Corporation (2001) *ACT Tourism Masterplan 2001–2005: ACT Wine Tourism Strategy*.Canberra Tourism and Events Corporation, Canberra, Australia.

Charters, S. and O'Neill, M. (2001) Service quality at the cellar door: a comparison between regions. *International Journal of Wine Marketing* 13 (3), 7–17.

Cronin, J. and Taylor, S. (1992) Measuring service quality: a re-examination and extension. *Journal of Marketing* 56, 55–68.

Ho, F.N. and Gallagher, M. (2005) *International Journal of Wine Marketing*, 17 (1), 44–55.

Lovelock, C., Patterson, P. and Walker, R. (2001) *Service Marketing: an Asia–Pacific Perspective*. Prentice-Hall, Sydney, Australia.

O'Neill, M. and Charters, S. (2000) Service quality at the cellar door: implications for Western Australia's developing wine tourism industry. *Managing Services Quality* 10 (2), 112–122.

O'Neill, M., Palmer, A. and Charters, S. (2002) Wine production as a service experience – the effects of service quality on wine sales. *Journal of Service Marketing* 16 (4), 342–362.

Parasuraman, A., Zeithaml, V. and Berry, L. (1985) A conceptual model of service quality and its implications for future research. *Journal of Marketing* 49, 41–50.

Parasuraman, A., Berry, L. and Zeithaml, V. (1991) Refinement and reassessment of the SERVQUAL scale. *Journal of Retailing* 67 (4), 420–451.

Tourism New South Wales (2002) *Wine tourism research – cellar door survey June 2002*, Tourism New South Wales, Sydney, Australia.

Tourism New South Wales (2003a) *Wine Tourism Fact Sheets* – Creating appeal: a visitor friendly cellar door (available at: http://www.corporate.tourism.nsw.gov.au/scripts/, accessed 30 June 2003).

Tourism New South Wales (2003b) *Wine Tourism Fact Sheets* – Customer service and quality standards: putting a face to the wine label (available at: http://www.corporate.tourism.nsw.gov.au/scripts/, accessed 30 June 2003).

Tourism New South Wales (2003c) *Wine Tourism Fact Sheets* – Providing a total visitor experience: motivations and expectations of visitors to wineries (available at: http://www.corporate.tourism.nsw.gov.au/scripts/, accessed 30 June 2003).

Winemakers' Federation of Australia (2003a) *The Cellar Door Experience 1 – What do Visitors Expect?* (available at: http://www.wfa.org.au/, accessed 30 June 2003).

Winemakers' Federation of Australia (2003b) *The Cellar Door Experience 2 – Creating a Successful Cellar* Door (available at: http://www.wfa.org.au/, accessed 30 June 2003).

Winemakers' Federation of Australia (2003c) *The Cellar Door Experience 3 – Cellar Door Checklist* (available at: http://www.wfa.org.au/, accessed 30 June 2003).

Winter, M. (2003) Is your tasting room ready for the crowds? *Wine Business Monthly* (available at: http://www.winebusiness.com/html/MonthleyArticle.cfm, accessed 30 June 2003).

Part III

Wine Marketing and Wine Tourism

8 Influences on Post-visit Wine Purchase (and non-purchase) by New Zealand Winery Visitors

RICHARD MITCHELL

Department of Tourism, University of Otago, PO Box 56, Dunedin, New Zealand
E-mail: rdmitchell@business.otago.ac.nz

Introduction

Several authors have noted the significance of winery visitation for wine distribution, customer satisfaction and positive brand and image development at both the individual winery and regional level (e.g. Morris and King, 1997; King and Morris, 1999, undated (unpublished report); Hall *et al.*, 2000; King, 2000 (unpublished report); Mitchell *et al.*, 2000; O'Neill and Charters, 2000a, b; Charters and Ali-Knight, 2002; Houghton, 2002; O'Neill *et al.* 2002; Mitchell, 2004; Mitchell and Hall, 2004). Despite widespread recognition that the winery visit plays an integral part in ongoing wine consumer behaviour, only a few studies have attempted to track visitors' post-visit behaviour (e.g. King and Morris, undated; Mitchell, 2004). For example, Mitchell and Hall (2004) have published findings that suggest, in New Zealand at least, almost half of all winery visitors purchase wine subsequent to their visit to the winery.

However, little empirical evidence has been published for the reasons why individuals may choose to purchase a winery's wine post-visit (or indeed why they do not). This chapter presents the findings of a study of New Zealand winery visitors undertaken in 1999 (see Mitchell, 2004) that highlights some of the reasons for post-visit purchase (and non-purchase), as well as links to other wine behaviour and the visitor's intention to make a subsequent purchase at the time of their visit. First this chapter briefly introduces the reader to the small body of literature on post-visit wine purchasing behaviour.

Literature Review

Winery visitation is part of what Mitchell and Orwig (2002) describe as 'consumer experience tourism' (CET), where companies invite visitors to the site of production, allowing visitors to witness the production of their favourite wine (Mitchell and Hall, 2004). According to Mitchell and Orwig (2002), the results of CET can include increased brand loyalty, greater understanding of the product, reinforcement of brand image and increased word of mouth about the product and the visit. According to Mitchell and Hall (2004, p. 41):

> In the case of a visit to a winery … a visitor has ample opportunity to have first-hand experience of several aspects of the production process. For example they can interact with staff who, in the case of many smaller wineries, will be intimately involved in all operations of the winery and/or vineyard and not just front-of-house operations. Similarly, unlike other manufacturing processes, wine is made at the site of production of the raw material and as such the vineyard itself is a part of the process. The fact that the cellar door is often part of the winery can also mean that the smells, sights and sounds of various wine-making activities can be viewed without a formal tour occurring. As a result, by simply visiting a winery and vineyard, visitors may gain several of the elements of CET.

Just two studies have studied this apparent ongoing behaviour of winery visitors (see King and Morris, undated; Mitchell, 2004). Both studies took place in the late 1990s, one in Western Australia (King and Morris, undated) and the other in New Zealand (Mitchell, 2004), with quite different results. While Mitchell (2004) found that 46% of New Zealand respondents made at least one other purchase of wine made by the winery of survey in the 6–8 months post-visit (see also Mitchell and Hall, 2004), King and Morris (undated) found that just 13% of visitors to Augusta/Margaret River wineries stated that they made a post-visit purchase of wine from the winery of survey over a period of 19 months (see also King and Morris, 1999).

As a result, King and Morris (undated, p. 8) concluded that this should be of some concern for wineries and that the 'cellar door is more tourism related than related to subsequent retail sales'. However, they continue, there may have been a number of intervening factors that limited post-visit purchases from this wine region, including: (i) the higher price of some of the Augusta/Margaret River wines; (ii) higher prices precluding this wine from 'everyday drinking'; and (iii) a lack of distribution in retail outlets. Mitchell and Hall (2004, p. 48), on the other hand, conclude that 'King and Morris' (undated) concern that a cellar door visit does not reflect wider purchasing of a winery's brand may not be warranted'.

Mitchell and Hall (2004) also suggest that the importance of the cellar door is further reinforced by the fact that repeat visitors to a winery are also more likely to be post-visit purchasers at locations other than the winery and that there are high levels of positive word-of-mouth behaviour amongst winery visitors.

O'Neill *et al.* (2002) have also suggested that, despite high levels of performance across both tangible and intangible elements of the winery visit (see also O'Neill and Charters, 2000b):

> Importance–performance scores for tangible dimensions of a winery visit, including the quality of the wine itself, failed to distinguish between [intended] purchasers and non-purchasers. By contrast, dimensions which related to contact with personnel and their responsiveness indicated that satisfied customers were more likely to purchase the winery's wine.
>
> (O'Neill *et al.*, 2002, p. 352)

Herzberg's (1966) 'motivator–hygiene factor theory' can be used to shed some light on the findings of O'Neill *et al.* (2002). According to Mersha and Adlakha (1992, after Herzberg, 1966), 'hygiene factors' are those product or service attributes that, if absent, may lead consumers perceiving the product or service as being poor, but the presence of these attributes does not necessarily substantially improve the perceived quality of the service or product. In essence, hygiene factors must be present to avoid dissatisfaction, but their presence is unlikely to improve levels of satisfaction and/or ongoing positive behaviour towards that particular product or service. Only the presence of true satisfiers/motivators will result in ongoing positive perceptions and behaviour of the product or service.

Balmer and Baum (1993, p. 33) have applied Herzberg's 'hygiene factors' to hotels, suggesting that 'the tangible product supplied by the hotel comes largely under the category of 'hygiene factors', as would incentives regarding price and free gifts. The intangible 'service'-related factors would be the true satisfiers'. O'Neill *et al.*'s (2002) findings suggest that this may also be the case for visits to wineries.

The King and Morris (undated) and Mitchell (2004) studies outlined above provide an interesting, albeit inconsistent, insight into the post-visit purchase behaviour of winery visitors in two different locations, but to date there are no published data on why individuals purchase or, indeed, why they do not purchase. O'Neill *et al.*'s (2002) research also provides a useful insight into intended behaviour and some aspects of the winery experience, however it did not establish any relationship with actual post-visit behaviour, as it was limited to collection of on-site behaviour, perceptions and future intentions. As such a number of questions still remain about the role of the cellar door experience in this ongoing behaviour. For example, is ongoing purchasing related to more tangible elements of the wine and winery or do less tangible (experiential) elements of the visit also play a role? Or, indeed, are there hygiene factors at play? Similarly, does this behaviour reflect the wider wine purchasing and consumption behaviour of the winery visitor? Or, are those with a higher level of intention to purchase post-visit more likely to actually purchase? The findings of Mitchell's study presented in this chapter go some way to answering these questions.

Research Method

This chapter presents the results of part of the second phase of a tracking study of New Zealand winery visitors that took place in 1999. Phase 1 of the study gathered a sample of 1090 respondents from 33 wineries across New Zealand. Phase 1 respondents were asked if they would be willing to take part in a follow-up survey and the 636 respondents that indicated that they were willing to receive the questionnaire were sent a mail-out–mail-back questionnaire 6–8 months after their visit to the winery of survey. The resulting Phase 2 sample totalled 358 usable questionnaires, giving a response rate of 56.3% and a sample of 32.8% of the Phase 1 sample. Included in the follow-up survey were elements of ongoing purchase and consumption of wine, as well as more experiential elements such as recollection of the visit, word-of-mouth behaviour and enduring levels of satisfaction (Table 8.1).

The focus of this chapter are data pertaining to the reasons for purchase or non-purchase (Table 8.1). These data were gathered by way of a five-point scale asking the respondents the degree to which they were influenced by a series of product-related attributes and experiential factors (see Table 8.1). Also discussed in this chapter are data relating to the intention to make a future purchase gathered at the time of the Phase 1 survey.

The data from both phases of the survey were entered into a single SPSS database so that all information from the Phase 1 questionnaire could also be utilized in the Phase 2 analysis. This was done to enable a comparison of the sample characteristics and behaviours (both on-site and post-visit) between the two phases, as well as to minimize the duplication of data collection and data entry in Phase 2. The measurement of the standard error difference between the proportions of a number of variables within each sample reveals that only the upper income respondents and those purchasing more than 12 bottles per month were over-represented in the Phase 2 sample. As such, the Phase 2 sample is largely representative of the original Phase 1 sample.

Table 8.1. Reasons for purchase and non-purchase of wine post-visit.

Product-related reasons	Experiential reasons
For purchase	For purchase
The taste of Winery X's wine	The service I received during my visit to Winery X
The availability of Winery X's wine	The memory of my visit to Winery X
The price of Winery X's wine	The memory of my visit to Region X
The packaging of Winery X's wine	The service I received during my visit to Winery X
(e.g. bottle/label)	The desire to share my experience at Winery X with others
	The desire to share Winery X's wine with others
For non-purchase	For non-purchase
The taste of Winery X's wine	The memory of my visit to Winery X (i.e. unenjoyable)
The availability of Winery X's wine	The service I received during my visit to Winery X
The price of Winery X's wine	I have had no reason to purchase any wine since my visit
I have Winery X's wine remaining from my visit	Lack of knowledge on where to buy Winery's wine

Findings

Reasons for post-visit purchase

The taste of the wine has the strongest influence on the purchasing of wine, with 65.3% of the 167 respondents that had made a post-visit purchase stating that taste was a strong influence (mean score 4.51, median 5.0) (see Fig. 8.1). This finding is perhaps not very surprising, as it is logical to suggest that if the wine is not to an individual's taste, they are unlikely to purchase it and this also reflects the findings of Dodd and Gustafson (1997), who found that taste was the most influential element in the on-site winery purchase at Texas wineries.

Importantly, in line with the findings of O'Neill and Charters (2000b) and O'Neill *et al.* (2002), it can be suggested that taste in itself does not provide

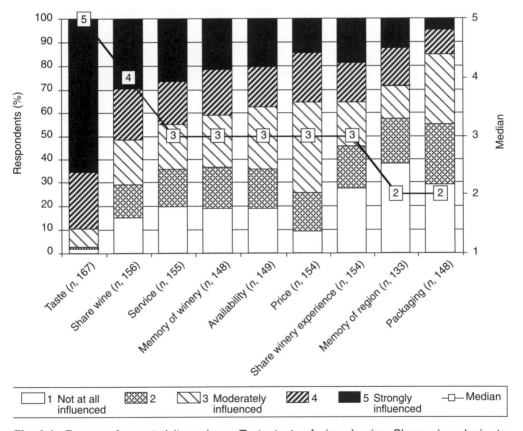

Fig. 8.1. Reasons for post-visit purchase. Taste, taste of winery's wine; Share wine, desire to share winery's wine with others; Service, service received during the visit to the winery; Memory of winery, memory of the visit to the winery; Availability, availability of winery's wine; Price, price of the winery's wine; Share winery experience, desire to share the experience of the winery with others; Memory of region, memory of the visit to the region; Packaging, attractiveness of the winery's wine bottles/labels.

the necessary motivation to purchase any given brand of wine, as there are potentially thousands of wines with a similar flavour profile. As wine is also associated with experiential consumption (Mitchell *et al.*, 2000; Mitchell, 2004), it could be suggested that this distinction between the more tangible hygiene factors (e.g. taste, price and packaging) and the intangible satisfiers is appropriate here.

Assuming then that taste can be eliminated as a true satisfier/motivator, the most important motivator of post-visit purchase was sharing the wine with others, with more than half of the respondents indicating a stronger than moderate influence (mean score 3.38, median 4.0). This is perhaps because of the generally social nature of wine consumption and, when combined with the high degree of word of mouth observed in this study (see Mitchell and Hall, 2004), has important implications for the marketing of the wine. Service at the winery, memory of the winery experience, sharing the winery experience with others and the availability of wine and price (both also hygiene factors) all have a moderate influence on post-visit purchase (mean score ranging from 3 to 3.2, median 3.0).

Importantly for wineries, there are a number of variables here that relate to the on-site winery experience and not to the wine. In particular, more than one in four respondents stated a stronger than moderate influence for the service at the winery and the memory of the experience, with a further one in five indicating a moderate influence for these variables. Sharing the winery experience was an additional experience-based influence that showed a moderate degree of influence, but it should be noted that more than one in four stated that this did not influence their purchase. Importantly, for wineries it appears that the cellar door experience is an important element in motivating post-visit purchase. This provides some evidence to support Mitchell's (2004, p. 13) assertion that:

> There is more to … wine tourism than the simple consumption of a beverage (albeit a hedonistic pursuit) or that this experience is limited to the senses and emotions associated with the wine alone. Wine tourism experiences (as with most tourism experiences) are much more than this, relying on the setting in which they occur, socialisation with the personalities of wine, and interaction with other elements of the experience such as food, accommodation and other visitors.

Memory of the region and packaging were the least influential variables, with most respondents stating a less than moderate influence (mean score approximately 2.5, median 2.0). The latter suggests that the often-cited (but yet to be proven) situation that most wine purchasers purchase wine at a retail outlet on the basis of the label may not hold true for winery visitors. Fourteen other reasons were provided, six of which related to the quality of the wine and/or reputation for quality.

Table 8.2 highlights a number of statistically significant differences in the strength of reasons observed between several of the segmentation criteria. Two variables showed regional differences: price and sharing the wine with others. Auckland and Hawkes Bay respondents rated price significantly higher than their Central Otago counterparts (Bonferroni significance 0.033 and

Table 8.2. Breakdown of reasons for post-visit purchase.

Reason for purchase	Product variables						Experiential variables		
	Taste (mean (median))	Price (mean (median))	Availability (mean (median))	Packaging (mean (median))	Service (mean (median))	Memory of winery (mean (median))	Memory of region (mean (median))	Share wine (mean (median))	Share winery (mean (median))
All New Zealand (139 ≤n≥ 165)	4.50 (5)	3.18 (3)	3.07 (3)	2.44 (2)	3.18 (3)	3.09 (3)	2.59 (2)	3.43 (4)	2.88 (3)
Regions		SSD							SSD
Auckland (21 ≤n≥ 26)	4.31(5)	3.63(3)	3.33(3)	2.38(2)	3.22(3)	2.73(3)	1.86(1)	2.84(3)	2.37(2)
Bay of Plenty (9 ≤n≥ 12)	4.25(5)	3.30(3)	3.50(3)	3.45(3)	3.50(3)	3.92(4.5)	2.78(2)	3.91(4)	3.50(3)
Hawkes Bay (32 ≤n≥ 34)	4.62(5)	3.58(3)	2.88(3)	2.22(2)	2.76(3)	3.00(3)	2.75(3)	3.36(4)	2.52(2)
Central Otago (36 ≤n≥ 44)	4.66(5)	2.76(3)	2.76(3)	2.50(2.5)	3.62(4)	3.47(4)	2.61(2)	3.70(4)	3.37(4)
Marlborough (29 ≤n≥ 33)	4.36(5)	2.94(3)	3.12(3.5)	2.24(3)	3.15(3)	2.93(3)	2.90(2.5)	3.42(3)	2.97(3)
Winery category	SSD	SSD	SSD		SSD	SSD		SSD	SSD
Category I (79 ≤n≥ 100)	4.61(5)	2.89(3)	3.09(3)	2.57(2.5)	3.43(4)	3.29(3)	2.66(2)	3.73(4)	3.20(3)
Category II (26 ≤n≥ 30)	4.47(5)	3.59(3)	2.96(3)	2.34(2)	3.03(3)	2.97(3)	2.58(2.5)	3.23(3)	2.38(2)
Category III (31 ≤n≥ 35)	4.23(4)	3.59(3.5)	3.09(3)	2.18(2)	2.61(2)	2.65(3)	2.44(2)	2.79(3)	2.44(2)
Country of origin	SSD		SSD				SSD		
New Zealand (124 ≤n≥ 150)	4.49(5)	3.21(3)	3.19(3)	2.51(2)	3.23(3)	3.06(3)	2.53(2)	3.39(4)	2.86(3)
Overseas (11 ≤n≥ 11)	4.55(5)	2.55(3)	2.00(1)	1.91(2)	2.91(2)	3.64(4)	3.36(3)	3.91(5)	3.27(3)
Gender				SSD		SSD		SSD	
Male (62 ≤n≥ 71)	4.35(5)	3.00(3)	2.94(3)	2.12(2)	3.03(3)	2.83(3)	2.40(2)	3.12(3)	2.63(3)
Female (75 ≤n≥ 92)	4.61(5)	3.31(3)	3.16(3)	2.68(3)	3.29(3.5)	3.31(3)	2.77(2)	3.70(4)	3.09(3)
Wine knowledge				SSD				SSD	
None or Basic (37 ≤n≥ 45)	4.33(5)	3.14(3)	3.15(3)	2.56(3)	2.90(3)	2.43(2)	2.88(3)	2.98(3)	2.71(2)
Intermediate (81 ≤n≥ 99)	4.57(5)	3.19(3)	3.09(3)	2.54(2)	3.40(4)	2.74(2)	3.28(3)	3.59(4)	3.06(3)
Advanced (18 ≤n≥ 19)	4.63(5)	3.28(3)	2.83(2.5)	1.63(1)	2.68(2)	2.37(2)	2.72(3)	3.63(4)	2.53(3)

Taste, taste of winery's wine; price, price of the winery's wine; availability, availability of winery's wine; packaging, attractiveness of the winery's wine bottles/labels; service, service received during the visit to the winery; memory of winery, memory of the visit to the winery; memory of region, memory of the visit to the region; share wine, desire to share winery's wine with others; share winery, desire to share the experience of the winery with others; SSD, one-way ANOVA or Independent Sample T-Test significant to at least the 95% level, except taste and share wine where a Mann-Whitney was used and this was significant at the 95% level.

0.022, respectively). The desire to share the winery's wine with others also varied according to region (Kruskall-Wallis significance 0.020), with Bay of Plenty and Central Otago respondents having a higher rating, and Auckland respondents having lower ratings.

The largest number of differences was observed between winery categories, with six of the nine variables exhibiting statistically significant differences (see Table 8.2). Four of the six differences are the experiential variables that relate to the winery of survey (i.e. the service received during the visit to the winery, the memory of the visit to the winery, the desire to share the winery's wine with others and the desire to share the experience of the winery with others). For all of these variables, respondents visiting the smaller Category I wineries (i.e. those producing less than 200,000 l per annum) were likely to report stronger influences than their larger Category III counterparts (i.e. those producing more than 2 million l per annum).

This appears to suggest that some of the differences in the nature of the experience observed in Phase 1 of the survey (see Mitchell, 2004) are borne out in the post-visit decision-making of winery visitors. In particular, Category III wineries appear to have a greater focus on the wine itself and learning about wine (although service is still important), while Category I wineries are as much about the experiential elements (atmosphere, setting, service and socializing) as they are about the wine (Mitchell, 2004). Mean scores for taste were slightly decreased as the size of the winery grew, but overall the scores remained high. Overall price was less important for Category I respondents, perhaps reflecting the higher pricing for many smaller producers.

International respondents reported a significantly lower level of influence for the availability of wine than their New Zealand counterparts. This is largely to be expected as there was a low number of international post-visit purchasers (*n*, 11). The lack of availability was the most influential variable for international visitors not making a post-visit purchase (see below). The only other variable to exhibit a statistically significant difference for domestic *versus* international respondents was that of the memory of the visit to the region, which was more influential for international respondents, perhaps reflecting both the importance of the 'exotic' nature of the region visited by international visitors and the relative familiarity of the region for New Zealanders.

Three gender differences were also observed, two experiential and one product-related. Females had higher mean scores for the desire to share the winery's wine with others and the memory of the winery visit. This also reflects differences in the way females perceive their winery experience, with Mitchell and Hall (2001a, p. 71) reporting that 'Females were also around twice as likely to enjoy elements of the ambience of the winery, including the inviting or relaxed nature of a winery, socialising with friends at the winery and sunny weather and alfresco dining'. It appears, then, that differences in the way females experience wineries have an impact on their post-visit behaviour (see also Mitchell and Hall, 2004). Females also reported a higher mean score for attractiveness of the winery's wine bottles/labels (i.e. packaging), but both male and female mean scores were less than a moderate influence.

The only other statistically significant differences observed relate to the level of wine knowledge. Those with advanced wine knowledge appear to be less influenced by wine packaging than their basic and intermediate wine knowledge counterparts, although all mean scores remain relatively low. The second statistically significant difference relating to wine knowledge shows that those with basic wine knowledge have a lower mean score for the desire to share the wine with others than those with an intermediate level of knowledge.

This difference raises interesting questions with respect to the reason why individuals might wish to share the wine with others. For example: is this more important for those with intermediate knowledge because they use the sharing of wine with others as a way of expressing who they are? Or is it simply because wine is considered to be a more social drink by this segment? The answer to these questions perhaps lies in identifying the nature of wine consumption for each level of wine knowledge and, in particular, the level of wine involvement each level has.

It is also important to note that there are no statistically significant differences between the different generations. This is interesting given some of the other differences observed in relation to the on-site experience and general wine habits and behaviour (see Mitchell, 2002). It is also important to note that there were no differences between wine-motivated visitors and non-wine-motivated visitors. In both instances this has implications for wineries in terms of who they see as the most important winery visitor in terms of ongoing purchases, and how they treat them while they are at the cellar door.

Other influences on post-visit purchase

It is also important to explore the relationship between intended purchasing behaviour and actual purchase behaviour, as well as how the wider wine consumer behaviour of the individual might be related to the post-visit wine purchase. Using a five-point scale (no intention to strong intention), Phase 1 respondents were asked to indicate the strength of their intention to purchase the winery of survey's wine at a range of retail categories (i.e. restaurants, specialist wine shops and mail order), and the relationship between these data and actual purchase is discussed here.

Table 8.3 reveals significant differences between purchasers and non-purchasers across each retail category. In each situation purchasers had a high mean and median intention to purchase post-visit. It should be noted that the very low number of mail order purchasers (*n*, 7) makes this figure somewhat unreliable. Despite this there is strong evidence to suggest that there is some relationship between intention to purchase and actual future purchase at both restaurants and specialist wine shops. In particular, around two out of three purchasers at these locations indicated greater than some intention at the time of their visit to the winery, with a further one in four indicating some intention. This suggests that many of those making a post-visit purchase at these locations are influenced to do so at (or before) the time of the visit to the winery.

Table 8.3. Intention to purchase of purchasers and non-purchasers.[a]

Variable	Purchasers	Non-purchasers	Statistical significance
Intention to purchase at a restaurant	(*n*, 63)	(*n*, 270)	T-Test sig., 0.000
Mean	3.78	3.07	
Median	4	3	
Intention to purchase at a specialist wine shop	(*n*, 54)	(*n*, 281)	Mann-Whitney – U sig., 0.000
Mean	4.04	3.22	
Median	4	3	
Intention to purchase by mail order	(*n*, 7)	(*n*, 313)	T-Test sig., 0.000
Mean	3.29	2.07	
Median	3	1	

[a] On the five-point scale used: 1, no intention; 3, some intention; 5, strong intention.

Figure 8.2 shows that frequent visitors were also much more likely to make a post-visit purchase. In particular, the majority of those that visit more than twice a year had made a purchase in the ensuing 6–8 months, suggesting a high degree of loyalty amongst frequent winery visitors. Only subsequent purchases at the cellar door showed any statistically significant difference between repeat visitors and those that had never or rarely visited the winery of survey. Subsequent purchases directly from the cellar door were made by more than half of those that had visited the winery more than twice a year prior to the survey, compared to less than 20% of those that had visited fewer than three times per year.

A range of wine purchase and consumption behaviour also appears to have an influence on post-visit purchases. For example, Table 8.4 shows that post-visit purchasers buy more bottles per month than their non-purchasing counterparts, and they are more likely to purchase more than three bottles of wine during their visit. Meanwhile non-purchasers are more likely to be

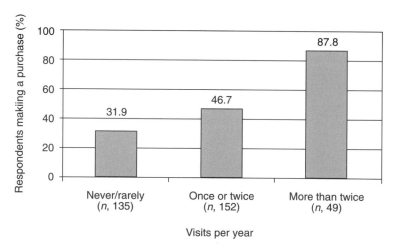

Fig. 8.2. Post-visit purchasing and frequency of visit.

Table 8.4. Purchase and consumption behaviour of post-visit (non-) purchasers.

Variable	Purchasers	Non-purchasers
Bottles purchased per month[a]		
Median	8	6
Minimum	1	0
Maximum	60	50
Mean	10.16	8.46
How often drink wine[b] (%)		
Every day	21.7	17.9
At least once per week[c]	89.7	87.9
Less than once per week[d]	10.3	12.1
Less than once per fortnight	0.6	7.9
Purchase during visit [e] (%)		
None	6.1	16.1
1 or 2 bottles	44.9	51.9
3 or 4 bottles	23.8	15.5
5 or 6 bottles	10.2	7.5
7–12 bottles	10.9	6.3
More than 12 bottles	4.1	2.9

[a] Mann-Whitney-U, 0.027.
[b] Pearson's $\chi2$, 16.16; df, 5; P, 0.006.
[c] Includes those that consume wine daily, a few times a week and once a week.
[d] Includes those that consume once every two weeks, once every three or four weeks and only on special occasions.
[e] Pearson's $\chi2$, 13.47; df, 5; P, 0.019.

infrequent drinkers of wine (i.e. less than once a fortnight) and are more likely not to have made a purchase at the winery or purchase just one or two bottles.

These findings are perhaps as could be expected, since it is reasonable to suggest generally that more frequent purchasers of wine and those that purchase more wine are more likely to purchase from a particular winery anyway. However, this does not detract from the fact that the cellar door is clearly a part of the purchasing behaviour of these 'high-end' consumers. It is also worth noting that post-visit purchasers also made larger purchases while at the winery and, therefore, on the face of it, were more likely still to have wine from a visit to the winery, yet still purchased wine post-visit.

It is interesting to note that there is no statistically significant difference in the reasons for visiting the region of purchasers and non-purchasers. While it might be expected that those visiting the region for wine-related reasons (only one in four respondents) might be more likely to make a purchase, this was not the case for either on-site or post-visit purchases.

Reasons for non-purchase

While information on the reasons for purchase are important, it is equally useful to explore the reasons why people did not make a post-visit purchase, especially given that more than half of the respondents (53.6%) indicated that they had not made a purchase of the winery of survey's wine in the 6–8 months post-visit. Table 8.4 shows that non-purchasers buy fewer bottles of wine per month, purchase fewer bottles of wine while at the winery and consume wine less frequently, while Fig. 8.2 suggests that they also visit the winery of survey less frequently. As a result, it is possible to postulate that, for whatever reason, non-purchasers are less wine-orientated than their purchasing counterparts.

This is further reinforced by the fact that purchasers are more likely to have an advanced or intermediate level of wine knowledge, while non-purchasers are more likely to have only a basic level of wine knowledge (see Mitchell and Hall, 2004). Despite this, it is also useful to explore the reasons why respondents did not make a purchase in the 6–8 months post-visit.

Figure 8.3 shows that the two most influential reasons for non-purchase were the availability of the winery of survey's wine and a lack of knowledge of where to buy this wine, with 50% and 42%, respectively, stating a higher than moderate influence for these variables. This has important implications for wineries as it implies that distribution and awareness of distribution channels are important factors in post-visit purchase, and perhaps implies a latent demand for their wine. The price of the wine also had a degree of influence but only about one in five respondents stated that this had a greater than moderate influence.

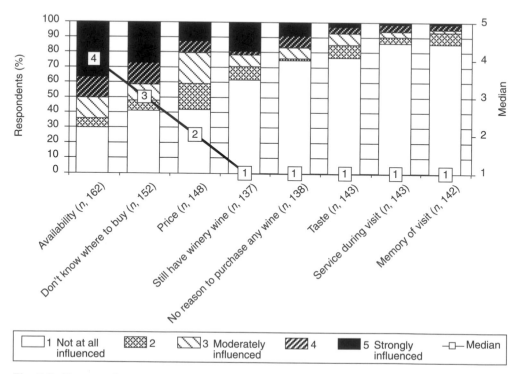

Fig. 8.3. Reasons for post-visit non-purchase.

The remaining variables were of little influence in the decision not to purchase wine post-visit. In particular, the taste of the wine, the service and the memory of their visit were the least influential variables, reflecting generally positive views and high levels of satisfaction with both the wine and the experience (including the service), both on-site and post-visit.

Twenty four other reasons were given by respondents for non-purchase, with the most frequently cited being: purchasing other wine (6); budget constraints (5); and had not returned to the region or winery (4). Further analysis reveals very few statistically significant differences between the segments used in this study. The main differences identified, as might be expected, are between international and domestic winery visitors. In particular, international respondents were more strongly influenced by the availability of the wine (mean 4.45 compared to 2.86 for domestics) and lack of knowledge of where to purchase the wine (mean 4.04 compared with 2.47).

Internationals appear to be less price sensitive (mean 1.70 compared with 2.41) and were less likely to be influenced by the fact that they still have wine from their visit (1.21 compared with 2.26). Those with a basic level of wine knowledge were also more likely to be strongly influenced by the fact that they had no reason to purchase any wine since their visit (15.3 compared with 5.7% for intermediates and 0% for advanced wine knowledge). This reflects the varying levels of wine purchasing and consumption amongst these three segments (see Mitchell and Hall, 2001b).

Implications for Wine Tourism

This chapter demonstrates that the cellar door does indeed play an important role in the ongoing purchase behaviour of winery visitors. In particular, it demonstrates that the experiential elements of the winery visit are important reasons given for making a subsequent purchase (e.g. service, memories of the visit to the winery and sharing the wine and experiences with others). This supports O'Neill and Charters (2000b, p. 120) assertion that:

> It is the favourable memories of the relational elements of the service encounter that rate more highly with customers. Clearly, customers rate these more relational factors as being as important as the wine tasted and/or subsequently purchased. Indeed, it may be surmised that the perceived level of service quality may in fact be a vital antecedent to any purchase being made.

These factors are particularly important for smaller wineries as visitors to smaller wineries cited these factors as being more influential than did visitors to larger wineries. While taste was cited as the most important factor influencing post-visit purchase, this chapter suggests that this a 'hygiene factor' and that it is the experiential elements that create a true point of difference for a wine brand.

As a result, while investment in maintaining high standards of winemaking is vital, it is also worth investing in the aspects of the cellar door that contribute most to this experience: staff training and the development of memorable experiences. This does not necessarily involve spending significant amounts of money on facilities (although these will undoubtedly be important hygiene factors), as it is the intangible, service-related elements that seem to lead to attachment to brand.

The social elements of wine are also highlighted as being important here (i.e. sharing the wine with others), and this could have important implications for the type of messages that wineries use to encourage ongoing purchases of their wines. This also suggests that there are significant spin-offs in terms of introducing other consumers to their wine.

The availability of wine or a lack of knowledge about where to find the wine when visitors return home were the most important reasons why respondents did not purchase post-visit. This was particularly significant for international visitors and reflects a lack of effort on the part of wineries to inform their visitors where they might purchase wine after they leave. This can easily be overcome by keeping a list of retail outlets that sell their wine in different markets both in New Zealand and around the world, and by supplying the appropriate list to visitors before they leave. It would also be a useful strategy to invite visitors to become part of a list that would inform them of events, tastings and promotions of the winemaker's wine in their region.

References

Balmer, S. and Baum, T. (1993) Applying Herzberg's hygiene factors to the changing accommodation environment. *International Journal of Contemporary Hospitality Management* 5, 32–35.

Charters, S. and Ali-Knight, J. (2002) Who is the wine tourist? *Tourism Management* 23, 311–319.

Dodd, T.H. and Gustafson, A.W. (1997) Product, environment and service attributes that influence consumer attitudes and purchases at wineries. *Journal of Food Products Marketing* 4 (3), 41–59.

Hall, C.M., Johnson, G.R., Cambourne, B., Macionis, N., Mitchell, R.D. and Sharples, E. (2000) Wine tourism: an introduction. In: Hall, C.M., Sharples, E., Cambourne, B. and Macionis, N. (eds) *Wine and Tourism Around the World: Development, Management and Markets*. Butterworth Heinemann, Oxford, UK, pp. 1–23.

Herzberg, F. (1966) *Work and the Nature of Man*. Thomas Y. Crowell Publishers, New York.

Houghton, M. (2002) Wine festivals: their effectiveness as a promotional strategy for wineries (a case study of the Rutherglen region). MA Thesis, La Trobe University, Victoria, Australia.

King, C. and Morris, R. (1999) Wine tourism: costs and returns in wine tourism – perfect partners. In: Carlsen, J., Getz, D. and Dowling, R. (eds) *Proceedings of the First Australian Wine Tourism Conference*, Margaret River (1998), Bureau of Tourism Research, Canberra, pp. 233–245.

King, C. and Morris, R. (n.d.) The flow on effects of winery cellar door visits. Unpublished report, Edith Cowan University, Bunbury Campus, WA.

King, J. (2000) Recognising and defining wine tourism. Unpublished report, Global Tourism and Leisure, South Australia.

Mersha, T. and Adlakha, V. (1992) Attributes of service quality: the consumers' perspective. *International Journal of Service Industry Management* 3, 34–45.

Mitchell, M.A. and Orwig, R.A. (2002)

Consumer experience tourism and brand bonding. *Journal of Product and Brand Management* 11, 30–41.

Mitchell, R.D. (2002) The generation game: Generation X and baby boomer wine tourism. In: Croy, G. (ed.) *Proceedings of New Zealand Tourism and Hospitality Research Conference*, Rotorua, 3–5 December 2002. Waiariki Institute of Technology, Rotorua, pp. 115–127.

Mitchell, R.D. (2004) Scenery and Chardonnay: a visitor perspective of the New Zealand winery experience. PhD Thesis, University of Otago, New Zealand.

Mitchell, R.D. and Hall, C.M. (2001a) The influence of gender and region on the New Zealand winery visit. *Tourism Recreation Research* 2, 63–75.

Mitchell, R.D. and Hall, C.M. (2001b) Wine at home: self-ascribed wine knowledge and the wine behaviour of New Zealand winery visitors. *Australian and New Zealand Wine Industry Journal* 16, 115–122.

Mitchell, R.D. and Hall, C.M. (2004) The post-visit consumer behaviour of New Zealand winery visitors. *Journal of Wine Research* 15, 37–47.

Mitchell, R.D., Hall, C.M. and McIntosh, A.J. (2000) Wine tourism and consumer behaviour. In: Hall, C.M., Sharples, E., Cambourne, B. and Macionis, N. (eds) *Wine and Tourism Around the World: Development, Management and Markets.* Butterworth Heinemann, Oxford, UK, pp. 115–135.

Morris, R. and King, C. (1997) Cooperative marketing for small business growth and regional economic development: a case study in wine tourism. In: Kunkel, S. and Meeks, M. (eds) *The Engine of Global Economic Development, Conference Proceedings of the 42nd World Conference International Council for Small Business*, San Francisco, June 1997.

O'Neill, M. and Charters, S. (2000a) Delighting the customer – how good is the cellar door experience? *International Wine Marketing Supplement* 1, 11–16.

O'Neill, M. and Charters, S. (2000b) Service quality at the cellar door: implications for Western Australia's developing wine tourism industry. *Managing Service Quality* 10 (2), 112–122.

O'Neill, M., Palmer, A. and Charters, S. (2002) Wine production as a service experience – the effect of service quality on sales. *Journal of Services Marketing* 16 (4), 342–362.

9 Electronic Marketing and Wine Tourism

JAMIE MURPHY

The University of Western Australia Business School, Stirling Highway, Crawley, WA 6009, Australia
E-mail: jmurphy@biz.uwa.edu.au

Introduction

Wine tourism is a winning solution for consumers, wineries and regions. For consumers, wine tourism goes beyond visiting wineries and vineyards to include unique social, cultural and leisure activities (Williams, 2001). For regions, wine tourism addresses a universal challenge – getting international visitors beyond gateway cities and into regional areas (Dowling, 2001; Beames, 2003) such as Western Australia (O'Neill and Charters, 2000). Wine tourism also boosts wineries' international and domestic sales (Ravenscroft and Westering, 2001; O'Neill *et al.*, 2002). A key element in wine tourism is the visitor's first contact, usually via the cellar door (O'Neill *et al.*, 2002). Websites and e-mail offer other doorways for that first contact.

However, despite a growing body of trade (Nielsen, 2000; Zemke and Connellan, 2001; Sterne, 2002) and academic literature investigating effective Internet (Hoffman and Novak, 1996; Nysveen *et al.*, 2002) and e-mail use (Murphy and Gomes, 2003; Nguyen *et al.*, 2003), unanswered questions abound. For example, what are effective online tools and the appropriate metrics to benchmark and investigate these tools (Kim *et al.*, 2002; Palmer, 2002; Scheffelmaier and Vinsonhaler, 2002–2003; Straub *et al.*, 2002a, b)?

Similarly, there are calls in hospitality and tourism research to investigate website features (Nysveen *et al.*, 2002; Chung and Law, 2003; Dubé *et al.*, 2003; Jeong *et al.*, 2003; Murphy *et al.*, 2003a; Fam *et al.*, 2004) and e-mail procedures (Gherissi-Labben *et al.*, 2003; Murphy and Tan, 2003; Schegg *et al.*, 2003; Matzler *et al.*, 2005). What website features and e-mail procedures should the wine tourism industry use? What website features and e-mail procedures does the wine tourism industry use? This study uses an online competitive analysis to help address these two questions, from both applied and academic perspectives.

Literature Review

The Internet's customer relationship capabilities and information access complement the information-intensive tourism industry (Rayman-Bacchus and Molina, 2001; Nysveen *et al.*, 2002; O'Connor, 2003). Providing information online is also important for wineries (Richardson, 2002), particularly as learning is a recurrent theme for serious wine tourists (Ravenscroft and Westering, 2001). If, as MacCannell (2002) argues, ego plays a vital role in tourism, knowledge is critical for wine tourism. Knowledge feeds one's ego and narcissism in the hopes that others will 'Look at me. Look up to me' (MacCannell, 2002, p. 148). For experienced based-travel such as wine tourism, market power lies in using information technologies to satisfy guests' knowledge-based needs (Olsen and Connolly, 2000).

Similarly, experiential branding in tourism – linking specific pleasurable experiences with a brand – also extends to wine tourism (Lockshin and Spawton, 2001; Williams, 2001) and the online environment (Dubé *et al.*, 2003). Websites and e-mail offer serious wine tourists another tool for their knowledge quest, and offer wineries another opportunity to position their brand experience and promote their wine sales (Richardson, 2002).

Research Method

Specific website features and e-mail policies should help wineries improve their online marketing via repeat customers, increased sales and stronger brand recognition. Using those features effectively and ensuring proper e-mail replies should satisfy guests' knowledge-based needs and complement the companies' experiential branding (Olsen and Connolly, 2000; Lockshin and Spawton, 2001; Dubé *et al.*, 2003; Jeong *et al.*, 2003; Murphy *et al.*, 2003a). A competitive analysis of Australian wineries in the Margaret River region highlights the importance of website features and replies to customer e-mails.

Selecting wineries

A local winery noted for its wine tourism suggested six nearby competitors for analysis. Given the importance of search engine rankings (Garofalakis *et al.*, 2002; Palmer, 2002; Drèze and Zufryden, 2004), results from the popular search engine Google yielded two additional wineries – the top listings for 'Margaret River Winery' and 'Napa Valley Winery'. These two wineries' top Google rankings should reflect above-average online practices. Given the Internet's California roots and leading edge practices in that state (Hanson, 2000), including a top California winery provides additional insights and international flavour to this study.

Website popularity and visibility

First, websites should be easy to find via search engine rankings and links to the site. Research suggests a direct relationship between search engine visibility and site visits (Drèze and Zufryden, 2004). Furthermore, links to a site increase site traffic, which then builds brand equity (Ilfeld and Winer, 2002).

Free toolbars available from two popular search engines, Google (http://www.toolbar.google.com/) and Alexa (http://www.pages.alexa.com/prod_serv/quicktour.html), provide reliable and valid measures of a site's popularity and visibility (Garofalakis *et al.*, 2002; Palmer, 2002). Google rank, a proxy for search engine visibility, ranges from zero to a maximum of ten for sites such as Microsoft and Yahoo. The higher a site's Google rank, the higher the site's listing on a Google search. Alexa rank, a proxy for popularity, ranges from number one for Yahoo to in the millions for rarely visited websites. Alexa also provides a visibility index via the number of links to a site.

Website features

Wine tourism operators choose from an ocean of possible features for their website and research suggests that websites evolve over three stages in their features and functionality (Hanson, 2000; Doolin *et al.*, 2002). First-stage websites provide basic information such as wines varieties and the physical address. Next, websites add interactive features such as newsletter subscriptions and downloadable brochures. Finally, sites add features related to processing and personalization via online sales and bookings.

A literature review, discussions with wine tourism operators and a preliminary investigation of several wine tourism websites yielded 37 features that wine tourism operators should consider for their website. The staged model of website usage helped classify these features into eight categories: (i) basic information; (ii) visual information; (iii) societal information; (iv) virtual information; (v) trust information; (vi) website navigation; (vii) customer relations; and (viii) sales. Five of those categories related to the first stage, providing information. Website navigation fell between the provision of information and the provision of interactivity. The final two categories, customer relationships and sales, fell between providing interactivity and personalization/processing.

Given information's importance in tourism (Mansfield, 1992), online tourism (Chung and Law, 2003; Jeong *et al.*, 2003) and wine tourism (Ravenscroft and Westering, 2001; MacCannell, 2002; Richardson, 2002), this study used five information categories. Basic and visual information includes winery awards and pictures. Visual cues such as pictures help overcome the Internet's lack of touch and feel (Nielsen, 2000; Veen, 2000). Societal information acknowledges community and environmental concerns; the latter extend globally thanks to the Internet (Sklair, 1999; Castells, 2001). Virtual information leverages the Internet's multimedia characteristics such as through videos and virtual tours.

Finally, trust-related information helps assuage consumer fears of the online environment (Hanson, 2000; Nysveen *et al.*, 2002). External links, copyrights and last updated information reflect confidence in the site (Nielsen, 2000). Branding is important to wine tourism (Lockshin and Spawton, 2001), and branded domain names – such as the hypothetical winetourism.com.au, rather than telstra.bigpond.com.au/ users/~winetourism – build brand equity and trust (Hanson, 2000; Murphy *et al.*, 2003a, b).

It does little good to provide information without providing easy website navigation; confused customers may never find the information or return to the website. Furthermore, ease of navigation can relate positively to attitudes towards the site and towards the brand (Bellman and Rossiter, 2004). To improve navigation, authors recommend including two static navigational features, site maps and Frequently Asked Questions (FAQs), and an interactive search function (Nielsen, 2000; Veen, 2000; Nysveen *et al.*, 2002; Palmer, 2002).

Given that visitors find and navigate their website, wineries should focus on customer relationships. Offline, good customer relationships increase wine consumption and seize market share from other retailers (O'Neill *et al.*, 2002). Newsletters are a good way to keep customers in contact with the winery and promote customer relationships (O'Neill and Charters, 2000). Other possible customer relationship features include wine clubs, as well as downloadable forms and brochures.

Depending upon the sophistication, sales features fall between the interactive and processing/personalization stages. A shopping cart – visitors add or subtract items to a real-time purchase – reflects processing/ personalization; online order forms reflect interactivity. Table 9.1 shows four sales features and 33 other features in the remaining seven categories.

E-mail response criteria

Despite its simplicity and spontaneity, organizations must treat e-mail as a business communication and sales tool (Zemke and Connellan, 2001). Table 9.2 shows five e-mail response categories based on business communication principles (Ober, 2001; Zemke and Connellan, 2001) and on past research (Strauss and Hill, 2001; Murphy and Tan, 2003; Murphy *et al.*, 2003a) – Prompt, Polite, Personal, Professional and Promotional – as well as technical and copy variables.

Similar to the tourism industry using mystery shoppers to test product and service quality anonymously, researchers pose as customers to test e-mail service quality. Their research suggests that tourism operations fail to treat e-mail communication as business communication (Gherissi-Labben *et al.*, 2003; Murphy and Tan, 2003; Murphy *et al.*, 2003a; Schegg *et al.*, 2003; Matzler *et al.*, 2005). Following their mystery shopper methodology, a standard e-mail asked each winery about buying their wines in a nearby suburb. A follow-up e-mail explained the study and shared the mystery shopping results with the eight wineries.

Table 9.1. Wine tourism website analysis.

	Winery 1	Winery 2	Winery 3	Winery 4	Winery 5	Winery 6	Winery 7	USA Winery
Popularity								
Google rank	3/10	5/10	5/10	4/10	3/10	3/10	4/10	5/10
Alexa traffic rank	550,495	3,838,512	672,793	2,206,395	2,339,460	1,322,254	No data	491,606
Number of links	18	51	122	8	3	54	7	142
Basic information								
Winery	√	√	√	√	√	√	√	√
Wine	√	√	√	√	√	√	√	√
Restaurant	√			√	√	√	√	NA
Functions	√			√	√			NA
Events	√	√	√		√	√		√
Contact information	√	√	√	√	√	√	√	√
Awards	√	√	√	√	√	√	√	√
Visual information								
Pictures of wine bottles	√	√	√			√	√	√
Pictures of wine labels	√	√	√			√	√	√
Pictures of estate	√	√	√	√		√	√	
Pictures of food	√				√	√	√	
Location Map	√	√	√	√	√	√	√	√
Societal information								
Environmental concerns			√					
Community and charity								
Virtual information								
Video downloads								
Virtual winery tours	√					√		
Trust information								
Branded .com name	√		√				√	√
Branded .com.au name	√	√	√	√	√	√	√	NA
Personal profiles	√	√	√	√	√		√	√
Privacy policy		√	√	√			√	√
Copyright							√	√
Last updates								
Links to other sites	√		√	√			√	√
Site navigation								
Search function								√
Site map								√
FAQs			√					
Customer relations								
News features		√	√	√	√	√		√
Downloadable forms								
Downloadable brochures								
Newsletter subscription		√	√	√		√		√
Wine club	√					√		

Table 9.1. *Continued*

	Winery 1	Winery 2	Winery 3	Winery 4	Winery 5	Winery 6	Winery 7	USA Winery
Sales								
Online order forms				✓			✓	✓
Gift vouchers			✓					✓
Online bookings	✓		✓	✓	✓			
Store locator			✓	✓	✓	✓		
Shopping cart		✓	✓				✓	✓

NA, not available.

Table 9.2. Wine tourism e-mail analysis.

	Winery 1	Winery 2	Winery 3	Winery 4	Winery 5	Winery 6
Prompt						
Working days to reply	2 days	1 day	same day	same day	1 day	same day
Hours and minutes to reply	48h 13m	19h 23m	7h 48m	6h 39m	22h 59m	4h 16m
Polite						
Opened with 'Dear/Dearest'			✓			✓
Thanked recipient for their interest		✓	✓			✓
Used 'please'			✓	✓	✓	✓
Closed with 'Best regards/Yours sincerely'	✓	✓	✓	✓	✓	✓
Personal						
Greeted recipient by name	✓	✓	✓	✓	✓	✓
Closed with sender's name	✓	✓	✓	✓	✓	✓
Included sender's title			✓			
Professional						
Answered the question	✓	✓	✓	✓	✓	✓
Used proper English	✓	✓	✓	✓	✓	✓
Promotional (included)						
Winery name				✓		✓
Winery website address				✓		✓
Winery physical address				✓		✓
Phone and fax numbers				✓		✓
Slogan or other promotional messages						✓
Branded e-mail address	✓	✓	✓			✓
Technical						
Used plain text e-mail			✓		✓	
Included attachment				✓		
Total e-mail size	4kb	6kb	3kb	156kb	4kb	13kb
Total attachment size				112kb		
Disclaimer						✓
Copy						
Use of first person	0	6	3	2	4	2
Use of second person	0	8	3	3	2	3
Ratio of second to first person		1.33	1	1.5	0.5	1.5

Website and e-mail research

Two researchers independently examined each winery's website for the presence of the 37 features. The researchers then double-checked five coding inconsistencies across the 296 (37×8) possible coding entries. Two third party tools, Google and Alexa, noted each site's visibility, popularity and links. The website analysis also culled an e-mail address for contacting each winery. None of the e-mail queries bounced. The researchers also coded the e-mail responses; there were no inconsistencies.

Findings

Website popularity and visibility

The US-based website led all other sites across the three popularity metrics: Google rank, Alexa rank and number of links. Google rank, a proxy for search engine visibility, ranged between three and five. Alexa rank, a proxy for user popularity, ranged from unavailable to almost four million. The number of incoming links to a winery ranged from three to 142. Operators should benchmark their number of incoming links and work to increase that number. Similarly, operators should chart their Google and Alexa ranks in order to mark their progress in online visibility and popularity.

Website information

While all sites contained a location map and basic – winery, wine, contact and award – information, most failed to provide other relevant information. Although they had restaurants, two wineries failed to mention the possibility of hosting functions. Six sites included pictures of their wine bottles, wine labels and the winery but only four sites featured pictures of their food. Most wineries could do more to highlight their restaurants.

Two sites offered virtual tours but none offered videos. While these features are expensive to add, a page with simple text is inexpensive to add. As just one winery noted its environmental concerns, wineries should consider adding an environmental or community page as a way of showing social concern and thus distancing their competitors.

While all Australian wineries used a branded name in Australia's .com.au domain, two Australian wineries also registered their name in the global .com domain. As visitors sometimes guess the website address (Roberts and Ko, 2001; Coyle and Gould, 2002), those guessing 'winetourism.com.au' or 'winetourism.com' arrived at the same site. If operators see overseas visitors as a target market, then they should invest about US$10 annually to register their name in the .com domain.

With regard to trust, all but one winery profiled key personnel, which makes the site more personal and increases trust (Nielsen, 2000). Five sites contained a privacy policy, an important element for consumer confidence (Culnan and Armstrong, 1999; Hanson, 2000; Phelps *et al.*, 2001). Five sites also linked to external websites. Despite the simplicity of adding a copyright or date of the last update of their web pages, just two wineries added a copyright and no site noted the last update of their pages. In addition to building trust, the last update can subtly remind site operators that it is time for a change.

Site navigation and customer relations

Only two sites included navigational features, an Australian winery with a FAQ page and the US winery with a site map and search function. In addition to being easy to implement, FAQs save wineries time in answering customer questions and a site map helps visitors navigate the site.

The sites fared better in customer relations. Six wineries offered online news to keep customers abreast of their latest happenings and five of these six offered newsletter subscriptions. websites act as online brochures, yet no winery provided downloadable brochures or forms. This downloadable information saves printing expenses for the winery and saves time for the consumer.

The Second Australian Wine Tourism Conference suggested wine clubs as a promotional vehicle for sharing wine awards, fostering a sense of community and interesting customers in the winery's affairs (Dowling, 2001), yet just two wineries offered subscriptions to their wine club. Wine clubs are also a good vehicle for increasing sales.

Sales

Disintermediation and distribution channel conflicts are Internet issues (Alba *et al.*, 1997; Hanson, 2000), particularly in tourism (O'Connor and Frew, 2002; Tse, 2003). Should and can wineries sell direct to consumers via their websites (Murphy and Rogers, 1998; Quinton and Harridge-March, 2003)? Seven wineries provided online sales, with one winery offering four separate ways. Three wineries included online order forms, two wineries offered gift certificates, four wineries offered function rooms and restaurant bookings, and four wineries had shopping carts. Four wineries also included store locator information in order to help customers find their wines. Wineries should reflect upon adding more sales features to their websites, particularly features that are simple and inexpensive to add such as order forms, gift certificates and booking enquiries via e-mail.

E-mail replies

Compared to clicking through a website, e-mail provides a more personalized interaction with guests. Similar to listing a telephone number in advertisements but not answering telephone calls, two wineries never replied to the inquiry about purchasing wine in a certain suburb. The remaining six wineries replied within two working days and five of the six replied promptly, within the recommended 24 hours (Zemke and Connellan, 2001; Murphy and Tan, 2003). Wineries not answering e-mail within one day should revisit their e-mail policies and procedures.

Just two wineries opened their e-mail politely, with 'Dear/Dearest', and only three wineries thanked the recipient for their interest. Four wineries used the word 'please' and all six authors closed politely with 'Best regards' or 'Yours sincerely'. All wineries personalized their replies by greeting the recipient by name and closing with their own name, but only one sender included their job title. The six wineries also replied professionally, answering the question and using proper grammar.

The wineries fared worse promoting themselves. Six wineries had branded website addresses but two wineries replied with a non-branded e-mail address. As branded e-mail addresses are usually part of the Internet service provider's hosting package, wineries should investigate their branded e-mail address options. Just two wineries included their winery name and contact details in the reply and only one winery included the company slogan.

Two wineries also used a plain text format, which reduces the size of e-mail in kilobytes and increases accessibility for users with older e-mail software, slower Internet connections and mobile devices such as cell phones or personal digital assistants. One winery included an attachment, which gives more information but balloons the number of kilobytes and requires the recipient to open another application. One winery included a formal disclaimer.

Finally, authors recommend using the second person you/your more often than the first person I/my/we/our in direct marketing, web pages and e-mails (Kilian, 1999; Tomsen, 2000; Usborne, 2002). The focus should be on the customer, not on the company. Four of the six wineries used the second person more often. As these e-mail and website results demonstrate, and the next section will show, there are myriad ways for operators to ameliorate their online presence.

Implications for Wine Tourism

Managerial implications

The results in Tables 9.1 and 9.2 illustrate suggested website features and e-mail responses. Wine tourism operations can benchmark themselves against these results as well as seeing how to gain competitive advantages in online wine tourism. Wineries improve their online marketing by providing customers with quick access to information through sitemaps or search engines, and anticipating user questions via FAQs (Palmer, 2002), yet only two sites offered these features. Successful hotel websites offer downloadable brochures (Murphy *et al.*, 2003a), but no winery offered brochures on their websites.

Based on this exploratory study, adding a sitemap and downloadable brochures is inexpensive and an easy step for wineries to distance the competition. As few wineries provided them, other inexpensive features that merit consideration include: (i) pages noting environmental or community concerns; (ii) copyrights; (iii) date of last update; (iv) wine clubs; and (v) retail store locations.

A successful wine tourism website should provide online avenues such as wine clubs to maintain customer relations and methods to promote sales such as online order forms. Sites should also increase trust, which is important for customer relations, repeat visits and online sales. Trust features include branded domain names (Murphy *et al.*, 2003a, b), providing reliable and updated information and including contact information (Nielsen, 2000; Veen, 2000; Chung and Law, 2003; Jeong *et al.*, 2003).

As expected, the California winery with the high Google rank led in the other traffic metrics – number of links and Alexa traffic rank. These results support the use of the Google and Alexa tools as metrics of website success (Garofalakis *et al.*, 2002; Palmer, 2002) and underscore the fact that wine tourism managers should solicit links to their website.

Wineries should grasp that e-mail communication is business communication and perhaps a customer's first impression of the winery. This study illustrates that wineries – Winery Six in this study – can gain an immediate competitive advantage with proper e-mail replies. Two wineries failed to respond and, of those that replied, most failed to respond politely or promotionally. Management should train their staff to answer e-mails politely and, given the poor promotional results, wineries should add signature files to their outgoing e-mails. This one-time process ensures that every e-mail includes contact details, the employee's title and a promotional slogan. Finally, given that the winery has a branded domain name, wineries should extend this branding to their e-mail addresses.

Research implications

The small convenience sample of wineries limits generalization of the results but does add to the small body of online wine tourism literature. The comparison of eight wineries' websites and e-mail responses helps benchmark current Internet practices and gives academics dozens of metrics for future research of online wine tourism.

The results in Table 9.1 suggest that these wine tourism sites are first-stage websites, providing information (Doolin *et al.*, 2002; Hanson, 2000). The sites are strong in providing basic, visual and most trust information, yet weak in providing societal and virtual information. The lack of virtual information may be due to financial hurdles and may not merit the extra expense. Wineries should focus on adding the previously mentioned inexpensive features. The lack of societal information hints at a gap between the growing environmental movement (Sklair, 1999; Castells, 2001) and wine tourism's connection with society and the environment (Ravenscroft and Westering, 2001; Beames, 2003). Wine tourism's role in society is one of several future research avenues.

That just two wineries had navigational features suggests that most sites failed to progress to the interactivity of Stage 2. Two sites mentioned their wine club but no sites provided downloadable forms or brochures. Paradoxically, most sites offered some Stage 3 features. Future research should explore this paradox by using a larger sample – in both Australia and abroad – and other website features, such as downloadable newsletters, estate plans and secure payment channels.

This type of research methodology, content analysis (Krippendorf, 1980), is difficult with websites (McMillan, 2000) and e-mail (Murphy and Tan, 2003; Murphy *et al.*, 2003a; Schegg *et al.*, 2003). Future research should test the reliability of human coders (Krippendorf, 1980; McMillan, 2000) and employ automated website analysis tools (Schegg *et al.*, 2002).

Finally, future research should examine the other half of the equation, consumers. Which website features and e-mail replies do consumers favour? In addition to survey-based research, qualitative research such as focus groups and in-depth interviews (Babbie, 1997) could help unravel why consumers prefer or dislike certain online initiatives.

References

Alba, J.W., Lynch, J., Weitz, B., Janiszewski, C., Lutz, R., Sawyer, A. and Wood, S. (1997) Interactive home shopping: incentives for consumers, retailers, and manufacturers to participate in electronic markets. *Journal of Marketing* 61, 38–53.

Babbie, E.R. (1997) *The Practice of Social Research*. Wadsworth Publishing, Belmont, California.

Beames, G. (2003) The rock, the reef and the grape: the challenges of developing wine tourism in regional Australia. *Journal of Vacation Marketing* 9, 205–212.

Bellman, S. and Rossiter, J.R. (2004) The website schema. *Journal of Interactive Advertising* 4, http://www.jiad.org/vol4/ no2/bellman/

Castells, M. (2001) *The Internet Galaxy: Reflections on the Internet, Business, and Society*. Oxford University Press, Oxford, UK.

Chung, T. and Law, R. (2003) Developing a performance indicator for hotel websites. *International Journal of Hospitality Management* 22, 119–125.

Coyle, J.R. and Gould, S.J. (2002) How consumers generate clickstreams through web sites: an empirical investigation of hypertext, schema, and mapping theoretical explanations. *Journal of Interactive Advertising* 2, http://www.jiad.org/vol2/ no2/coyle/

Culnan, M.J. and Armstrong, P.K. (1999) Information privacy concerns, procedural fairness and impersonal trust: an empirical investigation. *Organization Science* 10, 104–115.

Doolin, B., Burgess, L. and Cooper, J. (2002) Evaluating the use of the Web for tourism marketing: a case study from New Zealand. *Tourism Management* 23, 557–561.

Dowling, R.K. (2001) Second Annual Wine Tourism Conference. *International Journal of Tourism Research* 3, 158–159.

Drèze, X. and Zufryden, F. (2004) The measurement of online visibility and its impact on internet traffic. *Journal of Interactive Marketing* 18, 20–37.

Dubé, L., Le Bel, J. and Sears, D. (2003) From customer value to engineering pleasurable experiences in real life and online. *Cornell Hotel and Restaurant Administration Quarterly* 44, 124–130.

Fam, K.S., Foscht, T. and Collins, R.D. (2004) Trust and the online relationship – an exploratory study from New Zealand. *Tourism Management* 25, 195–207.

Garofalakis, J.G., Kappos, P. and Makris, C. (2002) Improving the performance of Web access by bridging global ranking with local page popularity metrics. *Internet Research: Electronic Networking Applications and Policy* 12, 43–54.

Gherissi-Labben, T., Schegg, R. and Murphy, J. (2003) E-mail customer service in the Tunisian hotel industry. *Tourism Review* 58, 18–26.

Hanson, W. (2000) *Principles of Internet Marketing.* Southwest College Publishing, Cincinnati, Ohio.

Hoffman, D.L. and Novak, T.P. (1996) Marketing in hypermedia computer-mediated environments: conceptual foundations. *Journal of Marketing* 60, 50–68.

Ilfeld, J.S. and Winer, R.S. (2002) Generating website traffic. *Journal of Advertising Research* 42, 49–61.

Jeong, M., Oh, H. and Gregoire, M. (2003) Conceptualizing web site quality and its consequences in the lodging industry. *International Journal of Hospitality Management* 22, 161–175.

Kilian, C. (1999) *Writing for the Web.* Self-Counsel Press, Bellingham, Washington.

Kim, J., Lee, J., Han, K. and Lee, M. (2002) Businesses as buildings: metrics for the architectural quality of internet businesses. *Information Systems Research* 13, 239–254.

Krippendorf, K. (1980) *Content Analysis: An Introduction to Its Methodology.* Sage, Beverly Hills, California.

Lockshin, L. and Spawton, T. (2001) Using involvement and brand equity to develop a wine tourism strategy. *International Journal of Wine Marketing* 13, 72–81.

MacCannell, D. (2002) The ego factor in tourism. *Journal of Consumer Research* 29, 146–151.

Mansfield, Y. (1992) From motivation to actual travel. *Annals of Tourism Research* 19, 399–419.

Matzler, K., Pechlaner, H., Abfalter, D. and Wolf, M. (2005) Determinants of response to customer e-mail enquiries to hotels: evidence from Austria. *Tourism Management* 26, 249–259.

McMillan, S.J. (2000) The microscope and the moving target: the challenge of applying content analysis to the World Wide Web. *Journalism and Mass Communication Quarterly* 77, 80–98.

Murphy, J. and Gomes, L. (2003) E-mail customer service by Australian educational institutions. *Australasian Marketing Journal* 11, 56–69.

Murphy, J. and Rogers, E. (1998) *The Wall Street Journal Interactive* (7 April).

Murphy, J. and Tan, I. (2003) Journey to nowhere? Electronic customer service by travel agents in Singapore. *Tourism Management* 24, 543–550.

Murphy, J., Olaru, D., Schegg, R. and Frey, S. (2003a) The bandwagon effect: Swiss hotels' website and e-mail management. *Cornell Hotel and Restaurant Administration Quarterly* 44, 71–87.

Murphy, J., Raffa, L. and Mizerski, R. (2003b) The use of domain names in e-branding by the world's top brands. *Electronic Markets* 13, 30–40.

Nguyen, D.T.H.C., Murphy, J. and Olaru, D. (2003) Investigating the adoption of electronic customer service by Australian businesses. *Managing Service Quality* 13, 492–503.

Nielsen, J. (2000) *Designing Web Usability.* New Riders Publishing, Indianapolis, Indiana.

Nysveen, H., Methlie, L.B. and Perdersen, P.F. (2002) Tourism web sites and value-added services: the gap between customer preferences and web sites' offerings. *Information Technology and Tourism* 5, 165–174.

Ober, S. (2001) *Contemporary Business Communication,* Houghton-Mifflin, Boston, Massachusetts.

O'Connor, P. (2003) On-line pricing: an analysis of hotel-company practices. *Cornell Hotel and Restaurant Administration Quarterly* 44, 88–96.

O'Connor, P. and Frew, A.J. (2002) The future of hotel electronic distribution. *Cornell Hotel and Restaurant Administration Quarterly* 43, 33–45.

Olsen, M.D. and Connolly, D.J. (2000) Experience-based travel. *Cornell Hotel and Restaurant Administration Quarterly* 41, 30–40.

O'Neill, M. and Charters, S. (2000) Service quality at the cellar door: implications for Western Australia's developing wine tourism industry. *Managing Service Quality* 10, 112–123.

O'Neill, M., Palmer, A. and Charters, S. (2002) Wine production as a service experience – the effect of service quality on wine sales. *Journal of Services Marketing* 16, 342–362.

Palmer, J.W. (2002) Website usability, design, and performance metrics. *Information Systems Research* 13, 151–167.

Phelps, J., D'Souza, G. and Nowak, G.J. (2001) Antecedents and consequences of privacy concerns: an empirical investigation. *Journal of Interactive Marketing* 15, 2–17.

Quinton, S. and Harridge-March, S. (2003) On-line wine – strategic or tactical? *International Journal of Wine Marketing* 15, 34–43.

Ravenscroft, N. and Westering, J.V. (2001) Wine tourism, culture and the everyday: a theoretical note. *Tourism and Hospitality Research* 3, 149–161.

Rayman-Bacchus, L. and Molina, A. (2001) Internet-based tourism services: *Business Issues and Trends. Futures* 33, 589–605.

Richardson, O. (2002) Utilisation of the World Wide Web by wine producers. *International Journal of Wine Marketing* 14, 65–79.

Roberts, M.S. and Ko, H. (2001) Global interactive advertising: defining what we mean and using what we have learned. *Journal of Interactive Advertising* 1, http://www.jiad.org/vol1/no2/roberts/

Scheffelmaier, G.W. and Vinsonhaler, J.F. (2002–2003) A synthesis of research on the properties of effective internet commerce websites. *Journal of Computer Information Systems* 43, 23–30.

Schegg, R., Steiner, T., Frey, S. and Murphy, J. (2002) Benchmarks of web site design and marketing by Swiss hotels. *Information Technology and Tourism* 5, 73–89.

Schegg, R., Murphy, J. and Leuenberger, R. (2003) Five-star treatment? E-mail customer service by international luxury hotels. *Information Technology and Tourism* 6, 99–112.

Sklair, L. (1999) Competing conceptions of globalization. *Journal of World-Systems Research* 5, 143–163.

Sterne, J. (2002) *Web Metrics: Proven Methods for Measuring WebSite Success.* John Wiley and Sons, New York.

Straub, D.W., Hoffman, D.L., Weber, B.W. and Steinfeld, C. (2002a) Measuring e-commerce in net-enabled organizations: an introduction to the special issue. *Information Systems Research* 13, 115–124.

Straub, D.W., Hoffman, D.L., Weber, B.W. and Steinfeld, C. (2002b) Toward new metrics for net-enabled organizations. *Information Systems Research* 13, 227–238.

Strauss, J. and Hill, D.J. (2001) Consumer complaints by e-mails: an exploratory investigation of corporate responses and customer reactions. *Journal of Interactive Marketing* 15, 63–73.

Tomsen, M.-I. (2000) *Killer Content.* Addison Wesley Longman, Inc., Reading, Massachusetts.

Tse, A.C.-b. (2003) Disintermediation of travel agents in the hotel industry. *International Journal of Hospitality Management* 22, 453–460.

Usborne, N. (2002) *Net Words.* McGraw-Hill, New York.

Veen, J. (2000) *The Art and Science of Web Design.* New Riders Publishing, Indianapolis, Indiana.

Williams, P. (2001) Positioning wine tourism destinations: an image analysis. *International Journal of Wine Marketing* 13, 42–58.

Zemke, R. and Connellan, T. (2001*) E-Service.* Amacom, New York.

10 Understanding the Impact of Wine Tourism on Post-tour Purchasing Behaviour

BARRY O'MAHONY,[1]* JOHN HALL,[2] LARRY LOCKSHIN,[3]
LEO JAGO[1] AND GRAHAM BROWN[3]

[1]Centre for Hospitality and Tourism Research, Victoria University,
Footscray Park, Melbourne, Australia; [2]Deakin Business School,
Deakin University, Toorak, Victoria, Australia; [3]University of South Australia,
North Terrace, Adelaide, Australia
*E-mail: Barry.OMahony@vu.edu.au

Introduction

For small and medium-sized wineries, setting up and operating a cellar door is an expensive proposition. These retail outlets are usually located on the winery property and make it possible to sell wine products directly to the public. In addition to the cash flow generated by across-the-counter sales, these activities offer exposure that can assist brand building, both in terms of enhanced awareness and potential repurchase of varieties of the brand.

The study described in this chapter seeks to understand more fully these longer-term implications of cellar door operations by focusing on wine tourists' purchasing and consumption patterns as a consequence of their visits to wineries. This involved investigating whether there is a positive link between the wine tourism experience and subsequent wine purchasing behaviour. Consumers were asked to identify changes in their wine consumption patterns three months after visiting a cellar door. As part of the analysis, the sample was segmented by involvement in the wine product category, since involvement has been shown to explain differences in wine consumer behaviour (Lockshin *et al.*, 1997, 2001, 2006; Quester and Smart, 1998; Aurfeille *et al.*, 2002).

Literature Review

The National Wine Tourism Strategy, launched at the Second Australian Wine Tourism Conference in Rutherglen in 1999, defined wine tourism as 'visitation to wineries and wine regions to experience the unique qualities of contemporary Australian lifestyle associated with the enjoyment of wine at its source including wine and food, landscape and cultural activities' (Dowling, 1999, p. 65). At that time it was projected that the Australian wine tourism industry would be worth Aus$1.5 billion by 2008 (Dowling, 1999).

In 2002, there were almost 4,000,000 domestic and nearly 470,000 international visitors to wineries in Australia (Table 10.1) and, between 1999 and 2000, wine tourism revenue is estimated to have been Aus$965 m. Almost half of this (47.5%) was spent in wineries on wine, food and accommodation, with the remainder (52.5%) being spent within the regional area.

Internationally, the development of wine routes has been presented as one of the most important features of wine tourism. In South Africa, Bruwer (2003) defined wine routes as '… the roadways to the core attractions in wine tourism, the wines and the wineries' (p. 424) and in Greece, wine trails are being used to counter intense competition from alternative drinks and a decline in the consumption of local wine (Tzimitra-Kalogianni *et al.*, 1999).

The importance of regional wine tourism was the focus of a strategy in Western Australia that has seen the establishment and development of wineries and growth of the tourism industry strongly intertwined. King and Morris (1997) asserted that winemakers and wineries in this state now see themselves as important to the tourism industry. This is consistent with the desired position of the Winemakers Federation, which has identified continual development of the wine tourism product as a priority for wineries. The belief was expressed that wine tourism can provide financial security and business growth for wineries that are able to capitalize on tourism demand.

It is becoming increasingly clear that unless many regional winemakers diversify their winery activities to develop additional income streams through a commitment to winery tourism, then their chances of growing and even their very survival could well be at risk (Winemakers Federation of Australia, 2005).

The dominant product focus of winemakers means that tourism is essentially a secondary or tertiary activity but it offers considerable scope for enhancement of sales, both directly and through longer-term associations. A visit to a cellar door makes it possible to develop wine knowledge '… in a

Table 10.1. Visitors to wineries (2002) (from BTR National Visitor Survey, cited in Winemakers Federation of Australia (2003)).

State	Domestic	International
QLD	261,000	171,110
NSW	953,000	253,727
ACT	19,000	34,567
VIC	1,021,000	208,966
TAS	89,000	25,359
SA	902,000	116,991
WA	702,000	159,869
NT	5,000	72,480
Total	3,952,000	1,043,069

QLD, Queensland; NSW, New South Wales; ACT, Australian Capital Territory; VIC, Victoria; TAS, Tasmania; SA, South Australia; WA, Western Australia; NT, Northern Territories.

friendly, social and unthreatening atmosphere' (Mitchell *et al.*, 2000, p. 108). Beverland *et al.* (1998) found that cellar door activities were an effective and low-cost product sampling mechanism for the consumer. If people are aware of a brand, they tend to like it more than brands they are less familiar with. Obviously, when people visit a winery, there is a powerful opportunity to create not only awareness, but also familiarity and affection.

There are commercial possibilities for wineries through direct sales and enhanced distribution channels (Macionis and Cambourne, 1998). The effective use of direct marketing material can be used to keep tourists informed and to provide a means of submitting orders by mail, telephone or Internet after a visit has been concluded (Beverland, 1999).

The concept of product involvement has been linked to product choice behaviour in previous research (Laurent and Kapferer, 1985; Slama and Tashchian, 1985; Zaichkowsky, 1985; Mittal and Lee, 1989; Steenkamp and Wedel, 1991; Ohanian and Tashchian, 1992; Flynn and Goldsmith, 1993; Kapferer and Laurent, 1993). Highly product-involved consumers spend more time and cognitive effort considering their product choices. The various definitions of product involvement used all tap the '... feelings of interest, enthusiasm, and excitement' consumers have about specific product categories (Goldsmith and Emmert, 1991, p. 365). Previous research on product involvement in wine consumption behaviour has shown differences in wine buying between high- and low-involvement consumers (Lockshin *et al.*, 1997, 2001, 2006; Quester and Smart, 1998; Aurfeille *et al.*, 2002).

Higher-involvement wine consumers pay more attention to details on the label and are able to associate these with particular styles of wine, while lower-involvement consumers tend to use single cues, such as price or brand, in their purchase decision making. Higher-involvement wine consumers have been shown to buy more wine and at higher prices than lower-involvement consumers. Other types of involvement, e.g. brand decision and situational involvement, have been measured for wine buyers, but little influence on actual purchase behaviour was found (Dean and Lockshin, 1997; Lockshin *et al.*, 1997).

We would expect to find differences in purchasing behaviour and recall of information regarding visits to wineries between lower- and higher-product involvement visitors, but it is not clear which of these two group's future behaviour would be more influenced by a cellar door experience. One could argue that higher-involvement visitors understand more and associate more of the details gained in a visit with their own wine preferences, so they would use this information in future purchasing. On the other hand, one could also postulate that lower-involvement visitors, having less knowledge and experience, would be more likely to remember their visit and use this information in their future purchasing.

Ali-Knight and Charters (2001) found that taste and price are the most important influences on consumers' decisions to buy wine at the cellar door and this was also consistent with the findings of a recent study by Brown and Getz (2005), which examined the relationship between wine preferences and visitation to wine regions. O'Neill *et al.* (2002) commented on the uniqueness of the cellar door experience compared to other service activities. It was pointed out that wine tourism involves the tourist visiting the vineyard to see the grapes growing, winemaking and experience the less tangible cellar door service process. Tasting the tangible product is a very important factor and reinforces the appeal of the whole experience.

It was also suggested that, although visits to the wineries may be short, the benefits to the winery can be of an extended duration. For example, visitors may seek out the product at a later date, may regularly purchase the product and make recommendations to friends. Positive outcomes of this kind are likely to be influenced by the quality of the service at the cellar door. O'Neill *et al.* (2002) suggested that operations, design, layout and appearance of the winery – as well as the appearance, friendliness, courteousness and knowledgeability of staff – are all of extreme importance.

These service quality dimensions represent a considerable investment for cellar door operators, however, and, anecdotally, some winery managers have expressed concern that they are making a greater contribution to the tourism industry than they get in return. It appears that this view is based upon the direct costs of running a cellar door operation *versus* the actual sales to visitors, and does not take into account the potential subsequent sales as a result of the winery visit. A key objective of this study is to examine the propensity of the consumer to purchase subsequent to the winery visit.

Research Method

The research employed what Tashakkori and Teddlie (1998) refer to as a sequential mixed method design. A series of quantitative studies were conducted, followed by an in-depth, qualitative research phase. This method was selected as the most appropriate to meet the objectives of the research and data were collected from three states within Australia (South Australia, Victoria and New South Wales). Seventy-two per cent of Australia's total cellar doors are located in these three states, making it possible to gain comprehensive coverage of the range of settings and consumption patterns associated with wine tourism behaviour.

In the first phase of the research, a review of previous studies was used to identify items for inclusion in the research instrument, before interviewing 207 respondents at cellar doors in South Australia, Victoria and New South Wales. Wineries were selected in order to cover a wide range of size, type, organizational structure and level of business success. Information about demographics, involvement levels, wine consumption and winery visitation history were collected, along with satisfaction with the service at the specific cellar door.

Based on the analysis of the initial 207 interviews and the themes and topics identified within the literature review, a second, more comprehensive questionnaire was developed in order to determine whether there had been changes in consumers' wine consumption patterns subsequent to the initial intercept interviews. Seventy-three of the initial 207 respondents had indicated that they were willing to be involved in further study and these respondents were contacted again 5 months after the first interview. Their recall of the wine region visit, wineries visited and purchase behaviour were all measured. Respondents were also asked to assess whether their consumption and purchase of wine in general, and brands in particular, had changed since the cellar door visit at which they were originally interviewed.

The second interviews indicated that 20% of respondents had changed their wine consumption behaviour since the original interview. The subsequent qualitative phase focused on those respondents whose wine consumption behaviour had changed. Further insight was sought about their wine purchasing behaviour, their perceptions of winery brands and their levels of recall of these brands as a consequence of their visits to wineries. Telephone interviews were conducted aimed at gaining more information about the increases, with questions such as: (i) had the increased consumption remained at the increased level? (ii) had further information been received or sought on the winery? and (iii) had the respondents experienced any other changes in relation to their consumption and purchasing patterns since visiting the cellar door? The interviews were transcribed and analysed and the results are reported below.

Findings

The demographic profile of the 207 cellar door visitors who participated in the initial phase of the study indicated that visitors' ages were well distributed throughout the age groups and ranged from young adults (18–24 years) to older citizens (over 65 years). Over 70% of respondents were between 25 and 64 years of age. The slight bias towards females in the sex of the respondents (56.5%) probably reflected the interviewee selection process and those who completed the visitor information records provided at the cellar door. In general, most cellar door visitors would have arrived in couples or groups, and one person in that group completed the visitor record.

Wine consumption segments

Using the factors related to frequency of purchase and price paid per bottle, an involvement dimension was constructed that reflected the wine consumers' behaviour. This segmentation applied to the cellar door visitors resulted in three primary segments: 'The Committed Consumer (CC)' (28.0%), 'The Traditional Consumer (TC)' (29.0%) and 'The Uninvolved Consumer (UC)' (43.0%).

Previous research has shown that UCs enjoy wine and drink it, but care little for the details concerning wine (Lockshin *et al.*, 1997). The CC purchases wine on a weekly basis and tends to buy the higher-priced wines. The TC buys regularly but tends to buy the middle-priced range of wines on a regular basis or the higher-priced wines less frequently. The UC tends to buy the lower-priced wines and buys them on an infrequent basis (see Tables 10.2, 10.3 and 10.4).

Table 10.2. Purchase frequency by involvement segments.

| | Wine involvement segments | | | |
	Uninvolved consumer (%)	Traditional consumer (%)	Committed consumer (%)	Total (%)
	(*n*, 89)	(*n*, 60)	(*n*, 58)	(*n*, 207)
How often do you purchase wine?				
Weekly or more regularly		55.0	86.2	40.1
Between weekly and monthly	34.8	45.0	8.6	30.4
Monthly or less regularly	65.2		5.2	29.5
Total	100.0	100.0	100.0	100.0

Table 10.3. Price paid by involvement segments.

| | Wine involvement segments | | | |
	Uninvolved consumer (%)	Traditional consumer (%)	Committed consumer (%)	Total (%)
	(*n*, 89)	(*n*, 60)	(*n*, 58)	(*n*, 207)
How much do you typically pay per bottle of wine?				
Less than $15 per bottle	71.9	55.0		46.9
$15 to $25 per bottle	28.1	45.0	77.6	46.9
More than $25 per bottle			22.4	6.3
Total	100.0	100.0	100.0	100.0

Table 10.4. Segment distribution by involvement segments.

| | Wine involvement segments | | | |
	Uninvolved consumer (%)	Traditional consumer (%)	Committed consumer (%)	Total (%)
	(*n*, 89)	(*n*, 60)	(*n*, 58)	(*n*, 207)
Weekly or more regular wine purchase				
Less than $15 per bottle		55.0		15.9
$15 to $25 per bottle			77.6	21.7
More than $25 per bottle			8.6	2.4
Total		55.0	86.2	40.1
Between weekly and monthly wine purchase				
Less than $15 per bottle	34.8			15.0
$15 to $25 per bottle		45.0		13.0
More than $25 per bottle			8.6	2.4
Total	34.8	45.0	8.6	30.4
Monthly or less regular wine purchase				
Less than $15 per bottle	37.1			15.9
$15 to $25 per bottle	28.1			12.1
More than $25 per bottle			5.2	1.4
Total	65.2		5.2	29.5

Table 10.5 shows the distribution of age groups by the level of wine involvement. This chart demonstrates that a purely demographic approach to segmentation can be misleading, as all involvement segments have a full distribution of age groups. The major difference is the bias the CC segment shows towards the 45–54-year age group, which is 36.2%, compared to only 15.7% for the UC Segment.

There are significant differences in the sources of information used by the wine consumer in the three involvement segments. The five main sources of information are newspaper, retailers, journals/magazines, friends and the winery or cellar door. The UC (25.8%) is much more likely to use electronic media (such as television and radio) than the IC (8.6%). Overall, 23.2% of cellar door visitors state that the winery or cellar door is one of their primary sources of wine information. This proportion rises to 31.0% for the CC and is only 18.0% amongst the UCs.

Changes in wine consumption after a cellar door visit

Five months after a visit to a winery located in a particular wine region, 20.5% of visitors claimed some changes to their wine consumption. The greatest change came in the quality of wine consumed, with 73.3% indicating that they now consumed higher-quality wines than in the past. This suggests that an educational impact occurs in going to a wine region and participating in the cellar door experience. In addition, 66.7% increased the quantity of wine purchased and 60.0% changed the wine style and type that they usually consumed. There was also a change in the average price of the wine, with 46.7% indicating that they were purchasing more expensive wines. Only 6.7% said that they had reduced the quantity consumed (Table 10.6).

These changes in consumption behaviour have, for most respondents, been multiple. Although the sample size is relatively small, these changes are interesting at a qualitative level. In all cases a particular change was associated with at least half of the visitors indicating that all other aspects of

Table 10.5. Age of cellar door visitor by involvement segment.

	Wine involvement segments			
	Uninvolved consumer (%)	Traditional consumer (%)	Committed consumer (%)	Total (%)
	(*n*, 89)	(*n*, 60)	(*n*, 58)	(*n*, 207)
Age of cellar door visitor				
18–24	7.9	5.0	3.4	5.8
25–34	28.1	23.3	27.6	26.6
35–44	22.5	23.3	19.0	21.7
45–54	15.7	21.7	36.2	23.2
55–64	15.7	18.3	8.6	14.5
65+	10.1	8.3	5.2	8.2
Total	100.0	100.0	100.0	100.0

Table 10.6. Nature of wine consumption change.

	(*n*, 15 (%))
Changes in wine consumption	
Increased quantity	66.7
Higher value	46.7
High quality	73.3
Changed type	60.0
Decreased quantity	6.7

their behaviour had changed. For example, of those who had begun to purchase higher-quality wines, 63.6% had increased both the quantity and value, and 72.7% had changed the types of wine consumed.

The competitive nature of retail marketing is a major factor in overall profitability for the small to medium-sized winery. Although only 20.5% of respondents changed overall consumption, there was a much greater impact on regionally based consumption changes, where 39.7% claimed to have changed behaviour. Only 4.2% thought their consumption had decreased after the visit to the wine region. In terms of the specific changes, quantity purchased and consumed from the region had increased for 62.5% of consumers.

Furthermore, 70.8% had chosen higher-quality wines and 66.7% had changed the type of wine they now bought from the region. Just over 54% of respondents had increased the value of the wines purchased, although 4.2%, said this had decreased. It was clear that cellar door visits have multiple influences on subsequent wine consumption behaviour for the region. In general, changes occurred for at least half the visitors in terms of quantity, value, quality and type.

The 73 respondents involved in the re-interview survey had visited a total of 135 identified wineries in their initial visit to the wine region. Using the same sample of visitors, a base of wineries was developed for which changes in purchasing patterns had been measured. These data can be used as a base for determination of the percentage of wineries that had increased their sales after the cellar door visit.

The proportion of those who recalled the cellar door visit at which they were initially interviewed was 72.5%. In addition, 94.8% of those recalling the visit were still able to give a description of or name of the wine purchased during that visit. It is also clear that for most cellar door visitors the involvement in wine tourism is something important in their lives and this was also evident in the qualitative findings.

Table 10.7. Change in consumption from region.

	(*n*, 15 (%))
Changes in wine consumption	
Increased quantity	62.5
Higher value	54.2
High quality	70.8
Changed type	66.7
Decreased value	4.2

Qualitative insights

Stage 3 of the data collection process involved qualitative research with a sample of 13 people who had completed both the cellar door survey and the second stage telephone follow-up survey. These respondents provided some detailed comments on particular areas of interest. The results provided here also help interpret some of the quantitative results.

The sources of information mentioned by the respondents were quite varied. The general media have already been described in relation to involvement levels, but it was also evident that more detailed information is found in wine newsletters, magazines, wine club publications and tasting notes from the cellar door or retail outlet. The search for information is one of the strongest indicators of true psychological involvement with a product. It is interesting to note that the information on wine is described, even by the wine consumer, as 'education' about wine and winemaking. The highly involved wine consumer wants two levels of education, first education about the winemaking and wine evaluation process and second about specific wines. The latter information is used to help them make a purchase choice.

> I enjoy drinking wine, but I have done no wine courses, and my knowledge is based on what they are explaining to me at cellar door, and by drinking it myself, so I do find that fairly useful … So those two things, tasting notes so there is something that I can take home with me, so I know that when I'm ready to reorder wine I can write notes on the tasting notes which one I like in particular.
>
> (NSW, female, 35–44 years)

In relation to the form of information participants prefer at the cellar door, the majority of respondents prefer a combination of reading the wine list with verbal interaction with the cellar door sales assistant. Many of the participants prefer to consult the list initially and then ask questions regarding particular wines from the list, as they feel that the staff can push them towards slow-moving products if they don't work from the list first. Other respondents do not use tasting notes and lists, as they prefer simply to talk to someone about the wine on offer at the winery. Nevertheless, they are keen to learn more about how best to cellar and serve the particular wine they intend to buy: 'We look for staff recommendations, tasting notes yes, look for cellaring advice, longevity of wine, is it drinking now or later, and any tips they may have in terms of that' (SA, female, 25–34 years).

The use of staff for information is a key feature of behaviour while visiting a cellar door. However, some visitors prefer to do evaluations and comparison free of any influence from staff. This latter group tends to exhibit 'higher involvement' behaviour and is generally guided by their experiences and tasting evaluations of the wines they select. A number of participants said that their purchases are based on what they have tasted, but can also be influenced by staff recommendations. 'Actually it's probably a mix – as if the staff say "this is a really good wine" I will taste it, but if I don't like it I will leave it. … however, they can influence the decision such as if they say it a great wine I will try it' (NSW, female, 35–44 years).

The findings indicate that this group of people, who showed a change (all increases) in one of the four factors, are seeking information and education on wine. They are also open to listening to staff about new wines to sample and take recommendations from staff; however, this may not always affect their final decision on purchasing.

Overall, respondents did learn more about wine from their visits to the wineries; however, it was clear from their comments that the information they wanted varied across the different groups of respondents at the cellar door. This information depended on each person's level of involvement and their level of knowledge, a feature that reflects the length of time they have been developing their interest in the product category. These interests extend from the established product characteristics, food and wine combinations to the winemaking process itself, and yet others were interested in learning about new varietals they had not tried before whilst others were interested in the storage and tasting of the wine. 'I don't know really what I learned. To be honest with you it was the last one we were doing, so I just knew I liked the flavours and taste that I was experiencing' (NSW, male, 25–34 years).

It is significant to note that wine experience is a shared experience, and opinions of others can have a bearing on attitudes. For example, the following comment was made about wine and food combinations. 'Matching wine with food? No, [my] husband doesn't believe in that. (VIC, female, 54–65 years).

The general impression based on the qualitative comments about the impact of a visit to a wine region and to a particular winery is that both winery and customer receive benefits in terms of knowledge, affection and loyalty. It should be noted that people in general are not very accurate when estimating global changes in behaviour over a lengthy period of time. The following comments should be interpreted as impressions rather than as hard facts.

There were many comments about re-visitation which seem to be encouraged by good past experiences. These positive experiences led to re-visitation to the wine region and to the specific wineries, as well as to increased purchases. There is also a direct flow to strong word-of-mouth recommendations to friends and family. As noted in the review of literature, when people visit a winery there is a powerful opportunity to not only create awareness, but also familiarity and affection (Beverland *et al.*, 1998). Respondents in this study confirmed that there is a great deal of affection developed for the winery and its products after pleasant experiences with the people who run the cellar door or winery tour facilities.

> I guess I do look for recommendations – depending on if its cellar doors that I go to, often you tend to know some of the staff there such as [name omitted] at De Luliis and [name omitted] at the Boutique Wine Centre. So I suppose I would take their recommendations, probably more because I know them and they know what I like as well, I guess it depends.
>
> (NSW, female, 35–44 years)

When asked about brand/region loyalty, about half of the respondents indicated they were loyal to favourite regions. Responses showed that participants were loyal to various regions and brands depending on the style/varietal of wine for which they were looking. If an experience is memorable and the wine is of suitable quality to the individual, they will often declare some loyalty to either the brand or the region. 'We go to that region several times a year, and as we explore more we get a better idea of what they have on offer and will certainly purchase what we are familiar with' (SA, female, 25–34 years).

In regards to changes in quality of wine consumed, various respondents indicated that the more wine they drank the more developed their palate became, and many are less likely to drink lesser-quality wine once they have experienced better-quality wines. One respondent stated: 'Some of the cheaper bottles that appeared to be quite good quality – for a cheaper bottle – don't seem to be as good quality, such as an $11 bottle which was good drinking. The wine today doesn't seem to be the same wine or standard' (SA, female, 25–44 years).

Overall, the amount spent on wine in most responses had remained more or less at the same level, with the exception of a few spending more over the Christmas season and a few spending marginally more, such as Aus$2–3 extra in order to purchase a better-quality wine.

During the series of in-depth interviews an assessment of the importance of various factors in the purchasing of wine was made. These factors, which were developed from the literature and previous research in the area, included:

- The image of the winery.
- Award received.
- Grape variety.
- Wine style.
- Wine brand.
- Price.
- Value for money.
- Knowledge of the wine.
- Knowledge of the winery.
- Knowledge of the wine maker.

Of course the purchase choice that occurs in wine buying is a very complex relationship between personal characteristics, past experience and product stimulus. It was confirmed that variety, style, price, value for money and knowledge of the winery can be very influential factors.

Value for money is a variable that is always a balance between the nature of the product and how much is paid for it, a balance which often shows an interactive relationship. That is, higher price is automatically indicative of higher quality. One respondent said that although she was happy to pay a higher price for a higher-quality wine, however, it was beneficial to taste the wine first before purchasing, because if you are paying Aus$50 for a bottle you want to know it is a good one. Another respondent noted that what he once thought were good wines at around Aus$10, he could not go back to drinking again as they tasted so poorly. Both of these examples show that value for money is an important factor, especially when one is prepared to pay more per bottle for a better-quality wine. Some wine buyers look for cellar doors that offer good value specials on some of their wines.

Price paid per bottle is an influential aspect when purchasing wine. Generally, when purchasing wine, the buyer has a good idea of how much to spend per bottle depending on the occasion. The indications in comments made by respondents were that the experience encourages them to spend an extra few dollars to get a better quality wine.

Implications for Wine Tourism

A major finding that emerged from this research was the high level of wine product involvement among cellar door visitors in general. These wine consumers typically engaged in some form of wine education activity, ranging from discussions and tastings with friends and colleagues to subscriptions to wine magazines. This search for information about wine is followed through on a winery visit, where sales staff or winery employees are an expected source of further information.

An implication for marketing activities is that these respondents seek information on wine and are receptive to the wine marketing message as long as promotional material is educational in nature. The challenge for wine marketers is to tap into their apparent desire for further knowledge about wine and to facilitate their move to Category 3 (committed wine consumers), whilst simultaneously developing brand awareness and consumer loyalty.

It is also useful to know that 80% of respondents claimed not to have changed their wine consumption behaviour after visiting a winery. This may be due to already high levels of involvement where the visit, as noted, merely added to existing knowledge and repurchase from favourite wineries. However, it should also be recognized that some respondents may not have declared an increase in wine consumption behaviour when in fact it had occurred, as such behaviour is not well regarded by some sections of society. Wineries may be expecting too much beyond the actual sale of wine at cellar door. It may be more important than previously thought to gain sales from as many visitors as possible in order to make a return on the running costs of a cellar door, rather than assuming future sales will occur. More research is needed to understand this.

Guidelines should be developed and provided to staff for handling the different wine consumer segments so that the right level of staff involvement in the tasting process is given. In other words, use experienced and knowledgeable staff for the segments for which knowledge and interaction are a major requirement of the visitor's expectations. Guidelines could include mechanisms for identifying previous visitors and buyers through such techniques as membership cards or newsletters, and for welcoming these visitors in special ways when they are revisiting or bringing friends and acquaintances.

Wine regions can also use these findings to better serve visitors to their area. It is important for wine regions to help member wineries train and motivate staff, because these costs are often too high for smaller wineries, and the outcome helps all wineries in the region (Thach and Olson, 2003). If gaining total sales from visitors is more important than relying on future sales, then wine regions have much to gain by promoting their region as a visitor destination. Organizing festivals and other drawcards may have greater importance in driving direct sales than originally thought. Improving overall promotions, education of staff and larger regional events should have long-term, positive effects for wine regions. The value of a well-known region has been shown to have positive effects on wine purchasing, especially for bottles over Aus$15 (Lockshin *et al.*, 2006).

This study indicates a need to gain further understanding of cellar door operations and their impact on wine tourists. Studies could examine the interaction and operations of the three key stakeholders – tourism authorities, winemakers and winery owners – as well as wine consumers. In particular, the following opportunities could be considered:

1. Complete the segmentation of the wine consumer with a broader use of the segmentation models as described in the literature.
2. Use case study techniques to evaluate the operating systems and the performance of cellar door operations, including an examination of the sequence and style of service, levels of visitor separation (based on interest), follow-up procedures and managing during busy times.
3. Further investigate the actual costs of operating various types of cellar doors and the monetary benefits.
4. Use the techniques of 'mystery' shopping, in which researchers act as normal purchasers and experience the full cellar door sales process from the perspective of a genuine consumer.
5. Organizational research into the systems, processes, management and planning in cellar door arrangements should be conducted.
6. Evaluation of the cooperative activities in regional tourism using case studies to establish both strong and weak practice.
7. A similar study that involves a larger sample of wine tourists may yield further useful insights.

Finally, since this study found that 20% of the respondents in the second survey had increased their consumption of wine after their winery visit, further qualitative research should be designed to explore whether it is possible to influence the remaining cellar door visitors to modify their behaviour in a similar manner. The finding that those respondents who did not indicate an increase in wine consumption over the survey period may be related to already high levels of involvement or consumption, or possibly a consequence of consumers not getting the information that they were seeking from the cellar door. As a result, an investigation that provides insights into the strategies or environmental conditions that might be utilized to persuade consumers to increase their wine consumption is merited.

References

Ali-Knight, J. and Charters, S. (2001) The winery as educator: do wineries provide what the tourist needs? *Australian and New Zealand Wine Industry Journal* 16 (6), 79–86.

Aurfeille, J.-M., Pascale, Q., Lockshin, L. and Spawton, T. (2002) Global versus international involvement-based segmentation: a cross-national exploratory study. *International Marketing Review* 19 (4), 369–386.

Beverland, M. (1999) Old world *vs.* new in wine tourism and marketing. *Australian and New Zealand Wine Industry Journal* 14 (6), 95–100.

Beverland, M., James, K., James, M., Porter, C. and Stace, G. (1998) Wine tourism: missed opportunities in West Auckland. *Australian and New Zealand Wine Industry Journal* 13 (4), 403–407.

Brown, G. and Getz, D. (2005) Linking wine preferences to the choice of wine tourism destinations. *Journal of Travel Research* 43, 266–276.

Bruwer, J. (2003) South African wine routes: some perspectives on the wine tourism industry's structural dimensions and wine tourism product. *Tourism Management* 24, 423–435.

Dean, R. and Lockshin, L. (1997) Situational influences on product involvement and service level in retailing relationships. In: Reed, P., Luxton, S. and Shaw, M. (eds) *Proceedings of the Australian New Zealand Marketing Educators' Conference*, Vol. 3, pp. 578–579.

Dowling, R. (1999) Marketing the key to successful wine tourism. *Australian and New Zealand Wine Industry Journal* 14 (5), 63–65.

Flynn, L.R. and Goldsmith, R.E. (1993) Application of the personal involvement. *Inventory in Marketing, Psychology and Marketing* 10 (4), 357–366.

Goldsmith, R.E. and Emmet, J. (1991) Measuring product category involvement: a multi-trait, multi-method study. *Journal of Business Research* 23 (4), 363–371.

Kapferer, J.-N. and Laurent, G. (1993) Further evidence on the consumer involvement profile: five antecedents of involvement. *Psychology and Marketing* 10 (4), 347–355.

King, C. and Morris, R. (1997) Wine tourism: a Western Australian case study. *Australian and New Zealand Wine Industry Journal* 12 (3), 246–249.

Laurent, G. and Kapferer, J.-N. (1985) Measuring consumer involvement profiles. *Journal of Marketing Research* 12 (February), 41–53.

Lockshin, L., Spawton, A. and Macintosh, G. (1997) Using product, brand and purchasing involvement for retail segmentation. *Journal of Retailing and Consumer Services* 4 (3), 171–183.

Lockshin, L., Pascale, Q. and Spawton, T. (2001) Segmentation by involvement or nationality for global retailing: a cross-national comparative study of wine shopping behaviours. *Journal of Wine Research* 12 (3), 223–236.

Lockshin, L., Jarvis, W., D'Hauteville, F. and Perrouty, J. (2006) Using simulations from discrete choice experiments to measure consumer sensitivity to brand, region, price, and awards in wine choice. *Food Quality and Preference* 17, 166–178.

Macionis, N. (1998) Wineries and tourism: perfect partners or dangerous liaisons? *Wine tourism – Perfect Partners: the First Australian Wine Tourism Conference*, Margaret River, Australia, Bureau of Tourism Research, Canberra.

Macionis, N. and Cambourne, B. (1998) Wine tourism – just what is it all about? *Australian and New Zealand Wine Industry Journal* 13 (1), 41–47.

Mitchell, R., Hall, C.M. and McIntosh, A. (2000) Wine tourism and consumer behaviour. In: Hall, M., Sharples, L., Cambourne, B. and Macionis, N. (eds) *Wine Tourism Around the World.* Butterworth-Heinemann, Oxford, UK, pp. 115–135.

Mittal, B. and Lee, M.-S. (1989) A causal model of consumer involvement. *Journal of Economic Psychology* 10, 363–389.

Ohanian, R. and Armen, T. (1992) Consumers' shopping effort and evaluation of store image attributes: the roles of purchasing involvement and recreational shopping interest. *Journal of Applied Business Research* 8 (6), 40–49.

O'Neill, M., Palmer, A. and Charters, S. (2002) Wine production as a service experience – the effects of service quality on wine sales. *Journal of Services Marketing* 16 (4), 342–362.

Quester, P. and Smart, J.G. (1998) The influence of consumption situation and product involvement over consumers' use of product attributes. *Journal of Consumer Marketing* 15 (3), 220–238.

Slama, M.E. and Armen, T. (1987) Validating the S-O-R Paradigm for consumer involvement with a convenience good. *Journal of the Academy of Marketing Science* 15 (1), 36–45.

Steenkamp, J.-B.E.M. and Wedel, M. (1991) Segmenting retail markets on store image using a consumer-based methodology. *Journal of Retailing* 67 (3), 300–320.

Tashakkori, A. and Teddlie, C. (1998) *Mixed Methodology: Combining Qualitative and Quantitative Approaches.* Sage Publishing, California.

Thach, L. and Olson, J. (2003) Customer service training in winery tasting rooms: perceptions of effectiveness by tasting room personnel. *International Wine Marketing Colloquium*, Adelaide, Australia, July, CD-ROM.

Tzimitra-Kalogianni, I., Papadaki-Klavdianou, A., Alexaki, A. and Tsakiridou, E. (1999) Wine routes in northern Greece: consumer perceptions. *British Food Journal* 101 (11), 884–892.

Winemakers Federation of Australia (2003) *Wine Tourism.* Winemakers Federation of Australia, Kent Town, SA, Australia (http://www.wfa.org.au/intro.htm).

Winemakers Federation of Australia (2005) *Wine Tourism.* Winemakers Federation of Australia, Kent Town, SA, Australia (http://www.wfa.org.au/intro.htm).

Zaichkowsky, J. (1985) Measuring the involvement construct. *Journal of Consumer Research* 12 (December), 341–352.

Part IV
The Cellar Door

11 Wine Tourists in South Africa: a Demand-side Study

Dimitri Tassiopoulos[1]* and Norbert Haydam[2]

[1]Centre of Excellence in Leisure and Tourism, Walter Sisulu University, Buffalo City, South Africa; [2]Cape Peninsula University of Technology, Cape Town, South Africa
*E-mail: dtassio@wsu.ac.za

Introduction

In 1994, the post-apartheid South African government undertook to make tourism one of the country's leading industries in the creation of employment and the generation of foreign income (Tassiopoulos et al., 2004). Studies undertaken by Cape Metropolitan Tourism (2000), WTTC (2002) and Grant Thornton Kessel Feinstein (2002) have indicated that the visitation of the wine routes by international and domestic tourists was ranked as the fourth (or, fifth in one winter study) most popular tourist attraction in South Africa.

Little empirical research, however, has been conducted in South Africa to determine the behavioural segmentation of wine tourists in the country from a demand-side perspective. Most demand-side information utilized by South African wineries in planning for wine tourism has been derived from various studies conducted outside the country, namely in Australia, New Zealand, Canada and the USA, amongst others.

Literature Review

The South African wine industry, according to Hands and Hughes (1997) and Bruwer (2003), is one of the oldest outside Europe, with some of the first vineyards having been planted and wine produced in the mid-17th century. South African vineyards are mostly found in the Western Cape Province, but other, smaller, production areas include the drier northern (Northern Cape Province) and central regions (Free State and Gauteng Provinces) of the country (Pienaar, 1999).

Considering that South Africa has been producing and marketing wines for a number of centuries, the development of South African wine tourism is, however, in its infancy and is not as well researched in South Africa as some more developed international wine tourism destinations. To date, most research undertaken by the South African wine industry has focused on product-driven research concerned with the wine production and marketing thereof, and little emphasis on demand-side wine tourism, although, according to Preston-Whyte (2000) and Nowers *et al.* (2002), the first South African wine route, namely, the Stellenbosch Wine Route, was established in 1971.

An understanding of wine tourism behaviour, according to Mitchell *et al.* (2000), is critical to understanding all marketing activity aimed at developing, promoting and selling wine tourism offerings. By understanding how wine tourists make decisions to purchase such offerings, it results in a better understanding of when marketers need to intervene in the decision-making processes of wine tourists. Appropriate interventions are thus used by wine tourism marketing organizations to persuade wine tourists to purchase a particular offering. Consequently, understanding wine tourism behaviour is crucial to the success of the activities of the wine tourism marketing organizations.

This type of research activity, according to Ali-Knight (2000), is important to the wine tourism industry as it assists in providing valuable insight into who the wine tourists are and what motivates them to visit a wine tourism destination and purchase wine offerings. It is underscored by Getz and Brown (2006) that various researchers have called for research into wine tourism preferences and behaviour. Some researchers, according to Charters and Ali-Knight (2002), have tried to give an overall impression of the wine tourist; however, there is no single, stereotypical 'wine tourist'. The wine tourist, according to Getz and Brown (2006), is seen to desire a broad travel experience that includes a regional bundle of benefits – wine tourism is rarely viewed as a discrete activity.

Although the existing South African research has provided considerable insight into wine tourism, much of it, however, has been from the wineries' (supply-side) perspective rather than from the tourists' (demand-side). South African winery owners and tourism operators have had difficulties in distinguishing the level of interest and commitment of the winery tourist to their region. The South African wine tourist is thus an important, but poorly understood and neglected, part of the wine and tourism market of South Africa. Some further issues are highlighted by Loubser (2004):

1. South African wine makers are seemingly more interested in cellar door sales, whereas wine tourists are looking for a total experience. There is seemingly a general lack of understanding about tourism, marketing and service requirements by winemakers.

2. National (and to a lesser degree local) tourism marketing authorities do not identify wine tourism as a marketing priority. The situation is compounded by a lack of integration between the various role players in the local and national tourism industry.

3. Wine tourism infrastructure is not appropriately developed, with wine tourism investments, at times, seemingly misdirected.

4. At local government level wine tourism is not considered a real priority, with local tourism development strategies being focused on other priorities.

5. An investment in wine tourism is often associated with taking a 'leap of faith' rather than the result of carefully formulated strategies based on thorough research. Research data are often not recorded; market research efforts are frequently fragmented and duplicated. Yet, large investments are being made to attract wine tourists to local wine cellars, estates and wine routes.

6. It is suggested that: 'In reality wine tourism is seen only as a secondary activity, although the industry often talks about it as if it is a main strategic approach to driving the wine industry into the future.'

7. Wine tourism is seen to be, at best, adding value to conditions already in place in the South African wine industry and it is not seen as a strategic business priority.

8. Unless wine tourism is integrated as part of the wine industry strategy that is market-focused, it will not be able to play its meaningful role in assisting the extraction of the maximum economic value of the South African wine industry and in building 'Brand South Africa'.

Against this background the aims of the research were, first, to develop a profile of South African wine tourists by shedding some light on demographic, trip-related and general wine tourism behaviour characteristics; secondly, to make recommendations to tourism policy planners and policy makers; and, lastly, to contribute toward the body of knowledge on wine tourism in South Africa.

Research Method

Study design

The study design was exploratory in nature and a quantitative approach was employed to provide an insight into the demographic, trip-related and general wine tourism behaviour characteristics of wine tourists in South Africa. This design was chosen because it provides a highly accurate picture of the phenomenon under study. The research was intended to be a demand-side pilot survey and was seen to be the initial phase of a longitudinal study, research funding permitting. It is crucial to emphasize that this study is the first of its kind in South Africa and hence it is exploratory in nature.

Sample

The target population covered four main areas, namely: (i) Stellenbosch (comprising of Stellenbosch Hills, Helderberg, Greater Simonsberg and Bottelary Hills wine districts); and (ii) the Paarl, Franschhoek and Constantia wine regions. In total, 34 wine farms and four Cape Winelands attractions were chosen randomly (primary sampling unit), from which wine tourist groups (final sampling unit) to the wine farms in the Cape Wine lands and Cape Town Wine lands and were intercepted using a systematic random sampling technique. In total, 165 wine tourists were interviewed, of whom 125 were interviews from Cape Winelands and 40 from various Cape Town Winelands attractions.

Almost 60% of the wine tourists were younger than 35 years and 58.8% were female. The majority of tourists were unmarried (57.6%) and they (84.3%) had no children under 16 years of age. Only 15.7% of tourists had children in their household and 58.0% of these people took their children with them on a wine route visit. About 50% had a professional occupation. The respondents were probed in regard to the years of formal education received: 53.3% had at least a tertiary qualification and an additional 18.2% had a post-graduate qualification, and 50.3% had a professional occupation.

In terms of place of origin, 9.1% of wine tourists were internationals who were mainly from Germany (53%) and the UK (26.7%). More than half of the respondents surveyed (56.0%) came from the Cape Town metropolitan area and 25.3% from within the Cape Wine lands. The rest of the Western Cape Province contributed another 5.3%. The major source of wine tourists outside the Western Cape was Gauteng Province, which contributes 9.3% domestic wine tourists to the South African wine tourism industry. The other provinces only make a marginal contribution toward wine tourism and require serious attention from the relevant tourism authorities if the wine tourism industry is to have a sustained growth.

Given a sample size of 165, the confidence interval for the study is ± 7.63% at a confidence level of 95%. In other words, there is a 95% certainty that the true percentage (p) of the population will deviate by ± 7.63% in each instance, where the confidence interval is calculated as p ± z.sp where sp = √p.(1-p)/n. As there is no/very little information about the population proportion, the value p can be conservatively estimated at 0.50 (Churchill and Iacobucci, 2002). The value of 0.5 makes provision for maximum possible variation in the population (Malhotra, 2002). Hence, for a 95% confidence level, the probability that the population mean will fall outside one end of the interval is 0.025 (0.05/2), which equates to a z value of 1.96. Replacing the values in the above-mentioned formula [1.96.√0.5. (1–0.5)/165] with the given sample size of 165, one arrives at p ± 0.763.

Research instrument

The research instrument used was a structured questionnaire adapted from a research instrument used for the 2000 Tasmanian winery visitor survey conducted by Tourism Tasmania, Australia (2000). A structured questionnaire was used because: (i) it has demonstrated the validity and reliability of measurement over the years; (ii) provides factual information on the subject under investigation; (iii) provides the respondents with an opportunity to give their own accounts of behaviour, attitudes and intentions; (iv) guarantees anonymity of response; and (v) reduces and eliminates differences in the way in which questions are asked and how they are presented. The questionnaire consisted of nine parts and included categories of questions on the following: (i) the origin of the tourist; (ii) wine route habits; (iii) trip-related criteria; (iv) information-related matters; (v) wine route development issues; (vi) expenditure issues; (vii) internet-related matters; and (viii) demographic criteria.

Procedure

The procedure adopted was that all interviews were conducted on a face-to-face basis. In all instances, permission was asked from the owner/manager or person in charge at the intercept point to conduct the respective interviews. Tourists were advised on: (i) their status as volunteers; (ii) their right to refuse to answer any question; (iii) the legal liabilities of their participation; (iv) confidentiality; and (v) the limitations of anonymity due to the nature of the study. A pilot study with ten wine tourists was undertaken. Thereafter, the wording of the original questionnaire was reviewed and modified accordingly. Ambiguity of meaning was eliminated; clarity, comprehensibility and simplicity of items were ensured.

The questionnaire was adjusted in order to accommodate cultural sensitivity of the participants. The fieldwork was conducted during the months of April to July 2003. Respondents surveyed in the non-wine key tourist attraction areas had to pass the screening question: 'Have you visited any wine farm in the Western Cape Province in the past 3 months?' before the interview commenced and these interviews were conducted from June to September 2003. Data analysis was done using the Survey System v8.1.

Findings

The demographic characteristics have already been presented under the sample details and they include age, gender, marital status, educational status, income and place of origin.

Buying and travel trip behaviour characteristics

The travel trip behavioural characteristics (or tripographics as per Hu and Morrison, 2002) of South African wine tourists are discussed in this section. These factors include aspects such as the accommodation preference of wine tourists, mode of transport used and the number of wine farms visited. In addition, the following buying characteristics were also considered: sources of information and general wine route habits. Areas for improvement and key aspects of the wine tourism destination are furthermore discussed below to shed some light on the key buying and general wine tourism behaviour patterns of the respondents.

Respondents were asked to provide an estimate of the total spending per travelling party. The study found the true mean per travelling party to be ZAR 564.00. In total, 53.1% of expenditure was spent on wine purchases, 26.1% on restaurants (including other providers of food) and 4.3% of all expenditure was on curios and gifts, with the international tourist, however, spending on average of 8.3% on curios and gifts.

The study probed the accommodation preference of the respondents during their visit to the wine route and found that the majority (73.2%) stated that they stayed at home and were considered to be day wine tourists for the purpose of this research. The study further showed that the most preferred forms of accommodation for those not staying at home were hotels (33%), staying with friends and relatives (31%) and bed and breakfast (11%). The study also suggests that the accommodation duration, on average, for wine tourists who stayed overnight is 7.0 days (true mean) on the Western Cape wine routes.

The findings indicate that more than three-quarters (75.8%) of respondents used their own vehicle for transportation to the wine tourism destination. Wine tourists also used the transport provided by friends and relatives (11.5%). The utilization of tour buses (6.1%) and minibuses (3%) were less popular choices.

The research showed that almost half (49.1%) of the respondents had visited one wine farm on a wine tourism excursion, a further 9.1% had visited two wine farms and 15.8% had visited three.

The study also determined how many wine routes tourists had visited in the previous 5 years, as well as in the previous 12 months. Positive responses showed that the Stellenbosch (91.9%), Franschhoek (64.9%) and Paarl (62.8%) Wine Routes had the highest incidence of visitations over the previous 5-year period. In the previous 12 months, the Stellenbosch Wine Route showed a high popularity, with 80.5% of respondents stating that they had visited this wine route.

The study shows that the mean for the total number of persons in a wine tourism travelling party was 2.1, with 90.9% of respondents stating that they did not travel with any children under the age of 16 years. Most respondents travelled with their family and friends (58.2%), and a further 20% indicated that they travelled with their spouse or partner. It was found that just over 93% of the wine tourists did not travel as part of an organized tour group. The study prompted the respondents for the main reasons why they had visited the wine route and the following key activities were given in descending order: sampling wines (64.2%), buying wines (52.7%), socializing with family/friends (30.3%), sightseeing (23.0%), eating at the winery restaurant (21.8%) and touring the winery (15.2%).

The study examined the issue of the information sources used by tourists with regard to making purchasing and non-purchasing decisions at wineries in the destination. Only three of the top seven information sources on wine tourism were published material – travel guides (17%), magazines (15.8%)

and travel publicity and brochures (11.5%). Recommendation from friends (38.8%) and previous experiences (35.8%) were the other four top sources of information. The Internet only recorded 2.4% as a source of information regarding wineries in the region, and this finding requires further research to determine the underlying reasons. The wine tourists indicated the following as hindrances to travelling to a wine tourism destination: (i) lack of adequate wine tourism information, trading hours and facilities available (48.6%); and (ii) signage (roads and maps) (36.1%).

Rating key aspects of the wine route

Respondents were asked to rate their satisfaction with regards to eight wine route variables. Two factors that were rated highly (extremely and reasonably satisfied) by the wine tourists were the quality of wines (79.3%) and the overall wine experience (75.4%). The following factors showed responses varying from satisfied to extremely satisfied: (i) road signs to the wineries; (ii) information regarding the wineries; (iii) staff service at the wineries; and (iv) winery promotional material about the wine route, but these indicate that there is considerable need for improvement in this regard. The results concerning the road signs to the wineries show that though there was a varied rating: it produced the highest dissatisfaction rating (reasonably and extremely unsatisfied, 16.6%) amongst respondents and requires the most urgent attention.

Areas for improvement

The study suggests that road signage and maps (29.8%), trading hours (17.3%) and improved service levels (14.4%) were the key areas of improvement recommended by wine tourists. When prompted on what aspect tourists found missing on the wine route excursion, the following emerged: (i) personal contact and socializing: namely, cellar tours (40.6%); meeting the winemaker (33.9%); wine events or festivals on the wine route (30.3%); historic tours (18.8%); meals and entertainment; and picnic facilities (29.1%); (ii) nature related: namely, nature trails and walks (23.6%); and (iii) accommodation: namely, overnight accommodation facilities (21.2%). The research highlighted the key strengths of wine tourism to be: nature related (37.4%), good-quality wine (37.4%) and the location of the wine farm (15.3%).

Discussion

It should be noted that because of the limited sample size, it is not possible to claim that the findings in this study are representative of the entire wine tourism population, as the sample size was determined in part by budget constraints, which inherently impeded the study. Furthermore, it should also be noted that the study was conducted during a period that can be considered to be the low season for the South African wine tourism industry, thus limiting the generalization of these wine tourism statistics. However, this study provides critical information for wine tourism development in South Africa. It is a ground-breaking study which could be explored further through longitudinal studies with larger samples.

The collection and interpretation of tourism statistics in South Africa can be described as being in its formative stage. There are no national data currently available to empirically quantify the number of foreign or domestic wine tourists. Surveys conducted amongst tourists have generally not included questions on the wine visitation habits of international and domestic tourists. There have been very few comprehensive empirical studies conducted on wine tourism statistics in South Africa. Various studies conducted by Grant Thornton Kessel Feinstein (2002), Bruwer (2003) and Demhardt (2003), amongst others, about the South African wine tourism sector, have used widely varying methodologies to determine the size of the South African wine tourism market, consequently making the determination of the actual wine tourism market size difficult.

For example: Bruwer (2003) estimates 5.151 million visitors to SA wineries in 2000 (approximately 14,511 visits per winery per annum). Demhardt (2003) estimates 478,000 'true visitors' to 76 Stellenbosch wineries in 1999 (approximately 1,672,000 individual visits that year). This study does not endeavour to provide a definitive study about the size of the South African wine tourism market. For the purposes of this research, the tourism figures provided Grant Thornton Kessel Feinstein (2002) were deemed the most reliable and were utilized to determine the size of the South African wine tourism market. It can therefore be deduced that the total market share for wine tourism in South Africa, during 2001, was about 425,600 wine tourists. This is derived as follows:

- The number of domestic wine tourists in 2001 was 210,000; in other words, in 2001 the Western Cape received 13% of total domestic tourists in South Africa, namely 4.2 million, of which about 5% indicated that they had visited wine attractions (as per Grant Thornton Kessel Feinstein, 2002).
- The Western Cape received 770,000 international tourists, of whom about 28% (the percentage of overseas tourists who had visited wine attractions, Grant Thornton Kessel Feinstein (2002)) were wine tourists, namely, 215,600.

The study further suggests that that the demographic profile of South African wine tourism are as follows: they are younger than 35 years of age (25–40 years old), most likely female and single, with no children and with a professional qualification. The results show that an overwhelming majority of wine tourists are day tourists (73%), with the majority (76%) using their own vehicle for transportation within the wine tourism destination. The findings in this regard have marketing and development implications for wine tourism in South Africa.

The South African wine tourism, as graphically illustrated in Fig. 11.1, can be structured on the basis of overnight *vs.* day-trips and mode of transport. As illustrated in Fig. 11.1, the South African wine tourism market is heavily reliant on day-trip visits (78%), of which the majority (94%) are conducted on a fully inclusive travel (FIT) basis. The majority of overnight visitors either stay at hotels (33%) or visit friends and relatives (VFR) (31%).

Wine tourists, it can be deduced, clearly know what they want: they seek to purchase quality wines and want an overall wine experience. To this end, they demand that information about the wineries, the quality of service at the cellar door, winery promotional material and the road signage within wine tourism destinations be given attention so that they can derive maximum value from their wine tourism experience. The research also found that socializing with friends and relatives was an important third dimension of the wine tourism experience and was the most popular reason for those tourists who visited four or more wine farms in a wine tourism excursion. Overall, the demographic and trip-related wine tourism behaviour results suggest remarkable similarity with the results of the Tourism Tasmania (2000) and South Australian Tourism Commission (2003) studies.

Implications for Wine Tourism

It is crucial that the tourism destination management organizations and tourism marketing authorities: (i) accurately segment South African wine tourism destinations, especially the less well-known ones, as destinations featuring the diversity of experiences available to the wine tourism target market; and (ii) position less well-known wine regions as holiday destinations which require more than one day to be experienced.

Further, there is a need to develop and promote wine tourism offerings which package wine visits with other top attractions and activities around the country. There is also a need to encourage the packaging of wine estate visitations with a diversity of tourist experiences available within the destinations.

In an increasingly competitive global wine tourism market, destination

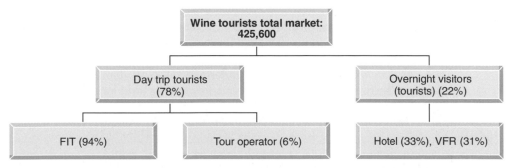

Fig. 11.1. South African wine tourism market structure; total market summary, 2001.

management organizations and tourism marketing authorities need to clearly define the needs, wants and characteristics of the wine tourism sector with accurate, relevant and up-to-date information concerning their target markets. In turn, this will lead to effective planning, management and marketing strategies for wine tourism destinations.

The study indicates, albeit not directly, the importance of the wine tourism experience delivered by winery and cellar door staff (owners and employees). It is crucial that such winery staff is adequately trained in order to ensure that they deliver the wine tourism experience that the wine tourist expects.

The South African tourism authorities have a number of major tasks to undertake in encouraging the development of wine tourism:

1. Innovative promotional strategies should be developed in partnership with provincial tourism authorities who provide an important multiplier for information dissemination, marketing and promotion and, especially, innovative international promotion of South African wine tourism.

2. Public tourism infrastructure needs, especially in the smaller wine producing areas, must be expanded to include tourist information and interpretive centres. These can be managed in a businesslike manner to cover ongoing running costs. They play an important role in attempts to gain the inclusion of wine regions into tourism wholesalers' itineraries.

3. Regional planning in wine growing areas, with particular focus on the smaller wine producing areas, can foster the development of regional identity, assist in growing businesses in both the wine and tourism industries and facilitate networking between these and individual providers of services.

4. The education and training of regional tourism operators and wine tourism employees is required.

5. The facilitation and promotion of cooperative ventures in the tourism and wine industries is required in order to improve the marketing performance of both sectors. A coordinated, cooperative and collaborative approach between the tourism and wine industries is essential to the efficient development of wine tourism.

6. There are substantial benefits from the development of innovative wine tourism publications, whereby a regional audit of tourism attractions and services can draw together wine experiences and the history and culture of the wine region.

7. There is a lack of appropriate market research into wine tourism in South Africa, and this needs to be rectified. There is a need to conduct longitudinal tracking studies of wine tourists. This has implications for the need to develop South African research capacity to undertake ongoing demand-and supply-side wine tourism research; to this end key public and private sector role players need to play a central role in resourcing such an endeavour for the long-term growth and sustainability of the South African wine tourism industry.

8. Wine regions should consider embarking on customer relationship programmes with different target groups, given the high incidence of recommendation from friends (38.8%) and that of previous experiences (35.8%).

The study thus recommends that more research be executed, i.e. the gathering of data is an integral part of the strategic marketing process. The strategic wine tourism marketing research plan (which supplements the strategic marketing plan) should be activated and the profile of the wine tourist should be tracked on a year-round basis; product and pricing research is also called for. This will assist with the target marketing and positioning of the South African wine tourism region. The wine tourism market is seen of growing importance as an emerging market within South Africa.

A strong relationship thus exists between wine and the decision to purchase wine tourism offerings and this renders it crucial that the tourism authorities clearly understand the needs and expectations of the wine tourist if they are to implement successful niche marketing strategies. Policies and strategies, according to Nowers *et al.* (2002), should be formulated toward the development of greater linkages between the wine and tourism industries and towards improvement in the ability to promote the regions so as to attract investment and encourage employment. Wine tourism is a rural-based industry that has the potential to contribute and serve as a strong base for the development of a healthy rural economy in South Africa.

References

Ali-Knight, J. (2000) In search of the grape: towards building a motivational framework for international wine tourists to Australia. In: Evans, N., Cong, P., Robinson, M., Sharpley, R. and Swarbrooke, J. (eds) *Motivations, Behaviour and Tourist Types.* Centre for Travel and Tourism (in association with Business Education Publishers Ltd., Sunderland, UK).

Bruwer, J. (2003) South African wine routes: some perspectives on the wine tourism industry's structural dimensions and wine tourism product. *Tourism Management* 24, 423–425.

Cape Metropolitan Tourism (2000) *Discover Cape Town Secret Season: Visitor Research Results,* May to September (winter).

Charters, S. and Ali-Knight, J. (2002) Who is the wine tourist? *Tourism Management* 23, 311–319.

Churchill, G.A. and Iacobucci, D. (2002) *Marketing Research – Methodological Foundations,* 8th edn. Harcourt College, Orlando, Florida.

Demhardt, I.M. (2003) Wine tourism at the 'Fairest Cape': post-apartheid trends in the Western Cape Province and Stellenbosch (South Africa). *Journal of Travel and Tourism Marketing* 14 (3/4), 113–130.

Getz, D. and Brown, G. (2006) Critical success factors for wine tourism regions: a demand analysis. *Tourism Management* 27, 146–158.

Grant Thornton Kessel Feinstein (2002) *Western Cape Tourism Trends.* Western Cape Tourism Board, Cape Town, South Africa.

Hands, P. and Hughes, D. (1997) *Wines and Brandies of the Cape of Good Hope: the Definitive Guide of the South African Wine Industry.* Stephen Collins, Somerset West, South Africa.

Hu, B. and Morrison, A.M. (2002) Tripography: can destination use patterns enhance understanding of the VFR market? *Journal of Vacation Marketing* 8 (3), 201–220.

Loubser, S.S. (2004) The role of wine tourism in establishing a successful South African wine industry, *Proceedings of the 2004 International Wine Tourism Conference*, Margaret River, Australia, 2–5 May.

Malhotra, N.K. (2002) *Basic Marketing Research – Applications to Contemporary Issues.* Prentice Hall, Upper Saddle River, New York.

Mitchell, R., Hall, C.M. and McIntosh, A. (2000) Wine tourism and consumer behaviour. In: Hall, C.M., Sharples, L. Cambourne, B. and Macionis, N. (eds) *Wine Tourism Around the World: Development, Management and Markets.* Butterworth Heinemann, Oxford, UK.

Nowers, R., De Villiers, E. and Myburgh, A. (2002) Agricultural theme routes as a diversification strategy: the Western Cape wine routes case-study. *Agrekon*, 41 (2) (June), 195–209.

Pienaar, J. (1999) *Introduction to Wine Growing Regions of South Africa.* VINPRO, Stellenbosch, South Africa.

Preston-Whyte, R. (2000) Wine routes in South Africa. In: Hall, C.M., Sharples, L. Cambourne, B. and Macionis, N. (eds) *Wine Tourism Around the World: Development, Management and Markets.* Butterworth Heinemann, Oxford, UK.

South Australian Tourism Commission (2003) *Cellar Door Market Research.* Adelaide, Australia.

Tassiopoulos, D., Nuntsu, N. and Haydam, N. (2004) Wine tourism in South Africa: a demographic and psychographic study. *Journal of Wine Research* 15 (1), 51–64.

Tourism Tasmania (2000) *Wine Survey: 2000.* Hobart, Australia.

WTTC (2002) South Africa: the Impact of Travel and Tourism on Jobs and the Economy. UK: World Travel and Tourism Council.

12 Younger Wine Tourists: a Study of Generational Differences in the Cellar Door Experience

STEVE CHARTERS[1]* AND JOANNA FOUNTAIN[2]

[1]*School of Marketing, Tourism and Leisure, Edith Cowan University, Western Australia;* [2]*Environment, Society and Design Division, Lincoln University, New Zealand*
E-mail: s.charters@ecu.edu.au

Introduction

The importance, for wineries, of visitation to cellar doors is recognized by both the tourism and wine industries (O'Neill and Charters, 2000). The quality of cellar door service plays a central role in the tourist's experience of a winery, the emotional attachments a tourist develops for a brand and, by implication, the future purchase intentions of that tourist (Dodd and Bigotte, 1997; Nixon, 1999; Charters and O'Neill, 2001).

Understanding cellar door expectations and experiences from the point of view of the wine tourist is essential to allow wineries to establish this loyalty (O'Neill and Charters, 2000). This chapter reports on research examining the perceptions and experiences of visitors to winery cellar doors in one wine region of Western Australia. It particularly focused on the perspective of younger wine tourists who, for current purposes, are defined as those that are members of the Generation X and Generation Y cohorts, and seeks to compare their experience and expectations of winery cellar doors with those of older wine tourists.

Literature Review

A number of articles have appeared over the past decade exploring the issue of visitor satisfaction with the service quality experienced at the cellar door (Morris and King, 1997; Ali-Knight and Charters, 2001). To date, however, very little research has explored the significance of age or generational differences of the wine tourist as a factor in the service quality experienced at the winery cellar door (exceptions include Mitchell, 2002; Treloar, 2002). While Mitchell's (2002) study found no significant generational differences in satisfaction with the winery experience, glimpses of age-related factors affecting cellar door experience have, at times, emerged from other more general investigations of the characteristics and experiences of wine tourists.

Dodd and Bigotte (1997) found evidence that older people were generally less critical of their winery experience than younger visitors, and that younger wine tourists rated service quality as a more important factor in determining their satisfaction with the winery visit than did their older counterparts. What has not been investigated, however, is whether the lower satisfaction of younger wine tourists was due to differing priorities and expectations at the cellar door or to differential experiences of service quality at the winery. This is particularly significant given the aging Baby Boomer generation and the growing disposable income of their offspring. In this context, there is a need to foster an interest in wine amongst Generation X and Generation Y in order to ensure the long-term survival of the wine industry (Beverland, 2001; Howard and Stonier, 2001; Bruwer, 2002; Mitchell, 2002; Treloar, 2002).

There is much disagreement about the start and end dates of Generation X, although the definition used in this context of people born in the period 1964–1978 is a widely accepted definition (King, 2001). Generation Y are defined as those born since 1979, meaning that at the time of this research (2004), the cohort of Generation X were aged between 25 and 40, while those in Generation Y were 24 and below. In this paper, these two age groups are referred to as 'younger wine tourists', and their experiences are compared with the 'older wine tourists', who were aged between 44 and 65 (and therefore members of the Baby Boomer and Mature generations).

It is recognized that the characteristics of Generation X are quite difficult to pinpoint (Beverland, 2001); however, some attempts have been made to identify their key characteristics. First, they are generally viewed as a generation marked by an independent spirit (King, 2001; Martin and Tulgan, 2001). They are a sceptical and non-committal generation, meaning that establishing brand loyalty with them is difficult (King, 2001). One defining factor of Generation X is their demand for recognition of their individual needs as consumers (Beverland, 2001). For this reason, experiencing the personalized service of a winery cellar door is a significant factor in the wine purchasing process, as are recommendations of family and friends (Howard and Stonier, 2001).

There is evidence also that Generation X wine tourists will be more likely to develop a relationship with, and brand loyalty to, a winery with well-trained and knowledgeable staff (Treloar, 2002). While Generation X are yet to register as significant consumers of wine, there is evidence that this cohort is beginning to recognize the appeal of the wine tourism experience and participate in wine tourism activities, particularly wine events and festivals, in greater numbers (Nixon, 1999; Houghton, 2001; Mitchell, 2002). To date, Generation Y, also referred to as the Echo-boomers or Millennium Generation, has been little studied in marketing or academic research, although this is beginning to change (Martin and Tulgan, 2001; Sheahan, 2005). The research that has been completed reveals that Generation Y are a confident cohort; comfortable with evolving technologies, self-reliant, ambitious, tolerant of others and eager for a challenge (King, 2001; Martin and Tulgan, 2001). They also expect validation from others, however, suggesting that the self-confidence mentioned above may not as yet be very robust (Sheahan, 2005). Generation Y have been raised to be demanding; they want 'instant gratification' and enjoy getting 'something for nothing', frequently seeing little connection between effort and results. They seek stimulation in both their work and leisure environments by way of multi-sensory experiences, entertainment, fun and variety (Sheahan, 2005). Their openness to change may provide an important opportunity and challenge to wine marketers and cellar door operators to be able to identify products and experiences which appeal to these young adults. Generation Y are currently irregular wine drinkers as, according to one report, 'when young adults begin drinking, wine doesn't factor into the equation at all' (Scalera, 2002, p. 2). This group's early experience of alcohol gradually begins with experimenting with alcoholic beverages in pubs, clubs and bars where the pressure to try wine is far less than it is to consume beer and spirits (Scalera, 2002; Treloar, 2004).

Nevertheless Treloar (2004) found that a significant proportion of Generation Y respondents showed an interest in wine tourism. More than half of his respondents had visited a winery at least once in the past and 60% of his sample viewed winery visitations as an appealing activity (Treloar, 2004, p. 137), suggesting a need for further research into this sector of the market.

Research Method

Quantitative studies exploring perceptions of cellar door service have been carried out in other regions using exit questionnaires (Charters and O'Neill, 2000; O'Neill and Charters, 2000), but in this instance it was felt a qualitative approach could yield a different perspective and shed new light on the cellar door experience. To this end, the researchers chose to make use of participant observers, fulfilling roles close to that of 'mystery shoppers', who would experience service at the cellar door and then report on it via a brief questionnaire, followed by input into a focus group discussion.

Mystery shopping is a form of covert participant observation in which researchers take on the role of customers or potential customers in order to 'monitor the processes and procedures used in the delivery of a service' (Wilson, 1998, p. 148). The potential of observational methods for investigating service provision is increasingly acknowledged (Grove and Fisk, 1992; Wilson, 1998), and mystery shopping has been used extensively in the services industry to investigate service quality. However, it has rarely been used in academic research on tourism to date (see Hudson *et al.*, 2001).

This research was conducted at cellar doors in the Swan Valley region of Western Australia. The Swan Valley is a small wine producing region about 40 minutes drive east of Perth. It has a long history of wine production, but is a hot region and in recent years its importance to Western Australian wine production has been eclipsed by Margaret River. Nevertheless, its proximity to Perth makes it a popular destination for day tourists and a number of organized visits to the region are offered by tourism operators.

To investigate cellar door service in the Swan Valley, 24 mystery shoppers were sent out in four groups. Each group consisted of three generationally defined pairs (one pair each of 'older wine tourists', Generation X and Generation Y). The pairs in each group made their visit to the winery at about the same time, thereby receiving the same temporal experience. Additional variables other than age that might influence the experiences of the participants were controlled as much as possible in the mystery shopping exercise, including travel party size and gender. The groups visited two wineries each; four wineries were visited in all. Consequently, there was a total of eight visits, with each winery being visited by 12 mystery shoppers (two groups of six). The mystery shoppers were given a general perspective on the study, but were not advised that age-related issues were important. They were advised to treat their visit as a normal, pleasurable exercise. On leaving the cellar door, each mystery shopper completed a short questionnaire about their visit.

While the mystery shopping exercise is useful for exploring the provision of service at the cellar door, this research set out to investigate the whole process of cellar door service, including both the service received by the mystery shoppers and their expectations of the cellar door experience. In order to explore the demand side of the service equation, the mystery shoppers were debriefed in a focus group setting. These focus groups discussed the cellar door experience in more detail, particularly the relationship between the prior expectations of the participants and their subsequent experiences.

Findings

Differences in expectations

There appeared to be some variation in the expectation that each generational group had of the cellar door experience. Critically, the younger wine tourists (Generations X and Y) appeared to place more emphasis on enjoying the entire experience, rather than explicitly focusing on the wine. Typifying this viewpoint, one Generation Y respondent wrote on his questionnaire that '[w]hen wine tasting with friends – having a good time ... is more important than tasting the wine'. During focus group discussions, this informant stated that while he didn't like the wines at one winery: 'I liked the atmosphere and would be keen to return to the winery with friends because it was not too "posh" or intimidating.' This perspective was mirrored on a number of occasions by the Generation Y and Generation X informants.

There was evidence also that the younger informants expected to interact with the staff at the cellar door more than their older counterparts. For these visitors it was important that the process involved a personalized service – perhaps even a relationship – rather than merely exchanging information or goods. This compared with the comments of the older visitors, who appeared to concentrate much more closely on their response to the wine tasted. A good example of this distinction focused on attitudes to personal space within the environment of the cellar door. One older visitor commented: 'Once they had given you the wine to taste they would actually stand back and allow you [to try it] … I liked that attitude of standing back, and allowing us to actually speak to each other, and also just taste the wine' (female, Baby Boomer).

This view was echoed explicitly by other older informants at different encounters. Yet a Generation X informant wrote of the same cellar door that she felt that the staff 'stood back and were not keen to serve'; and another, Generation Y informant, commented disapprovingly that the staff stood a long way away from them. The focus of younger visitors on the service experienced rather than on the wine tasted appeared to produce varying expectations of the organization of the cellar door encounter. Older visitors apparently preferred a more structured, 'systematic' approach to the tasting process. One Mature participant expressed satisfaction that the staff member serving her followed a set approach 'rigorously'.

This expectation contrasted with the preference of younger visitors who searched for a more flexible, rather than structured, experience. Younger wine visitors seemed to place a lot of emphasis on being asked their needs in the service experience and having those needs met. This seemed especially true of the Generation X group. For example, a Generation X informant enjoyed his winery visit, but felt more interest could have been shown in his needs, commenting: 'I just feel that … would be part of the service … [They should] try and find what the customer … would like. And then you could … direct them towards something.' Such comments were non-existent from the older visitors, but frequent amongst younger wine tourists, with a Generation X female expressing a similar opinion about service at a different winery: 'It was very *professional,* but I really didn't find that the chap had a lot of interest in what my needs were, what wines I like tasting, what my experience was of the previous wines I'd liked. [There was] no recommendation about anything else.'

Differences in treatment

One general point worth recording about the informants' experience at the cellar door is that the older visitors were generally far more satisfied with the experience than were the younger informants. Only in one out of the eight visits did a single older visitor appear dissatisfied with the experience. The younger generational groups were less sanguine. It seems possible that, in fact, the Generation X informants were marginally less satisfied with the experience than those from Generation Y.

In three out of the eight cellar door encounters, there was some suggestion that cellar door staff were inclined to treat younger visitors less positively than older ones; in two cases, the pairs from Generation X and Y were treated similarly, while in the other case it was the Generation Y mystery shoppers that were alone in being less well treated. In this latter example, all three pairs felt generally welcomed at the winery in question.

However, the cellar door staff appeared to discriminate against the Generation Y visitors in terms of the wines they were offered to taste. The winery has a flagship red wine (referred to here as 'the Icon'), which retails at around Aus$30 and is not generally available for tasting at the cellar door. However, on the afternoon of this visit, the wine could be tasted and was offered to both the older couple and Generation X pair, who commented approvingly on it. One of the Generation Y pair, who had explicitly expressed a preference for red wine, was interested in the Icon and noted the positive response of a Generation X female, so asked about the wine. The staff member, who had served the wine to the other two pairs, casually said 'oh, that's the Icon', but did not offer a sample to the Generation Y pair, who left without trying it.

It is worth noting that any instances of preferential treatment only seemed to occur when the cellar door was not busy. It is possible that preferential treatment to older visitors, where it exists, can only be the product of a cellar door with the luxury of time to make choices about how its visitors are handled. This observation, however, is based on a small sample; no definitive conclusions regarding differential treatment can be made and further research is required to investigate this issue.

Implications for Wine Tourism

It has previously been suggested that wine tourists are not a culturally homogeneous body (Mitchell *et al.*, 2000; Charters and Ali-Knight, 2002). This exploratory research implies that they are not generationally homogeneous either, having varying expectations of the cellar door encounter. The findings suggest that the older visitors place a greater emphasis on the product (shown also in their preference for 'space' in which to taste), while younger visitors (Generation X and Y) give more importance to the overall experience and the service they receive and can be explicit that the quality of the wine is secondary to them.

This suggests that Generations X and Y visitors require a different focus from those who staff the cellar door. They seem to say 'I want them to be interested in me', seeking a flexible, empathetic service rather than a transactional, structured one. Such an approach reflects the suggestion that Generation X require recognition of their individual needs as consumers, combined with a preference for the relaxed and the informal (Beverland, 2001). The more 'refined' cellar door may actually be off-putting to them, even if it is preferred by the older visitors. It is worth noting in this instance that Generation Y visitors seem especially ill at ease in the cellar door environment, perhaps belying the suggestion that they are a 'confident' and 'self-reliant' group (Martin and Tulgan, 2001). Younger visitors seem generally a bit more critical of cellar door service than older visitors, which may be especially true of the Generation X group, perhaps confirming their alleged 'scepticism' (King, 2001). It is, however, worth asking if older wine tourists are happier with the experience because they are better treated or because they come with different expectations of the encounter which are more easily fulfilled. It is natural to expect a winery to focus on the quality of the wine, rather than on the quality of the experience, and in doing so they may be overlooking the demands of younger wine tourists.

Nevertheless, it also seems that there may be instances when cellar door staff give preferential treatment to older visitors, a fact which may be noted by members of Generations X and Y. This occurred at three different wineries, but was not replicated in the second visit to any of those wineries. If this is correct, then two conclusions may be drawn from this. One is that there may be a culture of bias in some wineries, which is less apparent when the winery is busy. The other interpretation is that such preferential treatment is not built into the winery's culture, but is practised by individual members or teams of cellar door staff. In either case, however, it is the winery that has overall responsibility for such behaviour.

These issues are crucial for wineries providing a cellar door service. The future importance of Generation X as a customer base has been noted (Beverland, 2001; Howard and Stonier, 2001; Bruwer, 2002). Nevertheless, there appears to be some evidence that cellar door managers' 'ideal' customer is an older, professional male (Charters and O'Neill, 2000), a notion that supports only short- or medium-term brand development. An environment in which younger visitors feel at ease and which they leave satisfied is crucial to developing long-term brand loyalty for the business. Just as important to brand loyalty is ensuring that they give no appearance of preference for one group of customers over another.

It is necessary to observe that this research has clear limitations. It took place only in one small Australian wine region, it was exploratory in nature and, crucially, the gender balance of the Generation X and Y mystery shoppers was uneven. The study was too small-scale to allow an analysis of gender differences or other differentiating characteristics in varying generational responses to the cellar door experience, which is an issue that needs to be addressed in further research.

References

Ali-Knight, J. and Charters, S. (2001) The winery as educator: do wineries provide what the wine tourist needs? *Australian and New Zealand Wine Industry Journal* 16, 79–86.

Beverland, M. (2001) Generation X and wine consumption. *Wine Industry Journal* 16, 91–96.

Bruwer, J. (2002) Marketing wine to Generation X consumers through the cellar door. *The Australian and New Zealand Grapegrower and Winemaker*, December, (http://www.grapeandwine.com.au/dec02/07.htm, accessed 28 November 2004).

Charters, S. and Ali-Knight, J. (2002) Who is the wine tourist? *Tourism Management* 23, 311–319.

Charters, S. and O'Neill, M. (2000) Delighting the customer – how good is the cellar door experience? *Australian and New Zealand Wine Industry Journal: International Wine Marketing Supplement* 1, 11–16.

Charters, S. and O'Neill, M. (2001) Service quality at the cellar door: a comparison between regions. *International Journal of Wine Marketing* 13, 7–17.

Dodd, T. and Bigotte, V. (1997) Perceptual differences among visitor groups to wineries. *Journal of Travel Research* 35, 46–51.

Grove, S. and Fisk, R. (1992) Observational data collection methods for services marketing: an overview. *Journal of the Academy of Marketing Services* 20, 217–224.

Houghton, M. (2001) The propensity of wine festivals to encourage subsequent winery visitation. *International Journal of Wine Marketing* 13, 32–52.

Howard, R. and Stonier, J. (2001) Marketing wine to Generation X: the way ahead. *The Australian Grapegrower and Winemaker*, December, 69–71.

Hudson, S., Snaith, T., Miller, G. and Hudson, P. (2001) Distribution channels in the travel industry: Using mystery shoppers to understand the influence of travel agency recommendations. *Journal of Travel Research* 40, 148–154.

King, D. (2001) *Defining a Generation: Tips for Uniting our Multi-generational Workforce* (http://www.careerfirm.com/index.html, accessed 12 January 2004).

Martin, C. and Tulgan, B. (2001) *Managing Generation Y: Global Citizens Born in the Late Seventies and Early Eighties.* HRD Press, Amherst, Massachusetts.

Mitchell, R. (2002) The generation game: Generation X and baby boomer wine tourism. *Proceedings of the New Zealand Tourism and Hospitality Research Conference*, Rotorua, New Zealand, 3–5 December 2002, pp. 115–127.

Mitchell, R., Hall, M. and McIntosh, A. (2000) Wine tourism and consumer behaviour. In: Hall, M., Sharples, L., Cambourne, B., Macionis, N., Mitchell, R. and Johnson, G. (eds) *Wine Tourism Around the World: Development, Management and Markets.* Elsevier Science, Oxford, UK, pp. 115–135.

Morris, R. and King, C. (1997) Cooperative marketing for small business growth and regional economic development: a case study in wine tourism. *Proceedings of the USABE Annual National Conference – Entrepreneurship: the Engine of Global Economic Development*, San Francisco (http://www.usasbe.org /knowledge/proceedings/1997/index.asp, accessed 4 December 2003).

Nixon, B. (1999) The changing face of the winery tourist. *Proceedings of Wine Tourism: Perfect Partners – Australian Wine Tourism Conference*, Margaret River, May 1998, pp. 209–217.

O'Neill, M. and Charters, S. (2000) Service quality at the cellar door: implications for Western Australia's developing wine tourism industry. *Managing Service Quality* 10, 112–123.

Scalera, B. (2002) *New Ideas for a New Generation* (http://www.winexwired.com/archives/harpers2.htm, accessed 6 January 2004).

Sheahan, P. (2005) *Generation Y: Thriving and Surviving with Generation Y at Work.* Hardie Grant Books, South Yarra, Australia.

Treloar, P. (2002). An investigation into the significance of relationship marketing on the young winery tourist. *Proceedings of the New Zealand Tourism and Hospitality Research Conference*, Rotorua, New Zealand, 3–5 December 2002, pp. 128–185.

Treloar, P. (2004) *The youth market, wine and wine tourism: a behavioural context for wine tourism potential.* Masters Thesis, University of Otago, Dunedin, New Zealand.

Wilson, A. (1998) The use of mystery shopping in the measurement of service delivery. *The Service Industries Journal* 18, 148–163.

13 Survey Timing and Visitor Perceptions of Cellar Door Quality

MARTIN A. O'NEILL[1]* AND STEVE CHARTERS[2]

[1]*Department of Nutrition and Food Science, Auburn University, Alabama 36830, USA;* [2]*School of Marketing, Tourism and Leisure, Edith Cowan University, Perth, WA 6027, Australia*
*E-mail: oneilm@auburn.edu

Introduction

While much has changed on the tourism landscape over recent years, there continues to be one constant: service quality remains a complex construct to both conceptualize and measure. The measurement of service quality has been the focus for a considerable volume of published literature over the past two decades. Particular attention has focused on the following: (i) the components of service quality and its underlying factor structure (Parasuraman *et al.*, 1988); (ii) the relationship between service quality and customer satisfaction (Oliver, 1997); (iii) the processes by which consumers evaluate service quality (Bolton and Drew, 1991; Boulding *et al.*, 1993); (iv) the role of expectations in evaluation (Zeithaml *et al.*, 1993); and (v) the effects of service quality on repurchase intention and profitability (Rust *et al.*, 1999).

Not surprisingly, the tourism sector, which is typically very rich in critical service encounters, has been an extensive user of instruments to measure visitors' perceptions of service quality (for wine tourism-related research see Dodd and Bigotte, 1997; Charters and O'Neill, 2000, 2001). A number of conclusions have been drawn about the visitor's experience (see below). However, most surveys have tended to be administered during or immediately after taking part in a tourism activity. This paper focuses on a previously unexplored aspect of the measurement of service quality: the effects of survey timing on visitor measures of service quality at the cellar door.

Literature Review

Quality in wine tourism

It is now a well-accepted fact that the quality of service received by a visitor during their travels is just as important, if not more important, than the quality of other elements of the tourism experience. This is particularly relevant within the context of wine tourism. First, it is loyalty to the brand and not the location that the winery is ultimately trying to achieve. As such, the service received during the cellar door experience should serve to reinforce the customer's perception of the experience and the brand over the longer term.

Secondly, there is the issue of product (wine) as against service – with evidence that elements of the latter are of more importance to the visitor than the former (Charters and O'Neill, 2000). The fact that visitors are always chasing value-adding experiences continues to highlight the importance of the quality issue for both government and private sector developers alike.

In an attempt to achieve sustained competitive advantage, tourism organizations of all types have been investing in a range of quality improvement strategies best described as belonging to the Total Quality Management (TQM) movement. This approach stresses the fact that quality should be present throughout the chain of supply and places great emphasis on the quality efforts of 'everyone' and 'everything' that influences the end product, namely the visitor experience. To this end, the TQM approach espouses a number of clear principles, best represented in Fig. 13.1.

At its core is a belief that quality is all about satisfying the customer. As such, all company efforts must be tailored to both understanding and satisfying every customer requirement. This approach takes account of the

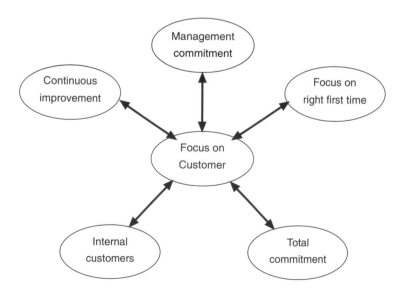

Fig. 13.1. Elements in a total quality management approach.

complicating characteristic nature of the service component of the typical tourism experience and stresses that equal effort should be applied to ensuring quality delivery of both tangible and intangible aspects of the visitor's experience. Those espousing a TQM approach go to considerable lengths to invest in their people. A very good example of this principle relates to the quality efforts of the winemaker not being best represented at the cellar door by front-line personnel who have little or no understanding/experience of the vinification or viticultural process.

The TQM approach also takes the view that quality delivery is a continuous journey and one that can only continue based upon informed decision making. To support this, a systematic approach to quality measurement is needed. Consequently, tourism organizations have been investing heavily in the development of an operational means of evaluating their product and/or service delivery systems (Hudson, 1998). This form of consumer research has the dual purpose of not only highlighting how the organization is performing in the eyes of its customers, but also allows for a better use of company resources through more targeted quality improvement initiatives. The central tenet of any such approach is the study of consumer perceptions of service quality or that process by which customers select, categorize and interpret purchase- and non-purchase-related stimuli which, in turn, may lead to either first-time, repeat or transferred patronage. Clearly, sustained and continuous quality improvement is not possible without some indication of quality performance.

A number of pieces of research have been carried out at the cellar door, examining the visitor's experience there. These include the importance of an educational component to the process and the visitor's desire to gain knowledge (Ali-Knight and Charters, 2000), the fact that the assurance and empathy the tourist gains from the encounter are crucial (Charters and O'Neill, 2000) and that older people tend to be more accepting of the service than those who are younger (Dodd and Bigotte, 1997). It has been suggested that tourists enjoy the chance to 'meet the maker' (Cambourne and Macionis, 2000). Generally, it seems, most visitors are positive about the experience (Morris and King, 1998; Charters and O'Neill, 2000).

The cellar door may be an excellent showcase for smaller producers or less well-known wine regions to display their products. In the mid-1990s, for instance, it was noted that over a 3-year period cellar door visits in the Canberra wine region had doubled (Cambourne, 1998). As a consequence cellar door managers have been advised to ensure that staff are alert to the needs of their visitors, especially those from different generational backgrounds (Howard and Stonier, 2002). Indeed, it has been suggested that the cellar door may be one of the best ways for marketing wine to Generation X (Bruwer, 2002). Critically, however, the cellar door must be used not merely to make money through immediate sales, but also as a means of developing a relationship with customers and building brand equity (O'Neill and Charters, 2000).

The influence of time upon cellar door perceptions

While much research has been reported which seeks to understand the processes by which consumer expectations of service quality are formed (Kahneman and Miller, 1986; Zeithaml *et al.*, 1993), relatively little attention has been devoted to an understanding of how perceptions are formed and sustained (Boulding *et al.*, 1993). Similarly, it has been claimed that while any sample's level of expectations may show a high degree of uniformity within the sample, perceptions are more likely to show greater levels of variability (Cronin and Taylor, 1994).

The subject is an important one to research, as it can be argued that wine tourist's repurchase intentions are influenced by their perceptions at the time of potential revisitation, rather than by those which prevail immediately following or during consumption of a tourism service. It follows that the preoccupation of many organizations with measuring perceptions during or immediately following service consumption may have little relevance to service quality perceptions which are important in subsequently forming future repurchase intentions, particularly with respect to the purchase of wine from a retail outlet offering many potentially competitive substitutes.

The literature presents a number of explanations as to why perceptions might change. One such explanation relates to the influence of time itself and the fact that perceptions of an event or service encounter are likely to become distorted over time as a result of memory selectivity and memory retention. (Asch, 1946; Abercrombie, 1967; Boulding *et al.*, 1999). Thus, an intercept questionnaire administered during or immediately following a service encounter – say at the cellar door – may give one indicator of perception. Through a process of selective perception, these may represent only a proportion of the stimuli that an individual is exposed to during a service encounter (Katz, 1968). Through a further process of selectivity, only a proportion of these will be retained intact.

A further explanation for changes in perceptions that can occur over time is founded in dissonance theory. Dissonance theory suggests that where there were dissonant elements arising from the original wine tourism experience (the negative aspects of the service consumed and the positive elements of the alternatives not consumed) there would, post-visit, be tension in the visitor's mind (Festinger, 1957; Oliver, 1997). This may have a moderating effect upon both the initial perceptual rating of a service at the time of consumption and any future perceptual rating.

The literature also suggests that consumers rarely approach a service experience such as wine tourism with a clear and open mind (Bloch and Richins, 1983; Sheth *et al.*, 1991; Solomon *et al.*, 1999). They normally bring with them all of their previous knowledge and experience, which they use to try and make sense of the mass of conflicting stimuli with which they have been bombarded (Chisnall, 1985). Consumer perceptions of service quality may, to a large extent, be influenced by the degree of prior experience the consumer has had or acquires in relation to a particular service product. Not surprisingly, it is likely that the degree of prior experience with a particular wine tourism service provider, the type of service provided or particular attributes of the service should also have some bearing on the extent of any perceptual change over time.

While a number of potential explanations have been alluded to, this paper seeks a better understanding of the links between survey timing and measures of service quality and the moderating effects of prior experience only.

The literature has suggested theoretical reasons why an individual's perceptions of a service encounter may be unstable over time, although the theoretical justification for a specific direction of change is less clear. One scenario is that we may look back at a service increasingly favourably through what has been described as 'rose-tinted spectacles'. This may be consistent with the extensive literature on cognitive dissonance (Festinger, 1957; Hausknecht *et al.*, 1998), which suggests that we are likely to rationalize away poor service delivery over time, and gradually improve our rating. An alternative view is that, with the passage of time, we tend to selectively forget elements of a total experience and perceptions will be influenced by subsequent exposure to related stimuli. As expectations rise, our perceptions of the quality of previous service delivery may decline (Zeithaml *et al.*, 1993).

For the purpose of hypothesis testing, two plausible alternative hypotheses are presented:

- Hypothesis 1a: an individual's perception of the quality of a wine tourism service encounter will decline with the passage of time after the encounter.
- Hypothesis 1b: an individual's perception of the quality of a wine tourism service encounter will increase with the passage of time after the encounter.

A proposition of many theories which seek to explain the effects of the passage of time is that as the frequency of an individual's involvement with an activity increases, the greater his or her propensity to recall an individual event associated with that activity (Hornick, 1984). It follows, therefore, that the schema of an individual with a high level of experience of a type of service encounter differs from an individual for whom the service encounter is a novelty. In other words, consumer perceptions of service quality may, to a large extent, be influenced by the degree of prior experience the consumer has had or has acquired in relation to a particular type of service over time; if they regularly visit a cellar door their perceptions of quality will be different from those who do not normally make such visits.

In the framework of this paper, experience is conceptualized as learning through previous encounters/visitation which has the effect of cognitive, affective and behavioural change. Through affective change, experience has the effect of changing the framework within which the quality of a current service encounter is assessed. The cumulative effects of experience will influence the stability of these perceptions over time, with the presumption being that an individual with a high level of relevant experience will be more inclined to maintain a stable level of perceptions of a service encounter with the passage of time after the encounter.

- Hypothesis 2: the extent of change in perceptions of the quality of a cellar door service encounter over time is negatively related to an individual's experience of that type of service encounter.

Research Method

The methodological framework comprised a longitudinal, quantitative study of visitor perceptions of the service encounter that occurred during a visit to a winery. Wine tourism has been a rapidly growing form of tourism in many of the world's chief wine growing areas, encouraged by higher levels of tourism expenditure in general and growing consumption (and knowledge of) wine in key tourism-generating markets. Wineries are a good area of tourism for testing the research hypotheses.

Visitors typically differ in their experience of wine that they bring to a visit. There is generally a long period of time between visits, during which perceptions of the initial visit may change. The wineries that participated in this study offered for sale to visitors wines that had been produced by the winery. All offered pre-purchase tastings and advice, and some offered additional facilities such as merchandizing, entertainment and food and beverage services.

Data collection for the first stage of this study was undertaken during April 2002 and comprised the interception of winery visitors as they departed from the site following their visit. Respondents were approached at random and the pertaining questionnaires were self-completion in nature. Research assistants were on hand to answer any questions that respondents might have. Those who agreed to participate in this stage of the research were asked if they would agree to be contacted again in one month's time for the purposes of further research. A small prize incentive in the form of a mixed dozen of locally produced premium wines was offered for respondents who agreed to take part in further research.

The second stage, follow-up survey was undertaken by post approximately one month after the original survey of departing visitors. As the Stage 1 data was collected over a 2-week period, Stage 2 surveys were distributed one month from the date of initial intercept. Six hundred questionnaires were administered at Stage 1, of which 493 were returned, representing a response rate of approximately 82%. Some 221 respondents provided contact information by way of participating in Stage 2 of the research and, of these, a total of 112 responses were received following the Stage 2 administration, representing just over 50% of those written to and 22% of the initial Stage 1 respondents. Once again, a small prize incentive in the form of a mixed dozen locally produced premium wines was offered for respondents who participated in Stage 2 of the research.

Scale development

The scales developed were based on the importance/performance analysis (IPA) direct disconfirmation technique (Ennew *et al.*, 1993; Joseph and Joseph, 1997) and took the form of a self-completion questionnaire For each item respondents were asked to rate their perceptions of the quality of elements of the service encounter on a five-point Likert scale anchored at strongly disagree (1) and strongly agree (5).

Scale items were based on the 22 items of the original SERVQUAL instrument. In the absence of a previously validated scale that had been applied to a winery, this appeared to be the best basis for a measurement scale. This scale has been widely replicated in both inferred and performance-only-based disconfirmation measures and the factor structure found to be appropriate to a wide range of consumer services, of which winery visits are typical.

The scale was modified extensively to take account of the particular wine tourism service setting in order to improve its content and face validity. This was achieved through an initial review of the published literature on wine tourism, which extracted common points related to consumer evaluation criteria. This was supplemented with five focus group discussions involving winery staff and customers. All discussions were recorded and subsequently analysed. The resulting analysis was then cross-checked against independently transcribed notes for accuracy and, where appropriate, item wording was changed to better 'fit' the context of the cellar door experience. These discussions led to the exclusion of two of the original SERVQUAL items due to 'cumbersome language'.

Two additional items deemed by participants to be highly relevant to the evaluation of service quality in the cellar door domain were included – scale items 5 and 10 (Table 13.4), which related to the range and quality of wines tasted and available for sale. An additional item was included as an overall measure of service quality for the purposes of assessing convergent validity. A final refined list of scale items was shown to two participating winery owners and agreement reached that the items were valid indicators of service quality in the context of winery visits.

Scale items used in the follow-up survey were identical to those used in the initial survey. Additional questions sought information about respondents' exposure to stimuli related to each of the wineries visited since returning home. Additional questions were also asked in relation to future behavioural intention.

Sample characteristics

Survey research was focused on twelve wineries in the Margaret River wine region of Western Australia. Wineries who agreed to participate in the research included: Evans and Tate, Island Brook, Clairault, Happs, Willespie, Ribbon Vale/Moss Wood, Hay Shed Hill, Voyager, Cape Mentelle, Leeuwin Estate, Sandalford and Howard Park.

Margaret River is a tourism destination about three-and-a-half hours' drive south of Perth, with a number of natural and ecotourism features, vineyards and wineries to attract visitors. Its reputation as a premium wine producing region has been forged over the last 25 years and it now has an international reputation for its wines – particularly based on the Cabernet Sauvignon and Chardonnay grape varieties. The region now has in excess of 150 wineries, of which just over 60 offer facilities for visitors. The selected wineries were chosen based on the extensiveness of their facilities for visitors and their willingness to participate in the research.

Visitors to the 12 wineries during a 2-week period in April 2002 were randomly invited to participate in the research as they departed from the winery. 493 responses were received in the first stage of the study and 112 at Stage 2. The principal demographic characteristics of the sample are shown in Table 13.1. Of the 493 subjects included in Stage 1 of the study, Table 13.1 shows an almost equal distribution of male and female respondents.

Respondents were categorized into one of five age groups. Subjects aged between 18 and 24 years accounted for 17.8% (88), 25–34 years for 35.9% (177), 35–44 years for 19.1% (94), 45–54 years for 17.2% (85) and 55 years and over for 9.1% (45) of the total. These figures are almost wholly replicated with respect to the Stage 2 sample. Approximately 73% of the sample were occupied in either a managerial or professional capacity, indicating a well-educated customer base. The majority of visitors were from Australia (just over 89%) and the remainder from overseas.

Of those surveyed, approximately 61% (301) were first-time visitors to the respective wineries. This is consistent with the observation that approximately 89% (439) of respondents visited wineries less than once a month. While this may seem to be a high proportion of occasional visitors, it is likely that when visitors do go to a wine region they visit a number of wineries over the period of visitation. Previous research indicated that 65% of visitors to the region had visited it at least twice, suggesting a high level of repeat visitation (King and Morris, 1997).

Table 13.1. Demographic profile of winery visitors.

Frequency of age groups				Frequency of Gender		
	Stage 1 n (%)	Stage 2 n (%)			Stage 1 n (%)	Stage 2 n (%)
18–24	88 (17.8)	14 (12.5)		Male	235 (47.7)	55 (49.1)
25–34	177 (35.9)	32 (28.6)		Female	257 (52.1)	57 (50.8)
35–44	94 (19.1)	22 (19.7)		Missing	1 (0.2)	
45–54	85 (17.2)	28 (25.0)				
55+	45 (9.1)	16 (14.2)				
Missing	4 (0.8)					
Total	493 (100.0)	112 (100.0)		Total	493 (100.0)	112 (100.0)

Note: Figures in parentheses refer to characteristics of the sub-sample that participated in stage 2 of the study. Percentages may not sum to 100 due to rounding.

While at first sight the fact that 89% of visitors visit wineries less than once per month might imply a low level of customer loyalty, it should be remembered that winery operators are attempting to achieve loyalty to their brand and not just to their visitor facilities. If brand loyalty has been achieved, customers can make future purchases at their local retail or speciality wine sales outlet, or by mail order.

Analysis

The modified SERVQUAL instrument performed well over both stages of the research, with strong reliability and validity indicators across all scales. Overall performance reliabilities were alpha = 0.97 and 0.91, respectively, for Stages 1 and 2 perceptions scales.

Discriminant analysis made use of the principal components OBLIMIN oblique factor rotation procedure. This failed to reproduce the five factor 'RATER' dimensions of the original SERVQUAL studies (Berry *et al.*, 1988).

Table 13.2 illustrates strong factor loadings (item to total correlations)

Table 13.2. Stage 1 factor analysis of the cellar door experience.

Variable	Component 1 Contact	Component 2 Tangibles	Component 3 Reliability
V1		0.728	
V2		0.865	
V3		0.759	
V4		0.633	
V5		0.623	
V6			0.635
V7			0.906
V8			0.813
V9		0.426	
V10	0.762		
V11	0.622		
V12	0.859		
V13	0.814		
V14	0.930		
V15	0.880		
V16	0.846		
V17	0.755		
V18	0.647		
V19	0.551		
V20	0.719		
V21			0.522
V22	0.618		
Eigenvalue	12.500	1.798	1.266
% of variation	56.817	8.173	5.573
Coefficient alpha	0.96	0.84	0.86

along three dimensions, with coefficient alpha scores ranging from 0.84 to 0.96. Extracted Component 1 is reflective of a combination of the dimensions of responsiveness, assurance and empathy from the original SERVQUAL instrument. Viewed in the context of a winery visit, Component 1 seems to relate to the contact issues (CONTACT) and the moment of truth. This factor seemed to focus on a winery's ability to quickly allay any fears that first-time visitors might have on being introduced to what is, for many, a new and potentially intimidating environment. This dimension is also reflective of the winery's ability to deliver its visitor services on time and as expected.

Component 2 is largely reflective of the tangible (TANGIBLES) dimension of the original SERVQUAL, which relates to the more physical aspects of the service encounter, for example the setting, décor, appearance of staff and the range of wines. Component 3 is reflective of the reliability (RELIABILITY) dimension of the original SERVQUAL and relates to the more time-related aspects of the service encounter.

The Stage 2 analyses revealed a much more complex factor structure, with five principal components being extracted. This factor structure seems to be more in line with that proposed within the original SERVQUAL model. Table 13.3 illustrates strong factor loadings (item to total correlations) along five dimensions, with coefficient alpha scores ranging from 0.76 to 0.92. Extracted Component 1 is largely reflective of the empathy dimension from the original SERVQUAL instrument, Component 2 of the tangible dimension, Component 3 of the reliability component, Component 4 of the responsiveness component and Component 5 of the assurance component of the original SERVQUAL model.

To analyse the hypotheses the first test involved summing each respondent's perception scores for each of the 22 items. This was done separately for the two survey stages, allowing an assessment to be made of the total quality score, but only for those respondents who had participated in both stages of the research (n, 112). The scales were all rated from 1 to 5, with 5 being indicative of the highest rating for all scales.

The total score at each sampling period was then divided by the number of items (22) to give a mean quality score (an adjustment was made for missing observations). The mean score at the first sampling point was 4.15, compared with 4.05 at the second sampling point. While there is a clear downward trend over the one-month time frame, a paired samples t-test revealed that the difference was not statistically significant at the level of 1% (t, 1.042; $P < 0.300$; df, 103). While these results lend support to Hypothesis 1a, they are not conclusive and therefore not generalizable to the population at large.

Mean quality scores had declined between the time of the original questionnaire and the follow-up survey, indicating that consumer perceptions were unstable. Further support for this hypothesis can also be gained from an analysis of the mean scores for individual scale items. These can also be seen to have changed between the time of the original questionnaire and the follow-up survey, further indicating that perceptions of quality had declined over the one-month time frame.

Table 13.3. Stage 2 factor analysis of the cellar door experience.

Variable	Component 1 Empathy	Component 2 Tangibles	Component 3 Reliability	Component 4 Response	Component 5 Assurance
V1		0.788			
V2		0.923			
V3				−0.503	
V4		0.772			
V5				−0.674	
V6			0.501		
V7			0.927		
V8			0.841		
V9					
V10				−0.515	
V11				−0.770	
V12				−0.618	
V13	0.864				
V14	0.858				
V15	0.796				
V16					−0.633
V17					−0.543
V18	0.627				
V19	0.777				
V20					−0.639
V21	0.779				
V22	0.846				
Eigenvalue	8.346	2.564	1.488	1.366	1.260
% of variation	37.963	11.653	6.763	6.209	5.727
Coefficient alpha	0.92	0.78	0.80	0.76	0.76

Table 13.4 indicates that this decline could not entirely be accounted for by random errors, with paired samples t-tests revealing that differences in four out of the 22 items were found to be significant at the 1% level ($P < 0.05$). These four items are denoted by asterisk in Table 13.4, with negative perceptual changes ranging from −0.26 (Winery staff were never too busy to respond to guests, Variable 14) to −0.38 (The winery had the best interests of patrons at heart, Variable 20). Each of these statistically significant differences relates to the more empathy-related dimension of the cellar door experience and clearly points to the need for further work in this area.

On a more positive note, respondent perceptions can also be seen to have increased over time with respect to certain variables, not least those related to the more tangible aspect of the cellar door experience. While the degree of change was not found to be statistically significant, Variables 1 and 3 have, none the less, registered sizeable increases, with +0.14 (The winery has good facilities to cater for visitors) and +0.18 (Winery staff appeared neat).

Table 13.4. Mean difference scores for items of service quality between Stages 1 and 2, ranked by mean difference in scores between Stages 1 and 2.

Item	Mean perceptual score time (t1)	Mean perceptual score time (t2)	Mean perceptual difference (t1–t2)
The winery had good facilities to cater for visitors	3.90	4.04	+0.14
The décor of the winery was visually appealing	4.20	4.09	−0.11
Winery staff appeared neat	4.23	4.41	+0.18
Brochures and signposting were visually appealing	3.85	3.75	−0.10
The range of wines available to taste was broad	4.21	4.06	−0.15
The winery showed a genuine interest in solving guest problems	3.82	3.74	−0.08
Getting things right the first time seems to be part of the winery's ethos	3.75	3.70	−0.05
The winery got things right the first time	3.68	3.77	+0.09
The opening/tasting times were convenient to me	4.20	4.07	−0.13
The quality of the wine tasted was high	4.27	4.30	+0.03
Winery staff were knowledgeable about opening and tasting times	4.26	4.33	+0.07
We did not have to wait excessively long for service	4.30	4.30	–
Winery staff were always willing to help guests	4.36	4.29	−0.07
Winery staff were never too busy to respond to guests	4.33	4.07	−0.26*
The behaviour of winery staff gave me confidence in the winery	4.32	4.20	−0.12
I felt secure in my dealings with the winery	4.27	4.16	−0.11
Winery staff were consistently courteous with guests	4.48	4.44	−0.04
Winery staff had the knowledge to answer guests' questions	4.39	4.34	0.05
As a whole, the winery made me feel like a special individual	3.99	3.70	−0.29*
The winery had the best interests of patrons at heart	4.07	3.69	−0.38*
Winery staff understood the specific needs of guests	4.03	3.68	−0.35*
Winery staff gave individualized attention to guests	4.29	4.05	−0.24

*, significant difference between perception scores at t1 and t2 at $P < 0.005$.

This is clearly reflective of the amount of investment in the service-scape at each of the participating wineries over the years.

The second hypothesis was concerned with the effects of respondents' previous experience on the stability of their perceptions of service quality over time. It had been hypothesized that experienced winery visitors would have had a schema that stabilized their perceptions within the context of its learned patterns of behaviour and responses. In order to test this hypothesis, respondents were divided into two groups:

1. Inexperienced: respondents who reported at Stage 1 that they *had not* previously visited a winery (*n*, 102).
2. Experienced: respondents who reported at Stage 1 that they *had* previously visited a winery (*n*, 9).

The first test involved summing each group's average perception scores for each of the 22 items for both stages of the research and subjecting these to paired samples t-tests. The mean scores for the two stages for inexperienced users were 4.22 (Stage 1) and 3.79 (Stage 2). These means were found to be significantly different at the level of 1% (t, 3.375; $P < 0.001$; df, 101). The mean perception scores for both stages for experienced users were 3.38 (Stage 1) and 3.58 (Stage 2). Unlike the results relating to inexperienced users, however, these results were not found to be statistically significant at the 1% level (t, -0.251; $P < 0.808$; df, 8). This lends support to Hypothesis 2.

Implications for Wine Tourism

This study has a number of implications for both academics and practitioners in relation to the management and measurement of service quality within the wine tourism sector. First, there is support for Hypothesis 1a, that perception of cellar door service quality scores decline over time. This research has demonstrated an effect of timing, but the methodological framework has not allowed a cause for this perceptual change to be identified. The finding would appear to be inconsistent with previous literature on cognitive dissonance that individuals have a tendency to revise upwards their attitude towards an unfavourable incident.

However, it should be noted that the overwhelming majority of respondents in this study were satisfied with their service encounter, and therefore there was probably very little dissonance to be reduced. Nevertheless, the wine tourist's perception of the quality of their experience has declined with time, which must be of concern to cellar door providers. This is not to say that consumer perceptions of cellar door service will always decline, rather this finding merely supports the fact that consumer perceptions are unstable and therefore must be accounted for with respect to the actual service encounter and future marketing and promotion efforts by the company.

Thus, the first practical conclusion for cellar door managers is that they should not merely rely on exit surveys for their analysis of how visitors felt about the experience. Whilst hard to implement, later surveys will give a better snapshot on the consumer's perspective about the brand and their long-term commitment to the winery, as opposed to merely the one-off cellar door experience.

Similarly, there is a tendency for winery managers to undertake visitor surveys at a time when it is most convenient for the company and not for its customers. However, this convenience has to be traded off against the quality of information that can be obtained. This study has demonstrated the instability of customers' perceptions, and managers should seek to measure perceptions that are the most likely to be valid at the time when the next purchase decision is made. The buying cycle differs between different types of wine tourism activity and this cycle should be fully understood in order that perceptions can be measured at the most appropriate time.

There is an extensive literature, which has suggested that it is quite unrealistic to talk about consumers having expectations for a service against which service delivery is assessed, when those expectations may be highly abstract. This research is consistent with these findings and suggests that inexperience may influence perceptions and affective change with respect to service quality. One visit to a winery may not have been sufficient to develop broader evaluatory criteria. It is essential for wine tourism operators to understand the role of experience in the formation of service quality perceptions so that they can be maintained and/or manipulated over time.

It is suggested, therefore, that tourism professionals seek to determine levels of visitor experience and differentiate accordingly when it comes to the cellar door service offering. This should inform segmentation efforts and related target marketing strategies. Additionally, winery managers should be seeking to create a number of encounters with their visitors in order to establish a consistent brand image in the mind of potential customers; relying on a one-off visit runs the risk that with time the recollection of that visit, of the wines and of the staff will be misremembered; a series of encounters may establish a positive attitude more firmly.

Further, this study lends support to the idea that winery owners should not be developing loyalty to the cellar door, so much as to the brand. Whilst the cellar door may be part of the organization's 'brand constellation' (Lockshin and Hall, 2003), the long-term success of the company depends not on cellar door sales but on overall brand equity and the consumer's long-term commitment to the product. This research shows how that commitment may wane after the cellar door encounter, and therefore marketing managers need to be alert to this, and implement strategies to overcome it.

This study has taken a longitudinal approach, but only two points of sampling were taken. Further research is needed to gain a fuller understanding of the decay processes of perceptions, and whether perceptual change follows a linear or non-linear pattern. Similarly, further research is needed to establish a link between the perceptions that are held at a point in time and the effects on buying intention and subsequent repurchase/ recommendation intention.

On a more practical note, the study has also demonstrated the value of such evaluation techniques to cellar door/winery operators in their continuous quality improvement efforts. The findings clearly point to a range of deficiencies with respect to this sample's cellar door experience and the fact that considered improvement is necessary in all cases. This is particularly true of the softer, more people-oriented side of the cellar door visit, where the results demonstrate a statistically significant decline in respondent perceptions regarding certain variables. The point being, that the magic of the vineyard and winemaker can very quickly and easily be undone by the unsympathetic efforts of unprofessional and uncaring cellar door employees.

References

Abercrombie, M.L.J. (1967) *The Anatomy of Judgement: an Investigation into the Process of Perception and Reasoning*, 4th edn. Hutchinson & Co. (Publishers) Ltd., London.

Ali-Knight, J. and Charters, S. (2000) Wine tourism – a thirst for knowledge? *International Journal of Wine Marketing* 12 (3), 71–82.

Asch, S.E. (1946) Forming impressions of personality. *Journal of Abnormal and Social Psychology* 46, 1230–1240.

Berry, L.L., Parasuraman, A. and Zeithaml, V. (1988) The service quality puzzle. *Business Horizons* 28 (5), 35–43.

Bloch, P.H. and Richins, M.L. (1983) A theoretical model for the study of product importance perceptions. *Journal of Marketing* 47, 69–81.

Blythe, J. (1997) *The Essence of Consumer Behaviour*. Prentice Hall, London.

Bolton, R. and Drew, J.H. (1991) A multistage model of customers' easements of service quality and value. *Journal of Consumer Research* 17 (4), 375–384.

Boulding, W., Kalra, A., Staelin, R. and Zeithaml, V.A. (1993) A dynamic process model of service quality: from expectations to behavioural intentions. *Journal of Marketing Research* 30 (1), 7–27.

Boulding, W., Kalra, A. and Staelin, R. (1999). The quality double whammy. *Marketing Science*, Vol. 18 No. 4: 463-484.

Bruwer, J. (2002) Marketing wine to Generation X consumers through the cellar door. *The Australian and New Zealand Grapegrower and Winemaker* (December), 67–71.

Boulding, W., Kalra, A. and Staelin, R. (1999) The quality double whammy. *Marketing Science* 18 (4), 463–484.

Cambourne, B. (1998) Wine tourism in the Canberra District. Paper presented at the *Wine Tourism: Perfect Partners – Australian Wine Tourism Conference*, Margaret River, Western Australia, May 1998.

Cambourne, B. and Macionis, N. (2000) Meeting the wine-maker: wine tourism product development in an emerging wine region. In: Hall, M., Sharples, L.,

Cambourne, B., Macionis, N., Mitchell, R. and Johnson, G. (eds) *Wine Tourism Around the World: Development, Management and Markets*. Elsevier Science, Oxford, UK, pp. 81–101.

Charters, S. and O'Neill, M. (2000) Delighting the customer: how good is the cellar door experience? *Australian and New Zealand Wine Industry Journal* 15 (4) (Wine marketing supplement), 11–16.

Charters, S. and O'Neill, M. (2001) Service quality at the cellar door: a comparison between regions. *International Journal of Wine Marketing* 13 (3), 7–17

Chisnall, P.M. (1985) *Marketing: a Behavioural Analysis*. McGraw-Hill Book Company (UK) Ltd., Berkshire, UK.

Cronin, J.J. and Taylor, S.A. (1994) SERVPERF versus SERVQUAL: reconciling performance-based and perceptions-minus-expectations measurement of service quality. *Journal of Marketing* 58 (1), 125–131.

Dodd, T. and Bigotte, V. (1997) Perceptual differences among visitor groups to wineries. *Journal of Travel Research* 35 (3), 46–51.

Ennew, C., Reed, C. and Binks, M. (1993) Importance–performance analysis and the measurement of service quality. *European Journal of Marketing* 27 (2), 59–70.

Festinger, L. (1957) *A Theory of Cognitive Dissonance*. Stanford University Press, Stanford, California.

Gronroos, C. (1984) *Service Management and Marketing*. Lexington Books, Lexington, Massachusetts.

Hausknecht, D.R., Sweeney, J.C., Soutar, G.N. and Johnson, L.W. (1998) After I had made the decision I … toward a scale to measure cognitive dissonance. *Journal of Consumer Satisfaction, Dissatisfaction and Complaining Behaviour* 11, 119–127.

Hornick, J. (1984) Subjective versus objective time measures: note on the perception of time in consumer behaviour. *Journal of Consumer Research* 11, 615–618.

Howard, R. and Stonier, J. (2002) Marketing wine to Generation X. *Australian and New*

Zealand Wine Industry Journal 17 (3), 78–82.

Hudson, S. (1998) Measuring service quality at tourist destinations: an application of importance–performance analysis to an alpine ski resort. *Journal of Travel and Tourism Marketing* 7 (3), 61–77.

Joseph, M. and Joseph, B. (1997) Service quality in education: a student perspective. *Quality Assurance in Education* 5 (1), 26–37.

Kahneman, D. and Miller, D.T. (1986) Norm theory: comparing reality to its alternatives. *Psychological Review* 93, 136–153.

Katz, E. (1968) On reopening the question of selectivity in exposure to mass communications. In: Abelson, I. (ed.) *Theories of Cognitive Consistency: a Source Book*. Rand McNally, Chicago, Illinois.

King, C. and Morris, R. (1997) Wine tourism: a Western Australian case study. *The Australian and New Zealand Wine Industry Journal* 12 (3), 246–249.

Lockshin, L. and Hall, J. (2003) Consumer purchasing behaviour for wine: What we know and where we are going. Paper presented at the *3rd Annual Wine Marketing Colloquium*, 26–27 July, Adelaide, Australia.

Lovelock, C., Patterson, P.G. and Walker, R.H. (1998) *Services Marketing*. Prentice Hall, Sydney, Australia.

Morris, R. and King, C. (1998) Delighting the wine tourist. Paper presented at the *Wine Tourism: Perfect Partners – Australian Wine Tourism Conference*, Margaret River, Western Australia, May 1998.

Oliver, R.L. (1997) *Satisfaction: a Behavioural Perspective on the Consumer*. McGraw-Hill, London.

O'Neill, M. and Charters, S. (2000) Service quality and brand loyalty at the cellar door – an exploratory study of Western Australia's wine tourism industry. Paper presented at the *Proceedings of the 5th International Conference on ISI9000 and TQM*, Hong Kong.

Parasuraman, A., Zeithaml, V.A. and Berry, L.L. (1988) SERVQUAL: a multiple item scale for measuring consumer perceptions of service quality. *Journal of Retailing* 64 (3), 12–37.

Rust, R.T., Inman, J.J., Jia, J. and Zahorik, A. (1999) What you don't know about customer perceived quality: the role of customer expectation distributions. *Marketing Science* 18 (1), 77–92.

Sheth, J.N., Newman, B.I. and Gross, B.L. (1991) Why we buy what we buy: a theory of consumption values. *Journal of Business Research* 22, 159–170.

Solomon, M.R., Bamossy, G. and Askegaard, S. (1999) Consumer behaviour: a European perspective. In: *Financial Times*, Prentice Hall, Harlow, UK, pp. 236–267.

Zeithaml, V.A., Parasuraman, A. and Berry, L. (1990) *Delivering Quality Service: Balancing Customer Perceptions and Expectations*. The Free Press, New York.

Zeithaml, V.A., Berry, L.L. and Parasuraman, A. (1993) The nature and determinants of customer expectations of service. *Journal of the Academy of Marketing Science* 21 (1), 1–12.

Part V
Wine Festivals and Events

14 Wine Festivals and Tourism: Developing a Longitudinal Approach to Festival Evaluation

RUTH TAYLOR

Curtin University of Technology, School of Management, GPO Box U1987, Perth, WA 6845, Australia
E-mail: ruth.taylor@cbs.curtin.edu.au

Introduction

Tourism development policy and strategies written at local, national and international levels all include the challenge of regional tourism development policy (Wine Industry Association of Western Australia and the Western Australian State Government, 1997; Collins, 2005). An increasing number of these strategies acknowledge wine tourism as a growth area for regional tourism development, which in turn can be enhanced through the development of events strategy and wine festivals (Getz, 1997; Macionis and Cambourne, 1998; Sparks and Malady, 2004; Queensland Government, 2006). Wine producing regions not only provide authentic spatial contexts for the development of wine tourism, but in many cases they can also provide the cultural context for the staging of wine and food festivals (WIAWA, 1997; Swan Valley Tourism Council and City of Swan, 2004).

Often, traditional events staged in rural areas are in the form of festivals, many of which celebrate past culture and heritage, or provide a corollary to current culture. A group of festivals exhibiting noticeable change is the increasing number of wine and food festivals being staged (Carlsen, 1999). This trend in increased staging of food and wine festivals presents an interesting area to be researched, as it not only provides information for the wineries in relation to their operational and marketing needs, but also provides information for supporting tourism and festival strategy development in regional areas.

Festivals and events staged in urban areas due to their location, size, economic impacts and media attention have received increased attention from both industry and tourism researchers (Hall, 1989; Getz, 1997); however, many regional festivals and events cannot claim this level of interest or attention (Getz, 1997, 1998; Foo, 1999; Delamare, 2001; Taylor, 2001;

Weiler *et al.*, 2004). This is an interesting point, as many of the festivals and events staged in rural areas are part of the local cultural scene and often staged on an annual basis. Being part of the local societal and economic fabric of regions (Australian Tourist Commission, 2004; Tourism Australia, 2005), it would appear that the cumulative effects and impacts of these events is worthy of discussion, as much as the one-off impact of a larger, urban event.

Whilst many festivals are annual or biennial events and many of the elements of the festival remain the same, no two events are ever exactly the same, and thus it is of interest to look at events from a longitudinal research and evaluation approach with the ability to develop the approach as the festival develops. This chapter will examine the evaluation techniques used during a longitudinal, triangulated study of both visitor experience and quality for an urban/regional fringe wine festival.

Literature Review

As Hall (1989, 2003) explained, many wine festivals and events can act as catalysts for repeat tourism visitation to wine regions, highlighting the perceived connection between wine festivals and wine tourism. Research in the area of wine tourists and wine tourism regions (Charters and Ali-Knight, 2002; Getz and Brown, 2006) is being undertaken in both Old and New World wine regions, and thus it is important to build upon this research in the area of wine festival visitor research. The importance of characteristics relating to the unique content and the context of the festival, and other elements such as service qualities, can provide valuable information for festival managers (Bowen and Daniels, 2005; Getz and Brown, 2006). Festivals and events can be characterized by three elements in terms of product, service and experience provision for the event visitor (Nicholson and Pearce, 2000; Getz *et al.*, 2001; Neirotti *et al.*, 2001; Taylor, 2001).

One of the key points in understanding wine festival attendance is to establish why people attend wine festivals amongst the congestion, queues and confusion of a festival when they can obtain many of the tangible tourism products if they visited the wine region at any time during the other 51 weeks of the year. This point is of even more interest when considering service quality. The absence of such actors as crowding and queues would be expected to provide a significantly higher level of service in the non-festival times. However, it is of worth to note that the third dimension, that of experience, appears to be important to the festival visitor (Cohen, 1996; Taylor and Shanka, 2002).

Murphy *et al.* (2000) present a model for a destination product and investigate service infrastructure, quality and value and the relationship with the tourist experience. The study showed that there were specific relationships between these constructs. Due to the fact that wine festivals staged in wine regions are very reliant on the destination as an integral part of the festival and a key provider of festival product and experience, it is therefore pertinent for researchers to investigate festival experience. As the demand for 'festival experience' assumes greater significance for the festival visitor, the way in which the three elements of a festival – product, service and experience – are defined and managed is of central importance to event stakeholders. Additionally, the approaches used to research these elements also need to be reviewed to provide a range of data and information for analysis.

Customer satisfaction and service quality are two event characteristics event managers can use to evaluate their festivals (Getz *et al.*, 2001; Taylor and Shanka, 2002; Weiler *et al.*, 2004). Fallon and Schofield (2004, p. 203) define customer satisfaction as 'post-consumption evaluative judgement that represents the "outcome" for the customer after the exposure to the service product', whereas 'quality refers to the service operation's "output"', i.e. the attributes of the product that are primarily under the control of the operation'. When considering the range of stakeholders involved in festivals and the number of ways events can be viewed (Getz, 1997; Allen *et al.*, 2005), it is realistic to assume that a number of approaches or methods can be used to provide a complete picture of the festival. It is also important to consider the life cycle of the festival and the relevance of the approach used to investigate the event (Getz, 1997, p. 145).

One way of achieving an appropriate cross-section of information is to use a triangulated approach to festival profiling and evaluation (Seaton, 1997; Carlsen, 2004). Descriptive surveys and correlational surveys are cross-sectional tools used for collecting data from visitors at one point in time. They are designed to measure such things as visitor demographics, visitor satisfaction and perception value (Punch, 1998). Questions can be designed with scales and categories to enable quantitative analysis of the data collected on demographic items or significance levels relating to satisfaction, whilst open-ended questions can be designed to provide qualitative information to such areas as importance levels of key festival characteristics, through content analysis of the responses. With three years of data collected by visitor surveys, it was proposed that in order to develop the festival it was necessary to investigate the quality of the festival offering.

Seaton (1997) and Carlsen (2004) both suggest that participant observation techniques are an effective tool when documenting event elements such as: (i) visitor composition and counts; (ii) initial impressions of the event; (iii) the event visual experience; (iv) the atmosphere and excitement of the event; (v) facilities and amenities; (vi) food and beverage; (vii) the event exit or departure; and (viii) operational characteristics such as queuing, crowding and congestion.

One tool used to investigate service quality at festivals and events is service mapping (Getz *et al.*, 2001). Bitner (1993, p. 362 cited in Getz *et al.*, 2001) suggests that service mapping 'visually displays the service by simultaneously depicting the process of service delivery, the roles of customers and employees, and the visible elements of the service'. It enables the intangible nature of the many customer service interactions and experiences at festivals and events to be written into a tangible form so as then to allow for analysis of service quality to be undertaken for managers then to develop strategy (Getz *et al.*, 2001). Thus, by gathering information through a number of approaches, visitor self-reporting, participant observation and mapping of service, a greater understanding of the festival and its elements can be brought together for event managers to determine planning, operational and experience stages of the festival.

Research Methods

Western Australia's oldest wine region's premier event, the 'Spring in the Valley' wine festival, has been staged annually for the past 15 years and has grown into what is now considered to be a premier wine tourism festival in Australia (Swan Valley Tourism Council and City of Swan, 2004). The Swan Valley wine region is located approximately half an hour's drive east of the Perth CBD area. Originally located along the north-eastern, urban/rural peripheral fringe of the city, it has now become enveloped in the rapidly spreading urban sprawl. Whilst traditionally an agricultural/viticultural area, it increasingly has to compete with housing and industrial developments and small hobby/leisure farms (Swan Valley Tourism Council and City of Swan, 2004).

A longitudinal study investigating this premier annual wine festival was carried out in 1999, 2000, 2001 and 2003 by administering a face-to-face questionnaire over a range of times across the 2 days of the festival each year. Due to the physical layout of the festival encircling a 32 km tourist loop, key nodes were chosen at random according to observed visitor numbers. These sites included a range of venues such as wineries, micro-breweries, cheese and chocolate factories, arts and crafts venues, fresh produce sellers and historic venues throughout the valley. The random intercept method was used to survey visitors.

The key information sought was visitor demographic information, visitor satisfaction levels and festival characteristic importance levels. The benefits of undertaking a longitudinal study as opposed to a cross-sectional study are that whilst they take more time, effort and cost, they can help to identify cause–effect relationships (Sekaran, 1992; Punch, 1998). Additionally, findings from each year can be analysed and any interesting results can be used to hone or add to questionnaires for the following year. Thus, whilst keeping the basic survey instrument the same for direct comparative purposes, each successive year can target previous year findings and thus provide for more in-depth analysis and richer results.

The basic format of the questionnaire across the 4 years was consistent in the collection of categorical demographic information; whereas the information collected regarding visitor satisfaction and festival characteristics importance was developed and refined over each successive year. This data were gathered in the form of both categorical and open-ended questions. Thus, direct comparison of quantitative analysis of visitor data has been analysed in SPSS where appropriate, and content analysis of qualitative data has also been performed where appropriate. The response rate for this study was 473 usable questionnaires (*n*, 473) for 1999, 326 (*n*, 326) for 2000, 249 (*n*, 249) for 2001 and 443 (*n*, 443) in 2003.

With the establishment of a profile of the festival and festival visitor from 3 years of data collection, it was proposed that in order to develop the festival further it was necessary to further develop the research approach. This is important when considering the festival life cycle of events, because as events change so may the need for event evaluation approaches to be considered (Getz, 1997, p. 145). Thus, in addition to the face-to-face questionnaire survey which had been successful in providing information regarding tangible elements of the festival, in 2003 a service-mapping approach was considered so as to provide greater information, particularly about the intangible elements of the festival (Berry *et al.*, 1994 cited in Getz *et al.*, 2001).

So, in the 2003 research project, service mapping was prepared by identifying key variables influencing quality from the qualitative responses collected during 1999–2001, having been validated by the local tourism council post-festival evaluation sessions. These included the process of service delivery, the relative interactions of customers and employees and the visible elements of the festival service. The service-mapping process developed in the study undertaken by Getz *et al.* (2001) was used as the framework for the research project. Additionally, by using this framework it could allow for comparison of findings across events. Getz *et al.* (2001, p. 389) suggested that 'It is concluded that service mapping can be adapted to any event formats, although testing at more complex events (i.e. with multiple sites and numerous activities) should be attempted'.

As this festival comprised of a range of individual site locations and venues, the number of which has been increasing over the 16 years it has been staged, service mapping was undertaken at 25 of the busiest locations to build an overall picture of the festival as perceived by the visitor attending the 'event'.

Results of findings and trends in festival visitors to this premier event are provided in the findings. The implications for wine tourism and events regarding festival product, service and experience provision by festival managers are then presented.

Findings

Wine festival visitor profile

The univariate descriptive analysis of frequency tabulation provides information concerning the demographic characteristics of visitors to the 'Spring in the Valley' festival (Table 14.1). The majority of the festival visitors in 1999 (45%) were in the middle-aged category, with a trend appearing across the years showing an increase towards younger aged visitors (54 to 61%). The older visitor market of 55+ years showed a continued decrease in numbers of visitors to the festival (16 to 10%) across the 4 years of the study. The gender of the festival visitors was fairly evenly split, with slightly more

Table 14.1. Demographic profile of 'Spring in the Valley' wine festival visitors.

Variable	1999 (n, 473) (%)	2000 (n, 326) (%)	2001 (n, 249) (%)	2003 (n, 443) (%)
Gender				
Female	58	57	51	58
Male	42	43	49	42
Age (y)				
18–35	39	54	50	61
36–55	45	34	38	30
55+	16	12	12	9
Origin of visitor				
Intra-state	91.4	91.3	89.4	91.0
Inter-state	3.2	3.4	2.2	3.6
International	5.4	5.3	8.4	5.4

females, ranging between 51 and 58% attending the festival each year. The vast majority of festival visitors (> 90%) came from Western Australia.

Whilst acknowledging the small number of international visitor respondents in the festival survey samples, the places of origin of those international visitors who were surveyed showed an interesting trend across the years, with the earlier festivals showing a higher proportion of visitors from the Asian region, and the later festivals showing a higher proportion of visitors from European countries.

Upon further univariate descriptive analysis of the data, a more detailed profile of the festival visitor can be established. Table 14.2 gives an insight into the visitation patterns of the 'Spring in the Valley' festival visitors. There is a relatively stable result for first-time *versus* repeat visitation to the Swan Valley region, with a trend to an increasing number of first-time visitors to the 'Spring in the Valley' festival. Word of mouth is the dominant source of information for the festival, with a small, however steady, increase in the use of the Internet from 1.5% in 1999 to 5.4% in 2003. The visitor group size showed three distinct clusters: around 1–5 persons (62–57%), 18–21 persons (24–19%) and 40–45 persons (4–11%). This in effect mirrors the vehicle size and type: private/hire cars (81 to 72%), minibuses and coaches (16 to 27%).

Whilst the majority of visitors travelled to the festival by private or hire car, a declining trend has been noticed over the years with an increasing trend in the use of minibuses, buses and coaches. The findings show that visitors are staying longer at the festival, with a decreasing trend for half-day visitor (56.3 to 40.0%) and an increasing trend for full day visits (39.0 to 55.3%).

Table 14.2. Visitation characteristics of 'Spring in the Valley' wine festival visitors.

Variable	1999 (n, 473) (%)	2000 (n, 326) (%)	2001 (n, 249) (%)	2003 (n, 443) (%)
Swan Valley Region				
First time visitor	34.6	29.2	29.8	31.7
Repeat visitor	65.4	70.8	70.2	68.3
SITV Festival				
First-time visitor	42.9	22.2	60.9	56.8
Repeat visitor	57.1	77.8	39.1	43.2
Source of information				
Word of mouth	51.2	55.4	60.8	63.3
Radio, TV, newspaper	33.1	29.2	31.3	23.7
Road signage	4.0	4.0	4.2	3.0
Internet	1.5	2.5	3.7	5.4
Other	10.2	8.9	0	4.6
Visitor group size[a]				
1–5 persons (standard vehicle)	70.8	62.5	60.9	57.3
6–20 persons (minibus)	20.4	24.4	19.3	18.9
21–45 persons (full coach)	5.5	8.7	11.7	12.8
46+ persons (multiple vehicles)	3.3	4.4	8.1	11.0
Mean visitor group size	8	10	12	18
Mode of transport				
Private car	72.2	70.2	67.4	59.4
Hired car	8.5	15.1	9.1	13.1
Coach/bus/river tour	16.5	10.7	23.1	27.1
Other	2.8	4.0	0.4	0.4
Duration of visit				
Less than 1 hour	3	2.1	0.8	3.8
Half day	56.3	55.9	59.4	40
Full day	39	40.8	38.6	55.3
Overnight stay	1.7	1.2	1.2	0.9

[a] grouped according to average vehicle seating capacity.

Wine festival visitor motivation

Direct comparison of statistical data cannot be reported due to the refinement of data collection over the longitudinal study period, but it is interesting to note the ordering of visitor motivations. A trend has developed towards a family/friends outing as the number one reason for attending the festival, followed by an interest in wineries/wine tourism, then participation in the festival itself (Table 14.3).

Significance of wine festival characteristics

During the reporting of information to the local tourism council it was decided to investigate more fully the characteristics of festivals, thus the 2001

Table 14.3. Ranked main motivations for wine festival visits.

Reason	Ranking[b] 1999 (n, 473)	Rating[a] 2000 (n, 326)	Rating[a] 2001 (n, 249)	Ranking[b] 2003 (n, 443)
Family/friends outing	28	4.16	4.39	30
Wine tourism/winery visits	33	4.10	4.27	22
Participating in the festival	44	3.88	3.76	24
Swan Valley's fine food	NA	3.47	3.36	7
The music/entertainment value	NA	3.31	3.22	4
An interest in arts/crafts	NA	3.28	3.15	4
It being part of an organized tour/group tour	6.4	2.78	2.57	11

NA, not available; [a] Likert scale: 1 = strongly disagree, 5 = strongly agree; [b] percentage of visitors reporting as being important.

and 2003 questionnaires provided a list of key festival visitor characteristics for visitors for evaluation on a Likert scale: 1 = poor, 3 = average, 5 = excellent. Table 14.4 provides an indication of the festival visitors' degree of satisfaction in the provision of these characteristics for the 'Spring in the Valley' festival.

In 2001 all the characteristics, except security, toilet facilities and public transport, received an above-average rating (> 3.5) for degree of satisfaction from visitors attending the festival. All visitors listed characteristics in 2003 with an above-average rating (> 3.5) for satisfaction. It is interesting to note that the order of the characteristics' rankings remained the same for the two years; however, the actual value, or level of satisfaction, of some of the characteristics indicated some changes. The more highly rated characteristics of atmosphere, location, timing of the event, service quality, and variety of

Table 14.4. Significance of wine festival characteristics.

Festival characteristic	Rating[a] 2001 (n, 249)	Rating[a] 2003 (n, 443)
Atmosphere	4.51	4.39 ↓
Location	4.42	4.20 ↓
Timing of the event	4.40	4.17 ↓
Service quality	4.04	3.96 ↓
Variety of attractions	3.98	3.94 ↓
Staffing levels	3.96	3.96 =
Parking	3.82	3.90 ↑
Crowd control	3.79	3.84 ↑
Information and signage	3.74	3.80 ↑
Amenities	3.61	3.71 ↑
Security	3.57	3.81 ↑
Accommodation facilities	3.31	3.79 ↑
Toilet facilities	3.28	3.61 ↑
Public transport	3.00	3.54 ↑

[a] Likert scale: 1 = Poor, 3 = Average, 5 = Excellent.

attractions all showed a decrease in rating, with staffing levels receiving the same rating across the two years. The characteristics of parking, crowd control, information and signage, amenities, security, accommodation facilities, toilet facilities and public transport all exhibited an increase in the ratings received from festival visitors.

It is worth noting that the lower-rated characteristics showing an increase in ratings across the time frame are factors highlighted to the tourism council in previous years' reports as those requiring attention. Perhaps due to this feedback and subsequent attention from the tourism council, these positive responses are the result. Many of these characteristics are also of importance in the overall development, and hence contributing to visitor satisfaction for not just a wine festival, but also imperative for a quality wine tourism destination.

However, of importance is the result that the three top-rated characteristics showed a decrease in visitor satisfaction rating. These characteristics are key aspects of festivals and events staging, and hence significant to the overall satisfaction of event visitors. The tourism council needs to monitor these characteristics, which all appear to be receiving a decrease in their ratings, particularly in light of the open-ended response indicating the importance that festival visitors attribute to these festival attributes.

Importance of wine festival attributes

Table 14.5 provides the content analysis from the open-ended responses to the question asking what the festival visitors enjoyed most about the 2003 festival. These findings attribute directly to the overall success of the festival.

Across all years of findings, the atmosphere generated for the 'Spring in the Valley' festival is considered a major key to the success of this wine festival. Thus, from the perspective of the festival visitor, the wine/wine tasting and atmosphere and opportunity to undertake a group outing (friends and family) are the acknowledged strengths of the 'Spring in the Valley' festival.

Service mapping the 'Spring in the Valley' festival

Figure 14.1 provides an illustrative record of the analysis of observations of primarily visual elements of the festival. From the recorded observations, it is also noted that the participant observers recorded olfactory and acoustic elements of the festival; these are important in that they, in conjunction with the visual elements, would all add to the 'experience' of the festival remembered by the visitors.

When analysing the observations, summation of the data across all the sites was undertaken due to the common observations recorded across the sites. The resultant sorting provided a number of clusters of observations. When viewed, these groups concurred with groupings established by Getz *et*

Table 14.5. Content analysis from open-ended responses investigating what the wine festival visitors liked most about the 2003 SITV festival.

Response	Percentage of responses[a] (n, 443)
Wine	25.1
Atmosphere	19.4
Spending time with friends/socializing	6.2
Variety of food/produce	6.0
Good entertainment	6.0
Great day out to relax	4.5
Beer	4.5
Everything	2.7
Weather	2.5

[a] multiple responses were allowed.

al. (2001, p. 386), thus it was considered appropriate to adopt the use of the four headings of that framework to develop the illustrative records as shown in Figs 14.1 and 14.2. The establishment that these four groups have resulted from two different events is a result in itself, and indicates the relevance of these categories across various types of events and hence determines its usefulness as a model for application in further research with a range of festivals.

The four headings include: (i) Physical Evidence – summarizing the key observations recorded from the 25 festival sites; (ii) Visitor Actions – providing a linear process and flow of key visitor movements throughout the festival; (iii) Visible Staff Contacts – indicating the observation of festival staffing; and (iv) Invisible Management Process – providing an indication of the key management activities needed for the continuation and maintenance of the festival during the staging of the event.

The impact on Visitor Actions observed through Physical Evidence related primarily to tangible elements of the festival such as poor/no signage to festival location, traffic congestions, lack of access for people with disabilities and distance from parking to venues. It was noted that many of these findings concurred when viewed with the responses of the open-ended questions from this and previous years' visitor survey findings.

Visible Staff Contacts reported where staff could be seen to be enhancing the visitor experience at the festival by their observed behaviours and presence or where there appeared to be a need for this to be sput in place. Examples included observations relating to lack of parking attendants, lack of staff guides and lack of staff friendliness. Many of these contribute to the intangible elements of the festival and are rarely commented on *per se* via visitor survey results.

Invisible Management Processes shown in Figs 14.1 and 14.2 provide an indication of where management functions can impact on visitor experience, remembering that these are processes observed by participant observers trained in the underlying theoretical knowledge of these functions when

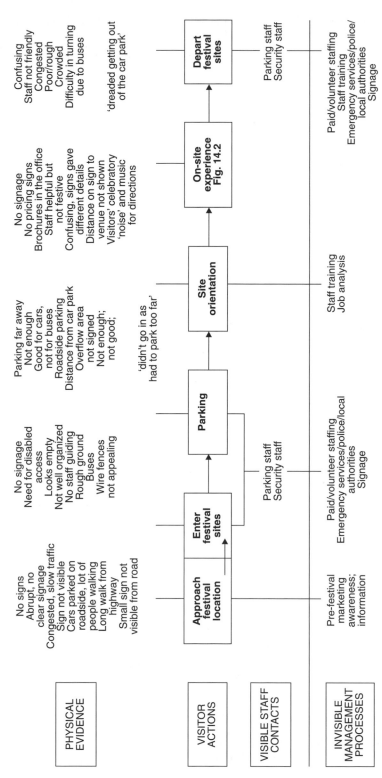

Fig. 14.1. Spring in the Valley wine festival. Stage 1: approach orientation and festival orientation.

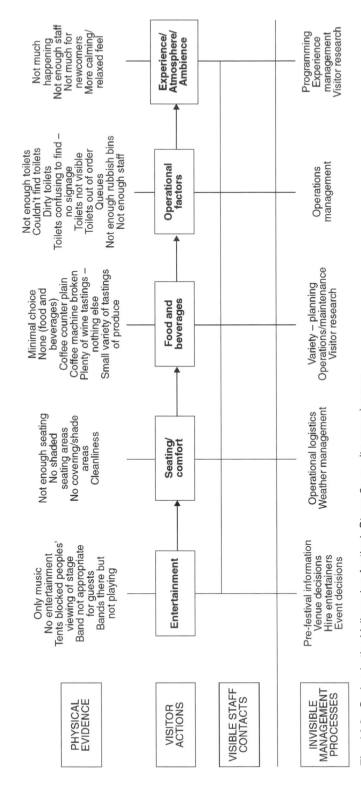

Fig. 14.2. Spring in the Valley wine festival. Stage 2: on-site experiences.

observing the festival. Many of these relate to staff management functions such as staff training requirements and job analysis, so staff know what they are supposed to be doing and when.

Table 14.6 summarizes the visitor satisfaction ratings of the 2003 festival grouped according to the service-mapping framework of elements. It shows that site elements received a larger proportion of comment on the service map and lower satisfaction ratings, while the other elements receiving a higher rating and less percentage of poor satisfaction was less observed on the service map. Thus, mapping of the service quality by observation provides event management with areas of key interaction with the visitors, which management can address in relation to improving service quality. The operational areas and staffing areas in this festival appear to require the most attention from management, evidenced by the visitor satisfaction responses and the observational evidence from service mapping (Table 14.6). As noted by Getz *et al.* (2001), these problems noticed by the observers did not appear to overly influence the general satisfaction of the visitor to the festival.

Implications for Wine Tourism

The univariate descriptive analysis of the festival reveals trends profiling the festival visitor. In essence, the results show a trend towards younger visitors, who travel in larger group sizes with increasing usage of buses/coaches for

Table 14.6. Satisfaction ratings from the 2003 visitor.

Festival characteristic	Rating[a] 2003 (*n*, 443)	Low satisfaction (%)
Site elements		
Parking	3.90	8.5
Crowd control	3.84	5.7
Security	3.81	7.6
Accommodation facilities	3.79	9.9
Information and signage	3.80	7.1
Amenities	3.71	4.9
Toilet facilities	3.61	7.5
Public transport	3.54	18.2
Other elements		
Atmosphere	4.39	1.7
Location	4.20	3.2
Timing of the event	4.17	3.3
Service quality	3.96	3.8
Variety of attractions	3.94	5.4
Overall quality of the 2003 STIV festival	4.30	1.0
Overall satisfaction with 2003 SITV festival	4.20	2.1
Staffing elements		
Staffing levels	3.96	4.7

[a] Likert scale: 1 = Poor, 3 = Average, 5 = Excellent.

transport to the festival and stay for a longer time at the festival. Whilst, anecdotally, this has been the observation of many festival participants (venues/tourism council/transport providers), the results of the study have been able to support these observations.

Thus building upon earlier typologies of wine tourists (Hall, 1996, cited in King and Morris, 1997; Charters and Ali-Knight, 2002), another segment to denote the wine festival tourist may need to be added to existing models of wine tourists. With the festival participants' first perceptions of wine festival attendees now changing, the marketing efforts can be developed to attract wine tourists and wine festival visitors to the various offerings within the wine tourism destination and calendar of events.

Content analysis of open-ended question responses to what festival visitors liked most about the festival consistently provided characteristics such as atmosphere, wine and spending time with friends and family. Content analysis of the open-ended responses, seeking to investigate visitors' suggestions for future festivals development, revealed that many of the operational variables requiring attention are those of significant importance not only to the successful staging of the festival, but also relate to successful year-round tourism. These included important wine festival and wine tourism characteristics such as public transport, signage, parking, toilets, shade, picnic eating areas and seating/seats areas.

As this study suggests, there is a high level of repeat local visitation to wine festivals, in particular from local populations, so not only is it noteworthy to investigate the satisfaction characteristics but, in addition, the importance attributed to the characteristics by the visitors could be investigated in further detail, to provide a more comprehensive understanding of wine festivals and the catalyst effect for repeat wine tourism and wine destination marketing and management.

Further research could investigate the festival life cycle in relation to the changing nature of the experience for the visitors, in particular repeat visitors. The festival organizers could consider the changes in the context of planned or unplanned nature of these experiences and the particular relevance to the festival with such a high level of repeat visitation. This research is possibly becoming more important, in particular to this particular festival. This is due in part to the fact that when the 'Spring in the Valley' festival was first staged it was unique and had minimal – if any – competition. However, recent years have seen the development and staging of many wine festivals which now either directly or indirectly compete for not only the wine festival market of visitors, but also the status of the festival and the image attributed to the destination via the festival.

Research could also be undertaken to evaluate wine tourism and wine festival strategies to evaluate the connections and impacts between these two niche markets. Additionally, operational management such as infrastructure needs and legacies could also be investigated. It is often assumed that all providers within regional areas wish to be involved in wine tourism and/or wine festivals; research could be undertaken into the stakeholders who do not wish to be actively involved and may or may not benefit from the staging of such events. The social ramifications within the community could also be investigated.

Another operational planning area to research is in relation to the importance of the high level of repeat visitation to urban fringe wine regions and to wine festivals. Whilst certain visitors may enjoy the familiarity or nostalgia of the festival each year, others may require a continuing higher level of service quality and variety in programming. The issue of 'nothing new' and 'boredom' were observed in the service mapping findings. The ability for regional wine festivals to 'keep up' with wine festival visitor needs, when compared to high-level urban events being staged, is important. The concept of value-perception and service quality would be appropriate to examine some of these research questions.

This chapter has presented a range of research approaches used to investigate visitor satisfaction and the quality of a regional wine festival from data collected over a 5-year period. The trends highlight the need for continuous research being undertaken using a triangulated approach to better understand the nature of festivals and events. Not only is the information gained valuable from a festival and event planning, management and marketing perspective *per se*, it is also of importance in relation to the high repeat visitation levels at many regional festivals and events and the potential catalytic effect in relation to wine tourism.

References

Allen, J., O'Toole, W., McDonnell, I. and Harris, R. (2005) *Festival and Special Event Management,* 3rd edn., John Wiley & Sons, Australia.

Australian Tourist Commission (2004) *Food and Wine Tourism Fact Sheet,* May 2004 (http://www.tourism.australia.com/content/Research/Factsheets/food_wine_may2004.pdf, accessed 10 January 2006).

Bowen, H. and Daniels, M. (2005) Does the music matter? Motivations for attending a music festival. *Event Management* 9 (3), 155–164.

Carlsen, J. (1999) The first Australian Wine Tourism Conference, conference report. *Tourism Management* 20, 367–368.

Carlsen, J. (2004) The economics and evaluation of festivals and events. In: Yeoman, I., Robertson, M., Ali-Knight, J., Drummond, S. and McMahon-Beattie, U. (eds) *Festivals and Events Management: an International Arts and Culture Perspective.* Elsevier, Butterworth Heinemann, Oxford, UK.

Charters, S. and Ali Knight, J. (2002) Who is the wine tourist? *Tourism Management* 23, 311–319.

Cohen, E. (1996) A phenomenology of tourist experiences. In: Apostolopoulos, Y., Leivadi, S. and Yiannakis, A. (eds) *The Sociology of Tourism – Theoretical and Empirical Investigations.* Routledge, London.

Collins, D. (2005) TRA niche market report no. 5, a profile of wine visitors in Australia 2003. *Tourism Research Australia,* Canberra, Australia.

Delamare, T.A. (2001) Development of a scale to measure resident attitudes toward the social impacts of community festivals, Part II: verification of the scale. *Event Management* 7, 25–38.

Fallon, P. and Schofield, P. (2004) First-time and repeat visitors to Orlando, Florida: a comparative analysis of destination satisfaction. In: Crouch, G., Perdue, R., Timmermans, H. and Uysal, M. (eds)

Consumer Psychology of Tourism, Hospitality and Leisure. CAB International Publishing, Wallingford, UK.

Foo, L.M. (1999) A profile of international visitors to Australian wineries. *Bureau of Tourism Research Report* 1, 1 August.

Getz, D. (1997) *Event Management and Event Tourism*. Cognizant Communication Corporation, New York.

Getz, D. (1998) Wine tourism: goal overview and perspectives on its development *Wine Tourism – Perfect Partners. Proceedings of the First Australian Wine Tourism Conference*, Margaret River, Western Australia, 7–9 May 2004.

Getz, D. and Brown, G. (2006) Critical factors for wine tourism regions: a demand analysis. *Tourism Management* 27, 146–158.

Getz, D., O'Neill, M. and Carlsen, J. (2001) Service quality evaluation at events through service mapping. *Journal of Travel Research* 39 (3), 380–390.

Griffin, T. and Loersch, A. (2004) The determinants of quality experiences in an emerging wine region. *Proceedings of the International Wine Tourism Conference*, Margaret River, Western Australia, 7–9 May 2004.

Hall, C.M. (1989) Hallmark events and the planning process. In: Syme, G.J., Shaw, B.J., Fenton, D.M. and Mueller, W.S. (eds) *The Planning and Evaluation of Hallmark Events*. Avebury, Aldershot, UK.

Hall, C.M. (2003) Consuming places: the role of food, wine and tourism in regional development. In: Hall, C.M., Sharples, L., Mitchell, R. and Macionis, N. (eds) *Food Tourism*. Butterworth Heinemann, Melbourne, Australia.

King, C. and Morris, R. (1997) Wine tourism: a Western Australian case study. *The Australian and New Zealand Wine Industry Journal* 12 (3), 246–249.

Macionis, N. and Cambourne, B. (1998) Wine tourism: just what is it all about? *The Australian and New Zealand Wine Industry Journal* 13, 41–47.

Murphy, P., Pritchard, M. and Smith, B. (2000) The destination product and its impact on traveller perceptions. *Tourism Management* 21, 43–52.

Neirotti, L.D., Bosetti, H.A. and Teed, K.C. (2001) Motivation to attend the 1996 Summer Olympic Games. *Journal of Travel Research* 39 (3), 327–331.

Nicholson, R. and Pearce, D. (2000) Who goes to events: a comparative analysis of the profile characteristics of visitors to four South Island events in New Zealand. *Journal of Vacation Marketing* 6 (3), 236–253.

Punch, K. (1998) *Introduction to Social Research: Quantitative and Qualitative Approaches*. Sage Publications, London.

Queensland Government (2006) Queensland Wine Industry Development Strategy, Department of Tourism, Fair Trading and Wine Industry Development (http://www.dtftwid.qld.gov.au/, accessed 16 January 2006) .

Seaton, A. (1997) Unobtrusive observational measures as a qualitative extension of visitor surveys at festivals and events: mass observation revisited. *Journal of Travel Research* 35 (4), 25–30.

Sekaran, U. (1992) *Research methods for business: a skill-building approach*. John Wiley, New York, .

Sparks, B. and Malady, J. (2004) Developing wine and food regions – product people and perseverance. *Proceedings of the International Wine Tourism Conference*, Margaret River, Western Australia, 7–9 May 2004.

Swan Valley Tourism Council and City of Swan (2004) *Swan Valley: Perth's Valley of Taste. Guide Brochure.*

Swan Valley Tourism Taskforce and State Planning Commission (1998) *Swan Valley: Tourism Development Implementation Strategy*. Western Australian Tourism Commission, Perth, Australia.

Taylor, R. (2001) Product, service, experience: what differentiates event visitors from everyday tourism visitors? *Touristics* 17, 1.

Taylor, R. and Shanka, T. (2002) Attributes for staging successful wine festivals. *Events Management* 7, 165–175.

Tourism Australia (2005) Wine Tourism In Australia, Niche Market Snapshot. *Tourism Research Australia* (http://www.tourism.australia.com/content/Niche/niche_snapshot_wine.pdf, accessed 16 January 2006).

Weiler, B., Truong, M. and Griffiths, M. (2004) Visitor profiles and motivations for visiting an Australian wine festival. *Proceedings of the International Wine Tourism Conference*, Margaret River, Western Australia, 7–9 May 2004.

Wine Industry Association of Western Australia and the Western Australian State Government (1997) *Western Australian Wine Industry Strategic Plan*. Wine Industry Association of Western Australia, West Perth, Australia.

15 Analysis of Motivational and Promotional Effects of a Wine Festival

Jingxue (Jessica) Yuan,[1]* SooCheong (Shawn) Jang,[2] Liping A. Cai,[2] Alastair M. Morrison[2] and Sally J. Linton[3]

[1]Department of Nutrition, Hospitality and Retailing, Texas Tech University, Lubbock, Texas, USA; [2]Department of Hospitality and Tourism Management, Purdue University, West Lafayette, Indiana, USA; [3]Indiana Wine Grape Council, Food Science Department, Purdue University, West Lafayette, Indiana, USA
*E-mail: jessica.yuan@ttu.edu

Introduction

Wine tourism is a newly emerged form of alternative tourism that overlaps both the wine and tourism industries. It has been recognized as part of agricultural tourism, rural tourism, cultural tourism, industrial tourism and special interest tourism (Yuan *et al.*, 2005). Wine tourism is also rapidly becoming a viable field of study for tourism researchers and practitioners alike, as many wine growing regions throughout the world are experiencing noticeable growth in the wine tourism sector (Macionis and Cambourne, 1998; Cambourne *et al.*, 2000).

Getz (2000) stressed that the conceptualization of wine tourism should be examined from three major perspectives: wine producers, tourism agencies and consumers. Thus, wine tourism is simultaneously a form of consumer behaviour, a strategy by which tourist destinations develop and market wine-related attractions and imagery, and a marketing opportunity for wineries to educate and to sell their products directly to consumers (Getz and Brown, 2005).

Researchers have acknowledged the role that wine festivals play in selling wine brands, promoting the attractiveness of wine growing regions, enhancing the image of the destinations and helping build customer loyalty toward individual wineries and their wines (Getz, 2000; Hoffman *et al.*, 2001; Bruwer, 2002). According to Getz (1991), festivals and special events are among the fastest growing forms of leisure and tourism-related phenomena. Wine festivals can accomplish a unique synergy between wine, special events and travel activities, adding more value to the tourism development of a wine region (Salter, 1998; Yuan *et al.*, 2005).

Yet few wine tourism studies to date have examined in depth the nature of a wine festival from either the demand or the supply side. For example, what are wine festival attendees' motivations and segmentation? What are the effects of a wine festival in promoting wine products and destinations? Visiting wine festivals is one important activity in the complete construct of wine tourism (Hall and Macionis, 1998). As a special event, a wine festival, if taking place at a convenient location, may attract attendees who do not intend to visit any winery and thereby would never be ascribed to the category of wine tourists (Yuan *et al.*, 2005).

Following the conceptualization of wine tourism by Getz (2000) and Getz and Brown (2005), this study attempts to analyse a wine festival from both the consumer behaviour and marketing perspectives. The overall goal of this study, therefore, is two-fold: (i) to examine wine festival attendees' motivations and subsequent segmentation; and (ii) to investigate the promotional effects of a wine festival through a cognitive model on consumers' decision process.

Literature Review

Wine tourism and wine festivals

When defined from the consumers' perspective, wine tourism is the 'visitation to vineyards, wineries, wine festivals and wine shows for which wine tasting and/or experiencing the attributes of a wine region are the prime motivating factors for visitors' (Hall and Macionis, 1998, p. 197). The changing trend and motivations in travel have driven wine tourism into more of a lifestyle and personal development experience than a primary recreational pursuit (Beames, 2003). Today's more educated and sophisticated travellers tend to experience a holiday with wine. Engaging in wine tourism enables them to look for authenticity, uniqueness, social contact, novelty and education (Hall and Weiler, 1992).

By fully understanding what their customers want, wine regions can provide the total wine tourism experience in a number of ways, the most notable being cultural heritage, hospitality, education and festivals and events (Charters and Ali-Knight, 2002). Wine festivals are the cultural resources of an area and organized to deliver a positive image of a place (Uysal *et al.*, 1993). Wine festivals also create a one-stop shopping opportunity for participants to sample wines from a particular region (Hoffman *et al.*, 2001). Attending festivals is recognized as the main reason and specific motivation for visiting wineries or wine regions (Hall and Macionis, 1998). Yuan *et al.* (2005) defined a wine festival, from the consumer's perspective, as a special occasion that attendees 'actively engage in for the satisfaction of their interest in wine and/or for the entertainment made available by other leisure activities' (p. 39).

Wine festivals take place at different locations (Getz, 2000). Taylor and Shanka (2002) examined a wine festival in the urban/rural peripheral zone of a Western Australian wine region. Their study demonstrated the importance of the location in contributing to the overall success of such an event. When a regional wine festival is staged in the centre of a city, it enables the convergence of rural setting (wineries and their products) and urbanity (city infrastructure and a connection with modern life). These festivals serve to promote the wine-growing region on a wider scale. They consequently appeal to a broader range of participants, who may be motivated by a wide variety of reasons.

Festival motivation framework

Festivals are themed and unique (Getz, 1991). The name of an event or festival can potentially influence motives and behaviour (Getz and Cheyne, 2002). The benefits attained through participation in festivals and special events are diverse. Accordingly, festival attendees attempt to satisfy one or more needs at the event (Iso-Ahola, 1982). The analysis of the underlying benefits sought for festival attendance is an important marketing tool for market segmentation and effective promotion (Lee, 2000).

With recognition of festivals and events as one fast-growing form of tourism attraction, researchers have examined motivations of visitors attending festivals and events. A review of the findings from these studies reveals some key festival motive dimensions: escape, excitement and thrills, novelty, socializing, family togetherness, and cultural exploration (e.g. Ralston and Crompton, 1988; Uysal *et al.*, 1993; Backman *et al.*, 1995; Schneider and Backman, 1996; Formica and Uysal, 1998; Lee and Lee, 2001; Lee *et al.*, 2004). In addition to the common motives and benefits, some of the studies also found unique dimensions of motivation attached to different festivals and events. The uniqueness is often associated with and specific to the theme of the festival or event (Scott, 1996; Kerstetter and Mowrer, 1998). Travel motivated by festivals and special events thus concerns seeking universal leisure experience as well as attaining unique benefits related to the theme of the event (Lee, 2000; Getz and Cheyne, 2002; Yuan *et al.*, 2005).

In their exploratory research on event motives and behaviour, Getz and Cheyne (2002) provided a general framework for evaluating motives to attend festivals and events. Multiple motives may apply to any given event visit. First, generic (common) leisure and travel motives incorporate the related theories (e.g. Maslow's hierarchy of needs). Secondly, event-specific motives stem from the inherent uniqueness of events and targeted benefits related to the theme and programme. An additional dimension encompasses a number of extrinsic motives that are unrelated to any specific appeal of the event itself (i.e. business, obligation and incentive). For instance, some people might attend a festival out of obligation because friends or family want to go. Generic leisure/travel motives, event-specific motives and extrinsic motives form an integrated framework that can serve as a foundation for the study of wine festival motivations.

A model of the promotional effects of a wine festival

Festival and special events can be used to enhance awareness of the destination and position it in a specific marketplace (Derrett, 2004). The decisions of staging a festival come from a special-interest group eager to educate a wider audience and to enhance the acceptance of the cultural practice at the destination. Festivals and events thus become a significant element in destination development by providing a medium for interpretation of the place (Getz, 1997). In recent years, festivals have become a viable component of both the wine and tourism industries. Getz (2000) proposed the roles of festivals and events in wine tourism as attractions, animators, image makers and catalysts for wine tourism.

Wine festivals are sometimes staged by winemakers to increase sales of their wine and to create product awareness (Houghton, 2001). Wine-related events, however, are more likely to be organized by wine and tourism industry associations and/or destination management agencies to promote attractiveness of wine regions and help build loyalty to the region and its individual wineries (Getz, 2000; Hoffman *et al.*, 2001). When having a good time at a wine festival, people may develop a positive image towards the wine tourism region and this image may lead to future visits to explore the tourist attractions at the destination. Wine festivals thus have increasingly become an effective promotional strategy for wine regions throughout the world (Collins, 1996).

Nevertheless, little empirical work has been expended to examine how marketers can utilize a wine festival to promote wine products and destinations. To help decipher the process, this study proposed a cognitive model of consumers' decisions by incorporating the concepts of perceived quality, satisfaction and behavioural intentions. According to the theoretical framework proposed by Lazarus (1991), attitudes might be linked to behavioural intentions following this sequence: appraisal is a function of emotional response, which leads to coping. Bagozzi (1992), in his application of the framework, asserts that individuals engage in activities (e.g. purchasing a product) typically because of a desire to achieve certain outcomes. If the individual's appraisal of that activity indicates that the person has achieved the planned outcome, an affective response (e.g. satisfaction) follows (Gotlieb *et al.*, 1994). The effect is then followed by a coping response (e.g. intending to purchase the product again) to maintain or increase the level of satisfaction.

This general theoretical framework can help explain the relationship among perceived quality, satisfaction and behavioural intentions. Definitions of perceived quality (a consumer's appraisal of a product's overall excellence (Zeithaml, 1988)) and empirical evidence (Parasuraman *et al.*, 1988; Bolton and Drew, 1991) indicate that it is an appraisal construct. Therefore, consumers are likely to judge perceived quality (i.e. appraisal), which will be followed by satisfaction (i.e. an emotional response). In addition, satisfaction has a direct effect on behavioural intentions (i.e. a coping response). It is a mediating variable that might link perceived quality and behavioural intentions (Baker and Crompton, 2000; Cronin *et al.*, 2000; Tam, 2000; Thrane, 2002).

Ample literature exists in the fields of marketing, consumer behaviour and hospitality exploring the causal relationship: perceived quality leads to customer satisfaction, which is a function of behavioural intentions. Some researchers also assert that service quality had a significant effect on behavioural intentions (Cronin and Taylor, 1992; Qu and Ping, 1999). This study thus developed a theoretical model. The model integrates perceived festival quality, satisfaction of the festival attendees and their subsequent behavioural intentions on wine products and destinations. Moreover, the study postulated attendees' awareness of wine and wineries as a mediator between: (i) festival quality and behavioural intentions; and (ii) satisfaction and behavioural intentions.

In the marketing field, awareness is seen as an important indicator of advertising effectiveness and essential for the communications process to occur as it precedes all other steps (Rossiter and Percy, 1987; Macdonald and Sharp, 1996). Awareness has also been hypothesized to play a crucial role in determining the consideration set in a consumer's purchase decision process (Howard and Sheth, 1969; Narayana and Markin, 1975). The proposed theoretical model is shown in Fig. 15.1, with six causal relationships.

- Relationship 1 (R1): Perception of the wine festival quality positively influences satisfaction with the wine festival.
- Relationship 2 (R2): Perception of the wine festival quality positively influences awareness of local wines and wineries.
- Relationship 3 (R3): Satisfaction towards the wine festival positively influences awareness of local wines and wineries.
- Relationship 4 (R4): Perception of the wine festival quality positively influences the behavioural intentions to buy local wines and to visit local wineries.

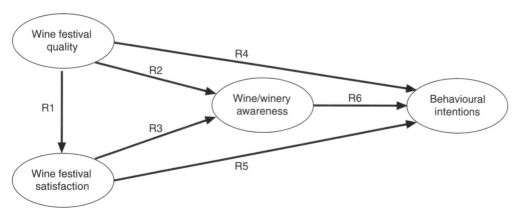

Fig. 15.1. A proposed model: the role of the wine festival in promoting product and destination.

- Relationship 5 (R5): Satisfaction towards the wine festival positively influences the behavioural intentions to buy local wines and to visit local wineries.
- Relationship 6 (R6): Awareness of local wines and wineries positively influences the behavioural intentions to buy local wines and to visit local wineries.

Research Method

Sample

A visitor survey was conducted at the 2003 Vintage Indiana Wine and Food Festival, a one-day event organized by the Indiana Wine Grape Council and taking place at downtown Indianapolis. It is Indiana's only statewide wine and food festival and was initiated in June 2000. The 2003 event featured live music, a variety of foods presented by local restaurants and wine and food educational sessions. Most importantly, 14 Indiana wineries offered free samples of more than 100 wines and also sold their wines by glass and by bottle. More than 6000 visitors attended the event in 2003. Ten trained field workers intercepted the attendees on the site of the festival and completed survey questionnaires through personal interviews. Only visitors above 21 years of age were selected. A total of 501 useable questionnaires were collected.

Measurement

A scale of 25 elements was extracted from the literature to measure motivations for visiting wineries/wine regions and for attending other types of festivals. Respondents were asked to indicate the importance of the reasons for attending the festival on a seven-point Likert scale, where 1 = not at all important and 7 = extremely important.

Scales were also developed to measure the four constructs in the conceptual model. Twelve items were used to assess perceived quality of the wine festival on a seven-point scale, where 1 = strongly disagree and 7 = strongly agree. A factor analysis was performed to reduce the 12 variables to three perceived quality dimensions labelled as facility, wine and organization. Two statements were developed to test the attendees' satisfaction level: (i) experience at the festival in terms of value for money (1 = very poor and 7 = very good); and (ii) overall satisfaction with the visit (1 = very dissatisfied and 7 = very satisfied).

The construct of awareness was measured by two items: (i) the wine festival increased the subject's awareness of local wines (1 = little and 7 = very much); and (ii) the wine festival increased the subject's awareness of local wineries (1 = little and 7 = very much). Two indicators were used to measure the construct of behavioural intentions: (i) likelihood of buying local wines after the wine festival (1 = very unlikely and 7 = very likely); and (ii) possibility of future visitation to a local winery after the wine festival (1 = very unlikely and 7 = very likely).

Data analysis

The analyses of the study consisted of two separate procedures. First, the 25 motivational elements were factor-analysed by using the maximum likelihood method combined with a Varimax rotation. The analysis resulted in a four-factor solution. This factor analysis was followed by a cluster analysis to identify the underlying segments on the basis of factor scores. A tracing of the ratio of intra-group to inter-group variance suggested a three-fold grouping as an appropriate compromise between generality and intra-group uniformity.

Secondly, the properties of the four constructs in the hypothesized model were tested with an AMOS procedure of structural equation modelling (SEM) (Joreskog and Sorbom, 1993). In the SEM process, the Maximum Likelihood (ML) method of estimation was adopted (Anderson and Gerbing, 1988). The overall model fit measures were employed to evaluate the structural model fit. Standardized solutions were used to report the casual relationships.

Findings and Discussion

Sample description

About 76% of the respondents at the festival had college or above degrees. Nearly 69% had annual household incomes of more than $40,000. The respondents were younger than the average wine consumer, as 29.5% of them were in the 21–29 age group and another 22.6% in 30–39 category; and a total of 74.1% were less than 50 years old. The percentages of male and female respondents were 35.9 and 63.7, respectively. Married (53.3%) and not married (46.5%) respondents were fairly evenly split.

Wine festival attendees' motivations and segmentation

The factor analysis on motivations produced a four-factor solution. The total variance explained was 53.0%. The total Cronbach's alpha value indicated that the model was internally reliable ($\alpha = 0.89$). The four dimensions were then labelled according to the variables that carried higher factor loadings within each particular factor. The factors were named as:

- festival and escape ($\alpha = 0.88$);
- wine ($\alpha = 0.81$);
- socialization ($\alpha = 0.73$); and
- family togetherness ($\alpha = 0.78$).

The first factor, 'festival and escape', consisted of nine variables: (i) enjoying special events; (ii) going for the festive atmosphere; (iii) enjoying a festival crowd; (iv) enjoying a day out; (v) changing pace from everyday life; (vi) enjoying the entertainment; (vii) for the uniqueness of the festival; (viii) getting away for a weekend; and (ix) trying something new. The second factor, 'wine,' included five variables: (i) experiencing local wineries; (ii) tasting wine; (iii) becoming familiar with Indiana wines; (iv) increasing wine knowledge; and (v) buying wines. The third factor, 'socialization,' included three variables: (i) meeting people with similar interests; (ii) exchanging ideas with wine makers; and (iii) visiting a place one can talk about when getting home. The last factor, 'family togetherness,' included two variables: (i) bringing family together more; and (ii) spending time with family.

The cluster analysis produced three distinct groups on the basis of the motivational factor scores. These three clusters were named after the highest cluster coefficient(s), respectively, as: (i) wine focusers (27% of the valid sample); (ii) festivity seekers (56%); and (iii) hangers-on (17%). The wine focusers geared their attention toward the wine-related experience at the festival. The benefits they were seeking were straightforward and clear-cut: wine was their primary pursuit. They did not care much about the other activities or entertainment available at the festival. The festivity seekers indulged themselves in almost every aspect of the festival with an evident enthusiasm for festivals and escaping. They seemed to consider wine as an add-on experience. Their major purpose at the festival was to enjoy a special event and its festive atmosphere, and to be entertained. The hangers-on group showed no interest in virtually anything at the festival. They were just hanging around at the festival site, making no evident attempt to get involved with the festivities. They particularly eschewed the wine theme.

Promotional effects of the wine festival

The results of the standardized parameter estimates for the structural model lend support for all the proposed relationships, except for Relationship 4. The perception of wine festival quality had a strong positive impact on wine festival satisfaction (standardized coefficient = 0.673) (R1), suggesting that perceived quality was an important antecedent of customer satisfaction in the wine festival setting. While the effect of perceived wine festival quality on behavioural intentions was not significant (R4), the festival quality significantly influenced the improvement of the awareness of local wine and wineries (standardized coefficient = 0.189) (R2).

At the same time, the awareness of the local wine and wineries had a strong positive effect on the behavioural intentions to buy local wines and to visit local wineries (standardized coefficient = 0.549) (R6). Thus, it could be interpreted that perceived festival quality did not have a direct impact on behavioural intentions, but it could motivate the customer intentions through awareness, indicating the mediating role of awareness between festival quality and behavioural intentions.

Wine festival satisfaction positively influenced both the awareness of local wine and wineries (standardized coefficient = 0.353) (R3) and the behavioural intentions to buy local wines and to visit local wineries (standardized coefficient = 0.270) (R5). Thus, satisfaction with the festival was found to have a direct and, simultaneously, an indirect effect through awareness on behavioural intentions. Satisfaction is also found to have two mediating roles: one that links festival quality to awareness and the other that connects festival quality to behavioural intentions.

Awareness, in the meantime, acts as a mediator between satisfaction and behavioural intentions. Thus, it could be concluded that if the festival quality is high enough to satisfy the visitors, the festival could improve the visitors' awareness toward associated wines and wineries and could subsequently motivate their behavioural intentions.

Implications for Wine Tourism

Visiting wine festivals is one activity class within the overall construct of wine tourism. For wineries and wine growing regions, wine festivals provide substantial public relations value, develop new markets by attracting a greater range of attendees and may have long-term effects on visitor numbers such as developing loyalty to the destination and its individual wineries (Cambourne and Macionis, 2000; Hoffman *et al.*, 2001). Based on Getz's (2000) and Getz and Brown's (2005) conceptualization of wine tourism, this study explored the nature of a wine festival from consumer behaviour and marketing approaches. Segments of wine tourists attending a regional wine festival on the basis of attendance motivations were first defined. The promotional effects of the wine festival on local wine products and wineries were then investigated.

Wine festival motivation and segmentation

Wine festivals attract a wide range of attendees who are not homogeneous in their motivations and, consequently, marketers need to adopt a segmented strategy. The study identified three different types of wine festival attendees, namely wine focusers, festivity seekers and hangers-on. The motivational segmentation corresponded with the postulation for structuring festival motives by Getz and Cheyne (2002), who stated that festival motives of any given event visit incorporated three interacting components, namely generic leisure and travel motives, event-specific motives and extrinsic motives.

The festivity seekers were primarily seeking to fulfil generic needs for a leisure experience. Their participation in the festival was motivated by common reasons that have been found in other festival motivation studies. The wine focusers were largely pursuing the wine and its related themes at the festival. Their motives stemmed from the inherent uniqueness of the festival and targeted benefits related to the theme. The hangers-on might have attended the festival out of obligation, which is considered an extrinsic motive unrelated to any specific appeal of the festival itself.

The segmentation approach in this study produced viable market segments that can be differentiated on managerially relevant variables. These findings should be valuable to the organizers of wine and food festivals and destination marketers in wine-growing regions. The festival atmosphere appealed successfully to a large group of attendees who were motivated by the prospect of enjoying a fun experience. The festival organizers should continue with the provision of the experience to retain this group of visitors.

Other attendees who were highly interested in wine found the festival an ideal venue to sample and buy local wines and get acquainted with local wineries. This is where the organizers may accentuate the unique wine theme to meet the needs of these wine lovers and to promote the regional wines. A small portion of the attendees (the hangers-on) came for a completely different set of reasons and had limited interest in the event. However, the exposure probably opened up the world of wine to them. Incentives may be offered to induce them to attend subsequently.

Promotional effects of a wine festival

This study extends previous research by specifically considering the possible ways in which a wine festival is used to promote associated products (wine) and destinations (winery). An empirical test upon the proposed model in this study indicated that perceived quality and satisfaction of the festival bring about or 'cause' product/destination awareness and subsequent behavioural intentions to buy the wines and visit the wineries exhibiting at the event.

A wine festival thus creates marketing opportunities for wineries and wine regions to educate their customers or potential customers. By developing a wine festival with good quality (e.g. entertaining live music, a variety of wine, being well organized), wine marketers may possibly help the attendees become aware of local wine products and those wineries that produce the wines. The increased level of awareness may subsequently lead into the attendees' intentions to buy the wine and visit the wineries as a destination. A wine festival with good quality could also produce satisfied attendees, who in turn would gather awareness of the wine and the wineries. The awareness would eventually contribute to heightening intentions to buy the wine and visit the wineries.

Wine festivals can act as attractions, animators and catalysts for wine tourism. Wine-related events present opportunities for wine regions to enhance the awareness of the products by individual wineries and to promote the attractiveness of the whole destination. The substantial role played by wine festivals in selling wine products and promoting wine-growing regions has thus been verified by this research study by using a cognitive model on consumers' decision process. Wineries, particularly small-scale businesses with limited marketing budgets, are encouraged to get more involved in wine-related festivals and events with good quality where they can seize sizeable marketing benefits.

References

Anderson, J. and Gerbing, D. (1988) Structural equation modelling in practice: a review and recommended two step approach. *Psychological Bulletin* 103, 411–423.

Backman, K., Backman, S.J., Uysal, M. and Sunshine, K.M. (1995) Event tourism: an examination of motivations and activities. *Festival Management and Event Tourism* 3 (1), 15–24.

Bagozzi, R.P. (1992) The self-regulation of attitudes, intentions, and behavior. *Social Psychology Quarterly* 55, 178–204.

Baker, D.A. and Crompton, J.L. (2000) Quality, satisfaction and behavioural intentions. *Annals of Tourism Research* 27 (3), 785–804.

Beames, G. (2003) The rock, the reef and the grape: the challenges of developing wine tourism in regional Australia. *Journal of Vacation Marketing* 9 (3), 205–212.

Bolton, R.N. and Drew, J.H. (1991) A multistage model of customers' assessments of service quality and value. *Journal of Consumer Research* 17, 375–384.

Bruwer, J. (2002) Wine and food events: a golden opportunity to learn more about wine consumers. *The Australian and New Zealand Wine Industry Journal* 17 (3), 92–99.

Cambourne, B., Hall, C.M., Johnson, G., Macionis, N., Mitchell, R. and Sharples, L. (2000) The maturing wine tourism product: an international view. In: Hall, C.M., Sharples, L., Cambourne, B. and Macionis, N. (eds) *Wine Tourism Around the World: Development, Management and Markets.* Butterworth-Heinemann, Oxford, UK, pp. 24–66.

Cambourne, B. and Macionis, N. (2000) Meeting the winemaker: wine tourism product development in an emerging wine region. In: Hall, C.M., Sharples, B., Cambourne, B. and Macionis, N. (eds) *Wine Tourism Around the World: Development, Management and Markets.* Butterworth-Heinemann, Oxford, UK, pp. 81–101.

Charters, S. and Ali-Knight, J. (2002) Who is the wine tourist? *Tourism Management* 23, 311–319.

Collins, C. (1996) Drop in for more than just a drop. *Weekend Australian*, 9 March, p. 3.

Cronin, J.J. and Taylor, S.A. (1992) Measuring service quality: a re-examination and extension. *Journal of Marketing* 56, 55–68.

Cronin, J.J., Brady, M.K. and Hult, G.T.M. (2000) Assessing the effects of quality, value, and customer satisfaction on consumer behavioral intentions in service environments. *Journal of Retailing* 76 (2), 193–218.

Derrett, R. (2004) Festivals, events and the destination. In: Yeoman, I., Robertson, M., Ali-Knight, J., Drummond, S. and McMahon-Beattie, U. (eds) *Festival and Events Management: an International Arts and Culture Perspective.* Elsevier Butterworth-Heinemann, Oxford, UK, pp. 32–50.

Formica, S. and Uysal, M. (1998) Market segmentation of international cultural–historical event in Italy. *Journal of Travel Research* 36 (4), 16–24.

Getz, D. (1991) *Festivals, Special Events, and Tourism.* Van Nostrand Reinhold, New York.

Getz, D. (1997) *Event Management and Event Tourism.* Cognizant Communication Corporation, New York.

Getz, D. (2000) *Explore Wine Tourism: Management, Development and Destinations.* Cognizant Communication Corporation, New York.

Getz, D. and Brown, G. (2005) Critical success factors for wine tourism regions: a demand analysis. *Tourism Management* 27, 146–158

Getz, D. and Cheyne, J. (2002) Special event motives and behaviour. In: Ryan, C. (ed.) *The Tourism Experience*, 2nd edn. Continuum, London, pp. 137–155.

Gotlieb, J.B., Grewal, D. and Brown, S.W. (1994) Consumer satisfaction and perceived quality: complementary or divergent constructs? *Journal of Applied Psychology* 79 (6), 875–885.

Hall, C.M. and Macionis, N. (1998) Wine tourism in Australia and New Zealand. In: Butler, R., Hall, C.M. and Jenkins, J. (eds)

Tourism and Recreation in Rural Areas. John Wiley and Sons Ltd., Chichester, UK, pp. 97–224.

Hall, C.M. and Weiler, B. (1992) Introduction: what's special about special interest tourism? In: Weiler, B. and Hall, C.M. (eds) *Special Interest Tourism.* Belhaven Press, London, pp. 1–13.

Hoffman, D., Beverland, M.B. and Rasmussen, M. (2001) The evolution of wine events in Australia and New Zealand: a proposed model. *International Journal of Wine Marketing* 13 (1), 54–71.

Houghton, M. (2001) The propensity of wine festivals to encourage subsequent winery visitation. *International Journal of Wine Marketing* 13 (3), 32–41.

Howard, J.A. and Sheth, J.N. (1969) *The Theory of Buyer Behaviour.* Wiley, New York.

Iso-Ahola, S.E. (1982) Toward a social psychological theory of tourism motivation: a rejoinder. *Annals of Tourism Research* 9 (2), 256–262.

Joreskog, K.G. and Sorbom, D. (1993) LISREL 8: structural equation modeling with the SIMPLIs command language. In: *Scientific Software.* Mooresville, Illinois.

Kerstetter, D.L. and Mowrer, P.H. (1998) Individuals' reasons for attending First Night, a unique cultural event. *Festival Management and Event Tourism* 5 (3), 139–146.

Lazarus, R.S. (1991) *Emotion and Adaptation.* Oxford University Press, New York.

Lee, C.-K. (2000) A comparative study of Caucasian and Asian visitors to a cultural expo. in an Asian setting. *Tourism Management* 21, 169–176.

Lee, C.-K. and Lee, T.-H. (2001) World Culture EXPO segment characteristics. *Annals of Tourism Research* 28 (3), 812–816.

Lee, C.-K., Lee, Y.-K. and Wicks, B.E. (2004) Segmentation of festival motivation by nationality and satisfaction. *Tourism Management* 25, 61–70.

Macdonald, E. and Sharp, B. (1996) Management perceptions of the importance of brand awareness as an indication of advertising effectiveness. *Marketing Research On-Line* 1, 1–15.

Macionis, N. and Cambourne, B. (1998) Wine tourism: just what is it all about? *The Australian and New Zealand Wine Industry Journal* 13 (1), 41–47.

Narayana, L.L. and Markin, R.T. (1975) Consumer behavioural and product performance: an alternative conceptualization. *Journal of Marketing* 39, 1–6.

Parasuraman, A., Zeithaml, V.A. and Berry, L.L. (1988) SERVQUAL: a multiple-item scale for measuring consumer perceptions of service quality. *Journal of Retailing* 64, 35–48.

Qu, H. and Ping, E.W.Y. (1999) A service performance model of Hong Kong cruise travelers' motivation factor and satisfaction. *Tourism Management* 20 (2), 237–244.

Ralston, L. and Crompton, J.L. (1988) Motivations, service quality and economic impact of visitors to the 1987 Dickens on the Strand emerging from a mail-back survey. *Report No. 3 for the Galveston Historical Foundation,* Texas A&M University, College Station, Texas.

Rossiter, J.R. and Percy, L. (1987) *Advertising and Promotion Management.* McGraw-Hill, Singapore.

Salter, B. (1998) The synergy of wine, tourism and events. In: Dowling, R. and Carlsen, J. (eds) *Wine Tourism: Perfect Partners: Proceedings of the 1st Australian Wine Tourism Conference,* Margaret River, Western Australia, May 1998, pp. 249–260.

Schneider, I.E. and Backman, S.J. (1996) Cross-cultural equivalence of festival motivations: a study in Jordan. *Festival Management and Event Tourism* 4, 139–144.

Scott, D. (1996) A comparison of visitors' motivations to attend three urban festivals. *Festival Management and Event Tourism* 3 (4), 121–128.

Tam, J.L.M. (2000) The effects of service quality, perceived value and customer satisfaction on behavioural intentions. *Journal of Hospitality and Leisure Marketing* 6 (4), 31–43.

Taylor, R. and Shanka, T. (2002) Attributes for staging successful wine festivals. *Event Management* 7, 165–175.

Thrane, C. (2002) Music quality, satisfaction,

and behavioural intentions within a jazz festival context. *Event Management* 7, 143–150.

Uysal, M., Gahan, L. and Martin, B. (1993) An examination of event motivations: a case study. *Festival Management and Event Tourism* 1 (1), 5–10.

Yuan, J., Cai, L.A., Morrison, A.M. and Linton, S. (2005) An analysis of wine festival attendees' motivations: a synergy of wine, travel, and special events? *Journal of Vacation Marketing* 11 (1), 37–54.

Zeithaml, V.A. (1988) Consumer perceptions of price, quality, and value: a means-end model and synthesis of evidence. *Journal of Marketing* 52, 2–22.

16 Strategic Planning for a Regional Wine Festival: the Margaret River Wine Region Festival

JACK CARLSEN[1]* AND DONALD GETZ[2]

[1]Curtin University, Perth, Western Australia, Australia; [2]Haskayne School of Business, University of Calgary, Canada
*E-mail: jack.carlsen@cbs.curtin.edu.au

Introduction

This chapter focuses on strategic planning for a regional wine festival. A case study of the Margaret River Wine Region Festival (MRWRF) illustrates the strategic planning process, with emphasis on the development of a 5-year vision for the festival. This process is of considerable interest within the context of wine tourism, but it also serves to generate recommendations for the planning of food and wine festivals in general. It begins with a review of relevant literature on wine festivals and their planning, marketing and management. Also as background, generic strategic planning for festivals is discussed, encompassing the important issues of organizational culture and the evolution of professionalism.

Most of the chapter is devoted to analysis of the MRWRF strategic planning process. The history and evolution of the festival is outlined, then details are provided on strategic planning process for the festival conducted in 2005. The authors were retained to advise the organizers and to help them formulate a strategy for the future to 2010. Previous visitor surveys were utilized as input to the process, along with a focus group comprising both internal and external stakeholders of the MRWRF Association (MRWRFA). The process also included expert input from the authors on matters of organizational development, marketing and branding, plus a SWOT analysis to place the festival in its competitive environment.

Recommendations made to the organizers, and their responses, are presented in the case study. The authors recommended that the festival needed repositioning in the marketplace, and needed strengthening in terms of its appeal and its ownership. A major aim was to elevate the festival's tourist attractiveness to at least that of a nationally significant event, while at the same time ensuring that all key stakeholders – especially the area's residents – would continue to feel ownership and commitment for the annual event. To achieve this repositioning and strengthening, a new name, mission statement and vision were recommended. Strategies for programming – and specific goals – were also recommended for adoption.

Literature Review

Wine festivals can stimulate visitation, raise awareness of a region and effectively promote regional wine tourism (Hoffman et al., 2001; Hall, 2003). Events can also maintain the profile of a wine region in key markets and assist in differentiating wineries and wine regions in a competitive market environment. The inclusion of events and festivals in marketing, branding and promoting wine regions has become so important that now practically every winery and wine region throughout the world hosts a wine festival and/or wine tourism event (Carlsen, 2002).

Frochot (2000, p. 67) found that promotion of wine festivals in France is often geared towards local and domestic markets. Houghton (2001) found that wine festival attendance increases the propensity for subsequent visits to wineries and attracting more visitors to wine regions in South Australia. Wine festivals attract mainly a local attendance and often lack the marketing and alliances needed to generate international tourism. For example, Toast Martinborough, one of New Zealand's most successful wine festivals (Getz, 2000), attracted only 3% of its visitors from overseas in 1999 (TRC, 1999). An estimated 10% of visitors to the 2000 Margaret River Region Wine Festival were from overseas and 5% from other Australian states (Carlsen, 2002).

There has seldom been a strategic approach to planning, marketing, managing and developing wine festivals or attracting target markets, promoting wine tourism, selling wine and maintaining awareness. This is despite the many benefits that such an approach could offer to wineries and wine tourism regions. For example, wine festivals generate immediate and substantial benefits to wineries in terms of sales, brand awareness and brand loyalty (Cambourne, cited in Hall et al., 2000). Wine festivals present an opportunity to identify the wine tourism market and the potential for target marketing to be employed (Carlsen, 2002). Wine festivals are also an appropriate environment in which to study wine tourism because visitors are mainly motivated by the opportunity to experience wine and wine-related activities, in line with popular definitions of wine tourism (Hall and Macionis, 1998, p. 197), specifically: 'Visitation to vineyards, wineries, wine festivals and wine shows for which grape wine tasting and/or experiencing the attributes of a grape wine region are the prime motivating factors for visitors.'

Wine events include new vintage releases, themed tastings and dinners, functions such as weddings at wineries, wine education programmes, conferences in wine regions and art exhibitions at wineries, viticultural field days and trade shows (Carlsen, 2002). Using a strategic approach, wine festivals and events could make a significant contribution to the marketing efforts of wineries and wine regions and support the increased consumption and sale of wine. A strategic approach to wine festivals can support the development of marketing strategies, improve the event and enhance the festival experience.

Getz (2000), in his book *Explore Wine Tourism*, discussed the major tourism-related roles of wine festivals, being that of tourist attraction (especially to overcome low-demand periods), image maker for the destination and catalyst for infrastructure development. 'Community wine festivals' were assessed, and this category applies to Margaret River. Their programming typically consists of education, entertainment, dining and drinking, commerce and trade (by and for the wine and tourism industries) and a variety of recreational opportunities. Profiles of community wine festivals were provided from Martinborough, New Zealand, and Grapevine, Texas, while the Leeuwin Concerts in Margaret River were featured as exemplar of private-sector wine events.

According to Getz (2005), strategic planning is a future-oriented process which seeks to attain goals through the formulation and implementation of broad, long-term strategies. A 'strategy' is an integrated set of policies and programmes intended to achieve the vision and goals of the organization. Strategy is rooted in a vision of the future and it outlines general ways to get there; it often leads to more detailed plans, policies and programmes.

Mintzberg (1994, p. 209) proclaimed that 'visioning' is at the heart of strategic planning. It is a process of setting the broad outline of a strategy, or identifying elements of a desired future. Every event organization should have not only a mandate, or statement of its purpose, but a vision statement which can motivate and foster unity of purpose among all stakeholders. At the heart of visioning is consideration of the ideal future state of the event and/or its organization. This vision can then be translated into goals pertaining to:

- desired size (e.g. attendance, volume, revenues, staff, volunteers);
- desired setting (e.g. the best venues, location);
- desired reputation and market position (e.g. the best and biggest event of its kind within a defined area);
- desired market mix (e.g. dominant and secondary segments attracted); and
- desired financial state (e.g. profit or surplus revenue and its uses, debt elimination, self-sufficiency for continuance or growth).

A good vision statement is one that reflects the organization's mandate or mission, is broad and general enough to attract widespread support, and sufficiently inspired and forward looking to stimulate innovation in its pursuit. Consultations with stakeholders will be important in shaping the vision, especially if they are to be asked to support the strategies and goals which flow from it.

Statements of mission or vision provide general direction for the organization, but not for specific programmes or management functions. Goal statements are needed to help translate the general direction of the organization into more tangible, results-oriented efforts. Once goals are formulated they must usually be translated into specific objectives which provide measurable targets and time frames. Objectives must be realistic and attainable, and it is generally useful to build in measures by which results will be evaluated, i.e. 'performance criteria' or 'key results'.

Key research support for strategic event planning includes the following: (i) ongoing consumer and market area research (to understand existing and potential market segments); (ii) situation analysis (stakeholder input and issues identification); and (iii) environmental and future scanning (what trends and forces are affecting us?). Analysis of Strengths, Weaknesses, Opportunities and Threats (SWOT) is a standard evaluation and planning tool. It can be performed internally, based on how the organization perceives itself, or by external consultants who will make comparisons to other events. The SWOT analysis is an excellent way of assessing the competitive position of the organization or its events. When tied to 'benchmarking', it can help the organization make specific changes for improvement.

Evolution of the festival is in keeping with the model of organizational change and professionalism as applied to events (see Getz, 2005, p. 207), in which the foundation stage is generally one of informality; a more formal organization then emerges, resulting in the professionalization of the event. This model is potentially reiterative, encompassing periods of growth and decline, higher and lower degrees of professionalization, depending in large part on available resources as well as competition. The life cycle concept can also be applied to wine festivals, giving rise to the expectation that change (both organizational, marketing and programmic) must be managed in order to prevent decline – especially in the face of rising competition.

Festival marketing

Although there is considerable advice available on how to market an event (see, for example, Hoyle, 2002; Masterman and Wood, 2006), little has been published in research journals on the subject of the marketing or tourism orientation of festival organizations. One relevant study was Mayfield and Crompton's (1995) examination of Texas festivals as to their visitor orientation, including their pre- and post-event evaluation of visitor experiences. Those researchers concluded that most organizers perceived themselves to be visitor oriented, but few did pre-experience evaluations (i.e. needs assessments or market segmentation). Sophistication in marketing appeared to reflect resources available, which is a similar conclusion to that made by Frisby and Getz (1989) regarding the evolution of professionalism in festival organizations in Ontario, Canada.

With similar findings, a study of small, community-oriented festivals in Norway by Mehmetoglu and Ellingsen (2005) concluded that they did not adopt a market orientation (specifically intelligence generation, internal dissemination and responsiveness to intelligence). The main reasons for not adopting the market orientation were found to be a lack of money and expertise, and the researchers concluded that holding a tourism orientation was closely associated with adoption of a true market orientation.

Larson's (2002) work on festivals in Sweden is also quite germane. Larson employed the concept of a 'political market square' in examining festival organization and marketing, with emphasis on interests, conflict and power. She found that certain actors (i.e. stakeholders) dominated the marketing process, and that five political processes could be observed: (i) gatekeeping (controlling entry to the festival); (ii) negotiation (which reflects relative power); (iii) coalition building (including formal alliances and interpersonal networks); (iv) building trust (based on reputation and past performance); and (v) identity building (the event's image or brand is a stabilizing force). All these processes appear to be inherent in many festival organizations owing to their multi-stakeholder nature. The more open they are, the more perspectives have to be accommodated, and this leads to a discussion of membership.

Festival membership

The typical not-for-profit festival organization (often a legally incorporated society) requires a committed and active membership. Members provide a base for committee and volunteer work, they elect and become directors, and are often charged with generating external support (Getz, 2005). Membership issues are also an element in external stakeholder management, because members are recruited from sponsoring companies, affiliated organizations, the audience and the community at large. The broader and larger the membership base, the more likely it is that the event occupies a sustainable niche in the community in terms of population ecology theory (see Donaldson and Preston, 1995). On the other hand, membership will often be deliberately restricted because of the various political processes identified by Larson (2002).

Virtually no research about event membership has been reported in the literature, so this remains an area in need of attention. Progress can be made through application of several theoretical perspectives, including stakeholder theory, population ecology and the political market square. Case studies of the type reported in this chapter can also contribute by identifying examples that fit into established theoretical frameworks (a kind of hypothesis-confirmation recommended by Eisenhardt, 1989) and by suggesting new hypotheses through application to new situations.

Case Study: the Margaret River Wine Region Festival

The first Margaret River Wine Region Festival (MRWRF) was held in 1990 and was a fairly informal festival, attracting mainly locals involved in the emerging wine and tourism industries. A period of growth ensued through the1990s and 'What started out as a small, mainly domestic affair has turned into an enormous event attracting many interstate and international guests' (MRWRF Association, 1999, unpublished).

From these informal beginnings the festival evolved over the next 5 years with the formation of the Margaret River Wine Region Festival Association (MRWRFA). This membership-based association is run by a management committee, comprising volunteers from wine and tourism industries and supported by a paid part-time secretary. In 1999 the association, in taking the final step to professionalism, appointed a festival director to develop a vision for the festival, market and promote the festival and to source corporate sponsorship.

The vision statement of the festival association 'envisions a world-class and internationally acclaimed festival which draws visitors from Australia and around the world to enjoy wineries, restaurants, music, arts, crafts and other attractions and activities of the Margaret River Wine Region' (McMillan, 2000, unpublished report). The festival association secured major sponsorship from *The Sunday Times* newspaper for 1999, 2000 and 2001. For the first time in the event's 10-year life, corporate sponsorship provided a platform to change the overall format of the event and afforded a level of resources that was unprecedented in the life cycle of the festival.

The MRWRF is a multiple-venue festival, that involved more than 60 events in 2000 at wineries, breweries and galleries, as well as community events with a dedicated bus service operating between most of the venues. The festival was held over one weekend until 1999, but was extended to 10 days and two weekends in November (10th to 19th) in 2000. Market research (Carlsen, 2002) in 1999 indicated that 75% of visitors would attend the festival again in 2000 and about 14% would attend over both weekends. The advent of the 10-day format was supported by marketing strategies designed to persuade visitors to stay during the week and enjoy the quality wine and services provided in the region. Extending the festival to 10 days over two weekends aimed for new programming to attract repeat visitors, as well as encouraging a longer stay in the region for the festival.

A period of rapid growth in the numbers of stakeholders, venues and events ensued, with the festival offering 185 separate events in 2002. It was immediately apparent that this number of events was not sustainable as there were too many competing events and, by 2004, the number of events was consolidated to 65 and it reverted back to the single-weekend format with a better mix of events. Festival Association membership had reached 80 wineries, tourism attractions, breweries and food producers, and stakeholders included regional tourist bureaux, Shire Councils (Augusta-Margaret River and Busselton) and the Margaret River Wine Industry Association. The 2005 festival boasted 60 events, including winemakers' dinners, cooking classes, music, art and community celebrations (*The West Australian*, 2005).

Research Methods

With this background, it is apparent that the festival was confronted with a number of options which could best be addressed using a strategic approach. The objective was to develop a vision for the festival based on existing research and information and taking into account the current views of the Festival Association membership. This required a focus on the future vision of the Association (Mintzberg, 1994) and the development of more detailed plans, policies and programmes (Getz, 2005), including specific strategies for repositioning of the festival.

Two related steps were employed in developing a strategic plan for the festival. First, early in 2004 a review of existing MRWRF research, documents and reports from previous years' festivals was conducted. This included market research, post-event reports and visitor profiles. The second step involved the conduct of a focus group, SWOT analysis and planning session with members of the Festival Association held in Margaret River in March 2005.

Review of existing documentation

Documented marketing strategies (MacMillan, 2000, unpublished report; McInnes, 2004, unpublished report)) focused on two target markets for the festival. First, 'young affluents' aged between 18 and 40, from predominantly professional and managerial backgrounds. Young affluents are not formally educated about wine, although they are keen to know more. They are also 'influencers' who will attract many more of their friends to the region and its wines. Secondly, 'serious wine lovers' tend to be older (35–65), also from professional and managerial backgrounds, highly educated, have high disposable incomes and are highly knowledgeable about their wines. Serious wine lovers tend to buy wines for cellaring, and are therefore likely to spend much more than the first group on a per-head basis.

In order to profile these markets, visitor surveys were conducted in 1999 and 2000 (Carlsen, 2002). In 1999, 299 useable interviews were conducted and, in 2000, 317 interviews and self-completed surveys were returned, comprising 200 useable interviews and 117 useable self-completed surveys. In both projects a convenience sampling method was used, so there is no measure of the statistical reliability or validity of the sample. Visitors from Perth are the predominate respondents in both samples, followed by visitors from other WA, NSW, Victoria and Queensland. Both samples included 10% international visitors, mainly from the UK/Europe.

Feedback from the 2004 event indicated that 65 events over a 2-day weekend may not be sustainable, as events compete with each other for patrons, resulting in some events being poorly attended and financial losses from hosting events, particularly the larger events. The majority of members indicated that their venue was not as busy as the previous year. A members' survey indicated that about half of the respondents would not host an individual event in 2005, but a new showcase event, 'Fusion', at which many of the wineries offered tastings, with some food and entertainment provided, was more successful. The 'Fusion' event is more financially viable than individual winery events as there is an entry fee to cover costs and about half of the wineries take wine orders at the event (McInnes, 2005, unpublished report). However, as the 'Fusion' is an all-day event, it competes with the individual winery events that are also part of the Festival. For example, there were some 15 events at wineries, galleries and other venues on the same day as the 2005 'Fusion' event (*The West Australian*, 2005).

The focus groups and planning workshop

A strategic planning worksheet incorporating goals identification, stakeholder networks and a SWOT analysis was provided by the authors. A total of 23 members attended the workshop, representing most of the key stakeholders, and input from each member was obtained as to the vision, structure and future development of the festival over the following 5 years. Particular emphasis was placed on: (i) developing a vision and mission statement; (ii) naming and positioning the festival; and (iii) identifying a number of goals and strategies to support the mission statement.

Participants reacted to the material presented by consultants, then through discussion formulated a number of recommended changes. The SWOT analysis (Box 16.1) is the result of this collective exercise, and it can be interpreted as both a kind of situation analysis and issues identification process.

Box 16.1. SWOT analysis for the Margaret River Wine Festival.

Strengths	Weaknesses
Debt-free	The Association needs a broadly based Board of Directors focused on governance, not on festival production
Professional, dedicated staff	
Evolving programme with popular elements	Need more local government support, especially in Margaret River itself
The Margaret River brand is strong	
Great wine, food and art product	Need for an attractive focal point in Margaret River
	Need for a themed, festival ambiance, especially in Margaret River
	Too many programme elements, lacking certainty and cohesion
Opportunities	**Threats**
Expand to a nationally significant event	Many other festivals in Australia offer similar product
Build resident support/ownership and demand	
Build younger and female audiences	Lack of community support can hurt growth potential
Use brand equity to its fullest (to attract sponsors, tourists, co-producers)	Grants and sponsorship revenue is not reliable
Bring all key stakeholders into an ownership position	

Outcomes of the Strategic Planning Process

The following outcomes from the review of existing documentation and focus group sessions were achieved. The findings are the culmination of various inputs from a wide range of sources dating back over the previous 5 years, as well as a creative visioning process looking forward to the year 2010. Some discussion as to the visioning process and subsequent implementation of strategies for the 2005 festival completes the case study.

The newly formulated mission statement defines the mandate or core purpose of the Association: 'To produce an annual festival that enables visitors to experience the unique and attractive lifestyle of the Margaret River region.'

This makes it clear that the Association exists primarily to produce an annual festival with a broad, appealing programme. The festival theme, as described in the mission and the following positioning statement, is a celebration of a unique and appealing lifestyle that is offered to visitors and shared with residents. Lifestyle is often what initially attracted the wineries and associated businesses to the region and, as such, provides the unifying theme for all stakeholders as prescribed by Mintzberg (1994). The programme fitting this theme will be diverse, encompassing food, wine, the arts and other ways of experiencing the region's lifestyle. This mission gives rise to a number of strategies:

- To ensure that all stakeholder groups, including area residents, local governments and the tourism and wine industries, feel ownership and commitment for the festival.
- To seek continuously to improve the experience for visitors as well as for participants in the festival.
- To maintain a board of directors that represent all the key stakeholders and consisting of individuals who are committed to sound governance of the Association.
- To employ professional staff to administer the Association and produce the festival.
- To engage in developmental activities, such as production of other events, to generate revenue and publicity for the annual festival.

In line with the future orientation of the strategic planning process (Getz, 2005), the 5-year vision for the Festival is: 'By the year 2010 The Margaret River Festival will be nationally recognized as a major lifestyle event, with sufficient appeal to specifically annually attract food, wine and arts lovers from all of Australia.'

This vision statement provides a clear indication of what the Association wants its festival to be in 5 years time, and leads to more detailed strategies in relation to positioning, programming, marketing and membership of the Festival Association.

Given the relatively low number of international visitors to wine festivals in other regions (TRC, 1999, unpublished report; Carlsen, 2000, unpublished report; Frochot, 2000), achieving international stature in this period is not realistic. However, it should be possible through repositioning, goals and strategies to become a major Australian wine festival that attracts visitors from the other states of Australia.

This vision will require considerable marketing and promotional effort in cities other than Perth, where the festival is now best known. Plans are in place to seek the following: (i) a major airline sponsor that can package a festival holiday and promote it through their networks; (ii) engagement of a public-relations company that can manage media releases and other promotional efforts; (iii) advertising in glossy magazines; and (iv) partnering with local, state and national tourism associations to promote the festival in their calendars of events. There is also an opportunity to link the festival to an annual wine and tourism conference in the region and to promote it at conferences leading up to the 2006 festival.

A unique selling proposition (USP) and fresh, appealing programme will have to be developed and effectively communicated to lovers of food, wine and the arts in particular. Margaret River will offer them a unique lifestyle event reinforced by the existing image as a producer of high-quality wines, food, art and entertainment. The current marketing theme appeals to the five senses and rotates through these over 5 years, with 'Taste It' having been the 2005 theme and 'Feel It' the 2004 theme.

Positioning strategies

The stakeholders considered that the Festival could be renamed as part of a positioning strategy. Some suggestions were *The Margaret River Festival* (drop 'wine' and 'region') and the *Margaret River Wine Festival* (drop 'region'). 'Margaret River' is a successful, unique brand, recognized nationally and internationally as a premium wine region. Including 'wine' in the name is not necessary for wine lovers who are already familiar with the region. Including 'region' in the name is unnecessary because most people already associate Margaret River with the wider south-west of Australia as a holiday destination. However, there was resistance to changing the name of the festival as much effort had been invested in 'branding' it as a regional wine festival, rather than with a focus on Margaret River township and surrounds. The festival name represents the desired market position of the festival and capitalizes on the reputation of the region for having appealing food, arts and lifestyle experiences, and is related to vision.

Positioning statements are used in marketing campaigns to communicate the USPs to target markets. They have to be sophisticated, yet not snobbish. The following statements emphasize a unique experience that only Margaret River can deliver and suggest that the community is united in inviting guests to share their way of life:

- Experience the Margaret River lifestyle.
- Our fine wine, cuisine and the arts are presented for you in the special ambiance of our annual Margaret River Festival.

This positioning and USP has to be backed by fresh, appealing programming, attractive settings (including all venues), high quality of product and service, and convenient packaging for tourists. Thus the positioning strategy addresses two of the elements of the vision, the desired setting and the desired reputation and positioning of the festival.

Programming strategies

To implement the mission and attain the vision, adoption of a series of goals and related strategies is required. These strategies, along with the marketing and organizational strategies discussed below, demonstrate the evolution of the event and that it is reaching the 'professionalism' stage of the event life cycle (Getz, 2005). Perhaps the most important of these pertain to programme development, or what the festival experience will be. The following are the main programming goals – representing in essence the strategic redesign of the festival.

1. Within 5 years, to build the festival to a 10-day, two-weekend format.

To become a truly national festival will require two weekends. Heavy publicity achieved in the first weekend can build demand for the second. Midweek should provide residents with more opportunities.

2. To set specific standards and criteria for the inclusion and production of all events within the Margaret River Festival.

The number of programmed events should be controlled through a set of application criteria and performance standards. Companies and associations desiring to hold events will be 'sanctioned co-producers' of the festival.

3. The Association should concentrate on three programme activities:

- Coordination and control of sanctioned programme elements.
- Production of the 'core festival element'.
- Creation of the desired festival ambiance, especially in Margaret River town.

The festival Association has to rely on other associations and companies to produce most of the festival, so its own efforts have to be focused.

4. The 'core programme element' produced by the festival association should meet the following criteria:

- Central (in Margaret River itself).
- Attractive (the town and venue should have a themed, festival ambiance; be the photogenic festival showcase).
- Predictable (same venue and dates every year; keep popular elements every year).
- Unifying (bringing all stakeholders, visitors and residents together).
- Creative (try a new element every year).
- Profitable (make money for the festival association).
- Affordable (sell multi-entry passes to residents, or provide discount).

It is highly desirable for any festival to have an attractive focal point, to be predictable as to time and place (this could mean the same weekends every year, not necessarily the same dates) and to combine traditionally popular elements with annual creativity to keep the programme fresh. '"Co-producers" should pay a fee for the privilege of using The Margaret River Festival brand or agree to profit sharing, and should be required to financially underwrite their event. "Co-producers" can be classified as "major" or "minor", with "major co- producers" being offered a seat on the Board of Directors.'

This model will limit the association's risk, generate revenue and allow it to focus on the core programme element. Major stakeholders should be brought into the association formally through director positions. This model might require the full 5-year time period to be fully operational.

Marketing and communications

The following recommendations are intended to complement the positioning and programming strategies.

1. Launch a national promotional campaign to promote the new name and using the new positioning statement.
2. Obtain major national sponsors to facilitate a national marketing campaign.
3. Use the Internet to its fullest potential, particularly by incorporating virtual experiences of the festival and encouraging online booking.
4. Foster exclusivity by restricting numbers to major programme elements and by requiring advance bookings; reserve a specific quota for tourists buying packages; work with wholesalers and retailers to sell packages.
5. Become more tourist oriented through the following actions:

- Offer a variety of attractive packages.
- Offer VIP service for premium prices.
- Ensure that every visitor is welcomed and made to feel special.

6. Target a younger segment and female with messages and programming designed for their preferences.

Membership

Recommendations for membership reform derive from the repositioning strategy and the need to ensure that the organization reflects its mission. There was a conscious intent to broaden the base in order to make the festival a true community event and not have it perceived to be just for and by the tourism industry.

Expansion of the membership should be a priority, to incorporate all stakeholders and especially the community at large. Membership could be in one of two categories: voting and non-voting (it might be wise to require a minimum number of years of membership in order to gain voting privileges).

Major stakeholders should be allocated voting memberships and seats on the directors' board to ensure a broad base of support and active involvement. Local government, chambers of commerce and professionals with expertise should be targeted to help in governance, along with wine and tourism industry agencies (not individuals) and community associations.

The Association has to be broad based, including all major stakeholders. While individual members should be able to vote and stand for office (after specified period of time), the Board of Directors should also legally incorporate representatives of key government agencies, and important community and industry groups.

Implications for Wine Tourism

The case study of the Margaret River Wine Festival demonstrates many practical lessons for wine tourism and festivals in general. The value of strategic plans for festivals is clearly linked to an ongoing need for renewal and improvement within a competitive marketplace. As the festival has evolved, questions have arisen concerning its mission, organization and programming, all of which required strategic appraisal. These issues are of considerable concern to the tourism industry and wine tourism in particular, given the festival's profile in shaping the image of the wine region and its ability to attract off-peak visitors.

The process of strategic planning is probably as important as the substance. Getting all stakeholders involved, resolving conflicts and working towards consensus are difficult, but vital, challenges. Obtaining external, expert analysis and recommendations can serve to focus the discussions and provide well-articulated alternatives. The case study also demonstrates the necessity of ongoing research to support marketing and strategic planning.

Situation analysis, environmental and future scanning are inherent in strategic planning. The festival has to be assessed in terms of its own development, its community and regional context, the wine and tourism industries, and real or potential competitors. A SWOT analysis is one tool in this exercise, but data are also needed on trends and competitors. Multiple stakeholders must be involved in this process. In this festival case, the tourism and wine industries and the community had to negotiate their respective goals for the festival and its organization.

Many events make the mistake of collecting information only from consumers, and while this constitutes valuable data it does not provide anything about potential customers or those who deliberately reject the product. Accordingly, market area surveys should periodically accompany visitor surveys.

Benchmarking should be pursued by festival organizers, through a process of systematic comparison with other, successful events. Events in other regions are more likely to cooperate, given the apparent lack of immediate competition. The process has not only to identify successful practices (such as attractive programming or effective marketing campaigns) but also must reveal the underlying organizational, managerial and resource bases of success. Benchmarking among festivals is, unfortunately, rarely practised.

Establishing performance indicators and an ongoing monitoring process are also inherent in strategic planning. The Action Plan, which implements strategies, has to provide concrete directions on how success and efficiency will be measured. The plan has to be revisited periodically, and this case clearly demonstrates that need.

Implications for wine festivals

The issue of industry *versus* community control is an important one. An industry-oriented and -dominated wine tourism festival runs the risk of alienating local support, resulting in loss of demand, volunteers and political support. Sustainability of all festivals rests on broad stakeholder support and the continuing ability of stakeholders to deal with arising issues, to negotiate mutually beneficial positions and to obtain necessary resources (see Larson, 2000).

By their very nature wine – or wine and food festivals – are a representation of local culture and lifestyle – they cannot merely be sampling or sales-oriented events. Each wine tourism festival should be unique in many ways, otherwise the sense of place that is an important part of the wine tourism product can be lost. Only broad community input and support can ensure that local culture and lifestyle are authentically incorporated. In the future, more emphasis will have to be placed on interpreting authentic cultural dimensions to visitors, and this in turn will reinforce uniqueness and authenticity.

Finally, life-cycle implications always have to be considered. Organizational culture evolves, competition tends to increase and programming over time tends to become stale. To retain competitiveness, the change process must be managed, necessitating strategic planning. As research on wine festivals increases, more will be learned about how successful ones adapt and become permanent – hallmark events representing the wine tourism destination.

However, it is difficult for community-oriented festivals to adopt and implement a true market orientation (Mayfield and Crompton, 1995; Mehmetoglu and Ellingsen, 2005), but the Margaret River Wine Festival is an example of how a tourism orientation and broad-based community involvement stimulates, or at least facilitates, this process. Visitor surveys are an important form of market intelligence, but this case also demonstrates the necessity of gaining a better understanding of non-customers, and using visioning and goal setting to select desired customers. Market intelligence is of little use unless it is disseminated internally (in this case study a planning workshop was used both to inform and involve the key stakeholders), and unless it is used in planning and marketing. For the MRWRF a repositioning process was initiated, including specific, recommended communication actions. Ongoing research will be necessary to determine if this strategy is successful.

This case study also makes it clear how membership, in the context of stakeholder theory (Donaldson and Preston, 1995) and the concept of a political market square (Larson, 2002), is integral to the marketing and strategic planning process. The festival plan made specific recommendations to ensure broad-based community and industry support, which is a difficult challenge for a tourism-oriented event that depends on volunteers, local government cooperation and local ticket sales. Reflecting the conclusions of Mehmetoglu and Ellingsen (2005), the MRWRF case supports their proposition that a market orientation is more closely associated with significant tourism demand and a tourism-oriented mandate, compared to small, community-oriented festivals.

The exact mechanism by which stakeholders are, or should be, involved in festivals is a matter for strategy, and relevant research has not been reported in the literature. The authors recommended that membership be expanded and that key stakeholders be asked to sit on the board of directors, thereby formalizing their commitment. At the heart of this strategy is the need to balance tourism and community interests, and this can probably be achieved most effectively within the 'political market square' of the organization. Accordingly, the organization must monitor its decision-making processes as carefully as it plans and implements its marketing strategy.

References

Cambourne, B., Hall, C.M., Johnson, G., Macionis, N., Mitchell, R. and Sharples, L. (2000) The maturing wine tourism product: An international view. In: Hall, C.M., Sharples, L., Cambourne, B. and Macionis, N. (Eds.) *Wine Tourism Around the World: Development, Management and Markets.* Butterworth-Heinemann, pp. 24-66.

Carlsen, J (2000) The Sunday Times Margaret River Wine Region Festival 2000 Visitor Survey. Unpublished report to the Margaret River Wine Region Festival Association.

Carlsen, J. (2002) Segmentation and Profiling of the Wine Festival Visitor Market. In: C. Cullen, G. Pickering and R. Phillips (Eds) *Bacchus to the future: An Inaugural Brock University Wine Conference.* St Catharines Ontario: Brock University.

Donaldson, T. and Preston, L. (1995) The stakeholder theory of the corporation: Concepts, evidence, and implications. *Academy of Management Review,* 20(1) pp65-91.

Eisenhardt, K. (1989) Building theories from case study research *Academy of Management Review,* 14 (4): 522-550.

Frisby, W., and Getz, D. (1989) Festival management: A case study perspective. *Journal of Travel Research,* 28(1): 7-11.

Frochot, I. (2000) Wine Tourism in France: a paradox? In Hall, C.M., Sharples, E., Cambourne, B. and Macionis, N. (Eds.) *Wine and Tourism Around the World: Development, Management and Markets,* pp 67-80. Oxford: Butterworth Heinemann.

Getz, D. (2000) *Explore Wine Tourism: Management, Development and Destinations.* New York: Cognizant Communication Corporation.

Getz, D. (2005) *Event Management and Event Tourism* (second ed.). New York: Cognizant Communication Corporation.

Hall, C.M. (2003) Consuming places: the role of food, wine and tourism in regional development. In: Hall, C.M., Sharples, L., Mitchell, R. and Macionis, N. (eds.) *Food Tourism.* Butterworth Heinemann, Melbourne.

Hall, C. M. & Macionis, N. (1998). Wine tourism in Australia and New Zealand. In Butler, R. W., Hall, C. M. and Jenkins, J. M. (eds.) *Tourism and recreation in rural areas* pp., 267-298. Sydney: John Wiley & Sons

Hall, C.M., Sharples, E., Cambourne, B. and Macionis, N. (2000) *Wine and Tourism Around the World: Development, Management and Markets*. Oxford: Butterworth Heinemann.

Hoffman, D., Beverland, M.B. and Rasmussen, M. (2001) The evolution of wine events in Australia and New Zealand: A proposed model. *International Journal of Wine Marketing*, 13(1): 54-71.

Houghton, M. (2001). The propensity of wine festivals to encourage subsequent winery visitation. *International Journal of Wine Marketing*, 21(3): 32-42

Hoyle, L. (2002). *Event Marketing*. New York: Wiley.

Larson, M. (2002) A political approach to relationship marketing: Case study of the Storsjöyran Festival. *International Journal of Tourism Research*, 4 (2): 119-143.

Masterman, G. and Wood, E. (2006). *Innovative Marketing Communications Strategies for the Events Industry*. Oxford: Elsevier.

Mayfield, T. and Crompton, J. (1995). The status of the marketing concept among festival organizers. *Journal of Travel Research*, 33(4): 14-22.

McInnes, P. (2004). *The Margaret River Region Wine Festival Business Plan*. Unpublished report to the Margaret River Wine Region Festival Association

McInnes, P. (2005). *The Sunday Times Margaret River Region Wine Festival 2004 Directors Report*. Unpublished report to the Margaret River Wine Region Festival Association

McMillan, R. (2000). *Action Plan for the 2001 Sunday Times Margaret River Wine Regional Festival*, Unpublished report to the Margaret River Wine Region Festival Association

Mehmetoglu, M., and Ellingsen, K. (2005). Do small-scale festivals adopt "market orientation" as a management philosophy? *Event Management*, 9(3): 119-132.

Mintzberg, H. (1994). *The Rise and Fall of Strategic Planning*. New York: The Free Press.

Margaret River Region Wine Festival Association (1999). Marketing Research Brief (unpublished),.

The West Australian (2005). Margaret River Region Wine Festival. November 13, 2005

Tourism Resource Consultants [TRC] (1999). Toast Martinborough Wine Food and Music Festival 1999 Visitor Survey. Unpublished consultants report to Toast Martinborough Ltd.

Part VI
Wine Tours and Trails

17 Nautical Wine Tourism: a Strategic Plan to Create a Nautical Wine Trail in the Finger Lakes Wine Tourism Region of New York State

MICHAEL Q. ADAMS

181 Wood Street, Flinders, VIC 3929, Australia
E-mail: mqa888@hotmail.com

Introduction

This chapter provides a preliminary report of an ongoing study on nautical wine tourism in the Finger Lakes wine region of New York State, USA. Nautical wine tourism results from the convergence of two distinct types of tourism, wine tourism and nautical tourism. There is a rich history of waterways and wineries coming together to create appealing visitor destinations, covering most of the world's major wine producing countries. The ancient barge canals of France, where Thomas Jefferson wrote fondly in 1787 of his Canal du Midi boat trip through the vineyard country, are just as popular today with wine tourists (Americans-in-France.Com, 2004). The wine cruise boats, which travel past the ancient Roman vineyards of the Moselle and Rhine regions in Germany, are another good example of nautical wine tourism (K-D German Rhine Line, 1991). In Western Australia, the Swan River provides opportunities for tourists to visit several area wineries on cruise boats (Captain Cook Cruises, 2004).

In the Finger Lakes Wine Tourism Region of New York State, both wine tourism and nautical tourism are quite well developed (New York State Canal Corporation, 2003b; New York State Office of Parks, Recreation and Historic Preservation, 2003; BoatU.S. Department of Public Affairs, 2004). However, they are presented as two completely separate tourism products, without a focused programme to combine them as a nautical wine tourism experience. It has become apparent to some of the wineries in the region and other stakeholders that this is a missed opportunity.

The project study is an exploratory effort to address the following questions related to implementing a successful nautical wine tourism product for the region.

- What is the definition of and components of a nautical wine tourism product?
- What are the potential benefits of establishing a nautical wine trail in the Finger Lakes?
- What are the issues and level of interest among the stakeholders in such a scheme?
- What costs are associated for stakeholders participating in a nautical wine tourism scheme?
- How could such a nautical wine trail be implemented successfully in the Finger Lakes?

This paper will define the concept, introduce the exploratory research conducted so far, describe the physical and market characteristics of the study site, categorize and quantify the stakeholders, identify findings which emerged during the research, suggest implications for nautical wine tourism and provide references for further research.

Definitions

Wine Tourism has been defined as 'travel related to the appeal of wineries and wine country; a form of niche marketing and destination development, and an opportunity for direct sales and marketing on the part of the wine industry' (Getz, 2000, p. 4).

Nautical wine tourism may be defined as the creation and promotion of a visit experience which includes, on the one hand, a winery, vineyard or wine-related activity and destination and, on the other, the visit itself; the latter is made either by means of water transport or occurs on or near the water. In other words, the destination is water-accessible. This definition would include visits to riverside or lakeshore wineries and vineyards, wine cruises, wine tastings at waterfront restaurants, etc.

Water-accessible implies a site that is on or near the water. This definition would also include sites where visitors arrive by boat, and then continue to the wine-related destination by foot, golf cart, bicycle, coach, etc. It is not unusual for a vineyard to be on or visible from a lake or river, but the tasting room itself may be 1–2 km away. Sometimes a local and convenient means of land transport is required for the destination to be considered water-accessible.

Examples of water-accessible, wine tourism-related destinations include the following: (i) Sandleford (sp) Winery in Western Australia; (ii) The Lake House Hotel and Restaurant in Victoria, Australia; (iii) Mitchelton Winery in Victoria, Australia; (iv) The Aurora Inn on Cayuga Lake, New York; (v) Sheldrake Point Vineyard on Cayuga Lake, New York; (vi) Belhurst Castle on Seneca Lake, New York; and (vii) the ancient port houses along the Duero River in Portugal, to name but a few.

The Finger Lakes study site

The study site covers three interconnected bodies of water and the land around their shores. The water bodies are Cayuga Lake, Seneca Lake and the Cayuga-Seneca Canal, which is part of the New York State Canal System. The region has a very strong brand image because of its scenic beauty, wineries and access to major population centres (D.K. Shifflet & Associates, 2001) (Fig. 17.1).

The lakes are long, narrow and deep (60 km long, 3–4 km wide and 132–188 m deep), with sloping banks rising gradually to spectacular vistas over the lakes, and dotted with vineyards. The two lakes are parallel, separated by about 11 km. The lakes are connected at their northern end by the 19 km-long Cayuga-Seneca Canal, which is also connected to the statewide Erie Canal system (New York Canal.Com, 2004; New York State Department of Environmental Conservation, 2004). These two Finger Lakes are classified by the state as being part of the Erie Canal system.

The Erie Canal, originally built in 1825 to open up the 'western frontier'

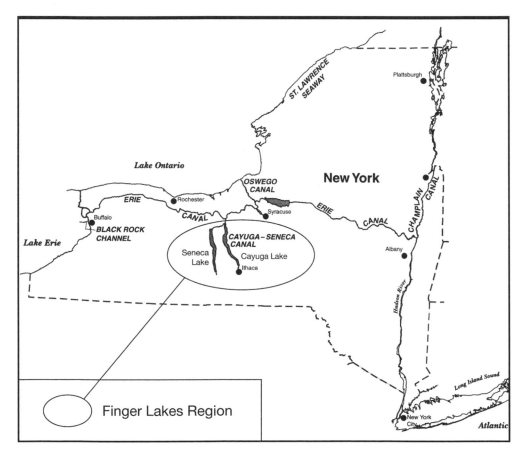

Fig. 17.1. New York waterways and canals.

of the day, has been redeveloped by New York State as a major international tourism destination for recreational boaters. It is now possible to cross the entire state (835 km) on the canal, through a network of locks. The canal also has connections to Lake Erie, Lake Ontario, the Finger Lakes, the Saint Lawrence Seaway and Canadian canal network, and via the Hudson River to New York City and the Atlantic Ocean. There are several companies that rent canal houseboats for visitors to do independent cruising, or boaters can bring their own boat to travel the canal system. Because of the extensive promotion of canal tourism by the state, there is an opportunity for the Finger Lakes to leverage those resources to promote nautical/winery adventures in its own region (New York State Canal Corporation, 2003a).

The extent of general tourism activity in the Finger Lakes region continues to grow rapidly. The visitor person-days reached 45 million in 2000 and visitor trips reached 23 million. The average length of stay is just over 4 days. The average distance travelled by visitors to the region is 835 km, which includes most of the north-eastern USA as well as Ontario, Canada. The population base in this half-day travel zone is more than 50 million people (D.K. Shifflet & Associates, 2001).

There are more than 50 wineries around the two lakes in the study area, each lake with its own wine trail – Seneca Lake Wine Trail and Cayuga Lake Wine Trail. Seven of the wineries have direct waterfront access, or have established an on-call shuttle service at a nearby boat dock. In addition to the wine tourists and recreational boaters, the study has identified more than 100 waterfront stakeholders in the study site, spread over ten general categories (see Table 17.1). It is an impressive list when combined, and provides a very comprehensive array of destination and service infrastructure for the nautical wine visitor.

While there has been extensive research conducted on wine tourism, very few references have been identified on the topic of nautical wine tourism. Nevertheless, much of the general wine tourism research appears to have potential relevance to this topic.

Wine tourism

Jaffe and Pasternak discuss the process of establishing new wine trails, including the need to motivate the visitors, building partnerships and alliances among the stakeholders, augmenting the winery visit experience, and branding and co-branding the new wine trail (Jaffe and Pasternak, 2004). They suggest co-branding food and wine, for example.

A similar approach could be used in the Finger Lakes to promote nautical wine tourism by combining boating and wine as key elements in the brand. One means of augmenting the wine experience in the Finger Lakes could be the opportunity to see boats pull up to a winery boat dock by the non-boating wine tourists. The nautical wine tourists and their boats could themselves become part of the attraction of the region. Jaffe and Pasternak also point out the importance of identifying a central coordinating organization to undertake

Table 17.1. Stakeholders: Finger Lakes Nautical Wine Tourism.*

	Cayuga Lake	Seneca Lake	Cayuga-Seneca Canal	Regional and state	Total
Wineries with water access	5	2			7
Marinas, boat launches, boat rentals and yacht clubs	12	8	11		31
Tour boat operators	3	4	2		9
Other tour operators	4	5	2		11
Waterfront restaurants	19	12	10		41
Waterfront accommodation facilities	13	7	4		24
State tourism, boating and natural resource organizations	–	–	–	8	8
Wine trail associations	1	1	–	2	4
Local/regional tourism organizations and chambers of commerce	11	11	2		24
Parks, campgrounds and historic sites	9	9	6		24
Towns with waterfront districts or harbours	4	3	2		9
Local boat owners					115,000
Traditional wine tourists to the region					1,600,000

* Data from Central Finger Lakes Marketing Group, 2000; New York State Canal Corporation, 2003a; New York State Office of Parks, Recreation and Historic Preservation, 2003.

the planning, coordination, research and marketing of a new wine trail. In the case of the Finger Lakes area, such a central organization would most likely exist within the regional tourism sector because of its existing relationship with the multiple counties and existing wine trails involved in the study area.

Morpeth describes a model of linked wine tourism together with cycle tourism as providing an alternative to traditional wine tourism. It offers a slower-paced and more nature-oriented form of tourism which draws on the benefits of both tourism segments. This linked model has important benefits for reducing automobile traffic in rural areas, encouraging neighbouring regions to integrate their planning and branding through policy networks, and enhancing rural economic development by bringing new visitors and operators into the wine regions (Morpeth, 2000). Several aspects of Morpeth's model of linked wine and cycle tourism can be applied to linked wine and nautical tourism. Of particular relevance to this project are the nature-oriented aspect of nautical tourism and the need to promote planning across two different wine trails and multiple county tourism authorities.

Donald Getz lists twelve critical success factors for wine tourism (Getz, 2000). Of particular relevance to nautical wine tourism are the following: (i) tourist-oriented wineries; (ii) adequate number of attractions to create a critical mass; (iii) protecting the scenic resources; (iv) accessibility to the region; (v) focusing on higher-yielding segments; (vi) organizational leadership and cooperation; (vii) consistency in wine branding; (viii) specialty events; and (ix) linking together of multiple segments such as wine, food, heritage, leisure, etc. All of these success factors appear to be highly relevant guidelines, which can be directly applied to the design of a new nautical wine trail.

The wine tourism visitor numbers for the Finger Lakes Wine Tourism Region are based on data from the New York Agricultural Statistics Service. For the year 2000, the winery visitor numbers totalled 1.2 million people, with average per-customer spending in the tasting room of US$20.30 and US$12.30 in the Cayuga Lake and Seneca Lake wineries, respectively. By 2003 Finger Lakes winery visitor numbers were estimated to have reached 1.6 million, showing an impressive growth rate of 11% per year (New York Agricultural Statistics Service, 2001).

The Finger Lakes wine tourists' motivations have been studied by Bruwer and the findings indicate that the most frequently cited attribute of the region is the scenic beauty, including the lakes and vineyards (Bruwer 2003, unpublished; 2004) (see Table 17.2). A nautical wine trail would complement these findings by including the boats traversing the lakes and docked at the waterfront wineries as an element in the scenic beauty of the region.

The other component of the nautical wine tourism opportunity assessment is the recreational boating market (see Table 17.3). There were 531,579 boats registered in New York State in 2002 and, in the specific region of the Finger Lakes, 115,818 boats were registered during the same period. There is also a means of tracking the boaters' use of the canal system in the

Table 17.2. Wine tourism characteristics, 2003.

	Responses (%)
Main purpose of wine tourists' visit to Finger Lakes wine region[a]	
Wine tourism (visit wineries and taste/buy wine)	46.9
Holiday	17.9
Just passing through	6.8
Visit friends and relatives	6.8
Business/conference	6.5
Recreation	6.2
Wine tourism and holiday	1.2
Wine tourism and visiting friends and relatives	1.2
Wine tourism and recreation	1.2
Other	5.3
Modes of transport used by the Finger Lakes wine tourist	
Own car	81.1
Rented car	7.4
Organized bus tour	4.8
Friend's car	3.4
Campervan/motorhome	1.2
Other	2.1
What are the Finger Lakes' main characteristics/elements	
Scenery/beauty/beautiful roads/scenic roads[b]	35.2
Next highest choice[c]	17.6

[a] n, 334; [b] n, 96; [c] n, 48.
Data from Bruwer (2003 unpublished, 2004).

Table 17.3. Recreational boating: market data.

BoatU.S. membership (2003) (national boating association)	550,000 (USA)
	48,000 (NY State)
Boat registrations: USA	12,854,054 (2002)
	11,132,386 (1992)
	9,073,972 (1982)
Boat registrations: New York	531,579 (2002)
	438,342 (1992)
	321,881 (1982)
Boat registrations: Finger Lakes region	115,818 (2002)
Canal pleasure craft permits: New York canal system	9,672 (2002)
Cayuga-Seneca Canal (2002)	3,859 (total boats)
Lock 2/3: Vessel lockings (entrance to the Finger Lakes)	317 (rental boats)
Boating facilities in the Finger Lakes (Cayuga-Seneca region)	
Marinas and boat launches	27
Yacht clubs	4

Data from BoatU.S., 2004; Central Finger Lakes Marketing Group, 2000; National Marine Manufacturers Association, 2004; New York State Canal Corporation, 2003b; New York State Office of Parks and Recreation and Historic Preservation, 2003.

region. Each boat that uses one of the locks on any part of the canal system is counted. By tracking the 'vessel lockings' (3859) at the point of access nearest the study site, it is possible to obtain a quantitative view of the canal boaters who may also be enticed to take a detour into the lakes to visit a winery. It is also possible to reach the local boating community through the primary boating association, BoatU.S., which has 48,000 members in New York State (New York State Canal Corporation, 2003b; New York State Department of Parks, Recreation and Historic Preservation, 2003; BoatU.S., Department of Public Affairs, 2004).

Nautical tourism can have both positive and negative impacts on the local area, particularly environmental impacts. For example, one of the most common pollution contributions of boaters is improper disposal of used motor oil and filters. A study in California found that boater education and awareness programmes were effective in correcting this behaviour (Public Research Institute, 2000). There is an opportunity for nautical wine trail member organizations in the Finger Lakes to help promote environmental awareness among the boating community by supporting coastguard and lake watershed association programmes. Participating wineries could distribute educational brochures and also offer their sites as venues for boater environmental awareness seminars.

A study of the economic impact of nautical tourism in the US State of Ohio found that the average annual trips taken by recreational boaters was 15.6, and the spending per trip totalled US$134, with food and lodging representing 41% of this expenditure. Additional expenditure on maintenance, fuel and docking totalled US$1200 per year. Boat purchases and financing represented another $2600 per year. The total spending per boat-owning household was US$5627 per year. It was also found that each 12 boating households results in one additional job for the state. The total economic impact of recreational boating in Ohio in 1998 was US$1.68 billion (US$673 million direct; US$1007 million indirect) and 19,500 jobs added to the state economy (Hushak, 1999).

A further study in New York State by Cornell University found that recreational boating had the very significant value of US$1.8 billion to the state and accounted for 18,700 jobs (Connelly *et al.*, 2004). Further research is needed to assess the potential economic impact of a new nautical wine trail in the Finger Lakes; however, the Ohio and New York studies provide a possible methodology (IMPLAN method) and points of reference.

Nautical wine tourism

In France most of the wine trails are situated along or nearby rivers, and there is a long tradition of visiting the wineries by boat (Wright, 1996). Wright further states that many of the rented canal boats include bicycles on board. Thus visitors can utilize a combination of boat and cycle to reach cellar doors that are not actually on the water.

In 1999 a study was conducted to evaluate the feasibility of implementing a Finger Lakes ferry service to connect wineries on opposite sides of Cayuga Lake (Phoenix Associates, Inc., 1999). Because of the seasonal nature of such a venture and the fact that it would primarily be used by visitors rather than local commuters, the concept was deemed to be unprofitable. The ferry idea has been retired for the time being. However, smaller *ad hoc* water transport could be established on a more economic basis by individual stakeholders or by some of the boat tour operators out of Ithaca and other locations.

In 1996 the New York State Department of Environmental Protection funded a study as part of a waterfront improvement project for one of the Finger Lakes waterfront towns on Seneca Lake. This study evaluated the feasibility of connecting all of the wineries in the region (50+) to a nautical tourism scheme. Since many of the area wineries are several kilometres from the waterfront, the concept would have required an extensive network of shuttle buses, at least on the weekends. The cost of such a transportation network was perceived as being too high, and could not be recovered from passenger ticket sales (Development Planning Services, 2002).

The Erie Canal Authority has begun to list winery locations on maps in its *Cruising Guide* for boaters (New York State Canal Corporation, 2003a). This is an effort to provide enhanced experiences and new destinations for the nautical tourists. It is also an indication of opportunities for more formal linking between the Finger Lakes wine tourism region and the Canal Authority.

Research Methods

Exploratory data were collected in telephone interviews from 15 of the estimated 100 major stakeholders in the region. These stakeholders represented wineries, marinas, boat owners, chambers of commerce and regional tourism authorities. The interviewees were randomly selected from listings in the *Canal Connections* brochure (Central Finger Lakes Marketing Group, 2000). These were open-ended interviews, which were intended to solicit a wide variety of comments that could be used in future phases of the project to build a more formal questionnaire for submission to all of the stakeholders. The responses were collected on templates by the caller. Following the interviews, the responses were organized according to the question categories.

The interviews included the following questions:

- Are you aware of nautical wine tourism locally or internationally?
- What is the scale of existing nautical tourism in the local region?
- What components could be included in a nautical wine tourism product from your stakeholder perspective?
- Are there any issues with nautical tourism in the region?
- Which are the individual stakeholder costs and activities associated with hosting visits from nautical tourists?
- What best practice guidelines can you suggest for successfully hosting nautical tourism visitors?
- What organizations could potentially host and manage a nautical wine tourism scheme in the region?
- Do you have an interest in participating in a formal nautical wine tourism scheme, if developed?
- Can you suggest other potential stakeholders in the region who may wish to provide inputs to this study?

Findings

The idea of nautical wine tourism is a good fit with the winery visitors' image of the natural beauty of the lakes, vineyards and wineries (Bruwer 2003, unpublished; 2004). Many of the wineries' vineyards are visible from the shoreline of the lakes. In the case of one winery interviewee, a 'decorative vineyard' has been planted between their boat dock and the tasting room so that boat visitors are able to walk through the mini-vineyard to reach the tasting room, thus enhancing the visual and sensual experience.

According to one interviewee in the local recreational boating community, boaters typically evaluate the following criteria when planning a day trip in their boats:

- 3–5 hour round trip;
- nice weather;

- experiences to share with friends;
- new destinations and new experiences;
- dining opportunities;
- shopping opportunities;
- entertainment opportunities (wine tasting, festivals, events); and
- able to conveniently and safely dock the boat near to the destination.

Nautical wine tourism satisfies most of the criteria on this list. In particular, the attraction of a new destination and new (fun) experience, coupled with a dining opportunity, is continually sought after by the boaters, according to several interviewees in the study area. Several of the wineries do have a food component to their winery visit product.

Awareness of current situation

More than 70% of the recreational boaters who were interviewed expressed surprise to find that there was such a variety of potential nautical destinations in the area. One of the challenges to success in nautical wine tourism will be to raise the awareness among the recreational boating community in the region.

Other components of a nautical wine trail product

The two boat tour operators that were interviewed suggested the addition of complementary nautical activities to enrich the list of possible product offerings. These included offering the following: (i) fishing boat excursions; (ii) lake ecology educational boat excursions; (iii) fishing lessons (both on boats and from the shore); (iv) small boat rentals; (v) wine cruises and charters; (vi) boat shuttles between partner stakeholders (for example between B&Bs and wineries); and (vii) beach cookouts and barbecues). Recreational boaters suggested that wineries could also host events of interest to the nautical tourists. These could include nautically themed festivals and events, workshops on boat safety or repairs, races, antique boat exhibitions and model boat clubs.

The needs of nautical visitors

The waterfront winery interviewees – as well as several boaters – shared their learning experiences of how to accommodate the nautical visitors and make their visit a positive experience. This advice will be useful to other stakeholder businesses as they consider the flow of the boat visitor traffic, including the arrival and departure process, ensuring that it is convenient, safe, visually appealing and enjoyable. The advice is presented in Table 17.4.

Table 17.4. Nautical visitor flow and needs.

Visitor process flow	Visitor needs	Suggested winery response
Visitor learns of the existence of the nautical wine trail destination	Easy to find and understand information, and it is complete and up to date	Pointer on winery website, with maps, details and photos; rules, if applicable
Visitor can easily find the winery from the water	Signage; landmarks; GPS coordinates; directions; map	Eight-foot name sign and wine trail sign; GPS measurement; nautical map and photos on website, showing landmarks
Visitor secures boat at dock/ mooring/anchorage	Adequate sized dock or mooring point with space available; adequate water depth	Adequate number of cleats; dock configuration to handle multiple boats; anchorage area for large boats; average water depth noted on website; for ferries or scheduled tour boats, reserve a slot at the dock
Visitor traverses dock and walks to winery or pick-up location	Clear directions of where to go; winery is conveniently located near the dock or a shuttle service is available; attractive landscaping of dock, foreshore and path; security of self and boat	Clear and attractive signage; road crossing signs for both pedestrians and cars; lighting, security cameras; meet-and-greet or pick-up/shuttle service for visitors, e.g. electric golf carts; possibly an intercom at the dock
Winery tasting, shopping or dining experience	Positive and memorable wine tasting or dining experience; wine and merchandise available for purchase	Attractive tasting and dining area, well-trained and friendly staff; quality products for tasting and sale; positive visual branding; recognition of the boating visitors through special events, products, souvenirs, etc.
Visitor has questions about activities in the area or other nautical destinations	Advice and directions on tourism, shopping, entertainment, dining and lodging	Maps and guides available; staff trained to assist the visitors with recommendations and directions
Visitor returns to boat via walking path or other conveyance method and departs	Clear directions of where to go; attractive landscaping of path, foreshore and dock; security of self and boat	Clear and attractive signage; road crossing signs for both pedestrians and cars; lighting; security cameras; meet-and-greet or pick-up/shuttle service for visitors, e.g. electric golf carts

Data from interviews with Finger Lakes waterfront wineries, boaters and marinas, 2004.

The physical facilities and costs of being nautical tourism-friendly

Based on stakeholder interviews, particularly with the wineries, data were collected on the physical requirements for a successful waterfront environment, together with associated costs. The data are presented in Table 17.5.

Table 17.5. Set-up costs for winery waterfront access.

Category	Format	Initial cost (US$)	Annual operation and maintenance (US$)	Other requirements
18-m boat dock	Wooden planks on steel pipe frame	15,000–50,000, depending on materials and configuration	500, power-washing, refinishing, repairs. 1,000, liability insurance	Need to reach a minimum water depth of 135 cm at end of dock, so length/ cost will vary with each site
Signage on dock and road crossing	2-m name sign and wine trail sign	500, including installation	50, cleaning and touch-up painting	Road /pedestrian crossing signs, if applicable; hours, phone number, safety info and rules
Landscaping of dock, beach and path		5,000	200	Include rubbish barrel and cigarette waste container, secured against weather and animals
Security	Security lights; camera; gate/fence	2,000+	100	Protects against vandalism and liability situations
Electric golf cart(s)	Four-person model	5,000 each	200, electricity and maintenance	Intercom for visitors to call for a pick-up/shuttle; walkie-talkie radios are also options for staff.
Staffing	If pick-up and drop-off service required	10-min pick-up/ drop-off	30-min/day clean up	Daily inspection, rubbish pick-up, sweeping, etc.
Totals		28,000–58,500	2,050	

Data from interviews with Finger Lakes waterfront wineries and marinas, 2004.

Issues

A number of issues were raised during the interviews with stakeholders. Indicative responses are listed below. The respondents did not wish to be identified in the report.

- *Are there liability concerns associated with serving wine to boaters?*
  Our insurance company advised us that they have much greater concerns about serving wine to automobile drivers than to boaters. We do not differentiate in our normal responsible consumption protocols between car and boat visitors.
- *Will the non-waterfront wineries in the region be concerned about being left out of a programme which is focused only on the wineries that do have waterfront access?*
  No, such a nautical wine tourism programme will attract the recreational boaters. This group is not currently being served by any of the area

wineries, because most of the boaters do not know that we are boat-accessible. Therefore, the programme will introduce incremental wine tourism to the region rather than cannibalizing customers from other wineries. So it will be perceived as positive for the entire wine region.

- *What organizational issues do you foresee for a Finger Lakes nautical wine trail if it were to be implemented?*

    The area of the two lakes and canal touches six counties, two wine trails and numerous chambers of commerce and tourism visitor organizations. The options for managing such a cross-boundary programme are limited. The most obvious options are a regional tourism organization or tapping into an existing cooperative team made up of several county tourism association, such as the group that produces the Canal Connections brochure on boating tourism (Central Finger Lakes Marketing Group, 2000).

Implications for Wine Tourism

The opportunity to establish and promote a successful nautical wine tourism product in the Finger Lakes Wine Tourism Region appears to be significant. There is strong economic activity in canal tourism, wine tourism and lake recreational boating in the region, but no sustained effort to unite these elements into a focused product. The number of wineries with waterfront access (seven) is already more than in many other successful nautical wine tourism regions, such as Tasmania (three), Western Australia (five) and Victoria (two). Also, many of the prerequisite elements for establishing such a new tourism product are now in place (beautiful lakes and canals, waterfront wineries; waterfront restaurants and B&Bs; marinas; waterfront parks and villages; large number of recreational boaters; strong interest in wine tourism). There is also enthusiasm among all categories of stakeholder interviewed to implement such a product.

The previous nautical wine trail study in the region, the Waterways and Wineries study, proposed including all of the area wineries into the scheme (Development Planning Services, 2002). This may have been too big a step. The current study has taken a much simpler approach, by suggesting that the project begin with only the wineries and other stakeholders that already have waterfront property or an established boater pick-up service.

Lessons from the previous studies in the region indicate the importance of minimizing barriers to entry for the stakeholders. For the stakeholders with existing waterfront access, there would be minimal cost to participate in the proposed programme. Such costs would include signage, landscaping, branding, promotion, maintenance and staff training, as identified in Table 17.5.

It is clear from the interviewees, as well as from the critical success factors identified by Getz, that an organizational 'home' and point of focus will be needed (Getz, 2000). The stakeholders cross several organizational boundaries, so this aspect is considered as being fairly important. Possible host organizations identified by the interviewees include a regional tourism authority or an existing cooperative group, made up of county tourism organizations in the target region.

Partnering and packaging will be critical in order to create a new and exciting tourism product for the consumer, since tourists in this programme have needs which go beyond the resources of individual stakeholders. Several ideas for packaging diverse components were provided by the interviewees, as well as being referenced in Getz's critical success factors (Getz, 2000). Suggestions such as links to tour boat operators, fishing instruction providers, B&Bs and marinas are quite relevant. Also, the idea was suggested of showing the nautical wine tourism visitors that they are recognized and valued. This could be accomplished by adding specialty events, nautical components to the winery gift merchandise, workshops and special packages as well as adequate boat docking and signage.

In response to the lack of awareness about the existing waterfront access by many of the interviewees, it is clear that the stakeholders need to do a better job of promoting their services to the nautical tourists. To address this need, a 'Stakeholders' Nautical Wine Tourism Start-Up and Promotion Kit' could be created and given to the stakeholders with appropriate explanation and training.

Regional tourism interviewees pointed out the scarcity of funding for new tourism projects by the State. Therefore, a phased approach to implementing a nautical wine trail is appropriate so that an immediate programme can be initiated with modest funding requirements. Implementing later phases of a nautical wine trail with more complexity would depend on the perceived success of the initial programme.

References

Americans-in-France.Com. (2004) *Barging Through the Ages*, http://www.americans-in-france.com/beginning.htm (accessed 23 February 2004).

BoatU.S., Department of Public Affairs (2004) *Membership Data*. Alexandria, Virginia.

Bruwer, J. (2003) *Finger Lakes Wine Region Wine Tourism Research Report* (unpublished confidential report).

Bruwer, J. (2004) Benchmarking key characteristics of wine and food festivals across New World wine countries. In: Carlsen, J. and Charters, S. (eds) *International Wine Tourism Research: Proceedings of the International Wine Tourism Conference, Margaret River*, Western Australia, May 2004. Vineyard Publications, Perth, Australia.

Captain Cook Cruises (2004) *Houghtons and Sandalford Famous Full Day Wine Cruise,* http://www.australia.travelmaill.com/travel-mall/tour/houghtons_and_sandalford_famous_full_day (accessed 20 February 2004).

Central Finger Lakes Marketing Group (2000) *Canal Connections: Cruise the Past, Unlock the Adventure*. Seneca County Tourism, Waterloo, New York.

Connelly, N.A., Brown, T.L. and Kay, D.L. (2004) *Recreational Boating Expenditures in 2003 in New York State and their Economic Impacts*. Cornell University, Ithica, New York.

Development Planning Services (2002) *Waterways and Wineries Final Report*. Thruway Authority, Albany, New York.

D.K. Shifflet & Associates (2001) *Finger Lakes Region, New York State: 2000 Year-end Domestic Travel Report*. New York State Department of Economic Development,

Albany, New York.

Getz, D. (2000) Explore *Wine Tourism: Management, Development and Destinations.* Cognizant Communications Corp., New York.

Hushak, L.J. (1999) Recreational *Boating in Ohio: an Economic Impact Study.* Ohio Sea Grant Publication OHSU-TB-040, Columbus, Ohio.

Jaffe, E. and Pasternak, H. (2004) Developing wine trails as a tourist attraction in Israel. *International Journal of Tourism Research* 6, 237–249.

K-D German Rhine Line (1991) *The Floating Wine Seminar: MS Austria 22 to 29 October 1991, Nijmegen-Basel.* K-D Lines, Koln, Germany.

Morpeth, N. (2000) Diversifying wine tourism products: an evaluation of linkages between wine and cycle tourism. In: Hall, C.M., Sharples, L., Cambourne, B. and Macionis, N. (eds) *Wine Tourism Around the World: Development, Management and Markets.* Butterworth Heinemann, Melbourne, Australia, pp. 272–282.

National Maritime Manufacturers Association (2004) *U.S. Recreational Boating: Domestic Shipment Statistics 1970–1998.* NMMA, Chicago, Illinois.

New York Agricultural Statistics Service (2001) *2000 New York Winery Survey.* NYASS, Albany, New York.

New York Canal.Com. (2004) *Cayuga-Seneca Canal,* http://www.nycanal.com/focuson cayugaseneca/content/cayugasenecacanal. html (accessed 23 February 2004).

New York State Canal Corporation (2003a) *The Cruising Guide to the New York State Canal System.* NYS Canal Corporation, Albany, New York.

New York State Canal Corporation (2003b) *New York State Canal System: Annual Traffic Report 2002.* NYS Canal Corporation, Albany, New York.

New York State Department of Environmental Conservation (2004) *Seneca Lake,* http://www.ohwy.com/ny/c/cayugalk.htm (accessed 23 February 2004).

New York State Office of Parks, Recreation and Historic Preservation (2003) *2002 Recreational Boating Report,* PRHP, Albany, New York.

Phoenix Associates, Inc. (1999) *Cayuga Lake Ferry Feasibility Study – Cayuga and Seneca Counties.* Phoenix, Rochester, New York.

Public Research Institute, San Francisco State University (2000) *Boating Clean and Green Campaign Pre- and Post-campaign Surveys of California Boaters.* PRI, San Francisco, California.

Wright, H. (1996) *Water into Wine: a Wine Lover's Cruise Through the Vineyards of France.* Kyle Cathie Ltd., London.

18 Wine Tourism in Portugal: the Bairrada Wine Route

LUÍS CORREIA[1]* AND MÁRIO PASSOS ASCENÇÃO[2]

[1]Polytechnic Institute of Leiria, School of Maritime Technology, Portugal;
[2]University of Applied Sciences, School of Hotel, Restaurant and Tourism Management, Finland
*E-mail: luis-correia@iol.pt

Introduction

> Do not be surprised if my handwriting is a little weird. There are two reasons for this. The first one is that this paper (the only one at hand now) is very smooth and my fountain pen slides too quickly on it; the second one is that I have just found, here at home, such a wine … splendid, from which I have opened a bottle and have already drunk half of it.
>
> (Fernando Pessoa, Portuguese poet, 1920, cited in Amaral, 1995)

Wine is a national treasure in Portugal and is a symbol of the country throughout the world. However, wine tourism is a relatively recent phenomenon in Portugal, as well as in other European countries with a long-established wine-producing history (Cambourne *et al.*, 2000). In recent years researchers around the globe have presented the advantages and disadvantages of wine tourism for wineries and the surrounding communities (King and Morris, 1997; Beverland, 1998; Szivas, 1999; Hall *et al.*, 2000), as well as the industry as a whole (Dodd, 1995; Fuller, 1997; King and Morris, 1997).

Because of the benefits that wine tourism provides, Portugal, an 'Old World wine country', has embarked on wine tourism following successful international examples. Wine tourism in Portugal is in its infancy; nevertheless recent years have seen significant developments. One tool employed is the so-called 'wine routes'. Wine routes emerged in Portugal from a movement which involved producers, oenologists, distributors, consumers, statutory organizations and other bodies connected to the industry.

This process of developing wine routes represents a new phase in the Portuguese wine industry, which is trying to reach those who have some interest in wine and are fascinated by the country's natural and cultural heritage. The wine route enables visitors to meet the wine producers as well as to participate in a variety of activities which are held in wine tasting centres and wine museums. To date, 11 wine routes have been created in Portugal under the Dyonísios Inter-regional Cooperation Programme in 1993. This is a European Union (EU) Programme intended to create economic and cultural exchange across eight wine regions in the EU, via knowledge transference in the areas of commerce, training and tourism.

The publication of the *Despacho Normativo n° 669/9*, a Portuguese government regulation, in this instance providing financial support for those involved in wine tourism, prompted a number of wine regions in Portugal to create wine routes. However, as a recent phenomenon, wine tourism in Portugal is a relatively new field of study so that little research has been conducted in the country. This research has two main objectives: first to make an evaluation of a specific wine route created under the EU Programme and Portuguese Government; and, secondly, to identify perspectives on its future potential.

Literature Review

The wine routes context

Wine routes have become important tourism products worldwide, as well as acting as a tourism promotional tool (Getz, 2000; Hashimoto and Telfer, 2003). In this way, wine routes can be seen as contributing both to the development and promotion of regional wine tourism (Marques, 2001), consequently contributing to the diversification of regional economies and increasing the reputation and image of wine regions and their wines (Cambourne *et al.*, 2000). While no research has formally established the critical success factors for a wine route, based on a number of studies some of which draw on more general tourism research (e.g. Getz *et al.*, 1999; Getz, 2000), a series of propositions can be made.

In general, a wine route consists of one or more designated itineraries through the wine region. The route should be clearly signposted as well as being marketed and interpreted via a leaflet and map, which notes the different vineyards and winemakers and provides information on sites of natural and cultural interest (Getz *et al.*, 1999; Frochot, 2000). Additionally, pictographic road signs are created using a common logo to guide travellers, and these should both be readily visible and easily read (Frochot, 2000; Getz, 2000). The route must be integrated into any national and regional framework, and must have easy vehicular access and navigation, as well as the ability to cope with the numbers of vehicle and visitors using it (Getz, 2000).

When developing a wine route, it is essential to create an organizational structure to manage and animate it. In Portugal, several wine routes were developed based on an independent structure, for example that under the aegis of the Port Wine Route Members Association. Other wine routes decided to become integrated into an existing institution, for example the Bairrada Wine Route is managed by the Bairrada Wine Commission, the local wine producers' organization. Thus wine route structure can be new or developed from an existing wine-related institution (Simões, 2003) but, ideally, it should involve both the public and the private sectors (Getz, 2000). A crucial part of this is ensuring appropriate evaluation of the route, and customer feedback (Getz, 2000). In addition, effective coordination and leadership are key prerequisites to wine tourism progress (Getz *et al.*, 1999).

According to Getz *et al.* (1999), Getz (2000), the following factors are key elements in successful wine tourism: (i) strong tourism marketing organization; (ii) cooperation between tourism and wine industry bodies; (iii) focused target marketing and communications; (iv) branding and image enhancement; and (v) packaging. All route members (wineries) must have quality wine and friendly and knowledgeable staff to ensure service quality for visitors, in order to ensure good reputation and repeat visits. Most importantly, it is necessary to have good-quality wine as visitors come to wineries primarily for the wine, although friendly and knowledgeable staff, and meeting owners and winemakers, are also considered part of the appeal (Getz *et al.*, 1999).

These can be facilitated by the development of major events which focus the attention of the key organizations involved in the delivery of wine tourism (Hashimoto and Telfer, 2003). Crucially, it is one of the paradoxes of a successful wine route that wineries need to work together – both formally and informally – with their commercial rivals if the route is to be successful (Telfer, 2001). This of course, goes against the grain for many wine producers who otherwise seek to gain competitive advantage over their neighbours.

Although the tasting of wine is the *raison d'être* of any route, this feature alone is unlikely to sustain tourism growth (Preston-Whyte, 2000). Consequently, wine route authorities can provide a source of marketing intelligence for wineries, organize activities and events such as wine fairs and contests, develop promotion/communication plans, conduct research, develop criteria for the selection of members and create tour packages (e.g. rural tourism accommodation plus visit to local wineries). They can also combine wine with other complementary activities, such as local gastronomy, architecture and heritage, mountain biking, sailing, golf, etc. (Dodd, 1995; Cambourne *et al.*, 2000; Frochot, 2000). Indeed, these links are essential, for wine on its own is unlikely to sustain the entire interest of a tourist (Getz, 2000).

The wine route can be a powerful instrument for developing long-term relationships with customers by utilizing customer databases. In addition, wine routes may create new jobs and generate commercial investment, at the same time as increasing wineries' sales and the prestige and image of the region's wine (Cambourne *et al.*, 2000; O'Neill and Charters, 2000). Furthermore it has been suggested that:

> An opportunity exists for the wine-grower to establish advantageous connections and a strategically important means of obtaining trade in high quality produce which encourages the development of direct sales and levels of awareness, and consolidates the image of products as well as creating a loyal consumer market.
> (Europäische Weinstrassen, undated, cited in Hall and Macionis, 1998, p. 206)

Crucially, a successful wine route should promote economic growth and employment opportunities in a region (Getz, 2000). For any of this to be successful, however, it is essential for the winery management to understand the nature and demographics of their visitors, by collecting information about them (Hashimoto and Telfer, 2003).

Visitors on wine routes tend to travel in groups (Preston-Whyte, 2000), therefore wineries must create 'added value' for them (O'Neill and Charters, 2000) – for example, food service amenities, accommodation, historical sites and arts and crafts facilities – in order to attract travellers (Gilbert, 1992; Zekulich, 1999). As a result, despite their advantages, wine routes demand significant levels of capital investment (at least at the outset) and their development will increase costs and demand management input (Dodd, 1995).

The Bairrada Wine Route

The Bairrada wine region had, in 2001, a population of just over 160,000 inhabitants. It is in the central northern part of Portugal (Fig. 18.1), between the rivers Águeda and Mondego. In 1979, the collaborative efforts of wine producers, trade, the Estação Vitivinícola (Vinicultural Station) and the Confraria dos Enófilos (Oenophilists Brotherhood) contributed to the designation of the Bairrada as a demarked wine region. The region has a significant number of producers of quality wines, as well as other tourist attractions including a tradition of fine foods and local spas.

There is a history – albeit limited – of visits to wineries for wine tasting. With the publication of *Despacho Normativo 669/94*, the Bairrada Wine Region decided to apply for accreditation as a recognized wine route. This application specified four objectives:

- to improve members' facilities and amenities;
- to install signage along the route;
- to elaborate promotional documentation about the route; and
- to develop complementary infrastructures and facilities for the route (interpretation centres and a museum).

As a result, in 1995 the Bairrada Wine Route Council (BWRC) was formed, comprising the four major regional city councils, the Bairrada Wine Commission, regional and national tourism commissions and the local Economic Development Commission. It was against this background that, in 1999, the BWRC finally created the Bairrada Wine Route (BWR), which includes 28 regional wine producers (members) and the BWRC itself.

With the establishment of the BWR, signage throughout the region has been improved to facilitate access to participant members and wine-related attractions. Three specific tours through the region have been created, and are advertised to visitors. Additionally, the 28 regional producers had to meet some basic standards for their facilities in order to be accepted as members, including accessibility, reception and the quality of provision.

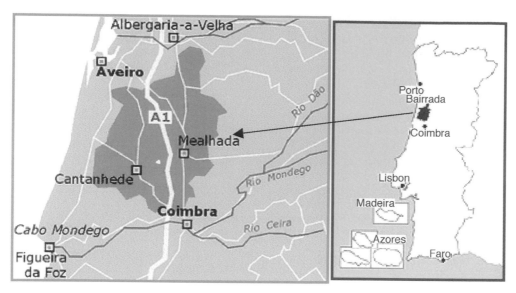

Fig. 18.1. The Bairrada wine region.

Research Method

As an exploratory study this study did not use any formal framework for the evaluation of the current success of the BWR. However, it did seek to assess the route in the light of the critical success factors already outlined above. The study therefore primarily focused on infrastructure issues – particularly effective signage, plus economic development, employment generation and promotion. Additionally, organizational cohesion – including administration, as well as relationships between wineries and with other tourism entities – is important. Crucially, the development of strong relationships with visitors and customers should be an important result of the success of the route. In carrying out the research the BWR was compared, in terms of the providers' perspective, with other benchmark studies (e.g. Frochot, 2000; Telfer, 2001).

The aim of this study was to make a complete evaluation of the BWR from its commencement in 1999 through to December 2003, based on the perspective of members involved in the route. In order to carry out this research, a practical study was developed which aimed to evaluate and assess the BWR and its future (Bruyne et al., 1991 cited in Pardal and Correia, 1995, p. 23; Bell, 2002). The methodology chosen for this study was qualitative, case-based research using the rich information that could be gained from interviews of the winery managers (Creswell, 1994; Yin, 1994; Carson et al., 2001). Case study research is appropriate for examining contemporary issues, such as in this study, that involve investigation of a dynamic, contemporary, pre-paradigmatic body of knowledge within its real-life context (Eisenhardt, 1989; Yin, 1994; Chetty, 1996; Carson et al., 2001).

Because case-based research involves the examination of events within their real-life context, properly designed research procedures are essential for the collection of appropriate and useful data. Thus, a two-stage methodological approach was used in this study. Exploratory interviews were used in the first stage, and case-based research was used in the second stage of this study through interviews and observations.

The first stage of the research was carried out from January to November 2003; the principal researcher conducted three in-depth, structured interviews with the President and the General Secretary of the Bairrada Wine Commission, in order to collect data and information about the route. In addition, during this stage of the study, the principal researcher participated in three meetings of the BWR Council to gain a better understanding of its function and operations.

In the second stage of the research, early in 2004, the researcher conducted a set of in-depth interviews with key industry players (14 wineries, all members of the BWR), followed by a visit to their facilities. The interviews, together with the observations, allowed rigour in the data collection. The selection of the respondents (members) was made using a systematic sampling method (Cannon, 1994; Pardal and Correia, 1995). From a total of 28 key players, 14 were selected, which were representative, in terms of organizational size, of all the members.

The interviews were structured in six sections:

- members' image, culture and style;
- wine tourism activity before they joined the BWR;
- members' activity after joining the BWR;
- members' evaluation of the cohesion of the BWR;
- the management of supply and demand by the BWR; and
- members' perspective on the future of the route.

During the interviews broad, open questions were followed by structured, probing questions which sought information on specific issues, such as the future of the BWR. Such questions helped to keep interviewees talking and the interview focused. In addition, using these questions enabled easy identification of the similarities to and differences from previous interviews. Occasionally closed questions were also posed in order to obtain basic information where a relevant – as well as variable – response to issues, in each case a Likert scale was used.

The data collected were recorded on a spreadsheet and basic descriptive statistics were produced for each variable such as frequencies, percentages and mean scores. The results of this study present analytic generalization, as opposed to statistical generalization. The focus was on a qualitative analysis of the data, giving depth of understanding rather than numeric generality – necessary given the small number of respondents. For confidentiality and identification reasons, each interview was numbered so, for example, interviewee number one is termed 'Member 1', interviewee number two is designated 'Member 2', and so on. Using this indexing method enables quick visual recognition of patterns in the data.

Findings

The wineries and wine tourism

The majority of the members are moderately sized family businesses. The size of the members is also reflected in the number of employees they have (Table 18.1, column 2). The majority of the members have more than 20 employees, whilst close to a one-third have less than five employees.

From Table 18.1 it is evident that there is a substantial disparity in numbers of employees. However, when considering the number of employees dedicated to wine tourism activities (Table 18.1, column 3), the differences are minimal. The majority of the members have at least one employee dedicated to the wine tourism activity.

The formation of the BWR

The initial objectives of the wineries which had become members of the BWR were mainly to increase the reputation of the region's wines and to increase wine sales. The development of partnerships with companies within the industry and the creation of a core group for the protection of the region's wines were also important objectives.

For wineries to be accepted as members of the BWR they had to fulfil certain requirements to ensure a basic standard for the facilities they offered. Therefore, the majority of the members needed to make a financial investment to upgrade their facilities, mainly to receive visitors (for instance, display rooms, shopping areas and museums). Only about half of the members resorted to state aid under *Despacho Normativo n° 669/94*, whilst the others obtained better financing deals from banks or other financial

Table 18.1. Number of employees and employees dedicated to wine tourism.

Case no.	Employees (n)	Employees dedicated to wine tourism (n)
Member 1	> 20	2
Member 2	> 100	2
Member 3	> 20	1
Member 4	> 20	1
Member 5	> 100	3
Member 6	> 40	4
Member 7	> 10	1
Member 8	> 10	1
Member 9	> 20	1
Member 10	< 5	0
Member 11	< 5	0
Member 12	< 5	1
Member 13	> 20	0
Member 14	< 5	0

institutions. The improvements were all made by companies within the region. However, those investments did not have a major impact on the creation of new jobs; only three jobs were created within the wineries as a result of the investment. The members instead redeployed their workforce, transferring existing employees to dealing with the wine tourism activities.

The performance of the BWR

At present, members recognize that the initial objectives are still far from achieved and only around one-third of the respondents feel that they have achieved some of the objectives set out at the foundation of the BWR. This limited success is believed to result from a number of constraints which have affected the BWR, such as problems with funding, diffuse focus and a lack of dynamism by the members. These constraints have contributed to the low level of approval for the current performance of the route, where the majority of members have no more than an average level of satisfaction with the programme, as outlined in Table 18.2.

Most members shared a common view on the management of the BWR: they suggested that the current structure is unwieldy. At present the BWR council determines policy for the route, but implementation is the responsibility of the Bairrada Wine Commission. The latter body does not implement the council's decisions effectively, and has no staff member dedicated to wine tourism. The members argued that the BWR needs to have a structure that organizes and invigorates the route in order to maximize outputs and optimize the use of resources using dedicated staff, and not focusing primarily only on wine.

The majority of the members are of the opinion that the current management model is not the most appropriate. Rather, the BWR should be managed by professionals within a specially dedicated organization. In addition, it is suggested that this new organization must be dynamic and market-led in its activities. Nevertheless, almost all accept the current level of financial contributions to the organization, and consider that these should continue if a new management model is implemented.

The wine route is a signposted itinerary through a limited, demarcated wine region (*Denominação de Origem Controlada*), aimed at discovering wine products in the region and the activities which are associated with it. The latter are carried out directly at the winery. The signage is fundamental in order to identify the location of the wine producers. The large majority of the

Table 18.2. Member satisfaction with the performance of the BWR.

☺ dissatisfied   ☺ average   ☺ satisfied

members do not agree with the current signage, and all see the need for it to be improved by its being more precise.

The future of the BWR

Despite the criticism of the management of the BWR, the interviews and observation data presented a picture of optimism in relation to the route as well as an urgent need to refocus the organization. For example, the members were positive about wine tourism as one of many means of selling wine, even though the members' focus is still very much on distributing to hotel, restaurant and café (HORECA) businesses, retailers and export markets. Currently, members do not liaise closely with each other in relation to international markets.

However, it is important to point out that several members recognize that the BWR may contribute to the development of formal or informal collaboration with other members which conducy business internationally. The BWR can play an important role in facilitating information about international markets and contributing to the minimization of the risk associated with exporting.

The majority of the respondents believe that in the future the number of consumers visiting the BWR will increase. The optimism is such that the majority of the members see a prosperous future for the route, and over half of them aim to invest more in wine tourism during the next 3 years. The investment will continue to be in physical infrastructure such as restaurants and bars, museums, shopping areas and an auditorium.

With the anticipation of such future growth in wine tourism, the members consider that the BWR must be transformed into a more formal organization. The organization must have a professional structure in order to capture more consumers, to develop cooperation between all the industry players and to engage in marketing activities. In addition, it is suggested by the members that this association must play an important role in obtaining greater exposure for the wines and the region.

The role of the members

Understanding the needs and motivations of wine tourists is crucial, and recording the details of interested visitors is important for those who wish to succeed in the wine tourism industry (O'Neill and Charters, 2000). Notwithstanding this, the interviews with the BWR members showed that only two members have a proper customer database. In 2003 one received close to 8000 visitors, whilst the other received approximately 5600. The other members accept the need to develop consumer databases in the near future.

Nevertheless, the majority of the members claim that they can identify the origin of their visitors. The majority of visitors are regional and national.

Foreign visitors are mainly from Europe (Spain, the UK, France, Germany and Belgium), Canada and Brazil. On average the number of persons per visit is between two and five (one or two families), or alternatively groups of around 30 visitors.

One member on its own is unlikely to attract many visitors; therefore, being part of the wine route can contribute to the creation of critical mass for the route and increase visitors per winery. Partnerships and collaboration with other organizations within the industry are also seen as vital in attracting more visitors. There are a very limited number of partnerships in the BWR. Only two members work together with travel agents, six have a relationship with catering services, two collaborate with hotels and two with regional tourism associations. These collaborations have proved to be important to the members' activity, and have also contributed to bringing together the local cuisine with Bairrada's wines.

Implications for Wine Tourism

Many factors influence the performance of the BWR as it competes for a share of the growing wine tourism market in Portugal. This chapter has examined a number of those aspects in order to evaluate the BWR activity. The study was exploratory in nature as there was no prior theory developed to evaluate wine tourism routes. Nevertheless, a number of tentative conclusions can be suggested, particularly in the light of the 'critical success factors' postulated for a wine route.

The first conclusions relate to the coordinating organization for the wine route. Some necessary aspects of the organization – for instance integration into a national framework (Getz, 2000) – have already been met. However, there are a number of constraints which have affected the development and growth of the BWR. These constraints have hindered members from achieving their initial objectives, and contributed to the low level of satisfaction with the route. Crucially the current management model is seen as not working, and there is a need for the creation of a new organization to manage the route more professionally in order to capitalize on the existing resources, confirming the assertions of Getz (2000) on the issue.

Another specific issue is that signage – already noted as important by Frochot (2000) – needs to be improved in order to facilitate access to wineries for visitors. It will also be noted that the initial investment made by the members did not have a major impact on the creation of new direct jobs. However, members' infrastructure was improved in order to receive visitors, reflecting a genuine interest amongst the members in developing wine tourism.

The second group of conclusions relate to the individual wineries themselves. There is a need to develop proper consumer marketing databases, based on accurate information about visitors, a point made by Hashimoto and Telfer (2003). In general, members do not collect and manage visitor information effectively. The lack of information about visitors may create difficulties in future planning and development for the route and members. Partnerships and collaborations are thought to be crucial (Dodd, 1995), yet in the BWR they are limited in number and scope, and need expanding. Yet, despite all this, the future of the route is perceived to be positive and there is the prospect of a reinvigorated dynamic in the route if a new organization is established. This optimism is associated with the intention to create new investment in infrastructure in future.

The results presented in this study need to be considered by both the management and members of wine routes, at least in certain parts of the world. It is clear that wine routes have scope for development, but it is necessary to have engagement and participation by the members in the organization of the route. In particular, it is of major importance that the management of a wine route shows professionalism and becomes more proactive in order to develop partnerships and collaborations with organizations within the industry, as well as developing marketing activities which will benefit the members and raise the route to another level (Hall *et al.*, 1998). The findings thus have more general applicability beyond Bairrada and Portugal.

Crucially, for newly developing wine tourism regions and wines routes, there needs to be a dynamic organizational leadership to drive the process forward. This leadership needs to have a clear focus, and the structure of the organization must be effective from the outset, allowing for that creative and dynamic leadership, whilst retaining the support and commitment of members. In the drive to promote collaboration and excitement, however, apparently minor but crucial practical issues must not be overlooked (in the case of the Bairrada region this was clear and consistent signage). In addition, if wine tourism is to be developed successfully, the individual organizations in the region must take responsibility for the success of the route. They need to collaborate effectively, and they need to ensure that their own systems are well planned (in this case, customer databases) to take advantage of their visitors. In short, wine tourism regions and wines routes need to adapt rapidly to new opportunities and changes in the market, as well as to be market-led in an environment of increasing uncertainty.

References

Amaral, J.D. (1995) *O grande livro do vinho.* Temas e Debates, Lisbon.

Bell, J. (2002) *Como Realizar um Projecto de Investigação. Um Guia para a Pesquisa em Ciências Sociais e da Educação,* 2nd edn. Gradiva, Lisbon.

Beverland, M. (1998) Wine tourism in New Zealand – maybe the industry has got it right. International Journal of *Wine Marketing* 10 (2), 24–33.

Cambourne, B., Hall, C.M., Johnson, G.,

Macionis, N., Mitchell, R. and Sharples, L. (2000) The maturing wine tourism product: an international overview. In: Hall, C.M., Sharples, L., Cambourne, B. and Macionis, N. (eds) *Wine Tourism Around the World: Development, Management and Markets.* Elsevier Science, Oxford, UK, pp. 24–66.

Cannon, J.C. (1994) Issues in sampling and sample design – a management perspective. In: Brent Ritchie, J.R. and Goeldner, C.R. (eds) *Travel, Tourism, and Hospitality*

Research: a Handbook for Managers and Researchers, 2nd edn. John Wiley and Sons Ltd., New York, pp. 131–143.

Carson, D., Gilmore, A., Perry, C. and Gronhaug, K. (2001) *Qualitative Marketing Research*. Sage Publications, London.

Charters, S. and Ali-Knight, J. (2002) Who is the wine tourist? *Tourism Management* 23, 311–319.

Chetty, S. (1996) The case study method for research in small and medium-sized firms. *International Small Business Journal* 15 (1), 73–85.

Cresswell, J.W. (1994) *Research design: Qualitative and quantitative approaches.* Sage Publications, Thousand Oaks, California.

Dodd, T. (1995) Opportunities and pitfalls of tourism in a developing wine industry. *International Journal of Wine Marketing* 7 (1), 5–16.

Eisenhardt, K.M. (1989) Building theories from case study research. *Academy of Management Review* 14 (4), 532–550.

Frochot, I. (2000) Wine tourism in France: a paradox? In: Hall, C.M., Sharples, I., Cambourne, B. and Macionis, N. (eds) *Wine Tourism Around the World: Development, Management and Markets.* Elsevier Science, Oxford, UK, pp. 67–80.

Fuller, P. (1997) Value adding the regional experience. *Australian and New Zealand Wine Industry Journal* 12 (1), 35–39.

Getz, D. (2000). *Exploring Wine Tourism: Management, Development and Destinations.* Cognizant Communication Corporation, New York.

Getz, D., Dowling, R., Carlsen, J. and Anderson, D. (1999) Critical success factors for wine tourism. *International Journal of Wine Marketing* 11 (3), 20–43.

Gilbert, D.C. (1992) Touristic development of a viticultural region of Spain. *International Journal of Wine Marketing* 4 (2), 25–32.

Hall, C.M. and Macionis, N. (1998) Wine tourism in Australia and New Zealand. In: Butler, R.W., Hall, C.M. and Jenkins, J.M. (eds) *Tourism and Recreation in Rural Areas.* John Wiley and Sons, London, pp. 267–298.

Hall, C.M., Cambourne, B., Macionis, N. and

Johnson, G. (1998) Wine tourism and network development in Australia and New Zealand: review, establishment and prospects. *International Journal of Wine Marketing* 10, 5–31.

Hall, C.M., Johnson, G., Cambourne, B. Macionis, N., Mitchell, R. and Sharples, L. (2000a) Wine tourism: an introduction. In: Hall, C.M., Sharples, L., Cambourne, B. and Macionis, N. (eds) *Wine Tourism Around the World: Development, Management and Markets.* Elsevier Science, Oxford, UK, pp. 39–42.

Hall, M., Sharples, L., Cambourne, B. and Macionis, N. (2000b) *Wine Tourism around the World Development, Management and Markets.* Elsevier Science, Oxford, UK.

Hashimoto, A. and Telfer, D. (2003) Positioning an emerging wine route in the Niagara region: understanding the wine tourism market and its implications for marketing. *Journal of Travel and Tourism Marketing* 14 (3/4), 61–76.

King, C. and Morris, R. (1997a) Wine tourism: a Western Australian case study. *Australian and New Zealand Wine Industry Journal* 12 (3), 246–250.

King, C. and Morris, R. (1997b) To taste or not to taste – to charge or not to charge. *Australian and New Zealand Wine Industry Journal* 12 (4), 381–383.

Marques, M.T. (2001) Enquadramento legal das rotas do vinho. *I Congresso das Rotas do Vinho de Portugal.* Estação Zootécnica Nacional, Vale de Santarém, Portugal.

McDougall, G.H.G. and Munro, H. (1994) Scaling and attitude measurement in travel and tourism research. In: Brent Ritchie, J.R. and Goeldner, C.R. (eds) *Travel, Tourism, and Hospitality Research: a Handbook for Managers and Researchers*, 2nd edn. John Wiley and Sons Ltd., New York, pp. 120–121.

O'Neill, M. and Charters, S. (2000) Service quality at the cellar door: implications for Western Australia's developing wine tourism industry. *Managing Service Quality* 10 (2), 115–122.

Pardal, L. and Correia, E. (1995) *Métodos e Técnicas de Investigação Social.* ASA Editores, Porto, Portugal.

Preston-Whyte, R. (2000) Wine routes in South Africa. In: Hall, C.M., Sharples, L., Cambourne, B. and Macionis, N. (eds) *Wine Tourism Around the World: Development, Management and Markets.* Elsevier Science, Oxford, UK, pp. 102–114.

Simões, O. (2003) A vinha e o vinho em Portugal: contributos para o desenvolvimento local e regional. In: Caldas, J.C. (ed.) Portuga Chão. Celta Editora, Oeiras, Portugal.

Szivas, E. (1999) The development of wine tourism in Hungary. *International Journal of Wine Marketing* 11(2), 7–17.

Telfer, D. (2001) Strategic alliances along the Niagara wine route. *Tourism Management* 22, 21–30.

Yin, R.K. (1994) *Case Study Research: Design and Methods*, 2nd edn. Sage Publications, California.

Zekulich, M. (1999) Growing wineries seek customers. *The West Australian*, 24 February.

19 Are We There Yet? How to Navigate the Wine Trail

DAVID HURBURGH* AND DICK FRIEND

Myriad Research Associates, Hobart, Tasmania, Australia
**E-mail: david.hurburgh@gmail.com*

Introduction

Satellite Navigation (SATNAV) units in Australian cars are becoming increasingly popular. It is estimated that in 2005 around 80,000 passenger vehicles, or approximately 8% of the total market, were sold with SATNAV units fitted. The majority of these units are found in prestige, luxury and sports utility vehicles. There is a strong alignment in demographics between people who are serious wine tourists and drivers of those vehicles that are likely to be equipped with SATNAV.

Wine tourism in the past 5 years has become an important new industry in many parts of regional Australia (Wine Makers Federation of Australia, 2003). The rapid growth in numbers of new cellar doors and wineries and the emergence of new wine regions in this period are well documented (Halliday, 2003). One of the key elements underpinning successful wine tourism is the availability of essential infrastructure items such as effective signage, informative brochures and websites and, most importantly, useful maps.

The ability of wine tourists to find their way with minimum effort to a cellar door is the essential starting point for an enjoyable cellar door experience. Even in mature wine tourism areas, maps and signage showing 'wine trails' and the locations of individual operations suffer limitations. This can be due to constraints such as the scale of a map, which may be unable to show precise locations, the complexity of the local road network or the practical limit to the number of signs at critical road intersections.

Two key reference texts covering the subject of wine tourism, Getz (2000) and Hall *et al.* (2000), have been reviewed. Although they discuss many aspects of wine trails (routes and roads) such as design and signage, they do not cover the recent emergence of SATNAV and other location-based service (LBS) technologies and their application to tourism infrastructure.

Applying the Statistically Improbable Phrases (SIPs) feature of amazon.com, which is attached to the Amazon entry for Michael Hall's (2000) publication, identifies at least 31 books which contain the phrases 'wine routes' or 'wine trails'. These titles represent an excellent resource for readers wishing to examine the subject of wine trails and routes in more detail.

Arrival of Global Positioning Navigation (GPS) technology in the early 1990s has made available very precise, low-cost and easy-to-use navigational and locational information tools across a wide domain of human activities. GPS-equipped devices are now ubiquitous and are rapidly becoming consumer items.

In-car SATNAV systems are the most familiar application of GPS technology. Many of the next generation of mobile phones (so-called 3rd Generation, 3G or smartphones) will contain embedded GPS chips, and manufacturers of hand-held computers (PDAs) are offering clip-on GPS units. With these advances, databases containing locational information (such as GPS-defined points of interest for the tourist) will become as valuable as phone directories are to telephone users.

The VineFinders™ Project was initiated in late 2003 as a research and data collection exercise. The prime objective was to physically locate and 'ground-truth', using GPS to a 4 m precision level, every cellar door entrance, winery and commercially significant vineyard in Australia. The information generated by this project is considered to be the most complete and up-to-date set of Australian wine-related locational information. The VineFinders™ data will become a key component of GPS, SATNAV and locational products serving the Australian wine tourism sector.

Research Method

Before the fieldwork commences in a particular region, all available reference sources to wineries and cellar doors are examined and a preliminary listing is generated. Key published resources identified by the project are:

- James Halliday's 2006 Australian Wine Companion – with 2001 winery (or wine producer) entries;
- WineTitles' Australian and New Zealand Wine Industry Directory (AWID); and
- regional vigneron associations' maps and brochures.

The two most useful on-line resources used for the pre-fieldwork research stage of the project were http://www.travelenvoy.com and http://www.winediva.com.au . Travel Envoy is a US-based site, and has the ambitious objective of having listings for all wine regions of the world. Although comprehensive, this site suffers from some quality control issues, with confusion and multiple entries for those wineries caused by 'labels' being seen as discrete wineries and changes of ownership. Much of the information on opening hours, facilities and contact details can also be out of date. Wine Diva is an Australian website, which has useful search tools allowing the visitor to filter a search query, for example, by grape variety and cellar door facilities. At the time of project planning, both these sites contained between 70 and 80% of the entries obtained by VineFinders™ during the fieldwork.

Regional tourism offices within wine regions are personally visited, where additional materials such as individual winery brochures are collected. Local tourist information staff – often volunteers – and their comprehensive knowledge of wine tourism amenities in their districts allow newer start-up wineries and cellar doors to be 'discovered'.

A wide range of additional data sources have been cross-checked when assembling the winery-related data sets used in the project. A rigorous process of verifying all available information sources generates the initial listing that is used in the field. Since the compiled databases form part of VineFinders™ intellectual property, disclosure of detailed listings is restricted for reasons of commercial confidentiality.

Data collection

A portable Magellan Meridian™ GPS receiver, capable of providing locational accuracy to around 4 m, is used in conjunction with the Australia-wide mapping data and software on Magellan's DiscoverAus – Streets & Tracks™ CD. Ahead of the fieldwork, maps of the region to be covered are up-loaded from a PC to the GPS unit. They are held on an internal Secure Digital™ (SD) memory card.

The latitude and longitude of each property entrance is marked as a 'way point' on the GPS and becomes a Point of Interest (POI). The GPS also records the altitude of the property – this is of interest to serious wine tourists in regions such as the Adelaide Hills and the Victorian Alpine Valleys.

A digital photograph is taken of the cellar door or winery signage at the entrance to each property. In combination with the GPS reading – also time/date stamped – these images provide an essential back-up and complement to the VineFinders™ dataset. The significance of the cellar door signage is discussed in the Findings section of this chapter.

After completion of the fieldwork in a particular region, the collected data are uploaded to a PC. The information is cross-checked by plotting on the DiscoverAus™ software-mapping package. The data are then aggregated into the VineFinders™ database.

In the 24-month period since fieldwork started, over 80,000 road kilometres in the wine regions have been covered.

Following the initial phase of research and fieldwork for each region, VineFinders™ continuously monitors the wine industry press for new developments, name changes and closures. Regular field trips to all regions are undertaken to allow continuous updating. Contact is also maintained with key local personnel throughout Australia's wine regions who monitor new wine-related ventures in their districts.

Findings

Although the prime purpose of the project is to develop a dataset to be used for SATNAV and related location-based (LBS) services, observations pertinent to broader wine tourism infrastructure issues have been made during the course of the fieldwork.

The research and fieldwork activities of the VineFinders™ Project has succeeded in identifying in excess of 35% more sites than are documented in leading industry directories.

The following example demonstrates the comprehensive coverage of the VineFinders™ Project's dataset. In south-eastern Queensland, where there has been spectacular recent growth in the wine industry, VineFinders™ had 140 cellar doors listed in late March 2004. This can be compared to the Australian Wine Industry Directory's 87 entries.

The database generated by this project thus represents one of the most definitive and up-to-date sources of cellar door and winery location information in Australia.

Most of the established wine regions in Australia have implemented some form of 'Wine Trail' – a recommended route that is systematically signposted and passes a range of cellar doors. Wine trails are often joint initiatives between regional vigneron associations and local tourism offices. To be truly useful, maps and brochures that specifically complement the trail should be readily available. The 'by-appointment-only' cellar doors can enjoy the benefits of signage if the protocols for visitors are publicized.

During the fieldwork activities of the VineFinders™ Project, constant consideration was given to the effectiveness (or otherwise) of established wine trails.

Wine regions can be classified according to the geometry of the road network. They range from a simple 'strip' like the Coonawarra, through the 'grid' layout of the Barossa Valley to the 'labyrinth' of roads found in the Adelaide Hills. The navigational demands put on the driver increase proportionally. Clearly, four-way fingerposts at every crossroad are impractical. It is in these situations where SATNAV and LBS tools are very useful.

Many smaller cellar door ventures do not appear on established wine trails. But often these lower-profile businesses have great appeal to the serious wine tourist, either for individuality or maybe for 'bragging rights' due to their lesser-known labels. LBS can be a prime tool for finding these more obscure and often out-of-the-way ventures.

Cellar doors on busy highways need multiple signs in advance of their gateway. Some local authorities are restricting the number of officially sanctioned directional signs on aesthetic or equity grounds (Mornington Peninsula Shire, 2003). Typically, they see wine trail signs as directional guides only, and not to be used as a form of advertising. From a safety point of view, drivers slowing down (or pulling over) while looking for a turn-off may frustrate or endanger other drivers. If they are tailgated in heavy traffic, the drivers may miss the turn entirely. SATNAV is the perfect solution to this dilemma.

Australian tourism authorities have identified signage as a key infrastructure issue. In November 2003 the Australian Federal Government released a tourism White Paper. This statement contained some major policy initiatives, which included proposed actions to improve tourism infrastructure. Among these was the formation of the National Tourism Signing Reference Group, which has the goal of delivering nationally consistent tourism signage. It can be anticipated that the results of this body's work will see improved signage in wine regions and assist in delivering the optimum experience for the wine tourist, including those aspects identified in this paper.

The demands of maintaining a full-time cellar door presence are often prohibitive to smaller operators. Most serious wine tourists respect the 'by appointment only' protocols that smaller vignerons must follow. However, attractive and informative signage – even for these low profile businesses – can build the brand.

Wine regions are often located in attractive landscapes, and many wine tourists get the aesthetic pleasure of enjoying the scenery and perhaps contemplating the *terroir*. With the strong appeal of 'estate-grown' wine, they like to see the 'home' vineyard of familiar labels. Many famous vineyards – such as Pewsey Vale in the High Eden (SA) – don't have wineries on the property, but they are definitely worth seeing. Signposting of these vineyards can add enjoyment to the wine tourism experience as well as loyalty to the brand.

The VineFinders™ photo database of cellar door signage contains in excess of 2200 images. Since the signs and structures at the gateway to a winery can provide both a useful initial visual image and information source about the business, it is planned that this database of images will be made accessible via the Internet. Seeing a winery's entrance in a photo ahead of a visit makes it easy for the interested tourist to turn off the highway and spend time at the cellar door.

Property numbering is often done on a very *ad hoc*, ambiguous and misleading manner. In the absence of prominent roadside directional signage ahead of a winery, address numbering is often the only guide to locating the business.

In the past two years Standards Australia (a Federal Government agency) has been approaching all local governments and advising them to introduce an Australia-wide system known as the Rural Address Numbering (RAN) standard.

This system involves initial agreement on unambiguous road naming across jurisdictional boundaries, such as shires and towns. The road numbering starts at a datum point such as a T-junction, with even numbers on the right-hand side of the road as you progress, with the numbers based on 10 m incremental units. For example, Tasmania's Meadowbank Winery Restaurant at 699 Richmond Rd, Cambridge, would be expected to be 6.99 km along the road to Richmond from the Cambridge turn-off. But the distances are wrong, the numbers are a jumble and they appear to start from the Richmond end but at no road junction! If the RAN system is widely and properly adopted, drivers will know immediately the distance they must drive to a given address.

Although property addressing may seem a very low-tech issue, the new system is in fact being tied into a new Australia-wide spatial dataset information system. Once most properties have adopted the new numbers, they will form part of the Geocoded National Address File, commonly known as G-NAF (see http://www.g-naf.com.au). This system is being introduced by the Public Sector Mapping Agency (PSMA – see http://www.psma.com.au), an arm of the Australian Bureau of Statistics (ABS) responsible for all public domain maps in Australia.

Ultimately, the G-NAF system will form a key part of all location-based services (LBS) in Australia. Searchable physical addresses will be tied to other parameters such as phone numbers, e-mail and web addresses. These will be accessed through devices such as GPS-equipped, web-connected smartphones.

VineFinders™ locational information based on GPS-SATNAV standards will provide valuable content for these new services.

Implications for Wine Tourism

Travel choices were traditionally planned months ahead after reading hard-copy books and magazines, talking with friends and colleagues and discussions with travel agents. The pace of life, wider access to travel, television and electronic bookings have largely replaced that with short stays based on recent information and planned and booked very close to departure.

The key benefit of delivery of LBS electronically is that locational information (such as roads, businesses and points of interest) can be constantly updated, rather than being reliant on annual or less frequent CD/DVD upgrades, the knowledge of travel agents or, worse still, books.

The excellent collaboration in early 2005 between the West Australian government departments of Primary Industry and Tourism with regional tourism bodies and the state's private wine industry body is a good example of producing maps with static information, whether in hard copy or as digital downloads. It is not updated live or linked dynamically to further information.

The website http://www.travelmate.com.au is an example of the new breed of online itinerary, route planning, distance–time-calculating, map-making and booking portals available to the home consumer (and of the wireless-enabled portable web browsers now available). Databases are interrogated in real time to deliver the most up to date information available.

The commercial rivalry between industry behemoths, such as:

- Google Earth and Microsoft's Virtual Earth, with their satellite views zooming in almost seamlessly to individual house 3-D views in the USA (and in Australia next year); and
- Telstra's Sensis/Yellow Pages/UBD/Search offerings, struggling to coordinate mapping and information data;

is sure to fuel consumer interest in LBS applications, and make them more integrated with our daily routines.

It is the authors' view that fixed, in-car CD/DVD-based SATNAV systems will be replaced over the next 3–5 years by lower-cost and more flexible delivery options. Mobile phone technology will drive this change and will mirror the way in which early cellular phones, which were hard-wired into vehicles, were replaced by truly portable devices. The convergence in capabilities of phones and computers is such that the latest generation of 'smart phones' has much the same features and performance as hand-held computers.

Already, in Europe, detailed road maps and navigational software are available as a web service delivered to 3rd-generation (3G) mobile phone handsets and PDAs. One such advanced service is provided by http://www.wayfinder.com. The locational information and software is provided by 'content providers' independent of the telephone companies. The appeal of this approach is that these SATNAV services work on a wide range of smart phone handset types as well as PDAs and other small computers, and are not dependent on one particular device.

From the tourism industry perspective, portable SATNAV and LBS delivered to portable devices will have a broad appeal. Interstate and overseas visitors are most likely to be using rental cars which, increasingly, are having GPS units as either standard equipment or as optional extras. Some wine districts are also popular with visitors using bicycles. The Clare Valley (SA) and King Valley (VIC) have great cycle paths (converted railway trackbeds) running through them. Portable SATNAV would be very useful to these categories of visitors.

In Australia, particularly in rural areas, the successful application of web-service delivery of SATNAV and LBS will rely on the continued rollout of high-bandwidth mobile telephone infrastructure.

Again, hard copy maps, brochures and signage will always be around to help tourists. However, GPS-defined locations, integrated with other information services and delivered through the next generation of smart phones, will provide a revolutionary advance.

Web-based delivery of locational information is very cost effective compared to the production and distribution of paper-based maps. Business models based on sponsored links to advertisers and the Google 'AdSense' associate programme generate revenue for web publishers that precludes the need for the site visitor to buy or subscribe to the map information.

The imminent launch of the G-NAF (Geocoded National Address File) system will piggyback off the new rural addressing standard. The implications for all users of locational information in Australia will be profound. Hopefully, the frequent sight of lost and bewildered tourists will no longer be seen at a crossroads near you.

References

Denso Australia (2003) Satellite Navigation. http://www.denso.com.au/dw/satnav/satnav_gen.htm

Getz, D. (2000) *Explore Wine Tourism: Management, Development and Destinations.* Cognizant Communication Corporation, New York.

Hall, C.M., Sharples, L., Cambourne, B. and Macionis, N. (2000) *Wine Tourism Around the World. Development, Management and Markets.* Butterworth-Heinemann, Oxford, UK.

Halliday, J. (2005) *James Halliday's Australian Wine Companion, 2006 Edition.* Harper Collins, Sydney, Australia.

Major, M. (ed.) (2003) *The Australian and New Zealand Wine Industry Directory* 21st annual edition. Winetitles, Adelaide, Australia.

Mornington Peninsula Shire (2003) *Directional Signage.* Peninsula Wide, Issue 43, p. 12.

Websites

Google Earth. A 3D interface to the Planet. http://www.earth.google.com/

LADS – Location Aware Devices and Services, http://ubikwitus.blogspot.com

Land Victoria. Rural addressing project. http://www.land.vic.gov.au/ruralroadnumbers

PSMA Australia. About G-NAF Project, http://www.g-naf.com.au/about.htm

Queensland Spatial Information Council (QSIC). *Rural Addressing,* http://www.qsic.qld.gov.au

Standards Australia. New standard to help you find your way, http://www.standards.org.au/NEWSROOM/NEWS%20RELEASE/2003-09-21/2003-09-21.HTM

The Age. National Map Project has swings and roundabouts, http://www.theage.com.au/articles/2003/08/25/1061663721571.html

The Australian. The internet comes home to roost, http://www.theaustralian.news.com.au/common/story_page/0,5744,16068379%255E36375,00.html

Wayfinders Systems AB. http://www.wayfinder.com/

Wine Makers Federation of Australia Wine Tourism. http://www.wfa.org.au/tourism.htm

Note: all web links are available as cached archives on http://www.google.com, if the key terms from the citation are used as search terms.

20 Conclusion: the Future of Wine Tourism Research, Management and Marketing

STEVE CHARTERS[1]* AND JACK CARLSEN[2]

[1]Edith Cowan University, 100 Joondalup Drive, Joondalup, WA 6027, Australia; [2] Curtin University, Perth, WA, Australia
*E-mail: s.charters@ecu.edu.au

Introduction

The aim of this book was to expand the knowledge base about wine tourism and, especially, to provide an outlet for applied academic research which would have an immediate relevance to those involved in the wine tourism industry as much as to other academics. The contributions have also been selected in order to develop the international debate about the nature and application of wine tourism. This chapter is designed to draw some overarching conclusions from the empirical studies which will help to focus the practical nature of the research, as well as to highlight areas where further research could usefully be carried out.

Each section of this chapter therefore both summarizes key issues arising from what has already been written and makes suggestions for where further investigation should be focused. As a preliminary, however, three contextual issues relating to the geographic focus on wine tourism research, the relationship of production and service industries and the potential for conflict within wine tourism, need to be addressed.

The rate of research into wine tourism is becoming ever faster. There have been a number of conferences around the world examining the topic, and at least two previous books devoted to it (Getz, 2000; Hall et al., 2000), as well as a dedicated issue of the Journal of Wine Research in 2004. Nevertheless, as is clear from previous publications as well as this book, there is an imbalance in the research. There is a distinct focus on wine tourism within the New World, especially Australia, New Zealand and North America; to a lesser extent South Africa also. The distinctive nature of the wine industry in those countries (Charters, 2006), and their Anglo-Saxon culture, means that our understanding of how wine tourism operates, the demands placed on it by visitors and the factors necessary to implement it effectively are limited.

It is clear that in Italy, for instance, there are wine tourists who do not fit into any of the categories noted by Tassiopoulos and Haydam (this volume, Chapter 11) and Yuan *et al.* (this volume, Chapter 15) (from the *Movimento del Turismo del Vino*, noted in Mitchell *et al.*, 2000). Of necessity, therefore, and despite the contribution here of Correia and Passos Ascenção (this volume, Chapter 18), any conclusions which may be drawn about how wine tourism is affecting winery or tourism operators, or how it can be more effectively utilized, are tentative and tend to apply more to anglophone cultures.

This, in turn, leads to a major – perhaps the most important – recommendation for further research. Given the disparate nature of the wine tourism offering in various regions and the shifting nature of the wine tourist in various places (Charters and Ali-Knight, 2002), it seems essential that more research is undertaken in Europe, examining what destinations offer, how they function, the relationship of wine tourism to the – in this case well-established – wine industry, and how consumers engage with the product.

Whilst there has been a limited amount of investigation in this field (Howley, 2000; Frochot, 2001; Correia *et al.*, 2004), it has been much more limited than research in New World countries, despite the fact that Europe produces over 60% of all world wine and that France, for instance, is the world's number one tourist destination. This disparity was also identified in the analysis of the CIRET database (see this volume, Chapter 1), which indicates that wine tourism, culture and heritage are dominant themes in the historic wine tourism literature yet rarely emerge as a discrete topic of study in the contemporary literature on wine tourism, which tends to be focused on New World wine regions.

This disparity gives rise to a number of questions for further research relating to comparisons between Old World and New World Wine regions, specifically:

- What is the nexus between wine, tourism, culture and heritage?
- What are the differences in the form and function of wine tourism?
- What are the relative numbers, demographic profiles, behaviour and preferences of wine tourists?
- What policy, planning and management regimes exist?
- How does the business and commercial environment for wineries and wine tour operators compare?

One important point needs to be reiterated, pertinent to those involved in wine tourism who come to it from the wine side. Wine production involves primary and secondary industries; that is, it involves agriculture – growing grapes – and then production; turning those grapes into wine. It is very much a product-focused business (Carlsen, 2004). As Fraser and Alonso point out (this volume, Chapter 2) on the fit of wine and tourism, those who enter the wine industry may have little desire to be involved in a tertiary business – the service industry of wine tourism (whether at the cellar door, the provision of a restaurant or organizing a festival at a winery). Even more significantly, the skills required for success at the primary and secondary industries are not necessarily those which make one successful in the service sector.

Unfortunately, there is some anecdotal evidence that many producers enter the wine industry because they love the product (Charters, 2001) but get drawn, sometimes reluctantly, into wine tourism because they need to develop further outlets for product distribution. The danger with this is that the wine tourism involvement is not thought out carefully and is sales-led, rather than truly service-led; the possible consequence of this is a poor-quality service provision which, in the long term, harms the very sales it was intended to enhance, rather than stimulating them. It takes a clear marketing plan to say – as, for instance, Moss Wood in Margaret River have – that the organization will not involve itself formally in wine tourism and will focus its promotional activities on other areas.

Once wine tourism researchers and wine industry managers recognize that wine and tourism are at opposite ends of the industrial spectrum, research issues and priorities become more salient. In effect, those wine managers and tourism destination management organizations need to understand and integrate the characteristics of both economic activities into their approach. Typical research questions to emerge could include:

- How do successful wineries manage to make the transition from a supply-led to a demand-driven business environment?
- Does wine tourism enable wineries to become price-makers instead of price-takers?
- Within a wine region, how and when does the locus of economic activity shift from wine production to tourism over time?
- How do wineries and wine regions diversify their products and services to meet the changing needs of visitors?
- What is the relative importance of capital growth compared to profit as wealth creation activities in wine regions?

The third contextual issue which frames this part of the conclusion revolves around the aspect of conflicts between wine, tourism and the wider economic, social and ecological environment. First, one can note the paradox of the competing requirements of small and large wine businesses. As Sparks and Malady suggest (this volume, Chapter 6), a successful wine tourism region benefits from having a large, well-known 'champion' to attract visitors. However, the large companies which make big-volume brands might not need to use wine tourism as part of their marketing strategy. If they do get involved then it may, in part, be due to their desire to benefit the region as a whole rather than from self-interest, and in the current competitive global environment for wine such altruism may not be enough to maintain that commitment.

Another potential conflict arises when wine tourism is highly successful. Williams *et al.* note in their contribution (this volume, Chapter 3) that the Napa Valley is now becoming saturated with tourists (as anyone who has been caught on Highway 29 on a Saturday morning can ruefully testify). Part of the appeal of wine tourism is a retreat to the rural and a desire for relaxation and a slower pace of life – yet if a region is successful in supplying those features its very success becomes self-defeating. At a slightly different level there is also a national variation of the same conundrum: how many wine tourism regions can a country sustain – especially if it has a comparatively low population and may be away from the main northern hemisphere population centres?

Finally, at the micro level, there is the issue of the viability of individual organizations. Successful wine tourism requires substantial resource input. The rewards may ultimately be high, but the demands can also be great; as Fraser and Alonso (this volume, Chapter 2) suggest, before starting out an operator needs to take a careful look at the viability of what they want to achieve. None of these issues, relating to the social, economic, organizational and demographic limits to wine tourism, have been explored in any detail, and it may be important for the future of the product that they are addressed urgently. Typical research questions could include:

- How do wineries and wine regions make the decision to develop wine tourism?
- What is the relative role of small, medium-sized and large wineries in wine tourism?
- What is the carrying capacity of wine regions?
- When is there a threshold for wine tourism flows?
- Is wine tourism development a viable option for all wine regions and wineries?

Market Knowledge

One way of ensuring viability is to have detailed knowledge of the market within which you work, both of competition and – crucially – of your customers. Thus one theme – which will be returned to again – is that anyone involved in wine tourism must have effective sources of information. As O'Neill and Charters make clear (this volume, Chapter 13), careful research can give nuances to your understanding of your market that might not otherwise be obvious. Merely because a visitor is enthusiastic about a wine at the cellar door does not mean that they will continue to purchase in the future. Research into what drives continuing brand loyalty is key to making a positive winery experience more than just a fleeting response.

However, even when information is available it has to be treated carefully. Tassiopoulos and Haydam note (this volume, Chapter 11) that some South African statistics may be unreliable, and Mitchell (this volume, Chapter 8) points out that even academic research may sometimes give only a partial or misleading picture. At the risk of seeming to promote academic self-interest, the answer is that wineries, wine tourism operators and wine regions should commission regular and detailed research to ensure that they understand their markets.

The Focus of Wine Tourism

A major issue is the question of what wine tourism is designed to achieve. At this point there is another potential area of conflict between different organizations involved in the process. For public authorities the key goal is probably regional economic (and perhaps social) development. For a tourism-focused organization wine tourism may be their livelihood, or a substantial part of it. For a wine producer it is an ancillary part of their marketing strategy – the main focus is on marketing or, possibly, selling the wine. Indeed, there is some evidence that wineries are sceptical about the value of wine tourism generally (as opposed to mere cellar door sales), thinking that it may do more to benefit tourism organizations than wine producers (Macionis, 1998). The potential for conflict about precisely what wine tourism is designed to achieve is thus substantial, and this can have a direct impact on how it functions on a day-to-day basis. There is no doubt that the wine industry has to refocus its ideas about the purpose of wine tourism in a number of ways.

A number of the authors in this book (for example Fraser and Alonso, Mitchell and Charters and Fountain, this volume, Chapters 2, 8 and 12, respectively) make the point that the primary focus should not in fact be on the wine; rather, a 'total experience is sought' (Roberts and Sparks, this volume, Chapter 4). That may seem counterintuitive to many in the wine industry but, as Mitchell emphasizes (this volume, Chapter 8), it is now well established that it is the quality of the service encounter and not the quality of the wine which is most important to visitors and which most informs their post-visit response to the winery (O'Neill and Charters, 2000; O'Neill *et al.*, 2002), and the work by Charters and Fountain (this volume, Chapter 12), which approaches service quality research from a different angle from past studies, reinforces this advice.

If you want to gain a more positive response to your wine then spend less time on the wine itself and more on the quality of the staff whom you employ, and on their training. That does not mean, as Mitchell also notes (this volume, Chapter 8), that wine quality is to be ignored – wines presented must have a good, basic level of quality. However, as Lockshin (1999) observed, 'wine which is technically superior is no longer enough; it is now merely an entry ticket to the ball. You have to learn how to dance too.' The 'dance' is the process of enticing the customer to drink your wine repeatedly, and it is adding value to quality which ensures that your partner leaves the dance both satisfied yet also wanting more.

A third issue revolves around the primary aim of wine tourism for the producer. Most wineries may see it as a means of selling their product (Macionis, 1998) and may, indeed, get involved in wine tourism when it becomes clear that selling stock is more difficult than anticipated (a major concern given the current oversupply of wine on world wine markets). However, selling and marketing are not the same and, as Fraser and Alonso suggest (this volume, Chapter 2): there is a danger if the focus is only on selling more wine. Many producers need to shift their emphasis from selling to marketing and – particularly – to building brand equity for their product.

A sale of one bottle or one case at the cellar door gives a slight and temporary income benefit. A loyal customer won, who returns for many years, provides an income stream for the winery, and may even act as an ambassador for its wines, promoting them and winning further customers in the future – as Roberts and Sparks suggest (this volume, Chapter 4): 'they come back'.

O'Mahony et al. testify (this volume, Chapter 10) to the way in which a positive cellar door experience may modify wine consumption behaviour, albeit for a limited number of visitors. This is an international strategy which the Champenois have been pursuing successfully for two centuries now and, whilst they do not neglect the quality of the champagne, their tourism and promotional strategy is focused on providing a great experience, and winning and keeping friends. Furthermore, as Charters and Fountain suggest (this volume, Chapter 12), such a strategy may require a shift in winery focus on customers.

Despite previous research challenging the idea (O'Neill et al., 2002), there still tends to be a perspective that the ideal visitor to the cellar door is male, professional and middle-aged, because they will spend most. However, in terms of the development of long-term brand equity for the winery, younger tourists may be more important. They may know less about wine, and be easily won over by the quality of the organization's product but, crucially, if they enjoy the experience, they may come back and search for the producer's wines elsewhere, for many years.

To this focus on the customer can be added the specific importance of consumer involvement as a driving factor in the wine tourism experience. Involvement level has already been established as a key driver for consumption behaviour with wine generally (Lockshin et al., 1997; Charters and Pettigrew, 2006), but O'Mahony et al. also highlight (this volume, Chapter 10) its importance within wine tourism. Yuan et al. (this volume, Chapter 15), although not using the same terminology, also effectively note different involvement levels.

Those active in wine tourism need to understand this, and to understand how to tailor their offering for those at different levels. The high-involvement 'connoisseur' will want different experiences to the medium-involvement 'festival seeker'. Indeed, there is anecdotal evidence that the most highly involved may eschew the indiscriminate and crowded nature of a wine festival and seek more intimate experiences which focus on their specific level of knowledge and interest.

Infrastructure and Land Use

A number of the contributors to this volume have made it clear that coordination of the development of a wine tourism region is essential; indeed, as Williams et al. suggest (this volume, Chapter 3), such coordination may have to be transnational if it is to be truly successful. At that level coordination is not just an issue for wine tourism organizations, important as their contribution is. Local, regional and national governments also have to be involved. Each of these has a different level of concerns, and each may be able to offer something different to the development of wine tourism, but each is crucial.

However, it can be hard to persuade governments of the benefits of wine tourism. In newly developing wine tourism regions local government often reflects the attitudes of long-established economic actors who may feel threatened by change, especially when it focuses on service industries and bringing in visitors from outside. At a higher level governments may be concerned about the financial commitment required by support for wine tourism (although, as the State of Victoria in Australia has shown, when it is carefully targeted it can have a positive impact). Nevertheless, as Williams *et al.* point out (this volume, Chapter 3), the key element which can be offered by government is the establishment of a conducive framework for local economic development. Crucially, all parties need to be aware that land-use issues are contentious and should be worked out, as far as possible, at an early stage, to allow a reasonable but equitable impact of new development on the region.

Sparks and Malady suggest (this volume, Chapter 6) that there is a difference between established regions and new ones trying to break into wine tourism. The Hunter and Napa Valleys and Champagne are highly reputed destinations, are keen to welcome tourists and have a well-developed infrastructure to deal with them. South Burnett in Queensland, the Snake River in Idaho and Duras in France have barely begun to explore the idea. The problem for each in the latter category is that they operate in the shadow of existing, successful regions. If someone wants a wine tourism experience then why would they choose the almost unknown, barely developed destination? This is increasingly important in light of the suggestion earlier that some countries may reach saturation in terms of the number of destinations which they can support.

As noted above, not everyone in the wine industry wants to be involved in wine tourism, nor do they all need to be, and this must be borne in mind in the early stages of developing a wine tourism strategy. More important than the involvement of all is the fact that those who do commit to the idea share a common vision, a point made both by Williams *et al.* and Gammack (this volume, Chapters 3 and 5, respectively).

Where a common vision is not a starting point – as, say, in the Bairrada region of Portugal – its absence may hamper the cohesive development of the region. A common vision implies that those involved in wine tourism will act cooperatively for the good of the region, a key success factor identified by Sparks and Malady (this volume, Chapter 6). This is predicated on the assumption that what benefits everybody will also produce some benefit for each individual organization. The need for this cooperative approach may be one reason why wine tourism has not developed as rapidly over the last 20 years in Europe as it has in the New World; again, some of the possible hindrances to this can be seen in the work of Correia and Passos Ascenção (this volume, Chapter 18).

Interestingly, one European wine region which has a very successful wine tourism industry – that of Champagne – has also had a very cooperative and cohesive wine production industry since the foundation of the Comité Interprofessionel du Vin de Champagne 65 years ago, a sense of cohesion which contrasts starkly with many other French wine regions.

Another key precondition for successful wine tourism, particularly at the level of the individual organization, is the need to be wholehearted about what you are doing. Both Sparks and Malady and Murphy (this volume, Chapters 6 and 9, respectively) make the point that if you are not committed to the process then it is less likely to be successful. The former authors make this point in the context of the overall development of a wine region, and comment that, for instance, generic information about a region may not be complete, which conveys the wrong impression about the readiness of the area to receive visitors and the determination of its key actors to deliver a high-quality service. Murphy (this volume, Chapter 9) endorses the point but at a micro-level. If a winery is not obviously committed to making life easy for the consumer why would the consumer utilize their service and, ultimately, buy from them?

Be Businesslike

Linked closely to the idea of commitment is the necessity for those involved in wine tourism to be businesslike in the way that they run their organization. Sparks and Malady repeat (this volume, Chapter 6) what has often been advised before when they urge operators to be 'open all hours', and to be open when advertised. As O'Neill and Charters observed (this volume, Chapter 13), consumers today expect service which offers that little bit extra, not service which is run to suit the whim of the business manager. Added to that is the need to deliver on what is promised. Murphy notes (this volume, Chapter 9) that if either of these (doing what is promised and doing extra) are not delivered, whatever the quality of the wine, customers will not stay and – where a winery is involved – they may also doubt the company's commitment to making a first-class product.

Being businesslike is not merely about projecting the right image to the customer; it is also about ensuring internal efficiency in the organization. Both Murphy and Correia and Passos Ascenção (this volume, Chapters 9 and 18, respectively) note the need to fulfil basic management requirements. Records have to be carefully maintained, signs and advertising kept up to date and databases regularly revised. These are not optional extras, ancillary to the core processes of winemaking, but are themselves the core. Without contact with customers, effective marketing and repeated sales there will be no chance to make wine. The Internet especially, as Murphy suggests (this volume, Chapter 9), is no longer some peripheral resource to be neglected with impunity, but must be used carefully and have its effectiveness maintained.

Sparks and Malady point out (this volume, Chapter 6) that this means it is crucial for wine tourism businesses to develop promotional, marketing and business skills; they must, for instance, learn to offer an experience, not just a tasting. Crucially, staff training which inculcates these ideas is a priority, as Tassiopoulos and Haydam suggest (this volume, Chapter 11).

Given the emphasis throughout the research in this book (note particularly Griffin and Loersch, Chapter 7) on the interaction with the consumer and the primacy of the service experience, staff must be selected not just because they are available (even less because they may not need to be paid much) but primarily because of their ability to engage with the consumer and project the image which the organization is aiming for. Staff training should not be, primarily, about the wines which are sold by the winery or in the region, but about how to deal with the visitor empathetically and to provide them with a secure, enjoyable experience.

The Wine Tourism Offering

What does wine tourism comprise? To some extent this has been examined in depth in previous studies (Hall *et al.*, 2000a), but a number of points have been reiterated here. The responsiveness and effectiveness of staff and the totality of the experience have been noted. Roberts and Sparks suggested (Chapter 4) eight key factors sought by wine tourists: authenticity and something which adds to their lifestyle are interesting propositions and will be considered in more detail below. The other six factors comprise: (i) value (though not necessarily the cheapest experience as people are willing to pay for something significant and of high quality); (ii) setting; (iii) a good interaction; (iv) an enjoyable product; (v) information; and (vi) the chance to learn (a factor reinforced by O'Mahony *et al.*, Chapter 10).

To those, Griffin and Loersch conclude (Chapter 7), can be added some tangibles: a pleasant tasting room, reasonable quality wine and good signage – although, as Hurburgh and Friend suggest (Chapter 19), traditional approaches to signage may be superseded in time by electronic media. Crucially, as suggested by Adams' contribution (Chapter 17), there is a need to think laterally about what is offered, and to link wine tourism to as many other attractive options as possible, to enhance the overall experience.

It is also clear that regional wine festivals are important, as Taylor, Yuan *et al.* and Carlsen and Getz stress (Chapters 14, 15 and 16, respectively). Just as with other elements of the wine tourism offering, it is essential that festivals, their consumer base and their potential impact are carefully researched. Failure to do this, and to re-research even where a festival is apparently successful, may produce an inappropriate product. Likewise, the commitment and focus on organization and delivery required in other areas of the wine tourism product are also necessary with festivals.

Authenticity and Lifestyle

As has already been observed, the investigation by Roberts and Sparks (this volume, Chapter 4) into the customer's experience of wine tourism explicitly noted that both authenticity and lifestyle were key goals of visitors, issues which were also raised – at least in passing – in a number of other chapters. With the impact of postmodernism, which places emphasis on the significance of both ideas in contemporary society (Featherstone, 1991; Goulding, 2000), these concepts are beginning to be seen as significant for wine generally (Demossier, 2004; Beverland, 2006; Charters, 2006).

Lifestyle seems to have become something of a catchword, both in practical marketing (including that of wine tourism) and for academics (Featherstone, 1991). Thus in South Africa, for instance, the long-established chenin blanc is being explicitly recreated as a 'lifestyle wine' (Wines of South Africa, 2004). Crucially lifestyle, whilst imperfectly defined, appears to include the facility for personal expression (Featherstone, 1991) and the enjoyment of serious leisure pursuits (Tomlinson, 1990). Lifestyle can be seen as a means of changing a banal and fraught existence into something more acceptable and enjoyable, with an emphasis on personal choice, control and the individual's private life. The focus may particularly be on understanding, intellectual and personal exploration and the pursuit of knowledge, and both wine and tourism offer substantial opportunities for these goals – especially when also linked to food, culture and heritage.

It can be argued that the 'postmodern', lifestyle-oriented consumer is becoming less interested in what is mass-produced and standardized (Beardsworth and Keil, 1992). In wine particularly the outworking of this focuses on the idea of the authentic. Wine tourism can both help to reinforce this authenticity and directly benefit from it. Thus tourism allows opportunities to enhance the 'authentic' nature of the product and itself grows when a region is seen to offer authentic wines.

It has been suggested that two of the main ways by which authenticity is imparted to wine are: (i) in establishing a close relationship between wine and the rural environment; and (ii) by developing a sense of tradition and history for the product (Charters, 2006). Both of these can be enhanced by the consumer's experience of wineries and wine regions. In particular, it has been noted in Europe that urban wine drinkers enjoy the links which wine affords to a traditional lifestyle, a slower-paced way of life and the rhythm of the seasons (Dimara and Skuras, 2003; Demossier, 2005). It also seems clear that vineyards as a physical place, which tend to be long-term undertakings, may give a sense of continuity and endurance which French consumers, at least, find attractive (Gade, 2004).

If this analysis is correct then there are implications both for wine tourism practitioners and academics. For the former a focus needs to be given to promoting the lifestyle aspects of their product offering. This is something which is being done overtly in some places – so that in Australia the national wine tourism programme explicitly refers to promoting wine in the context of lifestyle (Winemakers Federation of Australia, 2005).

Adams' contribution to this book (Chapter 17) highlights one way in which wine and tourism can be linked to other lifestyle interests – in this case boating. It is also true that more research needs to be carried out into precisely how wine fits into the drinker's concept of lifestyle, and how wine tourism can enhance the experience. Further, the notion of authentic wine needs further consideration, and again an understanding of the precise nature of authenticity needs to be developed; this, in turn, will enable wine tourism organizations to refine and improve what they offer to their consumer. The extensive body of literature on cultural and heritage tourism authenticity would be a logical starting point and framework for any investigation of authenticity and wine tourism. The analysis of the CIRET database (Appendix 1) of wine tourism publications suggests that enhancement of heritage is a major theme that has emerged in the wine tourism literature.

It may be, also, that if 'lifestyle' becomes a greater motivating factor for consumption generally and for wine tourism in particular it may change the way consumers engage with the product (Charters, 2006). Tomlinson (1990) makes a number of suggestions, some of which may be relevant here. The first is that as consumers seek to create a complete lifestyle for themselves, traditional opinion will be challenged more often and become less influential. Thus, the perceived quality of a wine region will no longer be automatically accepted because it has always been seen to be 'classic'. This is especially significant for some long-established wine regions in Europe, and research into the changing perspectives on what those regions have to offer would be academically interesting and practically relevant.

Secondly, consumers will increasingly be more serious about and focused on their hobbies and interests. The pursuit of knowledge and development of skill will be significant. It can be inferred, therefore, that wine education will become more significant and wine tourism may grow as a means of furthering that education. Those organizations that promote learning and understanding about wine may consequently benefit.

Thirdly, production-related factors will become less important for the consumer than issues affecting lifestyle. As a result, the consumer's focus may move from the way in which wine is made towards more experiential requirements. It has been posited that this has already begun to happen within the context of wine tourism, with the suggestion that consumers are focusing less on the ways in which wine is made and more on related recreational issues such as events, food and the overall experience of the vineyard (Williams, 2001).

These factors have been picked up by some of the contributors to this book. History, stories and cultural heritage, all of which add to the experience and underscore its authenticity, have been mentioned. Roberts and Sparks noted (Chapter 4) that the ability to buy boutique (not mass-produced or readily available), local (place-specific) wines is important to consumers. Indeed, there is a sense in the research of both Murphy and Carlsen and Getz (Chapter 9 and 16, respectively) that having wines available at all signifies their authenticity, whether at a festival or via the Internet.

Meeting people including, as Tassiopoulos and Haydam suggest (Chapter 11), the winemaker, adds to the sense of authenticity about a visit, and enhances the lifestyle experience. Finally, the opportunities for education and personal development are crucial, as Roberts and Sparks point out (Chapter 4). These factors all reinforce a key conclusion of past research into wine tourism, that it is not a discrete activity but operates in conjunction with other forms of tourism such as food, environmental and heritage tourism (Charters and Ali-Knight, 2002). It is always necessary to see wine tourism within that context.

References

Beardsworth, A. and Keil, T. (1992) Foodways in flux: from gastro-anomy to menu pluralism? *British Food Journal* 94 (7), 20–27.

Beverland, M. (2006) The 'real thing': branding authenticity in the luxury wine trade. *Journal of Business Research* 59, 251–258.

Carlsen, J. (2004) A review of global wine tourism research. *Journal of Wine Research* 15 (1), 5–13.

Charters, S. (2001) The structure of business in the wine industry. *Australian and New Zealand Wine Industry Journal* 16 (1), 97–100.

Charters, S. (2006) *Wine and society: the social and cultural context of a drink.* Butterworth-Heinemann, Oxford, UK.

Charters, S. and Ali-Knight, J. (2002) Who is the wine tourist? *Tourism Management* 23, 311–319.

Charters, S. and Pettigrew, S. (2006) Product involvement and the evaluation of wine quality. *Qualitative Market Research* 8, 4.

Correia, L., Ascenção, M.J.P. and Charters, S. (2004) Wine routes in Portugal: a case study of the Bairrada Wine Route. *Journal of Wine Research* 15 (2), 15–25.

Demossier, M. (2004) Contemporary lifestyles: the case of wine. In: Sloan, D. (ed.) *Culinary Taste: Consumer Behaviour in the International Restaurant Sector.* Elsevier Butterworth-Heinemann, Oxford, UK, pp. 93–108.

Demossier, M. (2005) Consuming wine in France: the 'wandering' drinker and the vin-anomie. In: Wilson, T.M. (ed.) *Drinking Cultures.* Berg, Oxford, pp. 129–154.

Dimara, E. and Skuras, D. (2003) Consumer evaluations of product certification, geographic association and traceability in Greece. *European Journal of Marketing* 77 (5/6), 690–705.

Featherstone, M. (1991) *Consumer Culture and Postmodernism.* Sage Publishing, London.

Frochot, I. (2001) French wine brotherhoods and wine tourism: a complex relationship. *Tourism Recreation Research* 26 (2), 53–62.

Gade, D.W. (2004) Tradition, territory and terroir in French viniculture: Cassis, France and appellation contrôlée. *Annals of the Association of American Geographers* 94 (4), 848–876.

Getz, D. (2000) *Explore Wine Tourism: Management, Development and Destinations.* Cognizant Communication Corporation, New York.

Goulding, C. (2000) The commodification of the past, postmodern pastiche, and the search for authentic experiences at contemporary heritage attractions. *European Journal of Marketing* 34 (7), 835–853.

Hall, M., Johnson, G., Cambourne, B., Macionis, N., Mitchell, R. and Sharples, L. (2000) Wine tourism: an introduction. In: Hall, M., Sharples, L., Cambourne, B., Macionis, N., Mitchell, R. and Johnson, G. (eds) *Wine Tourism Around the World: Development, Management and Markets.* Elsevier Science, Oxford, UK.

Hall, M., Sharples, L., Cambourne, B. and Macionis, N. (eds) (2000) *Wine tourism around the world: Development, management and markets.* Elsevier Science, Oxford, UK, pp. 1–23.

Howley, M. (2000) Wine tourism in the United Kingdom. In: Hall, M., Sharples, L., Cambourne, B., Macionis, B., Mitchell, R. and Johnson, G. (eds) *Wine Tourism Around the World: Development, Management and Markets.* Elsevier Science, Oxford, UK, pp. 175–189.

Lockshin, L. (1999) Wine marketing: science or science fiction? *Australia and New Zealand Wine Industry Journal* 14 (1), 65–67.

Lockshin, L., Spawton, A. and Macintosh, G.

(1997) Using product, brand and purchasing involvement for retail segmentation. *Journal of Retailing and Consumer Services* 4 (3), 171–183.

Macionis, N. (1998) Wineries and tourism: perfect partners or dangerous liaisons? Paper presented at the *Wine Tourism: Perfect Partners – Australian Wine Tourism Conference*, Margaret River, Western Australia, 5–7 May.

Mitchell, R., Hall, M. and McIntosh, A. (2000) Wine tourism and consumer behaviour. In: Hall, M., Sharples, L., Cambourne, B., Macionis, N., Mitchell, R. and Johnson, G. (eds) *Wine Tourism Around the World: Development, Management and Markets.* Elsevier Science, Oxford, UK, pp. 115–135.

O'Neill, M. and Charters, S. (2000) Service quality at the cellar door: implications for Western Australia's developing wine tourism industry. *Managing Service Quality* 10 (2), 11.

O'Neill, M., Palmer, A. and Charters, S. (2002) Wine production as a service experience – the effect of service quality on sales. *Journal of Services Marketing* 16 (4), 342–362.

Tomlinson, A. (1990). Introduction. In: Tomlinson, A. (ed.) *Consumption, Identity and Style.* Routledge, London, pp. 1–30.

Williams, P. (2001) Positioning wine tourism destinations: an image analysis. *International Journal of Wine Marketing* 13 (3), 42–58.

Winemakers Federation of Australia (2005) *Wine Tourism Programs* (http://www.wfa.org.au/tourismprojects.htm, accessed 24 February 2006).

Wines of South Africa (2004) *Wines of South Africa 2004* (Video presentation). Wines of South Africa, Cape Town.

Index